Social Foundations of Urban Education

Social Foundations of Urban Education

Harry L. Miller / Roger R. Woock

Hunter College, City University of New York

University of Calgary, Canada

THE DRYDEN PRESS INC.
Hinsdale, Illinois

Library of Congress Catalog Card Number: 79-110403

SBN: 03-089013-6, cloth; SBN: 03-089026-8, paper

Printed in the United States of America

0123 40 98765432

Cover photograph by Mark Feldstein. Grateful acknowledgment is made to the following:
For figure 1.3 from the *Harvard Educational Review,* page 23, Copyright © 1968 by President and Fellows of Harvard College; for table 1.10, page 26, reprinted with the permission of the National Association of Social Workers, Inc., publishers of *Social Work*; for quotations from "The Wrong Way to Find Jobs for Negroes," Copyright © by TRANS-action Magazine, New Brunswick, New Jersey; for figure 2.1, page 58, reprinted by permission of The Regents of the University of California; for quotations on pages 64-65 from "The Social Background of Teaching," Copyright by American Educational Research Association; for table 3.7, page 91, © Copyright 1965, 1966 by Oscar Lewis. Reprinted by permission of Random House, Inc.; for quotations from "When the Southern Negro Moves North," © 1967 by The New York Times Company. Reprinted by permission; for figures 3.1 and 3.2 on pages 102 and 103, "Median Equivalent Grades in Reading Comprehension for Central Harlem and New York City Pupils Compared to National Norms" and "Median Equivalent Grades in Word Knowledge for Central Harlem and New York City Pupils Compared to National Norms" from *Dark Ghetto* by Kenneth B. Clark (Harper & Row, 1965); for quotations from "It's Time for a Moratorium on Negativism," reprinted, with permission, from *The United Teacher*; for the unnumbered table on page 120, reprinted with permission of The Macmillan Company from *After Divorce* by William Goode. Copyright © The Free Press, A Corporation 1956; for quotations from "A Comparison of the Child-Rearing Environment of Upper-lower and Very low-lower Class Families" on pages 127-131, Copyright ©, the American Orthopsychiatric Association, Inc., Reproduced by permission; for figure 4.2 and table 4.5, pages 142 and 140 respectively, reprinted with permission of the National Association of Social Workers, Inc., publishers of *Social Work*; for table 4.6 and table 4.7 on page 144, copyright 1962 by the American Psychological Association, and reproduced by permission; for table 4.8, page 146, reprinted by permission of The Regents of the University of California; from *Teachers Talk: Views from Inside City Schools* by Estelle Fuchs. Copyright © 1967 by Hunter College of the City University of New York, 1969, by Estelle Fuchs. Reprinted by permission of Doubleday & Company, Inc.; for quotations from *The Autobiography of Malcolm X,* pages 180-181, reprinted by permission of Grove Press, Inc., Copyright © 1964 by Alex Haley and Malcolm X, Copyright © 1965 by Alex Haley and Betty Shabazz; for *Education in Depressed Areas,* edited by A. Harry Passow, pages 201-202, reprinted with the permission of the publisher (New York: Teachers College Press), 1963; for tables 6.1-6.3, pages 215-219, from the *Harvard Educational Review,* Copyright © 1968 by President and Fellows of Harvard College; for quotations from *Teaching Disadvantaged Children in the Preschool,* pages 230-233, © 1966. Reprinted by permission of Prentice-Hall, Inc., Englewood Cliffs, New Jersey; for tables 6.4-6.5, pages 237-238, courtesy of Charles C Thomas, Publisher, Springfield, Illinois; for quotations from *Realities of the Urban Classroom* by G. Alexander Moore, Jr. Copyright © 1964, 1967 by G. Alexander Moore, Jr. Reprinted by permission of Doubleday & Company, Inc.; for quotations on pages 282-284 and table 7.3, page 282, from "Expressed Motives of Teachers in Slum Schools" by William W. Wayson, reprinted from *Urban Education,* Volume I, Number 4 (1965), pages 230-232, by permission of the Publisher, Sage Publications, Inc., Beverly Hills, California; for figure 8.1, page 303, "Organizational pyramid for public-school administration," page 41, *Administration of Public Education,* Second Edition, by Stephen J. Knezevich. (Harper & Row, 1969); for table 8.1, pages 308-309, Copyright © by David Rogers. Reprinted by permission of Random House, Inc.; for various quotations from *Our Children Are Dying* by Nat Hentoff, Copyright © 1966 by Nat Hentoff, all rights reserved, reprinted by permission of The Viking Press, Inc.; for *The Supreme Court and Education* edited by David Fellman, pages 336-337, reprinted with the permission of the publisher (New York: Teachers College Press), 1960; for figure A-2, page 406, Prentice-Hall, Inc., Englewood Cliffs, New Jersey, © 1967.

PREFACE

Interest in the special problems of urban, and particularly of central city, schools has been sustained and intense for about a decade. During that period the flood of ideas, programs, and experimental funds has been so rapid that it was difficult to sort them out or to come to many well-based generalizations. Students of this field relied almost exclusively on a considerable number of books of readings that took occasional soundings in the available literature of the time.

The authors believe that at this point the major outlines of the field are sufficiently clear to permit an organized approach to an understanding of the basic structure of these problems and an assessment of proposed solutions. The many uncertainties still characteristic of the field of urban education, however, and our own view of training requirements, have led us to a format that differs in several important respects from the conventional texts in educational foundations:

1. Instead of presenting a consistent set of propositions and generalizations, as is often possible in a settled area of knowledge with a long history of development, we have emphasized the controversies that enliven our particular field of interest. In most cases we have tried to anatomize the important differences in viewpoints without attempting to settle the matter for the reader, though occasionally we indicate where our own biases lie. At various points in the text the reader will find such discussions on, for example, the definition of poverty, the effectiveness of various solutions for poverty, the validity of such concepts as "culture of poverty" and "cultural deprivation," the role of

family environment in achievement drive and school achievement, the influence of teacher expectation on the achievement of lower-class children, the effectiveness of compensatory education as a general approach, traditional nursery school approaches versus "verbal bombardment," the impact of school characteristics on academic achievement, the rationalist versus developmental proposals for school reconstruction, the effect of integration on achievement, school decentralization and community control.

We have tried to produce some clarity in all these issues, and others, without producing foregone conclusions that the student himself should arrive at, given the value conflicts underlying most of them.

2. In the process of arriving at judgments about issues such as those listed above, teachers and educators have generally tended in the past to ignore research findings, leaving the discussion of research adequacy and validity to the experts. In our view this attitude is becoming increasingly less defensible. With far better funding than ever before, and a growing number of well-trained investigators, educational research is now providing a body of evidence on many important issues that cannot be ignored in arriving at educational policy. One's assessment of the Coleman study for the U.S. Office of Education must influence a judgment of the potential for some types of compensatory programming, just as the continued funding of such large-scale programs as New York's More Effective Schools must in part depend on how one reads the evidence of objective evaluations of that effort. If the experts themselves argue about the validity of such studies, then teachers and administrators must grow accustomed to looking critically at the evidence.

Because we are convinced that school personnel must free themselves from the belief that they can make professional judgments of such intricate matters solely on the basis of their own particular and narrow experience, rather than by taking into consideration available research evidence, we have included detailed examinations of several crucial research studies. And, because education undergraduates lack the basic knowledge necessary for such an assessment, we have provided a discussion of the general criteria for research adequacy.

It is possible, of course, simply to skip over these often technical discussions of how much confidence one should have in the findings of some much-cited study, and, depending on the particular group of students, it may even be advisable. But our own experience has taught us that students are prone to overgeneralize to the point of gross error unless they are confronted with actual data; at this writing, Rosenthal's study of teacher expectations, for example, is being widely discussed, and the students we encounter are all convinced, without having read it, that the study conclusively proves that if teacher expectations are raised, pupil achievement will automatically improve.

We hope, then, that the users of this text will not too readily underrate their students' capacities for the examination of evidence. We talk a good deal about training children in critical thinking; if those who are going to be teachers are not given the opportunity to think critically about their own professional beliefs, it is unlikely that they will ever be able to help children to exercise judgment in the classroom.

New York City —H.L.M.
February 1970 —R.R.W.

INTRODUCTORY NOTE

This book makes extensive use of research findings in sociology, social psychology, and education. Studies are used to illustrate theoretical positions and a large number of educational controversies. All research bearing on a controversy or problem has not been reported. The authors have decided that it would be more useful and less confusing to report fewer studies in some detail.

The studies are *illustrative* rather than definitive of important research in our areas of concern. It is true that other studies might have been selected. The reader must keep in mind then that the research reported only suggests but does not provide the answers to important educational questions. Even the most exhaustive survey of research could not do this, for satisfactory answers are not available. If they were, there would probably be no need for this book.

New York City —H.L.M.
January 1970 —R.R.W.

CONTENTS

PART I

Social and Economic Influences on the Urban School

1

THE OPPORTUNITY STRUCTURE

This book is about the schools of urban America, the serious problems they face, and their response to the challenge posed to them by a public that believes firmly in the problem-solving powers of education. Only since the 1950s have professional educators paid much attention to urban schools as special phenomena. Before that time, and since the establishment of public schools for all in the first part of the 19th century, the stereotype of American education has been the rural or small-town school, as the movie image of the American teacher has been the "schoolmarm" confronting rows of freckle-faced children.

The nonurban focus of educational concern stubbornly persisted despite the steady shift of American society toward urbanism and despite the remarkable role played by a number of large city school systems in Americanizing the flood of European immigrants between the Civil War and World War I. Only when the schools of the large central cities failed dramatically to perform the same role with a different wave of immigrants, those completing the last great population movement from the farm to the city, did attention focus on urban schools. Even to an American educational establishment, whose strength lay in small town and small city America, it became clear that the new educational frontiers lay in the central cities of the large metropolitan areas.

The frontiers were there because by the 1950s a number of large-scale social and economic trends that had been proceeding at an individual pace converged at last and in their mutual interaction created a crisis not only for urban school systems but for the whole society. Shifts in occupational opportunities, the great migration from farm to city, and the rising anger of black Americans at their inequitable position resulted not only in a massive retardation among the school children of the central city slums but made the effect impossible to ignore. The same forces resulted in civil disorders in the 1960s that, many feel, threaten the disruption of a whole social order.

Both the social crisis and the school crisis are rooted in a formidable complex of forces, so complicated that the task of organizing a comprehensive approach to them poses severe problems that affect both the content and organization of this book. It may be useful to discuss a few of them:

1. The complexity of the problems have a serious effect on the development of effective public and educational policy concerning the urban crisis and the school. Simple solutions that appear on the surface to be logical and in accord with our experience may turn out not to be workable because a great many important variables were not initially apparent. Consequently, policy must take into account the findings of both basic and empirical research; that the research is imperfect, because we cannot control all the variables in human interaction, must also be considered. We find it necessary, then, throughout the book to discuss research findings often in considerable detail. The preface made this point at some length, but it is worth repeating. It is becoming increasingly difficult for educators, students, or professionals to take reasoned policy positions on problems in their field without giving serious and critical attention to relevant research findings. One cannot talk sensibly about the worth of approaches to compensatory education without considering the results of evaluation research, just as one cannot assume that the Job Corps, which looks like a first-rate attack on one important aspect of poverty, really works as well as we think it will. An additional demand on the reader imposed by the need to concentrate on often unfamiliar research procedures and terminology will be amply repaid by the gain in increased sophistication about the problems under review.

2. Although the general term *education* is used in the title, we will deal most of the time, and particularly in the last half of the book, with *schooling*. The distinction is an important one. The school is a formal institution committed to official purposes, and run by officially designated personnel who undertake specific educational roles. But the child's education, in a more general sense, consists of everything around him that influences his attitudes, his cognitive style, his aspirations, and his behavior. This is a truism, but one that education professionals, in our concentration on the school, often tend to minimize. Although a detailed look at the impact of schooling is postponed, the early chapters are nonetheless concerned with education: the socializing influences

of the child's position within the economic and social status system, the urban environment that immediately surrounds him, and the "curriculum" of the home.

3. The earlier focus on the economic and psychosocial environment of the urban school, instead of on the school itself, also indicates the authors' conviction that a better understanding of the tangled interrelationships between the two is obtained by first considering the more basic term in the relationship. More often than not the school *reflects* change, contradictions, and conflicts in the social order rather than initiating them. An important group of educators in this century would have it otherwise; they see the school as a key institution for reconstructing the social order in a more humane and democratic image. Whatever the future possibilities, however, the school as it exists mirrors society; it does not act upon society. We begin with one of the most powerful shaping forces, the distribution of opportunities in American society.

CONCEPTS: OPPORTUNITY STRUCTURE AND POVERTY

What the people in a society believe is sometimes more important than what they do; and the American nation has been shaped in many ways by a widely shared belief in the idea of equality. The religious tenets of the early settlers in the Northeast downgraded the authority of a priesthood in favor of individual and congregational responsibility. The vast land resources of a virgin continent encouraged a system of individual landholdings; where property meant status, large numbers of men had property and thus equal status. The Union was founded on ideas of political democracy that started from the assumption that "all men are created equal," ideas that were socially reinforced by the conditions of an expanding frontier far from the established institutions and hardening status lines of the well-settled East.

However the concept may have been violated in actual practice, the idea is firmly rooted in the American consciousness that one man is just as good as another, as one man's opinion and his vote has equal status with another's. The economic corollary slowly came to be accepted as well: Because most Americans defined the good life as that in which one was successful, every man should have an equal opportunity to achieve success and the good things of life.

It is not difficult to imagine a model of a society in which everyone really does have equality of opportunity to succeed, if we define success as Americans do: Having an occupation which others respect and an income that permits one to have a reasonable share of the comforts afforded by the society at any given time. Although we are all created equal politically, each man clearly differs in his aptitudes, his intelligence, and his ambition. Equality of opportunity ideally requires a state of things in which everyone, regardless of the circumstances of his birth, has an equal chance to compete for success with those at his own level of aptitude, intelligence, and ambition.

The American myth has always been that as a country we have reasonably approximated this ideal. But, although American life may have occasionally, in some places and at some times, roughly resembled the model, it is now clear that 20th-century America is far beyond those times and places. The myth supposes, for example, that one should be willing to bet at even odds on the chances for success of two boys born with equal genetic capability, wherever they may originate. It would be a reckless gambler indeed who would place such even odds if one of the boys were born to a black, sharecropping family on an Alabama farm and the other on the East side of Manhattan Island to the family of a corporation lawyer.

Opportunity has acquired a *structure,* a term that indicates that certain relationships or events occur more consistently than one would expect them to do by chance. The opportunity structure in the United States is not by any means as rigid as, say, that of the European medieval period; an ambitious, bright serf's son had only a small chance of climbing into the relatively fixed ranks above him; and a noble's son, no matter how stupid and passive, seldom sank below the status of gentleman. But neither is it as close as some Americans believe to the fluid, random model described above. Some of the circumstances that consistently tend to decrease opportunity are:

Geographical. To be born in the South of the United States, whether one is white or black, handicaps a person unless he happens to be fortunate in his family circumstances; the less-advanced economic level of the region and its poor educational systems depress the probabilities of success relative to other regions of the country. Also, within a given region the chances are better for those born in urban areas than in rural places.

Social class. Children born to relatively well-to-do families, with fathers engaged in high-status occupations, consistently do better than others. A later chapter will examine this in detail.

Ethnicity. To be born a nonwhite or to a family whose recent origins are not in the United States (unless those origins are in northern Europe) tends to depress access to opportunity, an effect that fluctuates with social attitudes toward the particular ethnic group.

Poverty

Although opportunity structure obviously is a complex phenomenon, attention has focused in recent years on one aspect of it, the uneven distribution of family income in the United States. Perhaps this is because poverty is the most visible aspect of those families that are least favored in the opportunity structure. It is a recurring concern in American life; the great national interest in doing something about the poor can be matched in several previous eras.[1]

One of the most difficult problems in discussing the concept of poverty is that the definition of "poor" is clearly a relative matter. Very few Americans are as poor, in absolute terms, as the mass of people living in underdeveloped areas of the world. Even in India, an economically advancing country, there are large numbers of city dwellers who do not even have shelter, families who put up a small piece of canvas in the street at night to protect them as they sleep and who do their cooking in small wooden sheds on a beach.

Though the majority of those considered poor in the United States are very well off compared to populations such as these, it is not very helpful to make such comparisons. The American who is poor does not compare himself to Indian standards but to what is roughly the average life style in his own country, which has been growing more comfortable at a very rapid rate.

Because of the relative nature of the term, some demographers prefer to define poverty simply as the lowest fifth of the income distribution, a definition that permits one to examine what kinds of people are among the poor from one period of time to another. From this point of view the pessimistic biblical observation that the poor will always be with us becomes a logical necessity. No matter how high living standards may rise, there will always be a lowest fifth of the families in the nation that can be considered disadvantaged in relation to the average.

Another approach is to compute an annual income necessary to maintain a minimum living standard, defining "minimum" in relation to prevailing ideas in the culture. At the beginning of the decade of the sixties, for example, such a computation based on living standards for a family of four persons applied the following categories: any income below $2000 was poverty; from $2000-4000 was a state of deprivation; from $4000-7500 was in the range running from deprivation to comfort.[2] By the end of that decade such figures need to be considerably re-

1. Robert H. Brenner, *Change and Continuity in Recent American Concepts of Poverty* (New York: Urban Research Center, Hunter College, mimeograph, 1962).

2. *Poverty and Deprivation in the United States* (Washington, D.C.: Conference on Economic Progress, 1962), p. 17.

vised, because according to the Bureau of Labor Statistics a four-person family living in one of our large cities needed an income of about $9000 to live in reasonable comfort.

When the federal government began a poverty program in the first half of that decade, it defined poverty at first in very general terms as an income of about $3000 for a family. It soon became clear that such a rough yardstick did not take into account living standard differences by size of community or family size, and the government now uses a very sophisticated, variable measure that considers family size, number of children, a nonfarm residence, as well as the amount of family money income. In 1966 the poverty level of nonfarm residents ranged from $1560 for a woman sixty-five years or older living alone to $5440 for a family of seven or more persons. It was $3300 for a nonfarm family of four with two children.[3]

Although the concern for such accurate definition often appears to be a futile exercise in hair-splitting, setting official poverty levels often has an important effect on policy. The income level of a family determines which persons are eligible for particular federally-financed programs and thus defines many of the problems those programs face. There are, for example, a number of youth agencies operating on federal funds committed to helping out-of-school and unemployed young people acquire skills and jobs. The professionals who administer the programs understandably want to show that they are effective, but if the population they serve must come from families only at the very lowest income level, those with the most severe problems, their rate of success will be low. Agencies are likely to argue, consequently, that income levels for admission to poverty programs should be set at a higher standard.

The other side of the policy dilemma is illustrated by Head Start, the preschool program for nursery-age children. Although its intention was to aid poor children in getting the skills and confidence necessary to do well in school when they entered, no income level was set for families that participated. There was a mild scandal when it was discovered, early in the program's history, that a number of children from upper-middle-class professional families were attending the summer programs; the government found itself financing free nursery schools for those who could well afford to pay for nurseries themselves. On the other hand, it was probably useful for many reasons to have a wide range of children in the program; it can certainly be argued that the disadvantaged child should be able to get a great deal of help from children his own age who are ahead of him socially and linguistically.

3. *Social and Economic Conditions of Negroes in the United States* (Washington, D.C.: Bureau of Labor Statistics Report No. 332, U.S. Government Printing Office. 1967), p. 22.

TRENDS IN POVERTY AND OPPORTUNITY

This section describes in some detail the distribution of poverty and occupational opportunity in the late sixties, and the trends within those distributions that seem to point to the future. It is impossible to understand the problems of the urban school without a general grasp of this broader social context in which those problems, and the challenge to the school, are embedded.

Table 1.1 Percent Distribution of Family Income in 1947, 1960, and 1966 (adjusted for price changes in 1965 dollars)

<table>
<tr><th></th><th colspan="3">Nonwhite</th><th colspan="3">White</th></tr>
<tr><th></th><th>1947</th><th>1960</th><th>1966</th><th>1947</th><th>1960</th><th>1966</th></tr>
<tr><td>Number of families (in millions)</td><td>3.1</td><td>4.3</td><td>4.9</td><td>34.2</td><td>41.1</td><td>44.0</td></tr>
<tr><td>Percent</td><td>100</td><td>100</td><td>100</td><td>100</td><td>100</td><td>100</td></tr>
<tr><td>Under $3000</td><td>65</td><td>44</td><td>32</td><td>27</td><td>18</td><td>13</td></tr>
<tr><td>$3000 to $4999</td><td>22</td><td>24</td><td>24</td><td>32</td><td>18</td><td>14</td></tr>
<tr><td>$5000 to $6999</td><td>7</td><td>16</td><td>17</td><td>20</td><td>23</td><td>19</td></tr>
<tr><td>$7000 to $9999</td><td>5</td><td>11</td><td>16</td><td>13</td><td>23</td><td>25</td></tr>
<tr><td>$10,000 to $14,999</td><td rowspan="2">2</td><td>5</td><td>9</td><td rowspan="2">8</td><td>13</td><td>20</td></tr>
<tr><td>$15,000 and over</td><td>1</td><td>3</td><td>5</td><td>10</td></tr>
<tr><td>Median income</td><td>$2284</td><td>$3441</td><td>$4481</td><td>$4458</td><td>$6244</td><td>$7517</td></tr>
<tr><td>Change, 1947-1966:</td><td></td><td></td><td></td><td></td><td></td><td></td></tr>
<tr><td>Dollar</td><td>*</td><td>*</td><td>2197</td><td>*</td><td>*</td><td>3059</td></tr>
<tr><td>Percent</td><td>*</td><td>*</td><td>96.2</td><td>*</td><td>*</td><td>68.6</td></tr>
</table>

* Not applicable.

SOURCE: U.S. Department of Commerce, Bureau of the Census. From *Social and Economic Conditions of Negroes in the United States* (Washington, D.C.: BLS Report No. 332, U.S. Department of Labor, October 1967), p. 18.

The distribution of family incomes between 1947 and 1966, as shown in Table 1.1, provides an important overview of the main dimensions of the problem. First, it suggests a reason for the current national concern with poverty, which may be found, paradoxically, in the increase in affluence. The proportion of white families with incomes over $10,000 quadrupled in the twenty-year period, an astonishing shift that places almost one out of three white Americans in a life style category one might call *comfort-affluence*. Many experts suggest that it is this spread of affluence that led intellectuals and then the general public to respond to such influential books as Michael Harrington's *The Other America*, which aroused widespread interest in the early sixties. A society that could produce such abundance and comfort for so many of its members, it was argued, ought surely to be able to do better for those still living in squalor and despair. Moreover, general prosperity for so many families is highly visible. Newspaper and magazine advertisements for gadgets intended for "the man who has everything" are read not only by the well-to-do but by those who have practically nothing.

Table 1.1 also indicates that the rise in income has been shared by white and nonwhite families and, indeed, the increase was proportionately greater for nonwhites, whose median income rose by almost 100 percent. But the *gap* between white and nonwhite median income has nevertheless grown larger than it was in 1947; the position of the nonwhites has improved substantially, but as a group they are losing ground because of the great original advantage held by the whites. It is easy to understand why black Americans feel that, though they are moving faster than the white, they are falling further behind.

At the lower end of the scale it is clear that a very considerable improvement has been achieved, if one regards poverty as an absolute rather than as a relative concept. The proportion of both white and nonwhite families below the poverty line has been cut in half. But again, about a third of the nonwhite families are still poor as compared to only 13 percent of the white families.

For a look at the kinds of people who are poor one has to return to the last complete census in 1960. There probably has been very little change, because the nature of the group occupying the lowest fifth of the income distribution has been remarkably stable. In the decade between 1950 and 1960, for example, the proportion of nonwhites in the lowest income fifth (21 percent) did not change at all, nor did the proportion who are aged; the percentage of female-headed families increased by only a few percentage points.[4]

A more detailed examination of the nature of this lowest income group reveals that for the most part their problem is an inability to be productive:

1. About 15 percent are low-income farmers, half of them living in the South. Only a small percentage are black, which is a very considerable shift in this group's composition, explained by the great migration of rural blacks since the forties to Northern cities.

2. One of the largest groups, 25 percent of the poor, is aged. About 2½ million low-income families, living primarily in metropolitan areas, are headed by a person over sixty-five. Most of them are white.

3. Another 15 percent are in fatherless families, almost all concen-

4. Herman P. Miller, *Rich Man Poor Man* (New York: Crowell, Collier, Macmillan Company, 1964), pp. 62-63.

trated in metropolitan areas. A third of these families consisting of mother and children are black, an overrepresentation that reflects the instability of the black family; one out of every five black children is born out of wedlock.

4. There were 1 million nonwhite families, about 10 percent of the total poverty group, headed by a man under sixty-five and living in or near large cities. Of these, 90 percent are black, and the family head is employed in a low-skilled job or is chronically unemployed. For him the problem of little education and skill is greatly complicated by racial discrimination.

5. Finally, the largest group, constituting almost 30 percent of the low-income group, includes white families headed by men under sixty-five living in metropolitan areas. Herman Miller points to the puzzling nature of this group when he says: "Explanations based on personal or environmental factors could be made for the farm poor, the aged poor, the widowed and divorced poor, and the Negro poor. What is there to say about the white poor?"[5] They are, it turns out, a very diverse group whose poverty is due to such different factors as low intelligence, physical disability, or just bad economic breaks. Almost a third of them, however, are in white-collar professional or managerial occupations, many just starting on their careers, and these may be expected to improve their economic position in time.

A later section of this chapter will consider a variety of social strategies proposed for improving the lot of all of these families. At this point it is necessary to note only that for the majority of those described, an educational strategy is clearly not relevant. As Miller points out, even the 3 million families in the last group represent a sample from 30 million similarly constituted families who happen to be at the lower end of an extensive range of incomes.

The group that does stand out is the 1 million nonwhite families headed by a productive male; his position cannot be explained by age, disability, or occupation in a marginal farm enterprise. It is this fact that underlies much of the militancy of the civil rights movement in this era—not poverty itself but the overrepresentation among the poor of black Americans out of all proportion to their numbers in the population. The inequity also gives social validity to the claim for redress, a validity that most Americans somewhat uneasily perceive. For, though the society does not believe as yet that everyone has a right to a decent standard of living, it does believe in equality of treatment, which clearly does not exist in this case.

That both education and racial discrimination are closely related

5. *Ibid.*, p. 78.

to the inequitable position of this group of families may be most readily appreciated by examining their occupational and employment position, the most significant index to opportunity. Table 1.2 gives the picture of the occupational distribution in the mid-sixties.

Table 1.2 Employment by Occupation and Sex, 1966 (percent distribution)

<table>
<tr><th></th><th colspan="2">Nonwhite</th><th colspan="2">White</th></tr>
<tr><th></th><th>Male</th><th>Female</th><th>Male</th><th>Female</th></tr>
<tr><td>Total employed (in thousands)</td><td>4655</td><td>3313</td><td>42,983</td><td>23,114</td></tr>
<tr><td>Percent</td><td>100</td><td>100</td><td>100</td><td>100</td></tr>
<tr><td>Professional, technical, and managerial</td><td>9</td><td>10</td><td>27</td><td>19</td></tr>
<tr><td>Clerical and sales</td><td>9</td><td>15</td><td>14</td><td>43</td></tr>
<tr><td>Craftsmen and foremen</td><td>12</td><td>*</td><td>20</td><td>*</td></tr>
<tr><td>Operatives</td><td>27</td><td>16</td><td>20</td><td>15</td></tr>
<tr><td>Service workers, except household</td><td rowspan="2">16</td><td>26</td><td rowspan="2">6</td><td>14</td></tr>
<tr><td>Private household workers</td><td>28</td><td>6</td></tr>
<tr><td>Nonfarm laborers</td><td>20</td><td>*</td><td>6</td><td>*</td></tr>
<tr><td>Farmers and farm workers</td><td>8</td><td>4</td><td>7</td><td>2</td></tr>
<tr><td>Other</td><td>**</td><td>2</td><td>**</td><td>2</td></tr>
</table>

* A few workers included in "other."
** Not applicable.

SOURCE: U.S. Department of Commerce, Bureau of the Census. From *Social and Economic Conditions of Negroes in the United States* (Washington, D.C.: BLS Report No. 332, U.S. Department of Labor, October 1967), p. 41.

The position of the black male is clearly the most disadvantaged in relation to the higher status white-collar occupations. His white counterpart has more than twice the representation in these jobs. Black women, many of whom are in teaching and who are also more acceptable in lower-level office jobs, are better off. Almost two-thirds of the nonwhite men are concentrated in unskilled industrial work or general labor and in service. Very nearly that same proportion of white men are concentrated in the occupations *above* that level.

Rising prosperity and, possibly, a greater social awareness of discrimination has brought some improvement. As unbalanced as this situation appears, it is a somewhat better one than was only recently the case.

As Table 1.3 indicates, nonwhites penetrated the white-collar occupations by substantial percentages in the first half of the decade of the sixties. Their numerical representation in those fields, of course, was so minor to begin with that even large percentage increases do not better their relative position by much. If the rate of increase of 50 percent in professional and technical jobs is maintained for succeeding five-year periods, they would achieve parity with whites in that category by about 1980, but only if whites did not enter that category at all.

Table 1.3 Employment by Occupation,* 1966, and Change, 1960-1966 (Numbers in thousands)

	Employed, 1966		Change, 1960-1966			
			Number		Percent	
	Nonwhite	White	Nonwhite	White	Nonwhite	White
Total	7968	66,097	+927	+6457	+13	+11
Professional, technical, and managerial	758	15,968	+251	+ 1893	+50	+13
Clerical	751	11,095	+244	+ 1791	+48	+19
Sales	149	4610	+ 36	+ 316	+32	+ 7
Craftsmen and foremen	602	8996	+187	+ 825	+45	+10
Operatives	1786	12,093	+371	+ 1537	+26	+15
Service workers, except private household	1558	5881	+326	+ 991	+26	+20
Private household workers	941	1308	− 66	+ 115	− 7	+10
Nonfarm laborers	934	2756	− 38	+ 72	− 4	+ 3
Farmers and farm workers	488	3389	−384	−1144	−44	−25

* Data on occupation are annual averages.

SOURCE: U.S. Department of Labor, Bureau of Labor Statistics. From *Social and Economic Conditions of Negroes in the United States* (Washington, D.C.: BLS Report No. 332, U.S. Department of Labor, October 1967), p. 39.

Job stability is a second significant dimension of the opportunity picture, and here the position of nonwhites has not improved at all. Not only are they concentrated in jobs that are by their nature unstable but the very existence of many unskilled positions is slowly being threatened by long-term trends in the manpower situation, as is shown in Figure 1.1.

There is some dispute about the immediate impact of these shifts in the nature of job opportunities, though they have obvious implications for the long-range future of educational institutions. But to the extent that there still does exist, as recent studies indicate, a sizeable pool of jobs requiring little skill or training, the dictum that the black is the "last to be hired and first to be fired" applies, as a comparison of unemployment rates reveals.

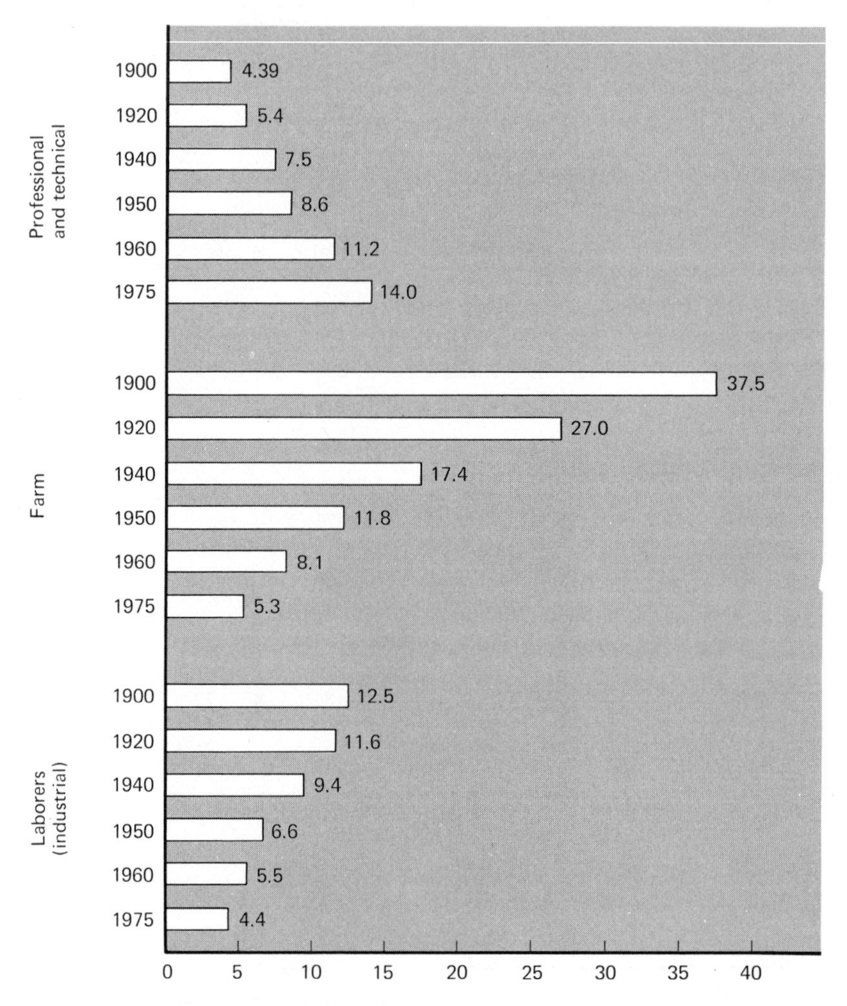

Figure 1.1 Occupational distribution of workers (actual 1900-1960 and estimated 1975).

SOURCES: Data for 1900-1950 from David L. Kaplan and M. Claire Casey, *Occupational Trends in the United States, 1900 to 1950* (Washington, D.C.: U.S. Department of Commerce, Bureau of the Census, Working Paper No. 5, U.S. Government Printing Office, 1958), p. 7.

Employment stability for the nonwhite has decreased over the past twenty years, then, and even the movement into more stable white-collar positions noted earlier has had no apparent effect on his relative positions. But these general figures for the group as a whole conceal some important differences. If one considers only married men, unemployment rates are considerably lower than the group average; they are actually halved. In 1967 the rate for married nonwhites was 3.4 percent, still double the rate for white married men but better than nonwhites generally. In troublesome contrast, Table 1.5 shows the unemployment rates for teenagers.

Table 1.4 Unemployment Rates,* 1949-1967

	Nonwhite	White	Ratio: nonwhite to white
1949	8.9	5.6	1.6
1950	9.0	4.9	1.8
1951	5.3	3.1	1.7
1952	5.4	2.8	1.9
1953	4.5	2.7	1.7
1954	9.9	5.0	2.0
1955	8.7	3.9	2.2
1956	8.3	3.6	2.3
1957	7.9	3.8	2.1
1958	12.6	6.1	2.1
1959	10.7	4.8	2.2
1960	10.2	4.9	2.1
1961	12.4	6.0	2.1
1962	10.9	4.9	2.2
1963	10.8	5.0	2.2
1964	9.6	4.6	2.1
1965	8.1	4.1	2.0
1966	7.3	3.3	2.2
1967 (First 9 months seasonally adjusted)	7.3	3.4	2.1

* The unemployment rate is the percent unemployed in the civilian labor force.

SOURCE: U.S. Department of Labor, Bureau of Labor Statistics. From *Social and Economic Conditions of Negroes in the United States* (Washington, D.C.: BLS Report No. 332, U.S. Department of Labor, October 1967), p. 30.

This shocking disparity between white and nonwhite rates of unemployment serves not only to pinpoint what is probably the major source for the social crisis of the sixties but brings the problem of disparities in opportunity structure closer to the school and to education as it affects opportunity generally.

Table 1.5 Unemployed Teenagers* and Percent Still in School, 1963, 1966, and 1967

	Unemployment		Unemployed: Number (thousands)		Unemployed: Percent still in school	
	Nonwhite	White	Nonwhite	White	Nonwhite	White
1963	30.2	15.5	175	708	22	34
1966	25.4	11.2	185	650	27	39
1967 (First 6 months)**	26.3	11.2	182	615	32	38

* "Teenagers" include those 16-19 years old. Full-time students are also counted as unemployed if they want a job and have been actively looking for work during the four-week period prior to interview in the monthly survey of the labor force.
** Not seasonally adjusted.

SOURCE: U.S. Department of Labor, Bureau of Labor Statistics. From *Social and Economic Conditions of Negroes in the United States* (Washington, D.C.: BLS Report No. 332, U.S. Department of Labor, October 1967), p. 33.

EDUCATION AND OPPORTUNITY

It seems merely a truism to say that there is a direct relationship between a man's occupation and his schooling, since it is an article of faith in our society that "if you want to get ahead" you must have a good education. For many occupations, particularly for the professions, level of schooling has a meaningful relationship simply because one cannot practice a profession without the required advanced degree. It is also true that if one examines general occupational levels one finds that the median years of schooling of those on each level follow a consistent trend, as in the following examples:

Occupation	Median years of schooling
Professional and Technical	over 16 years
Sales workers	12.3
Managers and proprietors	12.2
Craftsmen and foremen	9.3
Service workers	8.7

But the widespread belief that one cannot attain occupational status without a great deal of formal schooling, or that a certain amount of schooling automatically confers a job at a certain level, can only lead to simple-minded solutions for very complex problems. Although it is not the intention of this discussion, nor of the later treatment of the relation of education to social mobility, to attempt to prove that schooling is irrelevant, we do propose to substitute a more balanced view of the function of schooling in opportunity than one finds among the public generally.

The correlation between schooling and occupation is, in fact, only .32,*[6] a modest relationship suggesting that only about 10 percent of the difference in occupations is accounted for by the education of those holding the jobs. The correlation is lower than one might expect from the previous table of average schooling for groups of occupations because those averages do not tell us about the very considerable spread on both sides of that single value. Figure 1.2 presents a more accurate picture of the real situation. Occupational status scores represent an estimate of occupational prestige, based on a survey of national rankings of a wide variety of jobs.

In Figure 1.2 the width of the bar is proportional to the number of men in the population at the given educational level and its length represents the spread above and below the mean of the majority of men in each group. Thus, it is clear that although high-school graduation is generally assumed to give a man a poorer chance than college attendance, a considerable number of high-school graduates have better jobs than the average man who has one to three years of college. Half of those who leave college before graduating do as well as a majority of the men who finish college, and as well as at least half of those who go on to graduate work. At the other end of the scale half of the men who did not even complete grammar school are doing as well occupationally as many who finished high school. This data suggests that one must look more cautiously at other often-cited advantages of education for chances at a good life.

There is a similar relationship between education and income. It is possible, however, that the usual interpretation of this relation —that the more schooling one can get the higher one's income will be— reverses the true explanation, which may be that those men who will earn higher incomes for a number of reasons also happen to stay in school longer.

Some support for this alternative possibility may be found in recent estimates of education as an investment for both whites and blacks. The assumption of these kinds of analyses is that the time, effort, and money spent on a man's education can be computed and that his lifetime earnings represent a return on that investment. But suppose that instead of spending it on schooling he took the entire sum and bought a reasonable portfolio of stocks and bonds. How would his return compare to his investment in education?

* Before reading this section you may find it necessary to study the appendix, which deals with the interpretation of statistical measures with particular attention to the meaning of correlation coefficients.

6. Peter M. Blau and Otis D. Duncan, *The American Occupational Structure* (New York: John Wiley & Sons, Inc., 1967).

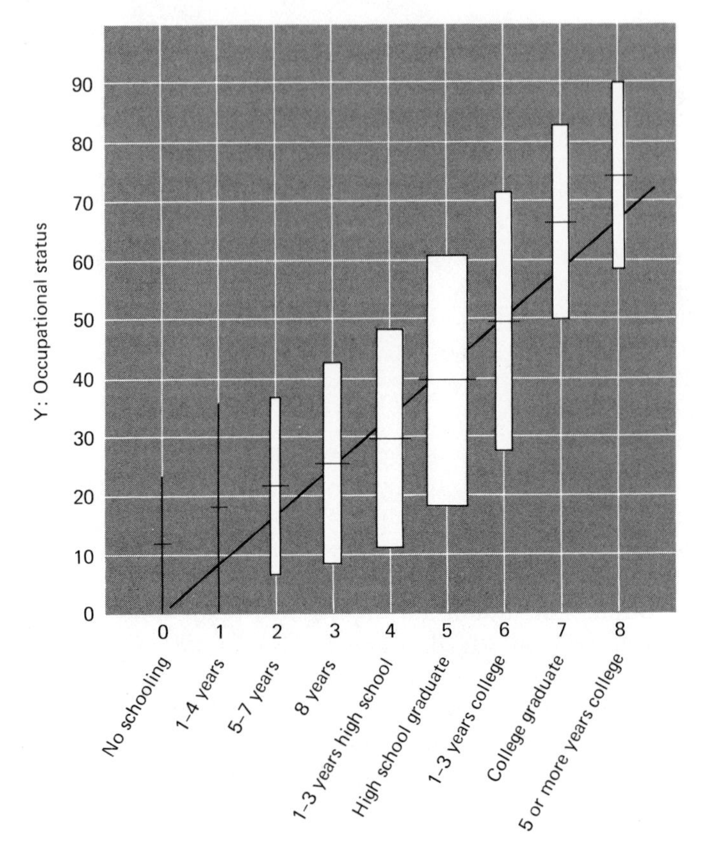

Figure 1.2 Bars represent ± one standard deviation from the mean of educational attainment for males 20-64 years old with nonfarm background. SOURCE: Peter M. Blau and Otis D. Duncan, *The American Occupational Structure* (New York: John Wiley & Sons, Inc., 1967), p. 144.

A recent projection of net lifetime income for men born in 1949 estimated that white men who attended college for four or more years are likely to earn $86,000 more than high-school graduates. This represents $17,000 more than they would make if they invested the cost of their schooling at 5 percent interest. But nonwhite males with the same amount of college earn only about $27,000 more than high-school graduates, and nonwhite men with only one to three years of college lose money. They earn only $1100 more, as against a possible gain of over $3000 from an equal investment at 5 percent.[7]

7. Melvin Borland and Donald E. Yett, "The Cash Value of College—for Negroes and for Whites," *Transaction* (November 1967), p. 46.

The relation between education and income is obviously a very uneven one and subject to considerable interference from other factors. In this case several factors are probably influential; discrimination in hiring and promotion policies, as well as the quality of higher education to which black Americans have access, play a part.[8]

Table 1.6 Median Income of Men 25 Years Old and Over by Educational Attainment, 1966

		Median income, 1966		Nonwhite income as a percent of white
		Nonwhite	White	
Elementary:	Total	$2632	$3731	71
	Less than 8 years	2376	2945	81
	8 years	3681	4611	80
High school:	Total	4725	6736	70
	1 to 3 years	4278	6189	69
	4 years	5188	7068	73
College:	Total	5928	9023	66

SOURCE: U.S. Department of Commerce, Bureau of the Census. From *Social and Economic Conditions of Negroes in the United States* (Washington, D.C.: BLS Report No. 332, U.S. Department of Labor, October 1967), p. 21.

Considering only the current data, in fact, increasing amounts of education seem to be a disadvantage for the black male in more ways than as a mere theoretical investment opportunity. Consider, for example, the relation of education to current income for this group alone in Table 1.6. A nonwhite with an elementary-school education has an income that is four-fifths that of comparable whites, but a college man's income falls to only two-thirds that of the comparable group of whites. That is not to say, of course, that college-educated blacks do not earn more than less well-educated blacks, only that their position is a less equitable one. Nor is it difficult to find explanations. Industrial unions probably play an equalizing role at the lower levels of education and occupation, for one. At the upper levels discriminatory hiring probably shunts many college-educated black men into jobs that are inferior to their preparation, thus depressing their income average as a group.

It is more difficult to explain the apparent irrelevance of schooling to employment opportunity at the beginning of work careers. A major theme of the sixties has been an insistence on the part of governmental

8. Christopher Jencks and David Riesman, "The American Negro College," *Harvard Educational Review,* Vol. 37, No. 1 (Winter 1967), pp. 3-60.

agencies and civil rights organizations that young men finish high school. One of the major attacks mounted on the school itself has been its inability to hold minority-group youngsters until graduation. Yet the evidence is far from clear that high-school graduation makes as significant a difference as is commonly thought.

Table 1.7 Unemployment Rates and Education of Persons 18 Years Old and Over, March 1967

	Male			Female		
Years of school completed	White	Non-white	Ratio*	White	Non-white	Ratio*
Total	2.7	6.5	2.4	4.0	8.4	2.1
Less than 4 years of high school	4.0	7.5	1.9	5.4	9.7	1.8
Elementary: 8 years or less	4.0	6.8	1.7	5.0	7.0	1.4
High school: 1 to 3 years	4.0	8.8	2.2	5.8	13.0	2.2
4 years of high school or more	1.8	4.7	2.6	3.2	6.9	2.2
High school: 4 years	2.3	5.4	2.3	3.7	7.7	2.1
College: 1 year or more	1.3	3.2	2.5	2.4	5.0	2.1

* Nonwhite unemployment rate divided by white unemployment rate.

SOURCE: *Educational Attainment of Workers, March 1967* (Special Labor Force Report No. 92, U.S. Department of Labor), p. 29.

There *is* a difference in officially gathered data for unemployment, as Table 1.7 shows. The interpretation of this data is complicated by recent evidence indicating that currently, at least, the high-school diploma has little overall impact on employment.

The report is from a very extensive, continuing study of education called Project Talent, which began in 1960 with a sample of 440,000 students attending over 1300 public and private schools.* In 1964 the project followed up those students who had been in the ninth grade at the original testing, comparing those who had dropped out before graduation with a random sample of control students selected from those who had graduated but had not gone on to college.

The authors of the report on the dropout phase of the study conclude that:

In 1964, the employment rates of dropouts and controls were quite similar. Ninety percent of the dropouts who did not continue their education after

* It is important in assessing these findings that the subjects were a probability sample of the United States student population. Only with this type of sample is it possible to estimate accurately the probability of error in the final results.

leaving high school were employed, 87% full-time, three percent parttime. The greatest percentages of dropouts were unskilled workers (drivers, laborer, miner, etc.), skilled workers (waiter, hairdresser, barber, etc.). The greatest percentage of controls were unskilled, skilled or clerical and sales workers. . . For the dropouts who were employed, the mean yearly salary was $3650; for controls it was $3500. The probable reason for this difference is that dropouts had been working longer than controls, in some cases four years longer.[9]

There are some differences in the level of jobs obtained between the two groups, and this may result in later gains for the graduating controls; but the picture as a whole for the dropout group does not seem greatly disadvantageous. Moreover, during the first half of the decade of the sixties the nonwhite youngster appeared to be rapidly closing the high-school educational gap, as Table 1.8 shows.

Table 1.8 Educational Attainment of Persons 25 to 29 Years Old by Sex, 1960 and 1966

	Male		Female	
	Nonwhite	White	Nonwhite	White
Median years of school completed:				
1960	10.5	12.4	11.1	12.3
1966	12.1	12.6	11.9	12.5
Percent completing 4 years of high school or more:				
1960	36	63	41	65
1966	53	73	49	74

SOURCE: U.S. Department of Commerce, Bureau of the Census. From *Social and Economic Conditions of Negroes in the United States* (Washington, D.C.: BLS Report No. 332, U.S. Department of Labor, October 1967) p. 46.

For whatever high-school graduation is worth, the nonwhite male has made considerable progress toward equality in those five years and improved his group's position in education beyond high school as well, though he still lags considerably behind the white. If one interprets this data as indicating a loss in significance of the high-school diploma and a parallel shift upward in the society's demands for schooling, it appears that well-meaning public relations campaigns are somewhat wide of the mark. For the sake of equity the emphasis should be on getting able nonwhite youth into junior colleges and universities rather than trying to prevent high-school dropping out.

9. Janet Combs and W.W. Cooley, "Dropouts: In High School and After School," *American Educational Research Journal,* Vol. 5, No. 3 (May 1968), pp. 343-363.

To summarize, school appears to be only a contributing factor in the complicated network of influences that determine opportunity and life chance, rather than the simple and direct causative agent it is often taken to be. For black Americans it seems to be an even less potent factor than for the society as a whole, and it seems likely from the data that the high unemployment rates of nonwhite youth previously noted are due as much to discrimination and a congery of other factors as to failure in school.

Schooling *is* a factor, however, whether one sees it as the main, or only a contributing, one; and whatever the larger society may do to improve opportunities must be accompanied by efforts to equalize school success for minority groups.

The magnitude of the effort required to do so may be estimated by examining on a very broad scale the academic retardation of minority-group children, as shown in Table 1.9.

Table 1.9 Nationwide Median Test Scores for First- and Twelfth-Grade Pupils

Test	Puerto Ricans	Indian-Americans	Mexican-Americans	Oriental-Americans	Negro	Majority
First grade:						
Nonverbal	45.8	53.0	50.1	56.6	43.4	54.1
Verbal	44.9	47.8	46.5	51.6	45.4	53.2
Twelfth grade:						
Nonverbal	43.3	47.1	45.0	51.6	40.9	52.0
Verbal	43.1	43.7	43.8	49.6	40.9	52.1
Reading	42.6	44.3	44.2	48.8	42.2	51.9
Mathemathics	43.7	45.9	45.5	51.3	41.8	51.8
General information	41.7	44.7	43.3	49.0	40.6	52.2
Average of the 5 tests	43.1	45.1	44.4	50.1	41.1	52.0

SOURCE: *Equality of Educational Opportunity, Summary Report* (Washington, D.C.: U.S. Department of Health, Education and Welfare, 1966), p. 20.

These scores have been standardized so that the average is 50 and the standard deviation is 10. Thus, half of any normal group should fall below 50, and about 34 percent should be between 50 and 40, one standard deviation below the mean. The average for black students on general information, therefore, means that almost 85 percent of these students scored below the average of the white majority students.

It is evident that only Oriental-American youth at the twelfth-grade level come close to majority-group achievement norms. It is also interesting and important to note that black children not only lag behind the other minorities in general but that by the end of high school their verbal scores are below those of Puerto Ricans, many of whom start school with the initial handicap of a lack of knowledge of the English language.

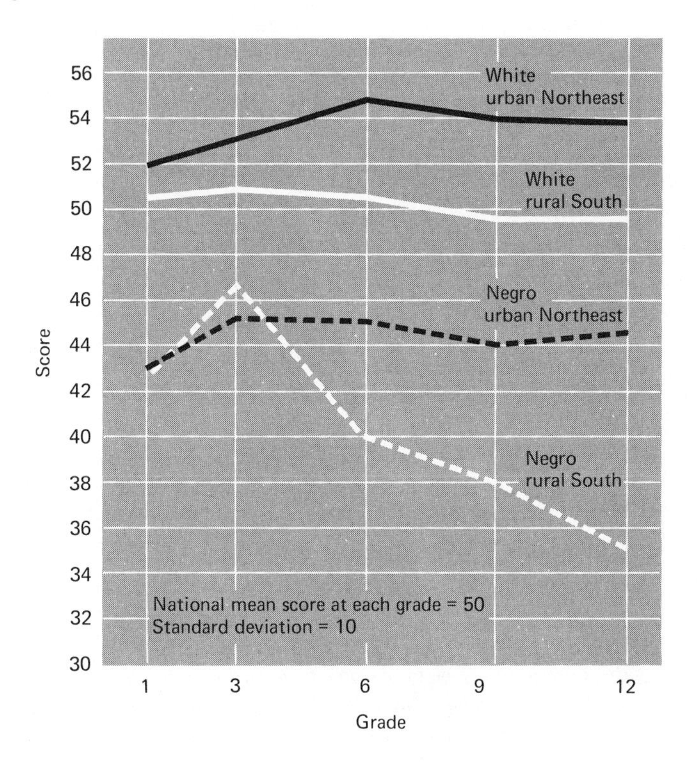

Figure 1.3 Patterns of achievement in verbal skills at various grade levels by race and region.

SOURCE: James Coleman, "The Concept of Equality of Educational Opportunity," *Harvard Educational Review,* Vol. 38, No. 1 (Winter 1968), p. 20.

As is the case with access to opportunity in general, both regional and urban-rural differences strongly influence these achievement levels, particularly for the black, but, as Figure 1.3 shows, even to some extent for the white majority child. James Coleman, from whose study this data is taken, argues that these curves are a rough measure of the school's failure to compensate for the differences in background that give minority-group children unequal access to opportunity in the first place. Some school professionals might view them as proof of the proposition that environment and early training are such strong forces that the school simply cannot overcome them. This central issue is a theme which will appear consistently throughout the second half of this book, as the role of the school in the central city is examined in depth.

ERADICATING POVERTY: PROPOSALS AND PROJECTS

If the structure of poverty and opportunity access so far described indicates the soundness of any generalization, it is that there are a large variety of different problems involved. Any one solution usually fits only one or two of the categories of poor or otherwise disadvantaged people. In the following discussions consideration of the role of formal schooling in the efforts to equalize opportunity requires some awareness of the broad spectrum of possible solutions. The serious proposals and on-going projects that are currently on the social scene will be grouped roughly into two major approaches, those for which the *structural* nature of the problem is paramount, and those that concentrate on *functional* disabilities of the socially disadvantaged.

There is an important general distinction between these terms. C. Wright Mills put the difference most succinctly in discussing two types of social issues when he wrote:

> When, in a city of 100,000, only one man is unemployed, that is his personal trouble, and for its relief we properly look to the character of the man, his skills, and his immediate opportunities. But when in a nation of 50 million employees, 15 million men are unemployed, that is an issue, and we may not hope to find its solution within the range of opportunities open to any one individual. The very structure of opportunities has collapsed. . . Consider marriage. Inside a marriage, a man and a woman may experience personal troubles, but when the divorce rate during the first four years of marriage is 250 out of every 1,000 attempts, this is an indication of a structural issue having to do with the institution of marriage and the family and other institutions that bear upon them.[10]

The approach to poverty and opportunity that looks fundamentally at structure assumes primarily that consistent personal patterns of behavior can best be explained not as individual problems but as responses to particular positions within the opportunity structure of the larger society, and, consequently, that they must be dealt with by changing broad social policy rather than on an individual basis.

Thus, it is clear that a large proportion of families are below the poverty level because of age or are unable to be productive and raise dependent children at the same time. These two large groups currently receive the major portion of their income from the government in the form of old-age benefits or aid-to-dependent-children payments. The rea-

10. C. Wright Mills, *The Sociological Imagination* (New York: Oxford University Press, 1959), p. 9.

son they are in poverty is that these payments are below the currently defined poverty line; all that is required to bring them above that line is to increase the present allowances.

Most of the remaining poor families owe their disadvantaged position to a variety of circumstances that decrease their productive capacity: Either the family heads operate marginal enterprises, such as uneconomical farms; or they are disabled; or have such low levels of skill that they are hired for only the lowest-paid jobs; or they are subject to social discrimination. Those who approach the problem structurally have advanced two major proposals to alleviate the plight of these families.

The first of these consists of various suggestions for manipulating the forces in the total economy with the aim of creating such a high demand for labor that even the unskilled will be pulled into the labor market at relatively high wages. The argument, in very simple terms, is that the government can, if it wishes to employ appropriate fiscal policies, encourage industry and business to increase their production to a point at which the productive resources of the economy are close to being fully employed. At such a point, theoretically, even the very unskilled and marginal worker can easily find jobs, and discrimination is lessened because employers, however prejudiced they may be, find it profitable to hire people.

Those economists who advocate this proposal point to the experience of Western Germany in the first half of the decade of the sixties as proof of their thesis. In that period production pushed so hard against labor capacity that unskilled workers from Italy and parts of Central Europe were imported to Germany in large numbers. Or, for another example, they cite the American experience during World War II, where industry working around the clock created a demand for labor that brought great numbers of both black and white marginal workers from the South to Northern cities.

An alternative solution of a structural sort is considerably simpler. The story goes that on a television panel show dealing with poverty the panel leader asked the University of Chicago economist, Milton Friedman: "We realize that dealing with poverty is an enormously complex and difficult problem, but can you tell us what *you* think provides the best solution?" To which Dr. Friedman succinctly replied, "More money." He was, in fact, perhaps the earliest advocate of a policy for simply instituting an income floor below which no American family should be permitted to fall. Nor is there any lack of concrete proposals for procedures that would successfully accomplish that end, ranging from family allowance systems, such as those operating in France and the Scandinavian countries, to a variety of suggestions for a negative income tax. Because this latter idea is likely to be the one that will be subjected to greatest public discussion, it is worth a closer examination.

Although there is little agreement among economists about where a minimum level of income should be set, most of the guaranteed income plans use the mechanism of the federal income tax as a device for carrying out the scheme. Each family will file a return showing its income, and will pay a regular tax if that income is above a designated figure. If the income falls below the set level, the family head would file a claim for a benefit in the amount of the difference between his actual income and the maintenance level. Table 1.10 illustrates how such a plan would work if one assumes a guaranteed income of $3000 a year for a four-person family; it was drawn up by Edward Schwartz of the University of Chicago. The cost of this plan would vary according to the income standard selected. At this minimum maintenance level the cost to the government would be $11 billion; at what Schwartz calls the economy level ($4000), $23 billion; and at a modest-but-adequate level ($5000), $38 billion. It must be noted that these outlays would substitute for very considerable expenditures for welfare benefits of various kinds (about $5½ billion) already being spent, so the net increase in government costs would not be as high as the figures actually cited.

Table 1.10 Income Allowance Plan Based on a Four-Person Family and Using a Minimum Maintenance Allowance Guarantee Level (in dollars)

Earned income	Family security benefits received or taxes paid	Total income
0- 999	3000-2400	3000-3399
1000-1999	2399-1700	3399-3699
2000-2999	1699- 900	3699-3899
3000-3999	899- 0	3899-3999
4000-4999	0	4000-4499
4500 and above	Tax on amounts above 4500	4500 plus

SOURCE: Edward E. Schwartz, "'A Way to End the Means Test," *Social Work* (July 1964), p. 9.

Although these minimum income plans would, in effect, eliminate poverty as currently defined, they would do little to help those family heads with low skills or marginal occupations get into the economic mainstream and give them some hope of bettering themselves.

Another type of proposal would accept some form of guaranteed income for those who cannot work at all (the aged, mothers with dependent children, and so on), but add to this devices to produce job expansion at the lower level of skills. The most attractive and far-reaching suggestion of this sort is that the government act as an employer of last resort.

Such a system of guaranteed employment would offer a job to any person who, because of low skill level or disability, could not find a job that would bring him a reasonable income above the poverty line. Nor would such a job have to be merely "make work." Daniel Moynihan, author of *The Negro Family* (*see* chapter 4), has calculated, for example, that if the post office returned to a system of two mail deliveries a day, which it abandoned earlier for reasons of economy, several hundred thousand jobs would be created overnight. More general estimates of the jobs that could usefully be done to improve the services of hospitals, museums, libraries, parks, and other public facilities run to several million nationally.

All of these proposals make a good deal of sense and have the great virtue of avoiding the creation of large government bureaucracies for administration. Critics have pointed out a number of flaws in all of them however.

There is considerable question, for instance, whether we have as yet enough skill for large-scale manipulation of the economy, as in the first proposal considered, without risking a runaway inflation as full use of the productive capacity is approached. In 1968 Congress had to be induced to pass a substantial tax increase in an effort to slow down production and spending to reduce inflationary pressures. It seems unlikely that conservative government fiscal experts will in the near future choose to take the risks demanded in heating up the economy.

Guaranteed income plans have come under fire for a number of reasons, the most important of which, doubts about their social consequences, is stated by James Vadakin, an economist, in this way:

> While undoubtedly not intended by their proponents, there is a pervasive suggestion emanating from these plans that the payments represent a sort of "social conscience money," as it is termed by Harry G. Johnson, paid by an affluent society to those of its members who do not share in a decent standard of living. Such payments of "conscience money" are easily justified on a short-term basis. But do we want them as permanent features of American society? Do we not wish to incorporate the poor into the mainstream of American life? Although there might be some small structural gains from such plans, as a result of altered habits and motivations of the poor once they come to enjoy more acceptable levels of living, the fact is that guarantee plans would do little to improve our human resources, to equip the able-bodied and nonaged poor to earn a better livelihood, and to contribute to our total social product.[11]

11. James C. Vadakin, "A Critique of the Guaranteed Annual Income," *The Public Interest,* No. 11 (Spring 1968), pp. 63-64.

Many other questions focus on what such an income floor would do to the incentive motive of the poor. Not much is known about how incentive operates in general, and it is obviously nonsense to talk about reducing the incentive to work on the part of the aged and infirm by providing them with a decent living standard. But large numbers of the welfare poor might well elect to accept a minimum income rather than perform low-paying and demeaning work.

Nor do such schemes fit very well into the ethical views of the American people. In a 1966 poll conducted in Minnesota only 24 percent of the respondents favored a negative income tax, and it is doubtful that even a majority of the poor, if consulted, would approve of it. Work is a central value in our culture, and the connection between income and productive work in the minds of most Americans is a very strong one.

Even more important, perhaps, than the ethical problems is the reaction of those Americans who themselves are gainfully employed and living on incomes not very much above the suggested minimum. A man earning $5000 a year and paying taxes on that income, thereby further reducing it, is unlikely to find a situation acceptable in which another able-bodied person is being given an income not very much less than his own net pay. Even if Congress were disposed to favor the idea of a negative income tax, which they are not, the hostile reaction of millions of constituents would act as an effective brake on such legislation.

This kind of objection does not apply to proposals for government guarantees of jobs, resistance to which appears to consist of a distaste left over from the thirties Depression for federally-created employment and, perhaps most important, to its cost. With peace in Vietnam and a redirecting of federal expenditure, it may yet turn out to be a workable answer to part of the problem of opportunity.

Functional Approaches

Programs that aim at the rehabilitation or improvement of the individual are, of course, the traditional American answer to the problems of poverty or lack of opportunity. An answer one sees most widely applied is the vast welfare system operated at local levels but largely federally funded.

The system has been under increasing attack throughout the sixties and is slowly moving toward a reform of its worst features. Criticisms have focused mainly on two unintended consequences of the way it is customarily administered. First, it is correctly claimed that the methods of making payment in general are demeaning to the recipients, making it impossible for them to retain any sense of self-respect and, in some ways, destroying family stability rather than working to improve it. A mother on welfare, for example, must spend her funds as dictated by welfare department budgets; if she needs new clothes for a child she must make an application for special funds. In many states a woman with children on welfare is not permitted to have a man in the house, which not only discourages her from marrying but encourages the bizarre practice of midnight raids by welfare departments to make sure that a man is not hidden in the apartment.

Second, the welfare bureaucracies are so busy investigating such matters as whether a recipient really needs a new shirt for her small son or whether she is spending her income precisely as budgeted, that little time is left for helping people solve the basic problems of their dependency and move toward self-sufficiency. Although there is a good deal of movement on and off welfare rolls, the system as such tends to encourage dependency among a large group of recipients for lack of anything else to do.

Recent reforms include Congressional authorization for aid to dependent children for those families with a working father in the home if his income is insufficient to support the family, a humane program that many states have adopted. It is likely, too, that more enlightened states will move toward a system in which a lump sum for clothes, furniture, and other items will simply be added to the basic allowance, permitting the recipient to make his own decisions about how to allocate funds and allowing the welfare department itself to use its personnel for more important tasks than checking rule-book expenditures.

Those tasks will inevitably involve education of one sort or another, primarily the improvement of skills to enable people to enter the labor force at a wage level where it makes sense for them to relinquish welfare. This aspect of urban education, though it does not involve the public schools in any significant sense, nonetheless is a problem of crucial importance that deserves some attention here.

The government has funded a number of training programs for both out-of-school youths, whose excessive unemployment rates were noted earlier, and for older adults, who need skill-upgrading and basic education. Only a very small proportion of the effort has been aimed at this latter group, and, though data is lacking, the general impression of most educators is that the adult programs have accomplished very little.

The most visible, and most controversial, of the training programs for youth is the Job Corps. This program was created by the Economic Opportunity Act to prepare youths aged 16 through 21 "for the responsibility of citizenship and to increase employability . . . by providing them in rural and urban residential centers with education, vocational

Table 1.11 Labor Force Status of Corpsmen, May 1967 (left Centers September-November 1966) — by percent*

	Working			Unemployed			In school and other**		
	Before entering Job Corps	Upon leaving Job Corps	6 months later	Before entering Job Corps	Upon leaving Job Corps	6 months later	Before entering Job Corps	Upon leaving Job Corps	6 months later
Total	44	53	58	44	39	34	12	9	11
Graduates	47	56	65	42	38	27	11	7	11
Dropouts	41	52	54	47	40	38	12	10	10
Discharges	46	53	55	42	39	38	12	10	11
Sex									
Men	47	55	59	42	37	33	11	8	10
Women	27	34	46	52	56	43	16	13	15
Race									
Negro	48	52	58	39	39	33	13	10	11
White	39	55	59	52	39	34	9	8	10
Length of time in Job Corps									
Less than 3 months	37	54	49	50	37	37	13	11	17
3-6 months	44	52	59	46	40	37	10	10	12
More than 6 months	52	55	67	36	41	26	12	5	8
Age									
16-17	39	50	55	45	37	40	16	13	16
18-19	43	51	54	45	42	33	12	10	10
20-21	52	59	68	42	38	29	6	3	6

* Figures may add up to more than 100 percent because some were both in school and working.

** About four of every five were in school. The survey fails to include former Corpsmen who entered military service. If the 7 percent of all former Corpsmen who were in the military were included, the overall distribution of their labor force status would have been: working, 54 percent; in school, 8 percent; in military, 7 percent; unemployed, 32 percent; other, 2 percent.

SOURCE: Louis Harris and Associates. *A Continuous Study of Job Corps Termination* (May 1967). Reproduced from Sar A. Levitan, *Antipoverty*

education, useful work directed toward conservation of natural resources, and other appropriate activities."[12] The key term in the act is "residential," for it was assumed that training was more likely to be effective if the participants were removed from environments that could only have a negative influence.

By the summer of 1967 there were 122 residential centers; 20 of these were for women; the majority of those for men were in rural rather than urban settings. In the first three years the total funds allocated totaled $715 million, during which time the centers enrolled almost 40,000 youths, 75 percent of them boys.

It is not an easy matter to assess the accomplishments of this program. Its early operations were subjected to a barrage of political criticism and to a bad press in general, due to conflicts between some residents and members of the local communities. There has been great confusion over the costs of the program, and the failure of the administrators "to explain the reasons for the high costs added to the impression that there were grounds for the charge that the centers were 'country clubs for juvenile delinquents.' "[13] In his study of the Job Corps, Sar Levitan cites as the latest estimate the figure of $8100 as the annual cost per enrollee.

Table 1.11 summarizes the impact of the Corps on one group of boys who left during a three-month period. Employability for both whites and blacks appears to have been improved by the period of training, but the improvement is far greater for women than for men. A significant influence on the benefits obtained from the Corps seems to be the length of time the trainee stayed at the Center. As a study by Harris notes: "The longer a corpsman stays in the Job Corps, the more likely he is to have changed jobs. Longer exposure to the Job Corps thus leads to higher employment and greater job stability."[14]

A crucial problem, then, is the low holding power of the Centers. Levitan's evidence suggests that about 40 percent of the Corpsmen drop out before three months, and that an additional third do so before six months. If the major benefit of the program accrues to those who remain longer than six months, only about a quarter of the total enrolled are getting those benefits. This is dramatically shown by comparing the Corpsmen with a group of youth who were selected for training but who never showed up at the Centers, in Table 1.12.

The "no shows" do better than all groups of Corpsmen except those who stayed in the Corps beyond six months. Since this is a minority

12. Quoted in Sar A. Levitan, *Antipoverty Work and Training Efforts: Goals and Reality* (Detroit: Institute of Labor and Industrial Relations of the University of Michigan and Wayne State University, 1967), p. 5.
13. *Ibid.*, p. 9.
14. *Ibid.*, p. 28.

of the total group, and since it is not unlikely that their staying power indicates superior motivation in general, the conclusion of a sophisticated cost analysis study that investment in the Job Corps passes the test of economic efficiency seems highly debatable. The study considered not only the 12 cent difference in average hourly wage gain on the part of Corpsmen over the control group but also the gain in education achievement, nine months at a center equaling 1.6 years of schooling. At a cost of $8000 a year these gains seem hardly substantial enough to justify the program.

Table 1.12 Labor Force Status and Wages of Former Corpsmen and "No Shows" (by percent*)

Corpsmen*	Employed	Unemployed	In school	Other	Hourly rate of those employed
More than 6 months	69	27	7	1	$1.50
3-6 months	56	36	11	1	1.40
Less than 3 months	49	43	7	1	1.39
No shows**	60	27	14	6	1.42

* Figures add to more than 100 percent because some were both working and in school.

** Former Corpsmen were interviewed in February 1967, six months after leaving Job Corps; no shows (accepted by Job Corps but not enrolled during 1965 and 1966) were interviewed January and February 1967, within 16 months after screening. Wage data may therefore not be comparable because federal minimum wage was raised from $1.25 to $1.40, effective February 1, 1967, after some no shows were interviewed. The extent to which the boost in minimum wages affected wage rates of former Corpsmen is not known.

SOURCE: Louis Harris and Associates, *A Study of August 1966 Terminations from the Job Corps* (March 1967) and *A Study of Job Corps "No Shows": Accepted Applicants Who Did Not Go to a Center* (February 1967). Reproduced from Sar A. Levitan, *Antipoverty Work and Training Efforts: Goals and Reality* (Institute of Labor and Industrial Relations of the University of Michigan and Wayne State University, 1967), p. 34.

Levitan's assessment of a second program, the Neighborhood Youth Corps, is even less encouraging. This program has two aims: to create parttime jobs for youths attending school, and a separate fulltime work program for idle 16-20 year olds, mostly high-school dropouts. A total of $773 million was allocated in its first three years of operation.

There is no doubt that the in-school program helped many young people by providing them with some income during the school year and particularly during the summer, but the evidence for its success in decreasing the dropout rate, which is the crucial test of its effectiveness, is not clear. A study of two groups of Neighborhood Youth Corps enrollees in the District of Columbia found that the dropout rate among these boys was only 10 percent of the rate that normally would have been predicted for them. In a more comprehensive survey in Pittsburgh, the dropout rate among NYC enrollees was exactly half that of the rest of the students.

Yet, as Levitan points out, a satisfactory case remains to be demonstrated, since it is possible that the program has attracted the more highly motivated among the children of the poor. Other evidence suggests that, in the words of a study conducted by the NYC itself: "The NYC summer program still is not an effective vehicle for attracting young dropouts back to school."[15] The same study found that one of every four enrollees dropped out of the project before completing his allotted time, yet the same proportions of this group returned to school as those who stayed with the project until the end.

The out-of-school program had apparently only a small impact on the employment future of the enrollees. An extensive survey that followed up a group of boys who had been in the program to determine what they were doing five to fifteen months afterward found that about three out of every five were engaged in some form of productive work or schooling regardless of the length of time they had spent in the program. And, although there was a greater tendency for those who had remained in the program for some time to be engaged in full- or part-time jobs, those who remained the longest also showed a lower rate of return to school. More than one in five was unemployed and not even looking for work, a group that included long-term enrollees as well as short-term ones.

Levitan concludes, with some justice, that NYC fulfilled a useful function in providing disadvantaged youth with jobs that gave them at least minimum support while they were still too young to do very well in the labor market. It can thus be viewed as an "aging vat," since unemployment rates for youth decline normally as they mature. But that the program delivered on its stated responsibility to help youth "to develop their maximum occupational potential" is clearly not the case.

The general failure of such training programs to achieve sizeably significant results, a failure which is matched in a number of similar large-scale training efforts, can be attributed to the operation of a number of factors. A clue to what is possibly the most important of these may be found in dramatic detail in an informal study of a California training program.[16] The students were twenty-five young men and twenty-five young women, most of them black, selected by a variety of

15. *Ibid.*, p. 54.

16. David Wellman, "The *Wrong* Way to Find Jobs for Negroes," *Transaction* (April 1968), pp. 9-18.

poverty programs in the Bay Area. Their ages ranged from sixteen to twenty-two. Having learned a lesson from previous training efforts, the program paid the young people $5 a day to participate.

The young sociologist, David Wellman, from whose report this account is taken sat in on the men's classes, and describes the participants and the nature of the program this way:

The young men who took part in TIDE had a distinctive style. They were "cool." Their hair was "processed." All sported sunglasses—very lightly tinted, with small frames. They called them "pimp's glasses." Their clothes, while usually inexpensive, were loud and ingeniously altered to express style and individuality. They spoke in a "hip" vernacular. Their vocabularies were small but very expressive. These young men, as part of the "cool world" of the ghetto, represent a distinctively black working-class culture.

To most liberals these young men are "culturally deprived" or "social dropouts." Most had flunked or been kicked out of school. Few had any intention of getting a high-school degree. They seemed uninterested in "making it." They had long and serious arrest and prison records. They were skeptical and critical of both the TIDE program and white society in general.

The TIDE workers were liberals. They assumed that if the young men would only act a little less "cool" and learn to smooth over some of their encounters with white authorities, they too could become full-fledged, working members of society. The aim of TIDE was not to train them for jobs, but to train them how to *apply* for jobs—how to take tests, how to make a good impression during a job interview, how to speak well, how to fill out an application form properly. They would play games, like dominoes, to ease the pain associated with numbers and arithmetic; they would conduct mock interviews, take mock tests, meet with management representatives, and tour places where jobs might be available. They were told to consider the TIDE program itself as a job—to be at the Youth Opportunities Center office on time, dressed as if they were at work. If they were late or made trouble, they would be docked. But if they took the program seriously and did well, they were told, they stood a pretty good chance of getting a job at the end of four weeks. The unexpressed aim of TIDE, then, was to prepare Negro youngsters for white society. The government would serve as an employment agency for white, private enterprise.

The program aimed to change the youngsters by making them more acceptable to employers. Their grammar and pronunciation were constantly corrected. They were indirectly told that, in order to get a job, their appearance would have to be altered: For example, "Don't you think you could shine your shoes?" Promptness, a virtue few of the youngsters possessed, was lauded. The penalty for tardiness was being put on a clean-up committee, or being docked.[17]

17. *Ibid.*, pp. 9-10.

Wellman goes on to describe the daily struggle "between white, middle class ideals of conduct and behavior and the mores and folkways of the black community." The boys engaged in elaborate forms of both "the put on" and "the put down." To put someone on is a form of hostility in which the "player" leads someone to believe that he is going along with what he says or wants done, while subtly rejecting or undermining it. The boys "put on" the instructional staff in a variety of ways—by pretending they didn't hear certain things, by playing dumb, by insisting on work-breaks and in many other ways. An example:

The program started at 9:30 A.M. The youngsters decided that their first break would be for coffee at 10:30. This break was to last until 11. And while work was never allowed to proceed a minute past 10:30, it was usually 11:15 or so before the young men actually got back to work. Lunch began at 12. Theoretically, work resumed at 1. This usually meant 1:15, since they had to listen to "one more song" on the radio. The next break was to last from 2:30 to 3. However, because they were finished at 3:30 and because it took another 10 minutes to get them back to work, the fellows could often talk their way out of the remaining half hour. Considering they were being paid $5 a day for five hours' work, of which almost half were regularly devoted to breaks, they didn't have a bad hustle.[18]

When they were not putting on the program, says Wellman, they were engaged in "putting down" the staff. The success of a "put down" depends on the victim *knowing* he is being made sport of in contrast to the put on's subtlety. An example of this tactic is the participants' response to an effort to train them for job interviews:

Actual employers, usually those representing companies that hired people only for unskilled labor, came to TIDE to demonstrate to the men what a good interview would be like. They did *not* come to interview men for real jobs. It was sort of a helpful-hints-for-successful-interviews session. Usually one of the more socially mobile youths was chosen to play the role of job applicant. The entire interview situation was played through. Some employers even went so far as to have the "applicant" go outside and knock on the door to begin the interview. The students thought this was both odd and funny, and one said to the employer: "Man, you've already *seen* the cat. How come you making him walk out and then walk back in?"

With a look of incredulity, the employer replied: "But that's how you get a job. You have to sell yourself from the moment you walk in that door."

The employer put on a real act, beginning the interview with the usual small talk.

"I see from your application that you played football in high school."

18. *Ibid.*, p. 11.

"Yeah."

"Did you like it?"

"Yeah."

"Football really makes men and teaches you teamwork."

"Yeah."

At this point, the men got impatient: "Man, the cat's here to get a job, not talk about football!"

A wisecracker chimed in: "Maybe he's interviewing for a job with the Oakland Raiders."

Usually the employer got the point. He would then ask about the "applicant's" job experience, draft status, school record, interests, skills, and so on. The young man being interviewed usually took the questions seriously and answered frankly. But after a while, the rest of the group would tire of the game and (unrecognized, from the floor) begin to ask about the specifics of a real job:

"Say man, how much does this job pay?"

"What kind of experience do you need?"

"What if you got a record?"

It didn't take long to completely rattle an interviewer. The instructor might intervene and tell the students that the gentleman was there to help them, but this would stifle revolt for only a short while. During one interview, several of the fellows began loudly playing dominoes. That got the response they were looking for.

"Look!" shouted the employer. "If you're not interested in learning how to sell yourself, why don't you just leave the room so that others who are interested can benefit from this?"

"Oh no!" responded the ringleaders. "We work here. If you don't dig us, then *you* leave!"

Not much later, he did.[19]

Wellman's conclusion from his observations is that the fiasco was wholly the fault of the white liberals who constituted the staff of the program. They did not understand that growing up in a racist society had made the boys deeply suspicious and hostile, and they acted on the naïve belief that the boys would respond in the same way that they themselves would. Thus, they blamed the participants instead of themselves for the failure of the training program. From the boys' point of view, says Wellman, the program was a sham because it tried to convince them that *if* they prepared themselves there would be attractive jobs waiting for youths who were black and had police records. And, he argues, the boys' suspicions were correct.

This interpretation makes some bitter sense, but it is not the only significant implication of the experience; there is something to be said

19. *Ibid.*, p. 12.

for the staff's belief that if you want a good job in this society you have to play society's game of politeness, punctuality, and good appearance. The boys were unwilling to control the expression of their hostility sufficiently to play that game rather than their own. The gratification of putting down the staff and visitors was so great that it prevented them from trying for a possible payoff for themselves later.

The girls in the program, on the other hand, though presumably no less hostile to a white society that looked down on them, played the program's game for all it was worth. They saw the boys' games as self-defeating, as in the following exchange when both groups were brought together to hear a talk from a black State Assemblyman:

> The moment Rumford finished speaking and asked for questions, one of the men jumped up and asked, "Hey man, how do we get a raise?" A male chorus of "Yeah!" followed. Before Rumford could complete a garbled answer (something like, "Well, I don't really know much about the procedures of a federally sponsored program"), the battle of the sexes had been joined. The women scolded the men for their "disrespectful behavior" toward an elected official. One said: "Here he is trying to help us and you-all acting a fool. You talking and laughing and carrying on while he talking and then when he finished you want to know about a raise. Damn!"
>
> "Shit," was a male response. "You don't know what you talking about. We got a *right* to ask the cat about a raise. We elected him."
>
> "We supposed to be talking about jobs," said another. "And we're talking about *our* job. If y'all like the pay, that's your business. We want more!"
>
> The debate was heated. Neither group paid any attention to Rumford, who wisely slipped out of the room.
>
> During the exchanges it became clear to me that the differences in clothing and style between the sexes reflected their different orientations toward the dominant society and its values. In the minds of the young women, respect and respectability seemed paramount. At one point, a young woman said to the men, "You acting just like a bunch of *niggers*." She seemed to identify herself as a Negro, not as a "nigger." For the men, on the other hand, becoming a Negro (as opposed to a "nigger") meant giving up much that they considered positive. As one young man said in answer to the above, "You just ain't got no soul, bitch."[20]

In the tangle of moral and social conflicts represented in this case one can at least clearly see that training without a real job as a goal is not likely to succeed with many of the young black men who are at the core of the problem of opportunity. There are several trends now emerging as a response to increasing recognition of this fact.

One is a reliance on training *on* the job, instead of before employment. Several large automobile companies in Detroit, as well as other

20. *Ibid.*, p. 14.

industries scattered throughout the country, are hiring members of the hard-core unemployed, putting them on specific jobs under training conditions, and paying them the going rate from the beginning. In some cases part of the work day is also devoted to basic education classes to bring participants up to high-school level in reading and mathematical skills. The most successful of these programs do not take for granted that even this immediate provision of job opportunity will be effective without a great deal of help for the individual. If one of the men does not show up for work someone goes out to find him; it turns out, in many cases, that the worker simply does not have an alarm clock, so unaccustomed is he to a regular work situation. The federal government has itself belatedly overcome its reluctance to support the private sector of the economy in such efforts and is now underwriting the training and turnover costs of a nationwide program of this type.

A second, and even more promising, approach is represented by the growing programs in subprofessional training, which represent one of the very few genuinely creative ideas about the expansion of opportunity in a whole decade of attention to that problem. In the report of a recent conference the idea is defined by the following characteristics:

> Subprofessional jobs consist of subsections of work, heretofore done by professionals, for which full professional training is not necessary, or of new functions that expand the scope of professional services.
>
> The jobs are designed at the entry level so that persons with less than the training or academic credentials that usually accompany professional status can, in relatively short periods, become sufficiently skilled to perform the work.
>
> The jobs allow opportunity for individual development, regardless of the traditional credentials or other arbitrary symbols of status, and permit advancement to duties of greater challenge and responsibility.
>
> Advancement is accompanied by increments of earnings and access to promotional avenues which are not dependent exclusively on full-time formal training financed by the individual.[21]

The fields in which most of the subprofessional job development is taking place are health, welfare, and education. A later chapter will consider in detail the use of teacher aides from the urban community itself in schools of the inner city. The broad possibilities inherent in the idea may be grasped by a look at the kinds of jobs that, unlike teacher aides, do not even exist at present:

> Social work aides to help with patients in communities and hospitals.
> Homemakers to help patients recover in their own homes.

21. Edith F. Lynton, *The Subprofessional* (New York: National Committee on Employment of Youth, 1967), p. 2.

Halfway house aides to care for those who no longer need hospital care but have no other place to go.

Community mental health workers to work with families, with individuals, and assist teachers in diagnosing children's problems.

Counseling aides, possibly themselves ex-addicts or ex-alcoholics, to deal with problems of alcoholism and addiction.

Health education aides.

Preventive medicine aides.

Medical aides to assist physicians in such tasks as taking histories.

Middle-management aides in hospitals to perform and supervise functions in record-keeping, supplies, and so on.

The practical problems involved in carrying through this idea have turned out to be severe, though probably surmountable. But as a means of opening access to real career opportunities for the socially disadvantaged, the approach holds such enormous promise that it is worthwhile wrestling with the problems. One fundamental advantage is that the employment focus is in the area of greatest occupational expansion, the service industries. We are moving away from a manufacturing economy to the point where two-thirds of the labor force is currently engaged in the production of services.

A second basic advantage to the idea is that it provides a way of breaking through what M.S. Miller has called "the credential society." By this he means the increasing demand by government and private industry for advance evidence of ability to perform a job before hiring, in the form of degrees, diplomas, or ability to pass a written test. Miller suggests that there are many able, intelligent people among the poor who, because of the circumstances of their bringing up are not able to present such credentials, though they probably could perform competently many of the jobs that require them. He proposes generally that employers of large working forces, as well as colleges and universities, reserve about 5 percent of the opportunities they control for those who cannot meet official entry requirements but who can demonstrate informally their probable capacity to succeed.

SOME GENERAL REFLECTIONS ON STRATEGY

This analysis of the outcomes and problems of a variety of proposals to make opportunity structure more accessible to the poor and the disadvantaged suggests that a mixture of both structural and functional programs is necessary, but that, wherever possible, the pure extreme of functionalism that attempts to work simply with individuals to make them "better adjusted" or "more employable" be abandoned.

The general principle involved in that suggestion has been described by Robert Levine as a preference for "less administered" over "more administered" programs.[22]

Levine notes the growing disenchantment among liberals with centralized federal programs aimed at overcoming social problems, but he argues that decentralization is not the answer. He writes:

The key, then, may not be decentralization as such, but the design of a system in which people make decisions for themselves in their own best interests, but in which the sum total comes out as a net increment to the social good—something like Adam Smith's "invisible hand." And if incentives or rules can be designed to induce the many "prime movers" in business, the states, and the localities to move in the same socially desirable direction at the same time, the cumulative impact of this movement would surely be greater than the power of the federal government to accomplish the same ends by administrative means.[23]

A good illustration of the difference Levine is pointing to may be seen in the contrast between two existing programs, public assistance and income tax. The welfare system depends on the application of detailed rules by an army of social workers and investigators in each individual case. Administrative costs are enormous and the human costs in degradation and "big brotherism" are even worse. The income tax system with all its abuses is, on the other hand, an efficient way of collecting revenue by setting general rules and allowing people to apply these to themselves. Where it has not worked well, Levine notes, it has been because of attempts to move toward a more administered system, as in the case of those with higher incomes.

One of the trends noted earlier in manpower training is a good example of the move toward less administration; the government encourages private industry to hire the unskilled by reducing the risk in doing so and possibly even making this profitable. There will, no doubt, be some abuses of the general rules, but random checks can keep them within limits and they are unlikely to be as expensive as a detailed system of supervision.

THE SPECIAL PROBLEM OF THE BLACK

A second issue of general strategy has to do with black Americans as a special target group in the general effort to improve access to op-

22. Robert A. Levine, "Rethinking Our Social Strategies," *The Public Interest*, No. 10 (Winter 1968), pp. 86-96.

23. *Ibid.*, p. 87.

portunity. The theme that runs through this chapter is the recurring insistence that in comparison with other groups the black man holds a particularly inequitable position in the opportunity structure and, consequently, that special efforts must be made for him.

It is commonly argued in reaction to this position that other groups, particularly European immigrants of various national backgrounds, have started at the bottom of the social heap and worked their way up by great effort and ambition, that America *is* the land of opportuniy for those who are willing to do their part. There are a number of very complex reasons why the experience of the European immigrant family cannot be compared with that of the blacks. The most important of these involves the interaction of both economic development and discrimination. The great flood of immigrants came at a time when the country was becoming an industrial society and needed a large pool of unskilled labor. By the time that immigration reached its greatest proportions discrimination had already relegated the newly freed blacks to nonurban, nonindustrial jobs. "Had it not been for racial discrimination, the North might well have recruited Southern Negroes after the Civil War to provide labor for building the burgeoning urban-industrial economy."[24] Instead, it was not until World War II that blacks began more often to be hired for industrial positions, and by that time unskilled labor had begun to be less essential.

Traditional patterns of discrimination also had a marked effect on the quality of schooling for blacks; because the majority grew up in the South, the amount and quality of their schools depended on allocations by local and state school boards and legislatures that saw no reason to provide even minimal levels of adequate schooling. The normal immigrant pattern of increasing periods of schooling over several generations thus had no counterpart for the average black family.

Finally, as the *Report of the National Advisory Commission on Civil Disorders* points out:

> Nostalgia makes it easy to exaggerate the ease of escape of the white immigrants from the ghettos. When the immigrants were immersed in poverty, they too lived in slums, and these neighborhoods exhibited fearfully high rates of alcoholism, desertion, illegitimacy, and other pathologies associated with poverty. Just as some Negro men desert their families when they are unemployed and their wives can get jobs, so did the mean of other ethnic groups, even though time and affluence has clouded white memories of the past.
>
> Today, whites tend to exaggerate how well and how quickly they escaped from poverty, and contrast their experience with poverty-stricken Negroes.

24. *Report of the National Advisory Commission on Civil Disorders* (New York: Bantam Books, Inc., 1968), pp. 278-279.

The fact is, among many of the Southern and Eastern Europeans who came to America in the last great wave of immigration, those who came already urbanized were the first to escape from poverty. The others, who came to America from rural backgrounds, as Negroes did, are only now, after three generations, in the final stages of escaping from poverty.

The immigrant who labored long hours at hard and often menial work had the hope of a better future, if not for himself then for his children. This was the promise of the "American dream"—the society offered to all a future that was open-ended. . . . For the Negro family in the urban ghetto there is a different vision—the future seems to lead only to a dead-end.

What the American economy of the late 19th and early 20th century was able to do to help the European immigrants escape from poverty is now largely impossible. New methods of escape must be found for the majority of today's poor.[25]

Recommended Reading

A good popular introduction to the analysis of census income data is Herman Miller's *Rich Man Poor Man* (New York: Crowell, Collier and Macmillan, 1964). Michael Harrington's *The Other America* (New York: Crowell, Collier and Macmillan, 1963) is still worth reading, though somewhat out of date. M.S. Miller and Frank Riessman have recently published *Social Class and Social Policy* (New York: Basic Books, Inc., 1968) which outlines a more contemporary and tougher approach to the problem. A good general collection of views on poverty may be found in Arthur Blaustein and Roger Woock's *Man Against Poverty: World War III* (New York: Random House, Inc., 1968).

An excellent source for a general picture of the economic and social conditions of black citizens is Bulletin No. 1511 of the U.S. Department of Labor (Washington, D.C.: U.S. Government Printing Office, June 1966). Another valuable and more detailed resource is the *Report of the National Advisory Commission on Civil Disorders* (New York: Bantam Books, Inc., 1968). Patricia Sexton's *Spanish Harlem: An Anatomy of Poverty* (New York: Harper & Row, 1965) provides a good picture of urban Puerto Ricans.

For the relationship of education to basic economic and social realities, see A.H. Halsey, Jean Floud, and C.A. Anderson's *Education, Economy and Society* (New York: The Free Press, 1961), an often technical but valuable collection of scholarly pieces.

25. *Ibid.*, pp. 281-282.

2

SOCIAL CLASS

In the first section of this chapter we will deal with a number of concepts which are important for understanding social class and the urban school. These concepts—including stratification, class, caste, class-value systems, culture of poverty, and group norms—are important in looking at the relationship between social class and achievement and education and social class mobility. They are also of central importance for considering aspects of urban education discussed elsewhere in the book.

STRATIFICATION

All societies past and present have some form of social stratification, a particular type of social differentiation that ranks individuals as higher or lower in terms of some criteria of preference. Kingsley Davis and Wilbur Moore argue that social stratification is universal, since all societies have unequal rewards attached to different positions.[1] There is great diversity among societies as to the criteria used and the complexity of stratification. However, all societies incorporate a differential reward system and hence exhibit social stratification. Davis and Moore argue further that stratification fulfills a functional role for society, since societies must concern themselves with motivating individuals to perform certain tasks and fill certain positions. The duties associated with the

1. Kingsley Davis and Wilbur E. Moore, "Some Principles of Stratification," *American Sociological Review 10* (April 1945), pp. 242-249.

wide range of positions in society are not all equally pleasant or important to the society or equally in need of the same ability or talent in performance. Following from these propositions, it seems reasonable to assume that a society must have rewards that can be used as inducements in persuading members to occupy certain positions; and it must have some way of distributing these rewards differentially according to position. In other words, those positions which are most important and which require longer training must be more highly rewarded than those which are not functionally important or which do not require long periods of training. Davis and Moore suggest that there are three different kinds of rewards which a society can offer as an inducement for its citizens in fulfilling social roles.[2] The first of these is wealth—the amount of income as related to the ability of people to obtain goods and services that contribute to their sustenance, comfort, and diversion. Second is power—the ability of an individual to exert his will even if it involves the resistance of others. The third is status—the ability of an individual to command prestige and esteem. These last two dimensions of status are perhaps important enough to be briefly defined. Prestige is the value attached to a position independently of the person who occupies it or how its requirements are carried out. The office of the President of the United States, for example, has attached to it a considerable amount of prestige regardless of citizens' judgments about the effectiveness of the current incumbent. The second kind of status, esteem, represents value which is attached to the individual according to how well or how poorly he carries out the requirements of his position, how well he plays his role. All college professors, for example, share a common level of prestige; however, esteem varies considerably, depending upon how the individual professor performs his role. His esteem among his peers is likely to be greater if he publishes.

Davis and Moore also suggest that in all societies within the system of stratification the most highly rewarded—whether by wealth, power, or status—are generally those people who are most functionally important to the society or those positions occupied by the most talented or qualified persons. That this proposition does not work perfectly in actual societies is quite obvious. One might compare the rewards of elementary- or secondary-school teachers and those of professional athletes and then judge the relative functional importance of their positions.

We have suggested so far that stratification is both universal and functional in that it supports the adaptation or the adjustment of the social system. It is important to realize that under certain circumstances

2. *Ibid.*, pp. 246-247.

stratification may be disfunctional. First, if social positions tend to be based upon inheritance they certainly serve to limit the possibility of using the full range of talent available within any society. Second, it is unlikely that the inequalities in rewards can be made fully acceptable to the less-privileged members of society or those on the lower levels of stratification. To the extent that this is true, and the differences are great, stratification may serve to produce hostility, distrust, and conflict between various levels in the system of stratification. Third, to the degree that the sense of membership in a society depends on one's rank in the hierarchial order social stratification may and probably does distribute unequally this sense of significant participation in the society. Later in this chapter we will look at Professor Oscar Lewis' theory of the "culture of poverty," which makes this point explicit.

SOCIAL CLASS

In looking at systems of stratification in societies social scientists define two general types which may be visualized on opposite ends of a continuum. At one end would be a society organized along caste lines, where the stratification is based entirely on inherited inequality. The Hindu castes of India are used as the most typical example of this type of stratification. The crucial feature of the system, as indeed of all caste systems, is that membership in a given stratum is ascribed and unalterable. It is given at birth and no individual actions can change the social position of a person during his lifetime. Rigid rules of avoidance operate, and marriage, for example, must take place within the caste.

At the other end of the continuum is a society which is based on equality of opportunity, where one's position in the system of stratification is entirely due to his own efforts and is not related to the position of his parents. The stratification system based on social class contains within it the concept of equal opportunity. It must be pointed out that no society, including that of the United States, approaches this "pure" social class-based system of stratification. Many of the arguments, and much of the research summarized in this book, for example, assume the importance of inheritance in terms of attitudes and values passed on from parent to child. In looking at the position of nonwhites in American society a strong case can be made for the use of the concept of caste in discussing racial relations.

In the discussion of social class which follows it is important for the reader to keep in mind that social class concepts and differences cannot be used to predict the behavior of individuals. Social class is a group concept and makes sense only for large groups. The teacher who uses it to classify individual students is guilty of gross oversimplification.

Joseph Kahl has identified seven major dimensions which he believes underlie the structure of social class in American society.

1. *Prestige.* Some people in the community have more personal prestige than others and are regarded by others with respect and deference.

2. *Occupation.* Some occupations are considered higher than others partly because they are more important to the welfare of the community, partly because they require special talents, and partly because they pay high rewards.

3. *Possessions or wealth or income.*

4. *Social interaction.* In a large community everyone cannot interact with everyone. Patterns of differential contact arise and people are most comfortable with "their own kind."

5. *Class consciousness.* The degree to which people at given levels are aware of themselves as distinct social groupings. Americans are said to be less class conscious than Europeans yet Americans, too, think of themselves as working class, or middle class, and a large proportion identify on the side of management or on the side of labor.

6. *Value orientations.* People differ about the things they consider different or important, and groups of people come to share a limited number of abstract values or value systems.

7. *Power, or the ability to control the actions of other people.* This variable, while it is important in determining social class, cannot be measured directly. It can be studied indirectly, however, by delineating the clique of important people in the community or by studying the people who control the capital wealth of the community.[3]*

In identifying these seven variables sociologists use three general approaches. Each implies a somewhat different conception of social class, but they are not necessarily mutually exclusive.[4]

1. *The objective approach.* The objective approach views social class as a statistical category. It is important to note that these categories are formed not by the people or the members of the classes themselves but by sociologists and in some cases statisticians. The sociologist employing the objective approach may decide, for example, to use a combination of occupation, education, and income as his criteria. Perhaps

* In a later chapter we will look at community power and at two views of community power structure in more detail.

3. Robert J. Havighurst and Bernice L. Neugarten, *Society and Education,* 3d ed. (Boston: Allyn and Bacon, Inc., 1967), p. 12, as summarized from Joseph A. Kahl, *The American Class Structure* (New York: Holt, Rinehart and Winston, Inc., 1957).

4. James W. Vander Zanden, *Sociology* (New York: The Ronald Press Company, 1965), pp. 274-281.

the most important advantage of this approach is that it is not usually necessary to conduct an actual survey to gain the information needed. Census data or other surveys may provide it. The disadvantage of the objective approach is, of course, that it does not include a number of the basic criteria listed by Kahl. It does not look at class consciousness, where people judge themselves to be on the social class scale. It cannot measure social interaction between members, and it says nothing directly about value orientation.

2. *The subjective approach.* This approach to social class views it as a social rather than a statistical category. That is, it assumes that an important element in social class is consciousness on the part of an individual that he *is* a member of a given social class. The method used is simply to ask the individual to evaluate his own class position. Although this method provides valuable information about an individual's judgment of himself, it has some disadvantages. For example, the class with which the individual identifies may be one to which he aspires rather than one to which he actually belongs. The skilled worker may wish to identify himself as middle class when responding to an investigator, while in fact certain objective criteria—that is, income, education, and occupation—would identify him as working class.

3. *The reputational approach.* This third approach to the study of social class was developed by W. Lloyd Warner, who was also important in originating categories used in what is identified here as the objective approach.[5] It requires the investigator to obtain judgments of other people's positions along the social class continuum. The reputational approach is reflected in Warner's definition of class as "two or more orders of people who are believed to be and are accordingly ranked by all the members of the community in socially superior and inferior positions."[6]

Warner and his associates in their community studies entitled *The Yankee City Series* engaged in intensive interviewing of large numbers of people. It was during this interviewing that Warner discovered that certain terms and concepts were used by individuals to describe other people who were above them, on their same level, or below them in the social structure. Warner says:

With the aid of such additional testimony as the area lived in, the type of house, kind of education, manners and other symbols of class it was possible to determine very quickly the approximate place of any individual in the

5. W. Lloyd Warner and Paul S. Lunt, *The Social Life of a Modern Community* in *The Yankee City Series* (New Haven: Yale University Press, 1942); and W. Lloyd Warner and Paul S. Lunt, *The Status System of a Modern Community* in *The Yankee City Series* (New Haven: Yale University Press, 1942).

6. *Ibid.*, p. 82.

society. In the final analysis, however, individuals were placed by the evaluations of the members of Yankee City itself, e.g., by such explicit statements as "She does not belong," or "They belong to our club."[7]

Out of these studies the sixfold standard social class designation was developed. Although in considering the problems of urban education we are more concerned with certain levels of the continuum, let us look briefly at the characteristics of these six social classes.

1. The *upper-upper class* represents a group that is both wealthy and has high status in the community based on birth. This social class is characterized by the possession of "old money" that has been in the family for a number of generations. Upper-upper class people tend to marry almost exclusively with other members of their class. Social relationships and involved and intricate codes of etiquette are extremely important. Although most of the men are employed, usually in businesses or in the more prestigious professions, the family wealth is inherited. This social class is by far the smallest in number in American society.

2. The *lower-upper class* shares many characteristics with the upper-upper class. The most important distinction has to do with the social position of the family or "prestige," and with the length of time which money has been in the family. The wealth of the lower-upper class is judged by people in the community as essentially "new money."

3. The *upper-middle class* includes occupationally the professions and middle and upper levels of business and management. This class is described reputationally as being made up of "solid, highly respectable" people, but not "society." Leadership in civic affairs comes primarily from this social class, including public education.

4. The *lower-middle class* is made up occupationally of small businessmen, clerical workers, and other lower level white-collar positions. This group tends to be proper, extremely concerned with middle-class values, especially respectability, and is conservative politically. They are generally labeled by others in their communities as "good, common people."

5. The *upper-lower class* tends to be made up occupationally of skilled and semiskilled workers—service workers such as policemen and firemen and small tradesmen. This social class lives in less desirable neighborhoods in the community, but is still viewed by other members of the community as "respectable."

6. The *lower-lower class,* unlike the upper-lower, is not judged by other members of the community as having respectability. They suffer from a "bad reputation." They may be viewed as opposites to "good

7. *Ibid.,* p. 90.

middle-class virtues." This group lives naturally enough in the least desirable neighborhoods and contains the unemployed and those on public assistance. The only occupational categories in this level are unskilled worker and farm worker, both sporadic and insecure jobs.

Warner, for his study of Yankee City, estimates the percentage of the population in each of these social classes as follows:

Class	Percent
Upper-upper class	approximately 1
Lower-upper class	2
Upper-middle class	7-12
Lower-middle class	20-35
Upper-lower class	25-40
Lower-lower class	15-25

In view of recent poverty studies in the United States, including Michael Harrington's *The Other America,* it may well be necessary to revise the percentage for the lower-lower class upward, if this class is defined as those living in a condition of poverty.[8] Harrington's estimate was about 25 percent, but others have ranged as high as 30 percent.

VALUE DIFFERENCES

Among those characteristics which differentiate social classes in American life, social class value differences are particularly important for teachers. This concept means that one's position in the social structure is related to how one values certain goals and objectives or what attitudes are held toward certain events. A number of writers have focused on the significance of social class value differences on learning in the school. Of particular importance are the writings of Allison Davis and Herbert Gans.[9] They identify at least four areas in which the difference between middle-class and lower-class values may be of particular interest for educators.

1. *Time orientation.* Lower-class life, with its uncertainties and unpredictabilities, focuses the attention of slum residents and especially the young on the immediate problems of life. In economic terms the

8. Michael Harrington, *The Other America* (New York: The Macmillan Company, 1963); *see* Appendices pp. 187-202.
9. Allison Davis, *Social Class Influences upon Learning* (Cambridge, Mass: Harvard University Press, 1948); and Herbert J. Gans, *The Urban Villagers* (New York: The Free Press, 1962).

possession of an unskilled job with the threat of layoffs and reallocations are all factors which prevent long-range planning in lower-class life. In the lower-lower class it may be true that even the next meal is an uncertain proposition. Certainly the next month's rent and whether the welfare check is forthcoming are the kinds of concerns which prevent lower-class individuals from focusing on those plans and projections which are central to middle-class life. The concept of thrift, for example, is essentially a middle-class virtue. One can be thrifty when one has some surplus with which to be thrifty and when one has time to plan for thriftiness instead of expending every moment on immediate concerns. The middle-class child is taught from a very early age—to use the psychological term—to "defer gratification." He is taught that a number of activities, such as going to school and studying, although perhaps restricting in themselves, will provide future benefits. This promise of future rewards is based on the experience of middle-class adults and children that, in fact, many years of education does pay off. The lower-class child, on the other hand, is not provided with this sort of model. He does not see, nor do his parents see, direct evidence of success from long-range planning. Although there is the occasional case of the cousin or brother who somehow "makes it" through education, more frequently the case is of a sibling, or a friend of the family, who although completing high school and perhaps even a year or two of college is nevertheless employed in a menial job. Given the general lack of supportive evidence it is not surprising that lower-class children are not enthusiastic about the prospect of long years of economic sacrifice in the hope that eventually greater rewards will result.

2. *Person orientation.* Lower-class youngsters tend to be more oriented toward interpersonal relations than the remote goals of achieving a high income or stable "career." For example, the stability that lower-class youngsters find in the neighborhood gang and in the extended family helps them to compensate for the unstable and unsatisfying relationships which they find in attempts to interact with the middle-class object-oriented world. This more personal orientation to the world probably relates to certain language disabilities of lower-class youngsters which are discussed in more detail in Chapter 4. Concepts such as "career" and "individual advancement" are by-and-large missing from the vocabulary of lower-class children, and represent a rejection of extremely important lower-class values of friendship toward one's peer group and loyalty to one's family. The middle-class assumption that an individual should be willing to leave friends and family to pursue a career and to get a considerably higher income is not only foreign to lower-class youngsters but violates the important value of friendship and personal relations. It follows, then, that the middle-class teacher's attempt to appeal to the lower-class student on the basis of

individual development and personal growth seem rather misplaced. Lower-class youngsters do not tend to respond to motivation on the basis of individual and career-oriented object goals.

3. *Self-image.* The self-image of lower-class youngsters is different from that of the middle class. Their position in the stratification system is lower and tends to be internalized and reflected in their own judgment about themselves. A fuller discussion of self-image in poor and disadvantaged youngsters is contained in Chapter 5. It is enough to state here that the image of one's own potential and ability is closely related to one's social class position. Lower-class youngsters tend to judge themselves to be less able in academic work than their middle-class counterparts.

4. *Physical aggressiveness.* The system of rewards and punishments differs across social class lines as well. The rewards which a school offers are much more relevant to middle-class children than they are to those in the lower class. The lower-class child does not respond favorably to the reward of grades, the value of which depends on the assumption that recognition and employment and increased income will come at some unknown time and in some occupation which is completely foreign to his present situation. The school as a middle-class institution fails, however, to recognize skills and the systems of rewards that are relevant to lower-class values. This is not to say that there is more aggression in lower-class life than in middle-class life, but rather that aggression in middle-class life takes more covert forms. Among middle-class youngsters it may take the form of gossiping, backbiting, and perhaps tattling to the teacher. The physical aggressiveness associated with lower-class values is, in fact, functional in terms of conditions of lower-class life. A youngster who lives in a slum area must be able to defend himself, to run fast, and to develop a range of physical skills in order to get along. Social class value differences are clearly present in the classroom. In *Elmtown's Youth* by August Hollingshead a clear relationship is found between adolescents' social class and their views on a whole range of value issues, such as clique formation, dates, religion, recreation, sex and marriage, and different beliefs about right and wrong.[10]

Another important dimension of social class value difference identified by Herbert Gans has to do with the difference in attitude toward what the author calls the "caretakers" in our societies.[11] The "caretakers" are those institutions designed to support, aid, and help citizens —such as police, fire department, social welfare groups, public schools, the courts and legal structure, and community medical facilities. Gans

10. August B. Hollinghead, *Elmtown's Youth* (New York: John Wiley & Sons, Inc., 1949), p. 9.

11. Gans, *op. cit.,* chapters 3-7.

suggests that the middle-class attitude toward these institutions is generally a favorable one. Children are taught to identify police, for example, as "our helpers in blue," and in general view all of the caretakers as supporting, helpful individuals. With lower-class youngsters and adults Gans believes that the situation is quite different. Here, a generalized hostility is expressed. Youngsters are taught to avoid contact with a variety of the caretaker institutions, especially the police department.

Value systems for any group of people of whatever social class are based on real experiences. It is crucially important for teachers to remember that lower-class value positions are based on a realistic evaluation of lower-class environment. The immediacy of time orientation is realistic when one understands the economic situation and the necessity for looking at daily problems which arise. The personal orientation is functional when one sees the importance of peer group and family relations for lower-class youngsters. The inferior self-image of lower-class children is realistic based on the general predominantly middle-class view of skills and abilities. Hostility toward the caretakers in society is justified by the experience of many lower-class people at the hands of social welfare workers, police, and doctors working for public health institutions. Ronald Corwin summarizes it very well when he says:

> Middle class persons, however, have difficulty understanding that values so clear and useful to them are not useful or appropriate to the slum boy who encounters other social dangers. And conversely that lower class value systems are functional in the slum environment. Ironically, teachers who resist other forms of standardization in the curriculum attempt to enforce a standardized value system on what they mistakenly define to be an immoral group. It is a moral one. What appears to the middle class teacher to be a negative attitude on the part of lower class children towards "self improvement" is in fact a positive orientation towards the peer group and a realistic assessment of the situation.[12]

THE CULTURE OF POVERTY

A slightly different perspective is offered on social class value differences by Oscar Lewis in his theory of the culture of poverty. Lewis, a cultural anthropologist, has studied poverty mostly in Latin America. In the introduction to his most recent book, *La Vida,* Lewis outlines his theory.[13] He begins by identifying the necessary conditions under which

12. Ronald Corwin, *A Sociology of Education* (New York: Appleton-Century-Crofts, 1965), p. 162.

13. Oscar Lewis, *La Vida* (New York: Random House, Inc., 1965), pp. xlii-lii.

the phenomenon known as the culture of poverty is found, the most important of which follow:

A society in which there exists a market economy and cash payment for work. This condition describes modern American society, as indeed it describes most non-Communist industrialized countries in the world.

A society in which there is both high unemployment and high underemployment. Unemployment, although by no means at an all-time high in the United States, has generally ranged between 4 and 6 percent and is double for nonwhite Americans.

A society in which there is no organization for low income groups either voluntary—organized, sponsored, directed, and controlled by low-income people themselves—or imposed—enforced by the government or some central authority.

A certain value possessed by the dominant group in society. The accumulation of wealth and property is emphasized and the failure of some individuals and groups to accumulate wealth and property is explained by reference to either individual or group inadequacy. Lewis seems here to be pointing to race prejudice or at least a kind of social class prejudice as an explanation for the existence of poverty in a society which is generally not poor.

The characteristics of the culture of poverty are analyzed by Lewis on four levels. Moving from the more general to the more specific he suggests that in relation to the larger society a culture of poverty is characterized by almost total separation from the larger society, including separation from its values. People living in a culture of poverty are aware of the larger society's values, may indeed pay lip service to them, but do not abide by them in their daily lives. This separation means that those living in a culture of poverty have no stake in the larger society. Lewis is particularly critical of research by sociologists, either questionnaire or interview, which suggests that there is a good deal of continuity in terms of certain values. For example, one of the authors of this book has conducted a study in central Harlem which showed that a large number of Harlem residents view "getting a good education" as an extremely important value for their children. Professor Lewis finds that the questionnaire survey simply does not get at real value positions. As an anthropologist he maintains that the necessary method is to live with and observe people over a considerable period of time. If this is done, he contends, it becomes apparent that people living in a culture of poverty do not in fact act out in their daily lives the values of the larger society.

Virtually no organized community exists among the people living in a culture of poverty. Lewis points out that primitive and preliterate peoples have developed a higher form of sociocultural organization than modern, urban slum-dwellers. This strong statement is supported to some extent by the experience of the Office of Economic Opportunity in its attempts to fight the "war on poverty." It is rather generally agreed that the part of this federal effort which has failed most dramatically is that calling for "maximum feasible participation of the poor." This includes attempts by the Office of Economic Opportunity to assist the poor in organizing themselves politically and socially. The legislation requires, for example, a certain percentage of poor to be represented on local poverty program boards. It has been extremely difficult to recruit members of poor communities to serve on boards, and in those communities in which elections have been held for board positions, the turnout has generally been light. This experience, while not proving the impossibility of organizing the poor, does suggest that Professor Lewis has hit on a crucial problem—the impasse of organizing the poor either from the outside or from within.

On the family level Professor Lewis finds the culture of poverty characterized by a high incidence of one-parent families, in most cases female-headed, and by a child rearing pattern that is considerably at variance from middle-class practices. He maintains that children raised in the culture of poverty do not know childhood as a long, protected period of life. Because of the economic and social environment, very young children are forced into assuming a variety of responsibilities for themselves, and in some cases for other family members, a situation from which middle-class youngsters are protected for years. The seven- or eight-year-old child in a slum area who is responsible for the care of an infant for considerable periods of time is not unusual. A small child may be required to prepare his own meals or get him or herself ready for school. Premature responsibility results, Lewis argues, in earlier patterns of sexual experience and earlier marriage and parenthood.

On the individual level the culture of poverty is characterized by psychological feelings of marginality, helplessness, dependence, and despair. Lewis points out that these feelings are in most cases directly related to reality. People living in a culture of poverty are marginal, relatively helpless, and in many cases dependent upon other people or the caretaker institutions of the society.

In considering possible solutions for the culture of poverty Lewis strongly believes that merely increasing money allotments in whatever form, direct payment or negative income tax, would not help break the established behavior patterns. When questioned directly about money payments, Lewis responded that although he was certainly not opposed to financial aid to the poor, the main effect would simply be to permit them to buy a better grade of wine. This harsh statement indicates Oscar Lewis' conviction that solving the problems of the poor is going to be complicated and will require a multifaceted approach rather than mere financial increment.

Not all of the world's poor live in the culture of poverty. In the introductory chapter to *La Vida* Lewis identifies those poor groups which he does not believe live within a culture of poverty. The lower castes and untouchables of Indian society are an example. Although many Indians live in extreme poverty, they are not separate from but integrated very closely into the larger society, with a clearly defined position and a shared value system. Eastern European Jews are another poor group who are not characterized as having lived in a culture of poverty. Lewis points out that although this group was certainly forced to be separate from the larger society, they nevertheless had an extremely strong community organization and family life. Studies of their ghetto existence provide no evidence of individual feelings of marginality, helplessness, or dependence. Primitive societies also fall outside the culture of poverty, although the entire society may be extremely poor, literally living from one harvest or hunt to another. The society is a firmly knit and all-inclusive structure.

Finally, Oscar Lewis suggests that Communist societies do not have within them anything that can be called a culture of poverty. He contrasts two visits to the same slum area in Havana, Cuba, to illustrate this point—the first, three years before the Castro revolution; the second, three years after. Physically, the neighborhood had changed very little, the only addition being the construction of a school. However, the neighborhood was still clearly an overcrowded slum and the people living there were obviously poor. The difference was that after Castro's revolution this community, and the poor in Communist societies generally, was organized and integrated into the structure of the larger society. This organization was imposed by the government and/or the Communist party, but it was there. They had a community representative, block representatives, and, Professor Lewis indicates, they did not reflect any of the individual or family pathologies associated with the culture of poverty.

Some American social scientists argue that the culture of poverty is not a completely satisfactory description and analysis of the nature of poverty in the United States. S.M. Miller, for example, partly in response to Lewis' theory, has developed a four-point typology of the poor.[14]

The "stable." Many poor families, whose income is relatively steady and stable although extremely low, have a family life which is also stable.

The "strained." Part of the general category of poor have a secure although very low-income economic pattern, but have unstable family patterns.

The "copers." Extreme economic insecurity may require this group of the poor to receive financial assistance from an outside agency. They

14. S.M. Miller, "The American Lower Classes: A Typological Approach," *Social Research 31* (Spring 1964), pp. 1-22.

nevertheless manage to achieve a good measure of family stability. Many single-parent families might fall in this category: A mother who because of the number of children in the house is unable to work must therefore be supported by a public or private agency, but still provides reasonably good care for her children.

The "unstable." Families in this category have neither economic nor personal security and stability. Social workers would probably describe them as "multiproblem families."

Miller believes it is this fourth type of poor which unfairly come to represent and stand for all of the economically deprived people in our society. He and Martin Rein go beyond the implied criteria of this typology and suggest that the emphasis on social class value differences and the theory of the culture of poverty include some errors of emphasis. They outline their own assessment of the poor as follows:

1. Great variation occurs among the poor [as indicated in the Miller typology listed].
2. Many of the middle class values like success are of less importance or have a changed character. Getting by is more important than getting ahead for most of the poor. More stress is placed on activity, on toughness. Unemployment is not as stigmatizing an experience among the low income population as among those better off. The poor are in economically vulnerable positions and recognize unemployment as a recurring possibility, mostly out of their control.
3. Although many of these patterns of orientations are carried from generation to generation, contemporary influences are important in maintaining them.
4. Some positive elements of strengths in coping exist as well in negative ones that make it difficult to handle life.
5. Many of the poor are open to change, to taking advantage of new possibilities; but in offering new possibilities their experiences and orientations must be considered.[15]

SOCIAL MOBILITY

Any consideration of social class, value differences, or the special problems of the poor naturally lead to a consideration of social mobility, and specifically the relationship between education and social mobility. Formal education, as we shall make clear later, is probably best viewed

15. S.M. Miller and Martin Rein, "Poverty, Inequality and Policy," in *Social Problems: A Modern Approach*, Howard Becker (ed.), (New York: John Wiley & Sons, Inc., 1967), pp. 492-493.

not as a cause of social mobility but rather as a means. Mobility, as we will use the term, may be defined as a movement of individuals or groups from one social class stratum to another. There are at least five factors in modern industrial society which have a direct effect on social mobility.[16]

1. *Changes in the number of positions available within a given social class.* In the last two decades within the United States, for example, certain technological developments have produced a tremendous increase in the number of engineers needed in our society. This increase provides opportunities for young people from other social classes to move into the position of engineer, an upper-middle-class professional position. Conversely, the decreasing percentage of the work force engaged in unskilled manual labor is undoubtedly a factor in forcing young men from families where parents are unskilled workers to consider other employment at higher levels in the social class structure.

2. *Different rates of fertility.* In all industrialized countries about which we have information there is an inverse ratio between the size of families and social class position. Lower-class families tend to be larger, while middle- and upper-class families are smaller. To some extent this tendency has brought about a shortage of young people to fill middle-class positions, which in turn creates an opportunity for lower-class young people to move into middle-class positions. There is some evidence that this factor has not been as important over the past decade, since the inverse relationship mentioned above is not as pronounced as it was twenty and thirty years ago.

3. *Changes in status of positions.* A particular kind of social mobility can be related to recent changes in the relative status of certain occupations. For example, the status of nuclear physicists and scientists in general has increased tremendously relative to other occupations since the early 1950s. Politicians, on the other hand, especially on state and local levels, have declined in relative status.

4. *Changes in the numbers of inherited social positions.* The evidence suggests that in modern industrial society there has been a decline over the last several decades in the number of inheritable positions. This is probably related to the decline in the number of small businesses and the rise of large corporations in which the managers are not the owners. The proprietor of the corner grocery store can pass his business on to his son, but the chairman of the board of General Motors cannot. The chairmanship is to some extent up for grabs, and may be filled by one of several qualified people from other social class strata.

5. *Changes in legal and political restrictions.* Many legal restric-

16. Seymour M. Lipset and Reinhard Bendix, *Social Mobility in Industrial Society* (Berkeley: University of California Press, 1959), pp. 57-60.

tions, which pertained to groups in the Middle Ages and earlier centuries, have been removed. In the United States both presidential executive orders and new legislation have had the effect of reducing

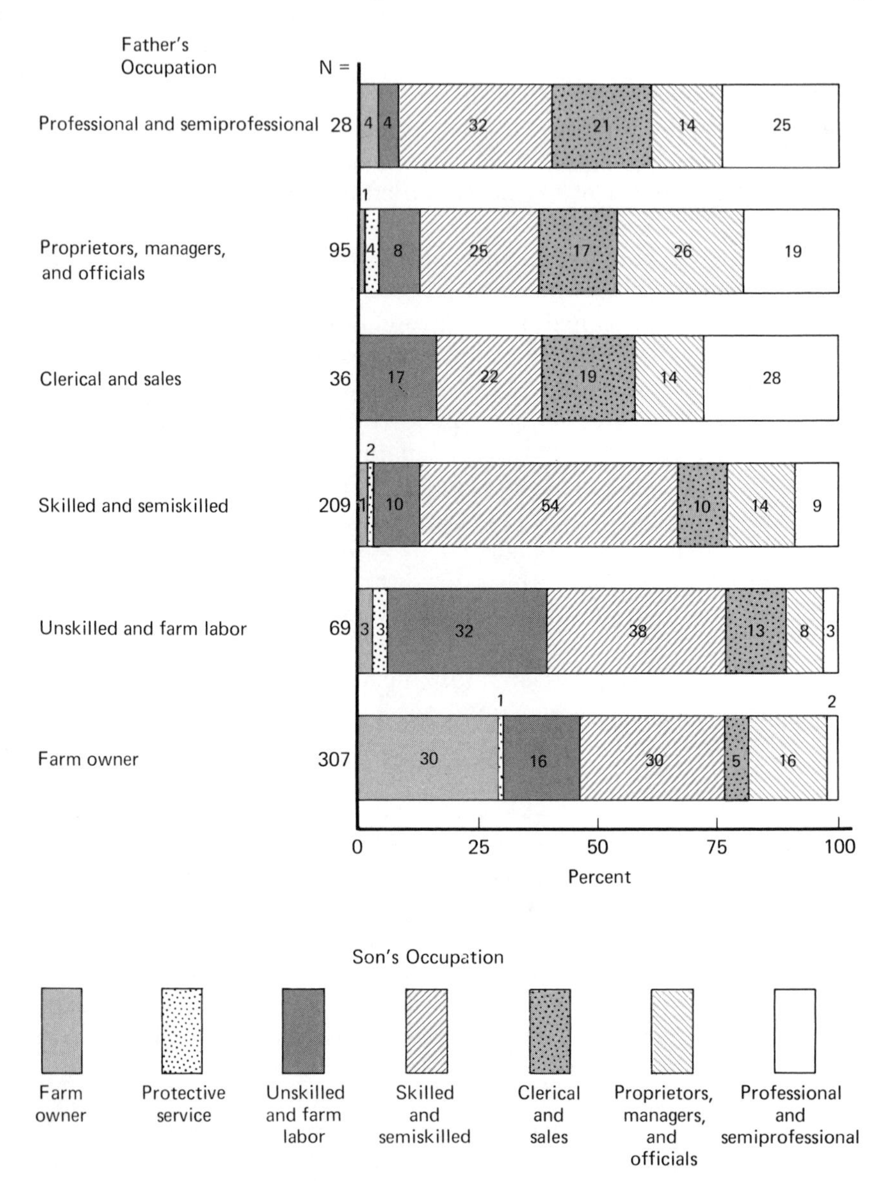

Figure 2.1 Occupational distribution of a sample of American males by their father's occupation. Protective Service omitted from "father's occupation" because of too few cases.

SOURCE: Seymour Martin Lipset and Reinhard Bendix, *Social Mobility in Industrial Society* (Berkeley: University of California Press, 1959), p. 89.

legal restrictions on the activities of minority group members in American society. There is some evidence also suggesting the decline of the quota system, a discriminatory device which restricted certain minority group members, most particularly Jews, from entering certain professions. One intention of the Supreme Court decision of 1954, *Brown* vs *Board of Education,* was to produce an educational situation for minority group members which would increase the possibilities for upward social mobility.

Figure 2.1 provides some information about the extent of social mobility and the kinds of social mobility existing in the United States. There seems to be no evidence to suggest that mobility has decreased over the past fifty years in this country. What evidence we have on this subject indicates that the movement has remained roughly the same over the last century. Studies by Havighurst and Neugarten, and Lipsit and Bendix conclude that the best general figure, including both upward and downward mobility, is about 33 percent.[17] That is, roughly one out of three individuals move from one social class position to another during their lives.

We have not yet mentioned downward social mobility. Estimates here vary, but certainly not more than 10 percent of the people in American society suffer downward social mobility. Two of the most important causes are: 1. downward mobility related to some form of personal maladjustment such as alcoholism, narcotics addiction, or a severe psychological neurosis or psychosis; 2. downward social mobility due to marriage. A middle-class girl, for example, whose father is a business executive, marries an assembly-line worker. This clearly represents downward mobility, since the social class position of the family is based to a large extent on the occupation, income, and education of the male head of the family.

SOCIAL CLASS AND ACHIEVEMENT IN SCHOOL

Most Americans would probably agree that under ideal conditions, intelligence and ability measured as accurately as possible should be the determining factor in who stays in school how long. Part of the democratic ethos seems to be that Americans have the right to be educated for as long as they are able to profit from the education provided. If one looks at the following table it can easily be seen that intelligence

17. Robert J. Havighurst, et al., *Growing up in River City* (New York: John Wiley & Sons, Inc., 1962); Richard P. Coleman and Bernice L. Neugarten, *Social Status in the City* (New York: Atherton Press, 1967); Lipset and Bendix, *Social Mobility in Industrial Society* (Berkeley: University of California Press, 1959).

as measured by IQ is indeed an important indicator of how many years of schooling one has. Of particular significance, however, is the number which appears in the lower right-hand corner, the 53 percent of the top quarter of intellectual ability who graduate from college. This figure suggests that a considerable loss occurs somewhere along the line that cannot be attributed to intelligence. One could assume that illness, both mental and physical, and a few personal decisions would keep some of the top quarter from finishing college. But certainly nothing like the 47 percent who drop out. What this loss suggests is that something other than intelligence is operating in determining who goes how far in formal education.

Table 2.1 Level of Education in Relation to Social Class of Youth in the Upper Quarter of Intellectual Ability (in percents)

	Social Class			
	Upper and upper-middle	Lower-middle	Working class	Totals
Composition of group	20	42	38	100
Do not finish high school	0	1	4	5
High school graduates; do not enter college	2	4	9	15
Enter college but do not finish	2	11	14	27
Complete a 4-year college program	16	26	11	53

SOURCE: Robert J. Havighurst and Bernice L. Neugarten, *Society and Education*, 3d ed. (Boston: Allyn and Bacon, Inc., 1967), p. 77.

In examining Table 2.1 one can see quite clearly that social class is an important factor. The reasons for fewer bright working-class boys and girls graduating from high school and going on to college are complex. Many poor youngsters simply cannot afford to go on to higher education or in some cases finish high school because of pressing current economic pressures. This is in spite of the argument that their life's income would be considerably increased if they stayed in school. Also important is a lack of motivation directly related to school performance on the part of some lower-class youngsters. A third important reason, however, and one that we propose to examine here in more detail, is the structure and pattern of school practices which contribute to the separation and the educational discouragement of lower-class youngsters. Robert Havighurst and Bernice Neugarten suggest that an important social function fulfilled by public education is sorting and selecting individuals into various categories.[18] They also suggest that although not

18. Havighurst and Neugarten, *op. cit.*, chapter 3.

consciously planned, this educational sorting and selecting produces a social class sorting and selecting as well. Educational policies widely used in American schools to separate youngsters into different classrooms, programs, schools, and school systems have the effect of separating them along social class lines. This sorting in turn discourages lower-class boys and girls from entering into the academic stream which will lead to college and professional education. They turn instead to technical or vocation education, or in some cases they drop out.

Havighurst and Neugarten suggest that this sorting takes place on a number of levels, beginning in the classroom itself. Ability grouping or "homogenous" grouping, the procedures under which pupils of the same level of ability are placed in the same classroom, although designed to facilitate the work of the teacher, also has the effect of grouping youngsters according to social class background. The authors argue that despite the increasing awareness on the part of school administrators of the need for finding able talent in any social class strata, by far the majority of youngsters in accelerated tracks or in honors classes are from the middle- rather than from working-class background.

High-school curricula themselves can be a basis for separating by social class. Within the typical comprehensive public high school there are several different courses of study. The academic course leads into college and into middle-class occupations. Other curricula lead to terminal programs, in some cases providing certain saleable skills for students. Still others, for example, the "general diploma" offered in New York City's public high schools, do not prepare the youngster either for entrance into any post high-school education nor does it give him any marketable skills. These different high-school programs are seen very clearly by students and faculty as ranging in status, with the academic curricula at the top, followed by the commercial and vocational, and, lowest, the general curriculum. Social status ranking is reflected in the numbers from various social class backgrounds who participate in the programs. The heaviest concentration of middle- and upper-middle-class youngsters are in the academic track, while the lower-class youngsters predominate in the general track.

The type of secondary school itself can be an important factor in sorting out youngsters by social class background. Especially in large urban school systems there tends to be a considerable variety in the type of schools, even where they are comprehensive. In New York there are academic high schools, such as Bronx High School of Science, with a heavily middle-class student population from which virtually everyone goes on to some form of higher education; and Benjamin Franklin High School, located in East Harlem, with a predominantly lower-class student body from which approximately 25 to 30 of each graduating class of 1400 go on to college or university. Comprehensive high schools in large cities generally tend to have attendance districts of their own.

Table 2.2 Socioeconomic Factors in School Achievement in High Schools of a Big City

School number	SER*	Achievement†	Low reading level**	Say will enter college††	Percent Negro enrollment
1	290	52	0	94	0
3	199	54	0	91	0
5	123	40	12	79	26
7	97	36	0	74	0
9	82	29	22	55	21
11	79	36	5	74	0
13	74	41	0	49	0
15	68	33	14	52	0
17	66	28	4	48	0
19	54	11	16	46	28
21	53	21	15	76	88
23	53	25	12	42	19
25	50	23	0	41	0
27	39	22	4	38	1
29	27	27	0	44	0
31	23	11	16	36	9
33	22	4	56	53	94
35	20	14	29	39	44
37	17	4	37	51	91
39	11	6	41	53	100

* Socioeconomic ratio of adults in the school's attendance area in 1960. Certain schools are not representative of the adult socioeconomic distribution because there is a selective factor in attendance at public schools.
† Percent of ninth and eleventh graders in top three stanines on standard tests of reading. For city as a whole, 23 percent are in the top three stanines.
** Percent of ninth-grade English classes in Basic English. Pupils are below sixth-grade level in such classes. In some high schools there are too few such pupils to form a trend though almost every high school has at least a handful of such pupils.
†† Students who will graduate in June are asked in the spring whether they expect to go to college. (Composite of data from 1962, 1963, and 1964.)

SOURCE: Robert J. Havighurst and Bernice L. Neugarten, *Society and Education,* 3d ed. (Boston, Allyn and Bacon, Inc., 1967), p. 85.

There then develops a natural social class difference between those comprehensive high schools located in middle-class and those located in lower-class communities (*see* Table 2.2).

Robert Havighurst and Bernice Neugarten comment on this table as follows:

The differences among such schools (middle class schools in middle class communities) are indicated in the above table which reports data on comprehensive high schools in Chicago. The schools are ranked according to the socio-economic ratio, sex, occupations of adult males in the school attendance area. The average achievement level is shown to be closely related to socio-economic level as is the proportion of students of low reading ability. These comprehensive schools practice ability grouping with as many as five levels or tracks aimed at adjusting the methods of teaching and the difficulty level to the ability of the students. However, a school located in a low status neighborhood with a generally low achievement level has difficulty in motivating the abler students to work as effectively as does a school with a generally high achievement level located in a middle class area.[19]

Another sort of selection procedure is found when one compares the social class background of youngsters attending private schools, as opposed to those attending public schools. An important distinction must be made between Roman Catholic parochial schools, which tend in general to reflect the social class background of the public school (with the difference that parochial schools enroll a smaller percentage from the lower working class), and independent private schools, which enroll boys and girls almost exclusively from the upper-middle and upper classes.

In addition to the selection which takes place within the formal school program, extracurricular activities also contribute to separation by social class. In the typical high school the leadership in almost all extracurricular activities is provided by middle- and upper-middle-class boys and girls. Participation is also primarily middle class, which may in part be economic. Working-class teenagers are more likely to have parttime employment and thus be unable to participate in activities after school. Another differentiation along social class lines is the comparison between lower-class and middle-class schools in terms of the extracurricular activities offered. Here one finds that, in general, middle-class high schools offer a wide variety of activities, while lower-class school offerings are more limited.

As was mentioned, one of the important ingredients causing lower school performance by poor children may be parental and community attitudes toward education. In an interesting study Richard Cloward and James Jones look directly at this problem.[20] They interviewed approximately one thousand residents of Manhattan's lower east side. Included in the interview was information about the social class position of the interviewee and his or her attitudes toward education, toward the school in the neighborhood, and toward the question of social mo-

19. *Ibid.*, p. 84.

20. Richard A. Cloward and James A. Jones, "Social Class: Educational Attitudes and Participation," in *Education in Depressed Areas*, A. Harry Passow (ed.), (New York: Bureau of Publications, Teachers College, Columbia University, 1963), pp. 190-216.

bility in relation to education. The findings relate to social class factors in educational achievement and the relationship between school and community in urban areas (*see* chapter 11). The authors conclude:

Two general findings, however tentative, emerge from this research. The first is that evaluations of the importance of education in the lower and working classes appear to be influenced by occupational aspirations. The point is not as has been so often suggested that low income people fail to perceive the importance of education as a channel of mobility. Rather that their level of occupational aspiration influences their evaluation of education much more than is characteristic of the middle class person. From a programmatic standpoint this suggests that public information programs designed to acquaint low income people with the rapid changes taking place in our occupational structure, especially the restricted numbers of unskilled and semi-skilled positions may have the effect of heightening occupational aspirations and thus the importance of education.

Second, our data suggest that participation in educational activities does influence evaluations of the importance of education and attitudes toward the school as an institution. The tendency of participation to heighten the emphasis on education is especially pronounced in the lower class. This suggests that efforts to involve lower class people in educational matters are quite likely to be rewarded by increased interest in the academic achievement of their children. Participation also tends to result in more critical attitudes in the school as an institution. These generally more negative attitudes, we noted, can be employed by school administrators as a basis for bringing about needed improvements in school facilities and programs.[21]

In general, the relationship between social class background and educational performance has been effectively summarized by Professor W. W. Charters in *The Handbook of Research on Teaching:*

It is proper to conclude that pupils of the lower classes will experience frustration and failure and pupils of the higher classes will experience gratification and success in their educational experiences. The evidence supporting this conclusion is overwhelming.

To categorize youth according to the social class position of their parents is to order them on the extent of their participation and degree of success in the American educational system. This has been so consistently confirmed by research that it now can be regarded as an empirical law. It appears to hold regardless of whether the social class categorization is based upon the exhaustive procedures used in Elmstown (Hollingshead 1949) or upon more casual indicators of socio-economic status such as occupation or income level.

21. *Ibid.*, pp. 215-216.

It seems to hold in any educational institution, public or private, where there is some diversity in social class, including universities, colleges, and teacher training institutions, as well as elementary and secondary schools. Social class position predicts grades, achievement, and intelligence test scores, retentions at grade level, course failure, truancy, suspensions from school, high school dropouts, plans for college attendance and total amount of formal schooling. It predicts academic honors and awards in the public school, elected school offices, extent of participation in extra-curricular activities and in social affairs sponsored by the school, to say nothing of a variety of indicators of "success" and formal structure of the student society. Where differences in prestige value exist in high school clubs and activities, in high school curricula, or in types of advanced training institutions, the social class composition of the membership will vary accordingly.

The predictions noted above are far from perfect inasmuch as the social class position rarely accounts for more than half the variance (See Appendix) of school success, the law holds only for differences in group averages, not for differences in individual successes.[22]

EDUCATIONAL AND SOCIAL MOBILITY

We have already noted in chapter 1 the rather low order of relationship between schooling and occupational position. We now turn to the allied belief, widely held in American society by both professional educators and the general public, that formal education is directly and causally related to social mobility. This relationship is generally understood to be one in which formal education itself is a cause or one of the causes of vertical social mobility. On certain levels this generalization seems true. Certain professions—medicine, law, and, increasingly, teaching—require a set number of years of formal schooling of a specialized kind. One cannot move into a position as doctor, lawyer, teacher, or engineer without this formal educational requirement. Whether one can say even in this case that formal education is a *cause* of achieving the professional position is a very debatable question. C. Arnold Anderson has rather effectively challenged the general assumption that vertical social mobility is caused by education through the examination of data relating to fathers' and sons' status in terms of occupation and education level.[23] Table 2.3 shows the distribution of socioeconomic status

22. W.W. Charters, Jr., "The Social Background of Teaching," in *The Handbook of Research on Teaching*, N.L. Gage (ed.), (Skokie, Ill.: Rand McNally & Company, 1963), pp. 739-740.

23. C. Arnold Anderson, "A Skeptical Note on Education and Mobility," in *Education, Economy and Society*, A.H. Halsey, Jean Floud, and C. Arnold Anderson (eds.), (New York: The Free Press, 1964), pp. 164-182.

Table 2.3 Distribution of Sons' Socioeconomic Status and Education Relative to Fathers'*

Son's education relative to father's	Son's status relative to father's			
	Higher	Same	Lower	Total
A. Actual distribution				
Higher	134	96	61	291
Same	23	33	24	80
Lower	7	16	22	45
Total	164	145	107	416
B. Minimum and maximum relative education association distributions and deviation of actual case distribution				
1. Random distribution				
Higher	115	102	75	291
Same	31	28	20	80
Lower	18	16	12	45
Total	164	145	107	416
2. Maximum relative education association distribution				
Higher	164	127	—	291
Same	—	18	62	80
Lower	—	—	45	45
Total	164	145	107	416
3. Deviations of actual from (1)				
Higher	19	−6	−14	
Same	−8	5	4	
Lower	−11	0	10	
4. Deviations of actual from (2)				
Higher	−30	−31	61	
Same	23	15	−38	
Lower	7	16	−23	

* Numbers do not add because of rounding.

SOURCE: C. Arnold Anderson, "A Skeptical Note on Education and Mobility," in A. H. Halsey, Jean Floud, and C. Arnold Anderson, *Education, Economy and Society* (New York: The Free Press, 1964), p. 167.

and education over one generation. Part A of the table is the actual distribution showing the relationship between the son's education relative to his father and the son's status relative to his father. As one might expect, in general the higher the son's education in relation to his father's, the higher the son's social status. Section B of the table represents two very interesting variations from the actual distribution. B-1 shows how the distribution would fall if education were totally random, that is, if the numbers in the actual distribution were simply spread randomly in the various categories. B-2 shows the distribution as it would appear if education were the sole determinant, the only way of fixing the son's status in relation to his father's. B-3 and B-4 show the differences between the actual and random distribution and between the actual and maximum, or total, education distribution.

From analyzing this table it is clear that the actual distribution of the son's education in relation to social status is closer to the random distribution than it is to the maximum education distribution. In every one of the nine cells the deviation of the actual from the "education as sole determinant" distribution is greater than the deviation of the actual from the random distribution.

In concluding his analysis of this research Anderson, referring to an earlier article, points out that according to his findings, from two-thirds to three-fourths of social mobility in the United States was congruent with intelligence differentials rather than educational improvement. He goes on to deduce that the findings of this particular study suggest that "ability (whether genetic or not)—and associated motivation—varying independently of school plays a powerful role in generating mobility."[24] Although Anderson has clearly done an excellent job of placing formal schooling in its proper perspective relative to social mobility, his final conclusion about the importance of ability and motivation does not contradict the findings of other writers on this subject. As has already been pointed out, the school itself may either dampen or encourage ability and depress or develop motivation in individual students. The important question for urban educators is just how the school can best perform the function of developing ability and motivation in youngsters of varying social class backgrounds.

THE TEACHER IN THE LOWER-CLASS URBAN SCHOOL

One important factor in improving the effectiveness of the urban school is the teacher. Robert Herriott and Nancy Hoyt St. John provide

24. *Ibid.*, p. 176.

a careful analysis of the nature, the background, the attitudes, the aspirations, and the competence of teachers in urban schools.[25] Their study is based on an extensive survey and a questionnaire distributed to over 500 principals and 4500 teachers in urban schools. The focus is on social class differences in terms of teacher characteristics, attitudes, and competencies. The schools surveyed in the study are divided into four social class categories. In this section we will describe the more important findings about teachers in urban schools, with particular attention paid to those teachers in the lowest quartile of socioeconomic status schools.

The important variable of teacher experience is one which has aroused a great deal of interest and concern in recent years, particularly from critics of urban schools. The generally held view that teachers in lower-class schools are less experienced was found to be true by Herriott and St. John. The lower the socioeconomic status of the school, the more brief is the total experience of teachers in that school. In addition to possessing less overall experience, teachers in lower-class schools have also been at their assignments for a shorter period of time. This suggests that more inexperienced teachers are to be found in lower-class schools; also their mobility rate seems to be higher. They do not remain in slum areas but move to other school districts, or in some cases leave the profession of teaching altogether.

Herriott and St. John asked teachers to place themselves on a scale running from honors to below average in terms of their college work. No significant difference was found on this variable between teachers in schools of the highest socioeconomic status when compared with those of the lowest. In examining the origins of urban teachers an interesting difference was discovered:

> Sixty-four per cent of the teachers in schools of highest SES grew up in communities smaller than the one in which they now teach. But only 49 per cent in school of lowest SES did so. This difference of 15 per cent is statistically significant. In terms of the community of their youth, the origins of teachers in schools of highest and lowest SES are clearly not identical. Those in schools of highest SES are more apt to be rural or small town immigrants to the city.[26]

Significant differences were also found when comparing the occupations of teachers' fathers between the highest and lowest school SES. The lower the school SES, the greater the proportion of teachers in blue-collar occupations, as opposed to middle-class managerial and profes-

25. Robert E. Herriott and Nancy Hoyt St. John, *Social Class and the Urban School* (New York: John Wiley & Sons, Inc., 1966).
26. *Ibid.,* p. 69.

sional occupations.[27] Another characteristic of urban teachers examined in this study was teacher-pupil congruity. That is, how do teachers match with their pupils on number of characteristics such as race, religion, and ethnicity. Figure 2.2 shows that the lower the school SES,

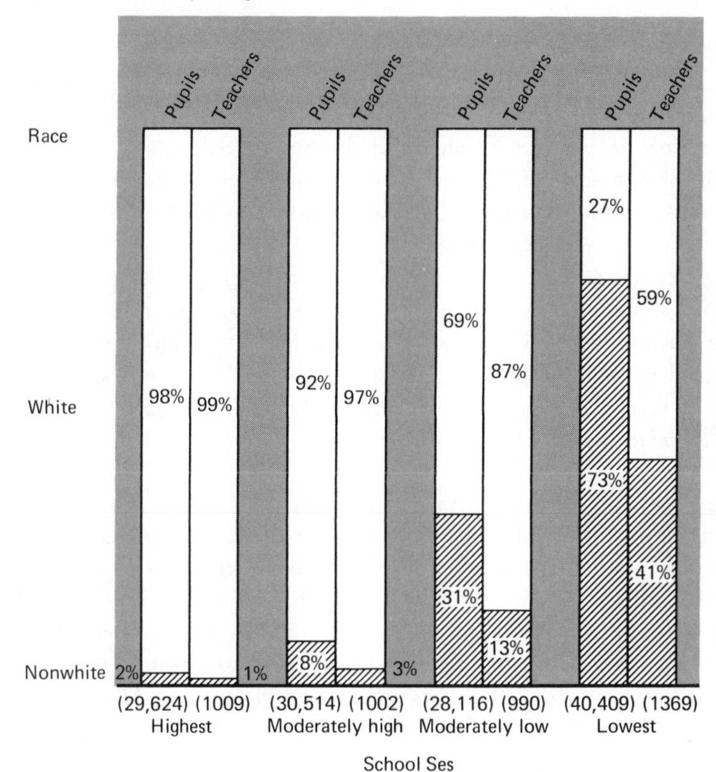

Figure 2.2 Proportion of pupils and of teachers who are white or nonwhite by school socioeconomic status.

SOURCE: Robert E. Herriott and Nancy Hoyt St. John, *Social Class and the Urban School* (New York: John Wiley & Sons, Inc., 1966), p. 78.

the less is congruency along dimensions of race. The authors point out: "As school SES falls the proportion of nonwhite teachers does not increase as rapidly as does the proportion of nonwhite pupils."[28] This factor, the overrepresentation of black pupils in lower-class schools and the underrepresentation of black teachers in terms of the student population, is one of the important criticisms which many civil rights organizations and black community groups make about urban schools. It should be pointed out that many urban school systems are now making serious attempts to recruit nonwhite teachers.

27. *Ibid.*, pp. 69-70.
28. *Ibid.*, p. 79.

Three other important characteristics of urban teachers viewed in this study are the aspirations of urban teachers, the job satisfaction expressed by urban teachers, and teacher morale in urban schools. Not surprisingly, in terms of job aspiration the authors find:

The lower the school SES the smaller the proportion of teachers who desire to remain in their present school for the remainder of their educational careers. The percentage of teachers who do desire to remain in their present school ranges from 68 per cent in schools of the highest SES rating to 49 percent in schools of the lowest SES rating, and represents a statistically significant difference. In order to assess teacher job satisfaction the teachers in this sample were asked to indicate whether they felt satisfied,—very, moderately, or slightly; or dissatisfied,—very, moderately, or slightly, with fourteen aspects of their present teaching situation. Nine of these items referred specifically to the present teaching situation of the teacher. On eight of these nine items expressed job satisfaction was less for teachers in lower class schools, and on seven of them this difference was statistically significant [see chapter 7 for a more detailed picture of dissatisfaction].

In assessing teacher morale both principals and teachers were asked to characterize their faculties in a number of ways. Principals were asked to estimate the percentage of their teachers who complain about how difficult students are to work with. Both principals and teachers were asked to estimate the percentage of teachers in the schools who seemed to enjoy their jobs. Principals were also asked to estimate the percentage of faculty who provided them with personal loyalty. The authors summarized the results in this area as follows:

To sum up, all of the six principal and the seven teacher reports relating to the aggregate satisfaction or morale of teachers in their schools are in the direction of lower satisfaction with lower school SES. All except three of these thirteen differences are statistically significant. Although on absolute terms no single difference is dramatic, the regularity of these results supports our interpretation that these differences are not random. We conclude, therefore, that teacher morale bears a positive relationship with SES.[29]

Besides questions of teacher backgrounds and attitudes toward work, there is a more direct measure which is extremely important in evaluating the effectiveness or ineffectiveness of urban schools—teacher competence. In reporting on teacher performance the researchers used judgments of principals and other teachers in the school. As reported by the principal, teacher performance varies significantly with school

29. *Ibid.,* p. 101.

Table 2.4 In the Average School of Lowest SES the Performance of Teachers, as Reported by Teacher-observers, Tends to Be Lower than in the Average School of Highest SES

	School SES			
Percent of elementary teachers in the average school who:	Highest ($N_m = 43$)	Moderately high ($N_m = 41$)	Moderately low ($N_m = 44$)	Lowest ($N_m = 41$)
1. are committed to doing the best job of which they are capable	87	86	85	82
2. take a strong interest in the social or emotional problems of their students	84	83	81	76
3. maintain an interest in improving the educational program of the school	83	83	82	79
4. try new teaching methods in their classrooms	73	73	69	68
5. provide opportunities for students to go beyond the minimum demands of assigned work	81	79	77	73
6. maintain effective discipline in their classes	84	86	83	81
7. plan their classes so that different types of students can benefit from them	84*	84	84	81*
8. do everything possible to motivate their students	81*	80	79	77*

* This highest-lowest difference is *not* significant at the .05 level.

SOURCE: Robert E. Herriott and Nancy Hoyt St. John, *Social Class and the Urban School* (New York: John Wiley & Sons, Inc., 1966), p. 114.

SES. The lower the school SES, the lower the proportion of teachers (as judged by their principals) who have mastered the skills necessary to present their subjects with high competence. The percentages range from 85 percent judged to have high competence in the highest quartile of school SES to 69 percent in the lowest quartile of school SES. This difference is statistically significant. The same general relationship was discovered when teachers were rated by their colleagues. As Table 2.4 indicates, on six out of eight variables class-judged teacher competence is significantly different. The authors conclude:

> The prediction that the performance of teachers in schools of lowest SES would be found to be poorer than the performance of teachers in schools of highest SES is supported by the data. This conclusion is based on the evidence of two independent sets of observers—principals and teachers—and it is supported by the trend across a large number of items and by the high proportion of statistically significant differences between schools of highest and lowest SES. Although it would seem safe to generalize this finding of SES difference in teacher performance to the population of schools from which this sample was drawn, it should be noted that in general the observed differences are not very large.[30]

In summary, then, we find a picture of the teacher in the lower-class urban school with the following characteristics: He or she is less experienced, tends to be more urban than teachers in middle-class schools, tends to come from a family in which the father was a blue-collar worker, is very likely not to be of the same race as the children, aspires to move from his present school, indicates less satisfaction with and lower morale in his present position and is judged by both the principal of his school and his colleagues to be less competent than teachers in middle-class schools.

Recommended Reading

A good general discussion of social class as it relates to education may be found in chapter 1 of Robert J. Havighurst and Bernice L. Neugarten's *Society and Education* (Boston: Allyn and Bacon, Inc., 1962). August Hollinghead's *Elmstown's Youth* (New York: John Wiley & Sons, Inc., 1949) and W. Lloyd Warner's *Social Class in America* (New York: Harper & Row, 1960) are classic studies useful for the serious student.

30. *Ibid.*, p. 115.

Herbert Gans' *The Urban Villagers* (New York: The Free Press, 1962), a study of a working-class community, and more recently *The Levittowners* (New York: Random House, Inc., 1967), a study of a lower-middle-class suburban community, explore in some detail the impact of social class value differences.

La Vida (New York: Random House, Inc., 1965) contains Oscar Lewis' theory of the culture of poverty; but a more successful and insightful book, although not dealing with poverty in the United States, is his *Children of Sanchez* (New York: Random House, Inc., 1961).

A very readable introduction to the thought and feeling of beginning urban teachers in lower-class schools may be found in Estelle Fuch's *Teachers Talk* (New York: Doubleday & Company, Inc., 1969). Professor Robert Nisbet raises some important reservations about the use of the concept of social class in chapter 6 of *Tradition and Revolt* (New York: Random House, Inc., 1968).

3

THE URBAN SETTING

The crisis in urban education that has featured turbulent school-community relations, desperate efforts by educators to make inner-city schools more effective, and battles over integration and decentralization is only one aspect of a broader urban crisis. A catalogue of the ills that afflict large cities can be composed from the pages of almost any day's edition of a metropolitan newspaper: rising incidence of crime and inadequate police forces; civil disorders and not enough money to solve the problems that cause them; nor enough money to modernize outdated schools, or clear the polluted air or water, or finance rapid transit systems that might help to unclog the traffic jams.

The mayors of large American cities make periodic pilgrimages to Washington to testify before Congress on the desperate needs of the cities, pleas to which Congress has for the most part turned deaf ears. The most powerful forces in the federal legislature are still rural, small town, or suburban and feel no commitment to aid urban areas, an indifference that is more than matched in the rural-dominated state bodies.

In their distrust and fear of the cities the legislatures are not alone, nor can one attribute the attitude merely to an uneducated and provincial know-nothingism. For, as Morton and Lucia White have pointed out, the American intellectual, too, has been traditionally anti-city:

Yet enthusiasm for the American city has not been typical or predominant in our intellectual history. Fear has been the more common reaction. For a

variety of reasons our most celebrated thinkers have expressed different degrees of ambivalence and animosity toward the city. . . We have no persistent or pervasive tradition of romantic attachment to the city in our literature or our philosophy, nothing like the Greek attachment to the *polis* or the French writer's affection for Paris. . . While our society became more and more urban throughout the nineteenth century, the literary tendency to denigrate the city hardly declined; if anything, its intensity increased. One of the most typical elements in our national life, the growing city, became the bete noire of our most distinguished intellectuals rather than their favorite.[1]

Many of the problems the cities face arise from the same sources that feed the distrust and animosity of rural legislators and intellectuals alike. They are also the sources of the urban school's dilemmas and challenges. This chapter will describe the large-scale trends that have created the urban structure of this decade, show what has happened to the urban school as a result of these forces, and examine some of the broad proposals for the future of metropolitan life and school systems.

CONCEPT: URBANISM

Sociologists have approached the urban condition from several different conceptual starting points, which are useful in developing an understanding of the city. The earliest of these conceptions—in the work of Tonnies, Simmel, and later Redfield—see the city as a distinct type of human community and proceed by developing an image of an ideal urban community as compared to an ideal small rural one.

This view emphasizes the differences primarily in human interaction between the homogeneous village or rural community and the large industrial city. The most fundamental contrast is between the *intimacy* of the small community and the remoteness of relationships in the urban setting, which are largely *contractual*. Compare, for example, what happens to a person who becomes ill in each of these communities.

The villager calls upon a doctor whom he has known for a long time and whom he trusts. Everyone in the community knows he is ill; there is likely to be a network of mutual aid in which he himself has participated in the past. Neighbors offer to take the children off his wife's hands for a period, or help with the cooking. Friends can be called on to perform the necessary work on the farm or at the store. There is a web of expectation and obligation based on personal relationship and a feeling of community.

1. Morton and Lucia White, *The Intellectual vs. The City* (New York: New American Library of World Literature, Inc., 1962), pp. 13-14.

The big-city dweller may not even know those living around him, and certainly is not likely to know them well enough to call on them for help. The doctor he sees probably has a professional rather than a personal relationship to him; it is far easier to go to a hospital where other unknown professionals and employees tend to his needs as part of their duties—if he can get in. If, during convalescence, his wife needs someone to care for the children, she will probably have to hire a person to do so or, if they are poor, to call upon a welfare agency.

The details of these contrasting situations conform to the differences one would expect from ideal types, but like all abstract models they tend to be too extreme. Although true in general, there are many relationships in urban society that are not merely contractual. Working-class neighborhoods in big cities come closer in many respects to the village community model than to the urban industrial one. Middle-class people living in large apartments may not know their neighbors but they do have intimate friends in other parts of the city. Though differences in the two milieus are, in general, significant, as anyone who has lived in both can attest, the ideal-type approach tends to exaggerate them.

Moreover, even sociologists can be prone to minimize the very real disadvantages of *gemeinschaft,* the term that stands for intimate relations of the small community. To know, and to be known, entails a lack of privacy that many find onerous; intimacy often demands a considerable amount of agreement on basic values that can restrict personal growth and individuality. One pays a price for the advantages of a sense of community.

Most urban sociologists in the United States analyze urbanism not by reference to ideal-type differences, but by categorizing the life of American communities at some point along the *rural-urban continuum.* Thus, Wirth has defined the city in terms of three major variables which are responsible for its special way of life: absolute numbers of population, density, and heterogeneity of population. As these three characteristics increase, it is postulated that one will find an increase in the following aspects of the community:[2]

1. Increasing complexity of both occupational structure and social stratification. Not only are there relatively few types of work in the rural community but the jobs themselves involve a variety of skills; the farmer farms and keeps his machinery in working order, often building his own structures. At the other end of the scale urbanism encourages a division of labor that results in an increasingly narrow specialization, finding its ultimate and most severe expression in the industrial assem-

2. Paul K. Hatt and Albert J. Reiss, Jr., *Cities and Society* (New York: The Free Press, 1957), pp. 18-19.

bly line. The professions, too, develop a system of specialties, as doctors find it profitable to become more expert than the general physician for some part of the body, and lawyers develop concentrated practices in corporation or maritime law. In the urban schools teachers' roles become more specialized also.

Social distinctions also sharpen and become more complicated. Where the majority are farmers it is unlikely that the community will differentiate among them except for such general groupings as "well-off" and "poor." In the complex urban system not only do people see such gross differences as those between white- and blue-collar workers but between the skilled and the nonskilled, the supervisor and the worker, top management and middle-management, and even the secretary and the file clerk.

2. Mobility of many kinds sharply increases. People move into the city and out of it and from one neighborhood to another and from one school to another with ease and frequency. Rural populations are kept relatively stable by ownership of land, by the strength of kinship ties, and by the advantages accruing to small businessmen from well-established ties with community members. It is the young people who move out in search of opportunity; movement into the community is restricted by its very stability.

Similarly, social mobility, the improvement of one's status by climbing the ladder of occupational prestige, is encouraged in the urban setting by the existence of a wide variety of occupations with small but significant differences in prestige value. The move from skilled worker to foreman can be negotiated fairly easily, as can many others, and with an increase in expectation, one finds increased pressure on the school to provide the basis for mobility. The poor sharecropper or a farmhand finds it much more difficult to accumulate the capital and credit necessary to buy a productive farm, which is about the only social move upward available to him.

3. The nature of social interaction not only becomes less intimate as urbanism increases, but the forms of interaction themselves shift. Neighborhood-anchored institutions, such as the church and the informal pattern of "dropping in" on neighbors, give way to voluntary associations focused on special interests and needs of individuals, transcending their purely geographical location in the city. The political club of the old city machine once played an important role in working-class neighborhoods, but its function has largely disappeared. The corner bar and grill in these areas is still a focus of local interaction for some, but the middle class goes to the "Y" for recreation, to the League of Women's Voters or the City Club for political action, and joins any one of the thousands of associations dedicated to furthering some particular interest or goal, from the American Civil Liberties Union to the

Woman's Christian Temperance Union. Not only do such associations draw on a city-wide membership but they are often linked together in national networks that go far beyond the local community. Thus, headquarters of large teachers' unions can influence the staffing of neighborhood schools in the city.

4. Instead of the relatively simple distribution of population in the rural area, with a few boundary lines separating farms from trading center, rich land from poor, perhaps cropland from dairy grazing, the city tends to segregate not only functions of many kinds but people as well. The larger the city, the more complicated are zoning regulations likely to become, separating residential from commercial areas and commercial from industrial. Recreational land becomes not only segregated but scarce, and the competitive struggle for it is often fierce. When a city becomes as complex as New York, one finds sections devoted to highly specialized commercial or industrial use; one street with fifteen or so shops devoted to wholesale florist supplies, six or seven blocks to the manufacture and sale of women's dresses.

Neighborhood lines sharpen. A black ghetto, a Puerto Rican *barrio,* a Chinatown, the Mexican section, an Italian working-class district, a Jewish middle-class area, the upper-class district—all can be drawn on a city map and are easily recognized by visible differences in life style, as well as by the presence of special food shops, restaurants, movie marquees, and special behavior patterns among children in the local schools.

5. All persons play many social roles. Even children must shift from the role of son or daughter to that of brother or sister, to pupil in relation to his teacher, to friend with his playmates. Adult roles are more varied and complex. Urbanism increases the separation of one role from another because these roles are not played out in the small and intimate context of a homogeneous community. City people, consequently, have greater difficulty in integrating the many roles they play; and because some of their roles involve impersonal relations at best, it is easy to develop divergent styles for different roles. The city teacher may be a sympathetic and loving mother, a supportive wife, and a member of associations interested in liberal and humane causes, but because her teaching is so separated from all of these, she can play a punishing and prejudiced role on the staff of a city slum school.

A large proportion of the contacts one has with other people in the city, moreover, are anonymous and are not shaped by role demands at all; that is, no one who is important to the person and whose expectations might influence his behavior is present. This fact goes far to explain the often-cited indifference of city people to the difficulties of others. Charles Addams once drew a cartoon of a small group of New Yorkers looking with mild curiosity at a man struggling in the tentacles of a giant octopus that had emerged from a manhole. And there are recurring actual stories of bystanders refusing even to call the police as they witness a crime.

6. But, as specialization and anonymity increase, so also does social tolerance. The city dweller grows accustomed to a wide range of behavior, and consequently the scale he uses to judge that behavior broadens. This does not necessarily mean that he approves of everything he perceives, but the realization that he has no social control over most of the others with whom he lives may lead either to acceptance or indifference, if the behavior is not too shocking. Urbanism thus creates the conditions for social change as well as for rapid shifts in taste and consumption patterns; but among many, as a later section will point out, it also creates frustration and fear.

7. The tolerance of difference is only one of the factors in cities that encourages greater variety of behavior than is found in the small community; the greater numbers of people and anonymity of life encourage many individuals to be different just to get attention and the feeling that they matter. City life commonly creates and tolerates a good deal of bizarre behavior. More fundamentally, though, what is involved here is that as communities grow larger one finds considerably more deviance from the shared beliefs of community members. Such deviance occurs from relatively unimportant norms, as well as from crucial ones. Standards of modesty and decorum are violated freely on city streets, and unless the violation is extreme, some passers-by turning their heads is the only consequence. Serious violations of the law, which also constitute deviance from community norms, is apt to occur with greater frequency in urban environments. The segmented life of the city permits the development of subgroups with standards of their own, as in the delinquent youth gang, often sharply different from or openly opposed to the general norms of the community. In the small community some control over such deviant behavior can be exerted indirectly by adults, but this type of control weakens in the urban environment and direct control of behavior is substituted—by police, truant officers, and social workers.

The size of the community alone may not be the essential element influencing many of the characteristics in the list above. In a series of fascinating investigations Robert Angell demonstrated that high rates of mobility, and the existence of cultural differences among the population are better predictors than size of how "good" a city is.[3]

He first had to develop a measure of "goodness," which he defined as "moral integration." He means by this term "a firm moral order to

3. Robert C. Angell, "The Moral Integration of American Cities," in Hatt and Reiss (eds.), (*ibid.*), pp. 617-630.

which people are loyal and in terms of which conflicting parties may be reconciled." It might be easier to think of it as the spirit, or morale, of a city. The basis of the integration index that Angell constructed was a measurement of crime rate, with crime defined only as murder and nonnegligent homicide, robbery, and burglary. To this he added an estimate of what he called "the welfare effort," computed from data on contributions to the Community Chest. This index measures three aspects of the welfare effort—the degree to which campaign goals were realized, the proportion of families in the community that contributed, and the economic sacrifice involved for the community considering its general level of economic activity. The welfare index correlated reasonably well with the crime index (r — .43), that is, those communities with a high crime rate tended to have a low welfare index.

Angell then tested several community characteristics against the resulting integration indices of a number of cities of over 100,000 population to determine what factors influenced the presence or absence of community integration. The two best predictors of integration turned out to be the heterogeneity of the population and the rate of movement into and out of the city. Table 3.1 shows the striking differences in heterogeneity for cities of varying degrees of integration.* When the proportion of foreign-born whites is added to that of nonwhites, the correlation between heterogeneity scores and the integration index becomes —.59, a fairly significant relationship.

Table 3.1 Ratio of Native-born Whites to Nonwhites in Fourteen "Consistent" Cities, Grouped According to Levels of Moral Integration

Well integrated		Moderately integrated		Poorly integrated	
Milwaukee	49.7	Hartford	16.8	Houston	2.6
Syracuse	82.2	Bridgeport	29.1	Columbus (Ohio)	7.3
Springfield (Mass.)	34.6	Canton	28.1	Dallas	4.7
Providence	31.4	Dayton	10.1	Birmingham	1.6
		Kansas City (Mo.)	7.9	Atlanta	1.9
Mean	49.5	Mean	18.4	Mean	3.6

SOURCE: Robert C. Angell, "The Moral Integration of American Cities," in Paul K. Hatt and Albert J. Reiss, Jr., *Cities and Society* (New York: The Free Press, 1957) p. 624.

The second significant factor, mobility rate, correlates with the index at a level of —.49. Rather surprisingly, population heterogeneity and mobility bear little relation to one another; it appears that Southern cities, which tend to be very heterogeneous, have low mobility rates, and the opposite is true of Northern cities. Because the two are inde-

* Since the study was done in the forties, these particular indices may have shifted.

pendent of one another, when they are combined, they yield a multiple correlation of —.79 with integration. That is, 63 percent of the variation in integration scores among the sample of 47 cities is accounted for by those two factors.*

Equally interesting are the city characteristics that do *not* appear to be independently related to integration, among them population size, the degree of absentee ownership of business, the proportion of church members, or the proportion of middle-class citizens.

URBAN TRENDS

A number of descriptive models have been applied to the way in which American cities grow. The simplest of these models will serve as an illustration of the pattern that many cities tend to develop; it views the city as a series of concentric zones around the central business district, which is where the city usually has begun its growth.

Encircling this downtown business area is a zone of transition, a mixture of business and light manufacturing and transient residential facilities composed primarily of rooming houses. In this zone one finds the oldest of the slums.

In the next zone are settled neighborhoods of working-class people, often with a particular ethnic or national flavor. In many of the larger cities these have been the particular target for urban renewal efforts, which have hastened the flight out of the city of previously stable lower-class populations.

Beyond this zone is one of better residences, single-family units and high-rise apartments, occupied predominantly by middle-class and the better-off working-class families. Then, often beyond the city limits, is a circle of suburbs of varying social composition that, during the past several decades in the larger cities, has expanded into several rings, as population growth has rapidly taken over areas that had been farmland.

In the discussion that follows, the term "central city" will be used to refer to those zones within the circle of suburban development, usually within the city limits. "Inner city" will designate those zones at the core of the concentric system, the area of deteriorated slum housing, greatest density, highest concentration of immigrants, and the pattern of urban pathology that includes high crime and disease rates, poverty, and alienation.

In order to get a general picture of the scope and nature of the current problems of urbanism, it is useful to examine the generally

* Technically speaking, most of these factors did correlate with integration scores, but their relationship to mobility and heterogeneity was so close that their influence was included in the already established relationship between those two original factors and the index, and they did not seem to operate independently (*see* the Appendix).

accepted proposition that in this century the United States has become "a nation of cities." This is a notion, says Daniel Elazar, "which conjures up a vision of nearly 200 million Americans living shoulder to shoulder along crowded streets, seeking their pleasures in theaters and poolrooms and suffering the pains of living under conditions of heavy congestion."[4] In fact, though over 70 percent of Americans do live in urban places, such a place is defined by the United States Census as any locality with a population of over 2500 persons.

Table 3.2 Population Growth in Central Cities and Outside Central Cities by Region, 1900-1960

Decade and area	North (percent)	South (percent)	West (percent)
1900–1910			
Central Cities	32.4	41.2	89.0
Outside Central Cities	21.7	18.3	64.7
1910–1920			
Central Cities	24.6	37.8	37.7
Outside Central Cities	20.8	10.3	39.2
1920–1930			
Central Cities	18.8	38.3	45.1
Outside Central Cities	31.7	19.6	63.8
1930–1940			
Central Cities	2.4	14.4	11.9
Outside Central Cities	9.7	23.7	29.3
1940–1950			
Central Cities	7.4	29.9	33.9
Outside Central Cities	24.9	43.5	79.3
1950–1960			
Central Cities	0.3	28.5	31.9
Outside Central Cities	43.7	47.7	65.9

SOURCE: U.S. Bureau of the Census, *U.S. Census of Population—1960, Selected Area Reports, Standard Metropolitan Statistical Area* (Final Report PC:1D).

Only about 10 percent of Americans live in cities with over 1 million population, and well over half are in rural areas or in cities under 50,000. Though there are more than 6000 legally constituted cities, only five of them have over 1 million people in them, and only 51 are over 250,000 in population. Furthermore, since the early decades of the century, while rural population has declined, that of urban places of

4. Daniel J. Elazar, "Are We a Nation of Cities?", *The Public Interest,* No. 4 (Summer 1966), p. 42.

Table 3.3 Population Growth in Metropolitan Areas with and without Central City Annexations, 1950-1960

Areas by size of population	Total change (percent)	Change without annexations (percent)
All SMSA's		
Central Cities	+10.8	+ 1.5
Outside Central Cities	+48.5	+61.7
Total	+26.4	+26.4
SMSA's, Population of:		
3,000,000 or more		
Central Cities	+ 1.0	+ 0.6
Outside Central Cities	+71.3	+72.2
Total	+23.2	+23.2
1,000,000 to 3,000,000		
Central Cities	+ 5.6	− 2.2
Outside Central Cities	+44.8	+52.7
Total	+25.0	+25.0
500,000 to 1,000,000		
Central Cities	+21.4	+ 4.8
Outside Central Cities	+57.4	+81.1
Total	+36.0	+36.0
250,000 to 500,000		
Central Cities	+16.2	+ 2.2
Outside Central Cities	+36.2	+51.9
Total	+25.6	+25.6
100,000 to 250,000		
Central Cities	+24.4	+ 4.6
Outside Central Cities	+27.6	+54.5
Total	+25.8	+25.8
Under 100,000		
Central Cities	+29.2	+ 8.6
Outside Central Cities	+10.9	+69.9
Total	+24.4	+24.4

SOURCE: U.S. Bureau of the Census, *U.S. Census of Population, 1960,* vol. I, *Characteristics of the Population,* Part A, Number of Inhabitants.

less than 50,000 has increased by 50 percent; in the period from 1920 to 1960 the population of cities over 500,000 has barely increased at all.[5]

Even disregarding city size, one can see more generally in Table 3.2 where growth of population has been increasing over this century. That the shift to the suburbs is accelerating can be seen in Table 3.3, which also clearly shows the difference in central city growth by size of city.

We are becoming, in fact, a nation of suburbs and small cities within large metropolitan areas. It can be argued that as long as the population growth occurs in what the Census Bureau calls Standard Metropolitan Statistical Areas the distinction makes no difference. But there are several considerations that must be kept in mind in regard to these SMSA's. One is their nonurban density. Density at an urban level is defined as at least 1000 persons per square mile; suburban density as 500 per square mile. Less than half of the states have even one county with an urban density, and three-quarters of all SMSA's contain fewer than 500,000 people even when central cities and suburbs are combined. Seventeen states do not have a single county that reaches suburban density, and only five of the small Northeastern states have more than 30 percent of their counties in the suburban density category.

A second important consideration has to do with the existence of any real cohesiveness within metropolitan areas. Although city planners have advocated cooperative metropolitan planning, and even the development of metropolitan governments since the thirties, they have made little headway against the resistance of the separate communities that make up SMSA's. The cities in the suburban rings value their autonomy and their identity, and in a number of the larger areas one can even begin to see a breakdown of the traditional dependence of the suburbs on the central city. Although the daily flow of people from the outer regions of the area into the city persists, in New York for example, centers of industry and commerce are developing in the outer rings, and there is a very substantial movement from one part of the ring to another.

This overwhelming preference for the suburbs may well be a response in part to the massive migration of minority groups into the central city, a second key trend, to be discussed below. But it is probably a mistake to interpret it only as flight. People moving to the suburbs give many likely reasons for their shift: "better for the children," "less congested," "cleaner," "larger lot," "lower taxes," and other specific advantages.[6]

5. *Ibid.*, p. 43.

6. Raymond W. Mack, "Suburb, Central City and Education," in Robert J. Havighurst (ed.), *Metropolitanism, Its Challenge to Education*, 67th Yearbook of the National Society for the Study of Education, Part I (Chicago: University of Chicago Press, 1968), p. 84.

In general, Americans appear to have maintained their anti-city bias and preference for rural values through the decades of their migration to the city; they continue, as Elazar puts it, to try to transform urban life to one that conforms more closely to that of the rural past. They want space, grass, storage space, play freedom, and small schools for their children. And, despite the derision of the intellectuals for the suburban life style and the complaints of metropolitan planners about urban sprawl, Americans in increasing numbers choose the low-density suburban ring in preference to the central city. One of the most interesting single indicators of American values can be seen in the fact that the percentage of families living in owner-occupied houses has increased from 43 percent in 1940 to 62 percent in 1960, and is thus approaching the percentage of owner-occupied *farm* housing in 1900, which was 64 percent.[7]

Table 3.4 The Ratio of Number of Families with Incomes over $10,000 to the Number of Families with Incomes under $3,000, per 100 Families, by SMSA Size, 1959

Population of SMSA	Entire SMSA	Central City (CC)	Outside Central City (OCC)	Difference in ratio (OCC — CC)
United States average	124.2	93.9	169.4	75.5
Over 3,000,000	183.0	126.7	311.5	184.8
1,000,000 to 3,000,000	160.5	97.3	238.9	141.6
500,000 to 1,000,000	95.6	73.8	129.3	55.5
250,000 to 500,000	82.8	78.6	87.4	8.8
100,000 to 250,000	70.3	73.1	66.6	– 6.5
Less than 100,000	67.0	76.3	41.0	– 32.3

SOURCE: U.S. Bureau of the Census, *U.S. Census of Population, 1960, Selected Area Reports, Standard Metropolitan Statistical Areas.*

It is also a mistake to regard the suburbs as homogeneously upper or upper-middle class. The stable working class has moved out of the central cities, as have lower levels of the white-collar population. In fact, the general public image of the prosperous suburbs, in contrast to the poverty-stricken central city, requires very considerable modification, as Table 3.4 shows. (Read it as: For every 100 families with incomes under $3000 in SMSA's of over 3 million population, there are 127 families with incomes above $10,000, and so forth.) The larger the metropolitan area, the better off its central city, but also the more affluent its suburbs. Thus, in the smaller SMSA's, the central cities are more affluent than the

7. Daniel J. Elazar, *op. cit.,* p. 47.

surrounding areas. And even in larger areas the ratio of affluent to poor families is only three-to-one.

Since central city populations have been relatively stable, it is obvious that there must have been substantial in-migration to fill the places left by the exodus to the outer rings of metropolitan areas. To a very considerable extent the gap has been filled as a result of the second key urban trend, the migration of rural Southern blacks to the cities of the North and West. The general extent of that movement is indicated in Table 3.5.

Table 3.5 Negro Out-Migration from the South, 1910-1966

Period	Net Negro out-migration from the South	Annual average rate
1910–1920	454,000	45,400
1920–1930	749,000	74,900
1930–1940	348,000	34,800
1940–1950	1,597,000	159,700
1950–1960	1,457,000	145,700
1960–1966	613,000	102,000

SOURCE: *Report of the National Advisory Commission on Civil Disorders* (New York: Bantam Books, Inc., 1968) p. 240.

This migration has proceeded along three major routes. "One runs north along the Atlantic seaboard toward Boston, another north from Mississippi toward Chicago, and the third west from Texas and Louisiana toward California." The effect of the migration on population patterns of the central cities is concisely summarized in the National Advisory Commission's report:

Almost all Negro population growth is occurring within metropolitan areas, primarily within central cities. From 1950 to 1966, the U.S. Negro population rose 6.5 million. Over 98% of that increase took place in metropolitan areas —86% within central cities, 12% in the urban fringe.

The vast majority of white population growth is occurring in suburban portions of metropolitan areas. From 1950 to 1966, 77.8% of the white population increase of 35.6 million took place in the suburbs. Central cities received only 2.5% of this total white increase. Since 1960, white central-city population has actually declined by 1.3 million.

As a result, central cities are steadily becoming more heavily Negro, while the urban fringes around them remain almost entirely white. The proportion of Negroes in all central cities rose steadily from 12 percent in 1950, to 17 percent in 1960, to 20 percent in 1966. Meanwhile, metropolitan areas outside of central cities remained 95 percent white from 1950 to 1960, and became 96 percent white by 1966.

The Negro population is growing faster, both absolutely and relatively, in the larger metropolitan areas than in the smaller ones. From 1950 to 1966, the proportion of nonwhites in the central cities of metropolitan areas with one million or more persons doubled, reaching 26 percent, as compared with 20 percent in the central cities of metropolitan areas containing from 250,000 to one million persons, and 12 percent in the central cities of metropolitan areas containing under 250,000 persons.

The 12 largest central cities (New York, Chicago, Los Angeles, Philadelphia, Detroit, Baltimore, Houston, Cleveland, Washington, D.C., St. Louis, Milwaukee, and San Francisco) now contain over two-thirds of the Negro population outside the South, and one-third of the Negro total in the United States. All these cities have experienced rapid increases in Negro population since 1950. In six (Chicago, Detroit, Cleveland, St. Louis, Milwaukee, and San Francisco), the proportion of Negroes at least doubled. In two others (New York and Los Angeles), it probably doubled. In 1968, seven of these cities are over 30 percent Negro, and one (Washington, D.C.) is two-thirds Negro.[8]

These trends suggest that the outflow to the suburbs, whatever its social class, must be composed of white families; and this appears to be the case. If the whites of the central cities had grown in the same proportion as the white population as a whole did, it would have increased between 1950 and 1966 by 8 million. It actually rose by only 2.2 million, which provides a rough estimate of the number that moved out of the central cities, about 6 million. The movement appears to be even more rapid during the first half of the sixties; almost 5 million whites appear to have left the central cities in the first six years of that decade.[9]

Within the central cities themselves patterns of segregation have forced nonwhites into inner-city ghettos that, during the decade of the sixties, exploded each year into civil disorders on a national scale (*see* chapter 11). Though it is true that the degree of segregation within the city has increased over the past several decades, this fact tends to obscure the kinds of change that have been occurring in the ghetto, in the central city, and in the surrounding metropolitan areas.

One of these changes has to do with the density of those areas in the cities where the minority poor have traditionally concentrated, areas which are now thinning out to some extent. A second dynamic is operating among the black populations in the central city, resulting in increasing diversity in the conditions of life among subgroups within that population. A special census study carried out in the Cleveland

8. *Report of the National Advisory Commission on Civil Disorders* (New York: Bantam Books, Inc., 1968), p. 243.

9. *Ibid.,* pp. 245-246.

ghetto in 1965, which concentrated on changes since the 1960 census, reveals a far from static situation.[10]

The survey identified three separate groups of blacks within the city as a whole: the inhabitants of the "Crisis Ghetto," the lowest income census tracts within the ghetto; those living in the "Rest of the Neighborhood," ghetto residents not residing in the crisis section; and those blacks living outside the ghetto altogether in other parts of Cleveland.

This last group had almost doubled in number in the first five years of the decade, from 22,000 to 40,000. It is probable that on the whole they are no less segregated than those blacks in the ghetto, but the study revealed that they had made spectacular economic gains as a group. In the five years under consideration their unemployment rate had declined by 21 percent and their poverty rate by 40 percent.

At the other end of the scale the poverty level in the Crisis Ghetto rose sharply within that period, up by 11 percent. Female unemployment was up 38 percent. Perhaps most significantly, the income gap between the Crisis Ghetto and the Rest of the Neighborhood widened. In 1960 the difference between the best-off census track in the Crisis Ghetto and the worst-off track in the Rest of the Neighborhood was $550. In 1965 that difference was about $1300.

During this period the Crisis Ghetto population declined by 20 percent, which suggests that the more able people moved into the Rest of the Neighborhood or into other parts of Cleveland. One would reasonably expect that such movements would result in a widening of the gap, as indicated. But there was an *absolute* increase, as well as a relative one, in the number of female-headed families in the Crisis Ghetto and, consequently, almost 4000 more children living below the poverty line than in 1960 in a general population that had declined by 36,000. "Them as has, gits," as the American folk saying puts it; and as the somewhat better-off part of the black urban population improves its lot, the lowest level appears to sink further.

THE FUTURE OF THE MIGRATION

From one point of view it is possible that the trend toward higher concentration of blacks in Northern cities will taper off in time. The rate of migration does seem to be falling (*see* Table 3.5) as is also the comparatively high black fertility rate. Indeed, middle-class black women produce children at a *lower* rate than their white middle-class

10. Walter Williams, "Cleveland's Crisis Ghetto," *Transaction,* Vol. 4, No. 9 (September 1967), pp. 33-42.

counterparts, and as greater proportions of blacks move into that class the rate of population increase should fall.[11]

Table 3.6 Percentage of Total North and West Gain from Southern In-Migration, 1950-1966

Year	Percentage
1950	85.9
1960	53.1
1966	28.9

SOURCE: *Report of the National Advisory Commission on Civil Disorders* (New York: Bantam Books, Inc., 1968) p. 241.

Although the migration tapered off considerably by the end of the decade of the sixties, it seems to be more than offset, at least in the foreseeable future, by the current differences in fertility, as can be seen in Table 3.6. A study directed by the National Commission on Urban Problems in 1968 amply confirms the estimate of the future made by the Commission on Civil Disorders several years earlier. Projecting for the next fifteen to twenty-five years, the later study came to the following conclusions:[12]

By 1985, central cities will have gained 10 million nonwhites, a 94 percent increase, while the suburbs will gain 53.9 million whites, a 104 percent increase. Although nonwhites are expected to increase in the suburbs, they "will still be all but lost in a sea of whites, with the nonwhite suburban population increasing only from 5 to 6 percent of the total."

By 1995 the central cities, which were 88 percent white in 1960 will be only 69 percent white.

By 1985 there will be a "startling" increase in the young labor force—persons between the ages of 15 and 44—by 57 percent nationally. But in metropolitan areas that group will increase by 67 percent for whites and 129 percent for nonwhites.

A massive change in fertility rates and in-migration would be necessary to change such sizeable trends materially. And, whatever may happen to the first of these, migration from the rural South is likely to continue, even if reduced in rate, because it does, in fact, represent an improvement in opportunity for those who move, white or black.

11. For an elaboration of this view see Robert J. Havighurst, *Education in Metropolitan Areas* (Boston: Allyn and Bacon, Inc., 1966), pp. 191-192.

12. "Wider Division of Races Feared in Urban Report," *New York Times* (July 17, 1968), p. 1.

In the first instance, as Blau and Duncan demonstrate in their massive study of occupational structure, the average occupational status of communities, that is, the relative number of higher-status positions available, varies with the size of the community:[13]

Community	Percent
Very large city (1 million and over)	40.0
Large city (250,000 to 1 million)	41.6
Middle-sized city (50,000 to 240,000)	38.9
Small city (2,500 to 50,000)	37.1
Rural nonfarm	32.9
Rural	17.5

The authors' study of the general relation of migration to occupational status leads to the following conclusions:

1. Men who live outside the region of their birth have jobs significantly superior to those occupied by men still living in that region. "It appears that something either about migration or about migrants promotes occupational success."[14]

2. Migration is clearly the prevailing pattern in this society; about three-fifths of all adult men now live in communities outside those in which they were raised.

3. Migrants to small cities are more successful and experience greater upward social mobility than those who move to larger cities.

4. Migrants' degrees of success, however, are influenced strongly by the size of the community in which they are raised. Generally speaking, the more urban the community of origin, the better the chance of achieving occupational status. Unexpectedly, this relationship is reversed for migrants to larger cities whose rural upbringing is less advantageous than for those who migrate to small cities; Blau and Duncan conclude that "the outstanding opportunities [of the large city] outweigh the educational handicaps of rural migrants."

5. Though rural migrants to large cities are better off than they would have been if they had not moved, they are not as well off as the natives or those who come to the city from urban places.

6. Both white and nonwhite migrants from the South to the North suffer occupational handicaps due to inferiority of education and early occupational experience.

13. Peter M. Blau and Otis D. Duncan, *The American Occupational Structure* (New York: John Wiley & Sons, Inc., 1967), p. 249.
14. *Ibid.*, p. 251.

Regional migration has different implications for the ultimate achievement of southern whites and Negroes. The white profits by remaining in the South, where he need not compete with the superior background, education, and experience of Northerners, and where stronger discrimination in employment against Negroes favors him. The southern Negro, on the other hand, profits by moving north, accepting the handicap of inferior education in exchange for escaping from the more rigorous discrimination in the South.[15]

Whatever the misery of their present position in the slums of Northern cities then, migration represents an advantage for the Southern black which he is unlikely to relinquish so long as it exists. The same is true of the Puerto Rican migrant to the large cities of the mainland, as can be seen in the income comparison cited by Oscar Lewis in Table 3.7.

Table 3.7 Annual Family Income of Sample Groups Studied in New York and San Juan

Annual family income	32 sample families La Esmeralda 1964 (percent)	All families La Esmeralda 1960 (percent)	100 sample families 4 Puerto Rican slums* 1964 (percent)	50 families of relatives in New York 1964 (percent)
Less than $500	15.7	22	20	0
$500–$999	31.2	15	20	2
$1000–$1999	31.2	32	32	4
$2000–$3999	18.8	27	18	50
Over $4000	3.1	4	10	44

* 25 families from La Esmeralda are included in the 100-family sample.

SOURCE: Oscar Lewis, *La Vida* (New York: Random House, Inc., 1968), p. xxxix.

THE SHOCK OF MIGRATION

The statistical promise of betterment, however, can do little to ease the pains of adjustment to a large city. In a sense those pains are a part of the human condition, at least from the development of civilized settlements four or five millenia before the Christian era. The story of man from that point is one of almost continuous flow from farm and village to centers of greater sophistication and opportunity. But, to the

15. *Ibid.*, p. 219.

people undergoing the experience, an objective, historical perspective, even if it were available to them, is of no comfort. The migrants' feelings are graphically portrayed by Robert Coles, the Harvard psychiatrist, describing the Carroll family who moved north to Boston:

. . . We knew we had it real bad down there, but to tell the truth we didn't want to leave, if we could help it. A lot of us had relations up there, and they'd write and tell us it was different—oh, yes, we sure knew that—because you were in the city, and there wasn't the sheriff to beat you up if you waited a second before obeying a white man. And you could get more relief money, and the big city hospitals took you in if you were real bad sick, whether you had a dollar or not.

But we also heard it was bad up there, worse even. They'd write and say they were glad to be out of the South and up there, but they wished they could get out of where they were, too, and come home. "Now I ask," my mother would say, "where will they go next? Move to the North, maybe, where there's ice and snow all year long, and where no one hates the poor colored man because there's no one around, period?"

That's the way I thought, just the way she did, until I got married. I was 15, and I started worrying about feeding my babies. And my husband Fred, he started looking to the future and wondering what we'd be doing 10 years ahead, and if we could even stay alive that long. But we thought we'd try, where we were, like all the people had before us, right in Marengo County, down there—and we did. We lived through 10 years and more even, and we lost three children that might have lived, but the others did stay alive with us —and you can see I have eight—even if it's hard to know what tomorrow will bring. (Usually, nothing is what it brings!). . .

Mrs. Carroll spends her days taking care of her children. . . Her husband comes and goes. He is not unfaithful to her, but only if he is gone can they qualify for relief. From what I can gather the social worker is particularly sensitive and flexible: She know he's around—I can tell—but she don't ask too many questions. She's better than the last one, who kept at me all the time, asking this and asking that and wanting to know about everything, until I told her she was worse than my 4-year-old girl, with her questions. I said, "Don't you ever get tired of asking?" And she said I was being rude and ungrateful, and I said she should go bother someone else with her asking, and I didn't care if we starved to death. So she called me a lot of names, and I told her I was going down to the Mayor's office and report her. And believe it or not, she got switched. I didn't do anything. All I knew was that a new worker came. I guess I scared the old one, or maybe she just got worried, finally. That's what she needed, to worry herself and not make us worry.

Mr. Carroll cannot keep as busy as his wife. She has eight children to tend. He cannot find work. He is essentially illiterate. He is no loafer, though; he tries. When he first came to Boston he immediately called on relatives, his wife's brother-in-law and a cousin of his own. He came North first, found a three-room apartment near his cousin, put just about everything he had into the first month's rent ($60) and sent for his wife and children, who came by bus. He borrowed everywhere, in Boston and Alabama, to pay for their tickets. He got a job helping his cousin, a janitor's assistant I suppose the "position" could be called.

"It wasn't bad," he recalls. "At least I was doing something, and it wasn't like back home in Marengo County where you worked for nothing and all the time, like you were a pet. (They'd be good to you if they liked you, but if they didn't you might as well be dead.)

"It was old buildings, like a lot of them in Boston, that I had to mind; and I took care of the garbage and tried to keep things clean, and if someone had done something wrong I reported it and they sent people right over to fix it. But then they sold the buildings, and the new 'bossman'—well, he was a company and had a 'janitor service' they called it. So I was let off and my cousin, too, and ever since then it's been hard, real hard—and touch and go. I'll pick up a job washing dishes and they'll get a dishwasher. I'll try sweeping out the movie theater late at night, and in the morning and they'll get a company to come over with machines. . ."

Mrs. Carroll has a lot in her way, apart from her husband. She is up at 5:30 in response to her infant's crying, and she is the last one to bed, about 11 o'clock at night. "All day long it's go, go, go. It's different here, different than down south, because there's so little room. Three rooms for 10 people. Beds piled up. There's the rats to keep away and they bite, and they don't give us screens that work, so it's a picnic the mosquitos have. I have to worry about food, where it's coming from. There's always something short, always. And clothes, they're the worst to find. They cost a lot and you really need them up here. You have to have shoes for everyone.

"With me it's just trying to keep us all alive. You don't have friends up North, you just see a lot of people, but you don't know them one bit. A lot of the time I wish I was back South, but I know my kids have it better here, maybe. They can go to the city hospital if they falls sick, and we see more money here—even on relief—than Daddy saw all year. You use it up fast, and you need a lot that you have no money to buy, but at least you don't starve, and we was near to it, I do believe. And we was more afraid, that I sure know.

"Up here I feel like I was on the moon, or a strange place somewhere, I mean I'm still not sure how to go about things. You don't know the store people and they insult you with their remarks as bad as they do in Alabama. You don't even get to know your next door neighbor too much. Everyone is to himself, and it's only the kids who meet other people. . .

"[the children] tell me they're ashamed of us, and they want to tear up the certificates we have that says they were born in Marengo County, Ala. They say we never should have lied down before the white people and let them walk all over us. I try to explain, but it does no good. Even my 7-year-old boy, he's all mixed up. One minute he tells me he wants to be a policeman and he'd shoot down all the niggers who tried to cause trouble. Imagine talk like that! Then, the next minute, he says he's going to kill a white man one day, he just knows it, and when he does it'll be about time. I scream him down and I hit him sometimes. I've got to. But I don't understand. I don't. We were brought up to live with the white people, because you have to, and now my children want to be away from them, and get rid of them. Maybe you can up here, where they live outside the city and we're inside, but they're still on top, I know that, and no matter what the kids say, that's true."

Her two sons took part in the riots that seized Boston ghetto this summer. Why? How did they get involved? Their mother cannot answer these questions. To her they were "two quiet boys." They had never taken part in any civil rights activity in Alabama—as some children and young teen-agers in the region had—nor have they done so since their arrival in Boston. Years ago they were both called "proper" by the Southern schoolteacher who taught them in a two-room rural school. ("It wasn't the best school, but they're not so good up here either," was Mrs. Carroll's way of making a comparison. "Actually, I think the school buildings here are twice the age of those we had in Alabama.")

It didn't take long for her "proper" boys to change. "First, they were kind of made dizzy by the street. They'd want to stay inside, or they'd come back from outside full of stories of what they saw; there'd be drunken men and people on dope, and there'd be a lot of sex, and just a lot of people standing around, and they'd see knives and things. Guns, I guess, too. You know, in the country it's not like that. We have a lot of bad colored people in Alabama, but they're not living all together, with no place to sit or take a walk, and with nothing but the sidewalk to rest on and the police to hide from.

"Well, my kids began to forget about everything they once knew—just like that! The streets grew on them, and they'd come and tell me all the stories, and then they stopped. That's when I knew they were *really* changed. It was all second nature, and they were all part of the scenery down there, I guess, so when the riot came, they seemed like everyone else."

Her sons don't quite put it as she does. The oldest youth speaks bluntly and sarcastically. He asks me as many questions as he answers: "Why do *you* think we riot? Don't you know? You must now, or you're pretty slow on the draw, pretty slow. We've had enough. They push you so far, then you can't let it go further. That's it. In Alabama, they keep us down with guns. Here they say we're 'free.' But if we try to act free, then they pull their guns, anyway."[16]

THE URBAN CRISIS

The sense of crisis that has infected American cities stems from the presence of many families, like the one just described, in the slums

16. Robert Coles, "When the Southern Negro Moves North," *New York Times Magazine* (September 17, 1967), pp. 94, 96, 98-100.

of the inner city; from the despair of those in the core of the black ghettos, as they see the improvement in those about them; from the anger of blacks of all classes at their inability to escape from the ghetto.

It is easiest to see the crisis in those terms, almost purely a matter of racial conflict, of greater concentrations of urban blacks demanding equity against the resistance and, often, backlash of whites. This is the way the situation looked to the Commission on Civil Disorders when it concluded that we are a nation divided, that racism and segregation must be overcome. And they surely must be, if American cities are ever to regain peace and order.

From another point of view this crisis can be viewed in a more general sense. James Wilson argues that it is necessary to examine more closely than we usually do the sense of unease that afflicts both blacks and whites in today's cities.[17] Scholars, he points out, are interested in poverty, but that is a national rather than a purely urban concern; the black is interested in racial discrimination, which is of less concern for the white, however much we want him to be interested.

The deepest concern of the ordinary urban citizen, as it emerges in poll after poll, is not with conventional urban problems—housing, transportation, pollution, and the like—a recent survey conducted by Wilson in Boston showed these to be significant problems for only 18 percent of those responding, a group that was disproportionately affluent and better-educated. Only 9 percent mentioned jobs and employment. "The issue which concerned more respondents than any other was variously stated—crime, violence, rebellious youth, racial tension, public immorality, delinquency. However stated, the common theme seemed to be a concern for improper behavior in public places."[18]

This perhaps was an expression among some white respondents of covert antiblack feelings, but the same feelings were expressed by blacks as well as whites, and by those who, in answer to another question, expressed the most willingness for the government to do more to help blacks. In Wilson's view, what these concerns have in common is a sense of *failure of community*. By this he does not mean a longing to return to the intimacies of the small community or a need for identification with a supraindividual entity but "a desire for the observance of standards of right and seemly conduct in the public places in which one lives and moves, those standards to be consistent with—and supportive of—the values and life styles of the particular individual."[19]

This thesis bears an obvious relation to Angell's idea of *moral integration,* for it is in cities with the greatest population diversity and higher rates of mobility that one can expect to find not only lower levels

17. James Q. Wilson, "The Urban Unease," *The Public Interest,* No. 12 (Summer 1968), pp. 25-39.
18. *Ibid.,* p. 26.
19. *Ibid.,* p. 27.

of moral integration but a breakdown of neighborhood controls, the same kinds of cities that concern Wilson. The rational concern for community, as Wilson defines it, is often attacked as conformity or an expression of prejudice or an overconcern for the trivialities of appearance. But, argues Wilson, the purpose of social sanctions on public conduct, from the most informal frown of disapproval to the official complaint to the police, is to handle what economists call "third party effects," the external and public consequences of private behavior:

> I may wish to let my lawns go to pot, but one ugly lawn affects the appearance of the whole neighborhood, just as one sooty incinerator smudges clothes that others have hung out to dry. Rowdy children raise the noise level and tramp down the flowers for everyone, not just for their parents.[20]

This is why people prefer to live in homogeneous neighborhoods; they can expect less deviation from common standards of conduct. An unfortunate result of this desire for community is that people are likely to assume different standards of conduct on the basis of purely external differences of skin color or accent. However undesirable, such assumptions change only very slowly, and the feelings behind them cannot be wished away. Anti-discrimination laws in housing are necessary and desirable, but they are unlikely to control feelings.

The preference for community, Wilson points out, is at odds with the idea of cosmopolitanism that requires the existence of diversity within the city. But only a minority really want that in a city—intellectuals, the young unmarrieds, who have come to the city for excitement, dropouts from society. It is a grave error, Wilson warns, to mistake the preference of the few for the needs of the many. Nor does this emphasis on the sense of community necessarily imply a defense of "middle-class values." The process is the same, whatever the neighborhood, to enforce any set of values.

> To be sure, we most often observe it enforcing the injunctions against noisy children and lawns infested with crabgrass, but I suppose it could also be used to enforce injunctions against turning children into "sissies" and being enslaved by lawn-maintenance chores. In fact, if we turn our attention to the city . . . we will find many kinds of neighborhoods with a great variety of substantive values being enforced.[21]

"Increasingly," says Wilson, "the central city is becoming made up of persons who face special disabilities in creating and maintaining a sense

20. *Ibid.*, p. 20.
21. *Ibid.*, p. 21.

of community."[22] These are affluent whites without children, who can at least isolate themselves in high-rise apartments; poor whites, economically unable or unwilling to leave their old neighborhood when it undergoes a change; blacks, whose segregation by color in enclaves of the central city means that various class levels among them have no spatial separation.

It is particularly in these segregated areas that the unease is greatest, because it is most difficult there to maintain different communal life styles. In such areas the breakdown of community controls leads inevitably to a demand for more direct external controls. Thus, one even finds ghetto schools under police control at times. But the police remain largely ineffective; it is simply not feasible for them to control all conduct in public places; and disorder often arises out of disputes *among* neighborhood residents over what ought to be standards of proper conduct. Until what hour of the night, for example, should one be permitted to sit on the steps playing a guitar and singing?

As Wilson points out, the problem is likely to grow rather than recede. Efforts to eliminate poverty in the city may only increase the flow of rural migrants to the city as the advantages of migration are increased, and make it more difficult to maintain a sense of community. From this point of view the black-and-white confrontation in the city is only one aspect of a greater problem that has to do with class more than color, and that will continue to afflict the schools of the central city after the present crisis passes.

THE URBAN SCHOOLS

The combined forces of in-migration, diffusion of whites toward the metropolitan periphery, and the loss of a sense of community that induces the white middle and working class to send their children to private schools has resulted in an increasing proportion of black and minority group children in public schools. How far that trend has gone in the mid-sixties can be seen in Table 3.8.

It is generally supposed that schools in low-income areas of the cities are much inferior in facilities to schools in better neighborhoods; indeed, this is one of the complaints of the national civil rights movement. As chapter 9 will show, minority group status *does* make a difference in the quality of school facilities available to children, though not consistently so. For economic status, independent of race or nationality, the conclusion is by no means so clear, and is, indeed, contradictory, as an analysis of Project Talent data indicates.

22. *Ibid.*, p. 30.

Table 3.8 Proportion of Negro Students in Total Public Elementary School Enrollment, 1965–1966

City	Percent Negro
Washington, D.C.	90.9
Chester, Pa.	69.3
Wilmington, Del.	69.3
Newark	69.1
New Orleans	65.5
Richmond	64.7
Baltimore	64.3
East St. Louis	63.4
St. Louis	63.3
Gary	59.5
Philadelphia	58.6
Detroit	55.3
Atlanta	54.7
Cleveland	53.9
Memphis	53.2
Chicago	52.8
Oakland	52.1
Harrisburg	45.7
New Haven	45.6
Hartford	43.1
Kansas City	42.4
Cincinnati	40.3
Pittsburgh	39.4
Buffalo	34.6
Houston	33.9
Flint	33.1
Indianapolis	30.3
New York City	30.1
Boston	28.9
San Francisco	28.8
Dallas	27.5
Miami	26.8
Milwaukee	26.5
Columbus	26.1
Los Angeles	23.4
Oklahoma City	21.2
Syracuse	19.0
San Antonio	14.2
Denver	14.0
San Diego	11.6
Seattle	10.5
Minneapolis	7.2

SOURCE: *Report of the National Advisory Commission on Civil Disorders* (New York: Bantam Books, Inc., 1968), p. 248.

The urban Northeast is the only urbanized area in the country in which per-pupil expenditures are less for low-income students than for others; excluding the largest cities, the figures are $362 for low-income students and $461 for higher-income students. In all other regions of the country the difference is no larger than $33. Even in the Northeast, in cities over 250,000 the difference in per-pupil expenditures between income groups is a matter of only a few dollars.[23]

There is a difference in the very largest cities of the country in the age of school buildings; low-income schools in New York, Los Angeles, Chicago, Philadelphia, and Detroit are distinctly older than schools in higher-income areas, in fact, almost twice as old. But, aside from these large cities, in the urban Northeast, urban Southeast, and urban West lower-income school buildings are newer; and in moderate-sized cities throughout (from ¼ to ½ million population) the average age of buildings is identical. Furthermore, in all areas, low-income students are *less* likely to be on double schedules than are higher-income students; and average class sizes are approximately the same.

The assumption that low-income city children have less experienced teachers, however, seems to be true. Although average teacher experience is about the same for all income groups in small and medium-sized cities, the larger the city, the greater the disparity. In medium-large cities, higher-income pupils have teachers with an average of thirteen years experience, against ten years for lower-income students. In the largest cities the figures are thirteen and six years respectively. The urban teacher career patterns that account for these differences will be explored in chapter 7.[24]

There is no question, moreover, of the retardation in achievement in basic skills among lower-class city children, both black and white. A recent study of the Chicago school system provides a good example of what is happening in central city schools;[25] some confirmatory illustrations from New York City are added.

A graphic picture of the results of the urban trends described earlier as they affect Chicago may be seen in school enrollments over a thirty-year period in Table 3.9.

The study estimates that "more than a third of the children now enrolled in Chicago elementary and high schools are affected by the factors included in a definition of 'socially disadvantaged.'" Differences in achievement levels by socioeconomic status and race are given in the listing of school districts in Table 3.10 (the lower the rank order, the higher the status). Note that there are many white children in some

23. Bernard Goldstein, *Low Income Youth in Urban Areas* (New York: Holt, Rinehart and Winston, Inc., 1967), p. 43.

24. *Ibid.*, pp. 43-44.

25. Robert J. Havighurst, *The Public Schools of Chicago* (Chicago: The Board of Education of the City of Chicago, 1964).

Table 3.9 School Enrollments in the City of Chicago, 1930–1963 (age 5 through 18)

	1930	1940	1950	1960	1963
Total Chicago school enrollment*	630,000	567,000	513,000§	686,000	740,000††
White and other	596,000	517,000	436,000	497,000	490,000††
Negro	34,000	50,000	77,000	189,000	250,000††
Chicago public schools**	470,000	420,000	350,000	476,000	536,000
White and other	440,000††	374,000††	276,000††	290,000††	286,000
Negro	30,000††	46,000††	74,000††	186,000††	250,000
Chicago Catholic schools†	157,000	143,000	184,000	232,000	234,000

* Data from the United States Census in the age group 5 through 18
** Data from the Chicago Public Schools
† Data from the Catholic School Board of Chicago
†† Estimated by the author
§ Kindergarten pupils were underenumerated in 1950.

SOURCE: Robert J. Havighurst, *The Public Schools of Chicago* (Chicago: The Board of Education of the City of Chicago, 1964), p. 54.

of the schools with considerable retardation, but that the picture is worst for the highly saturated black schools.

In a rougher comparison the same relationship can be seen by contrasting achievement levels in the schools of Central Harlem in New York with those for the city as a whole, in Figures 3.1 and 3.2.

One feature of the inner-city school has to do with a kind of mobility not yet mentioned; unlike in-migrant movements into the city and the movement from the central city to the suburbs very little is known about the large amount of moving that goes on within the city itself. But school administrators and teachers are sharply aware of its effects; teachers in some schools end the year with very few of the pupils with whom they began in September. In the largest cities the amount of pupil transiency can be shockingly high, as the data from the borough of Manhattan in New York City in Table 3.11 indicates.

Moving frequently from one school to another should logically affect children's school achievement negatively, but it seems, oddly, to do so only for lower-income children. Numerous studies of transiency in populations that are middle class or where class was not isolated as a variable for study show that there seem to be no ill effects from a

Table 3.10 Socioeconomic Status, School Achievement, and Race by School Districts

Rank order in SE status, district no.	IQ	Grade 6, 1963, achievement in reading and arithmetic, grade level	Grade 1, 1963, reading readiness, percent average or above	October 1963 percent of elementary pupils, Negro
2	111	7.5	75	0
18	104	6.8	74	37
1	112	7.8	89	0
17	108	7.4	74	7
16	101	6.4	67	77
4	107	7.1	78	1
3	107	6.8	74	0
14*	95	5.8	48	85
7**	94	5.8	44	48
5	109	7.2	85	0
15	109	7.2	79	16
10	96	6.0	48	67
20	93	5.7	47	100
12	103	6.7	65	1
6	99	6.3	52	69
21	91	5.5	41	92
8	89	5.4	33	81
11	92	5.5	45	96
19	93	5.6	45	61
13	90	5.5	42	100
9	90	5.3	34	81
City wide	99	6.2	55	—

* District contains University of Chicago, with many children going to the University School (private)
** District includes North Side "Gold Coast," with many children in private schools

SOURCE: Robert J. Havighurst, *The Public Schools of Chicago* (Chicago: The Board of Education of the City of Chicago, 1964), p. 54.

greater number of moves.[26] But within the city a high level of transiency obviously has a quite different meaning than it has normally, as is noted by the results of Justman's examination of reading test scores of pupils

26. John W. Evans, Jr., "The Effect of Pupil Mobility upon Academic Achievement," *National Elementary Principal* (April 1966), pp. 18-22.

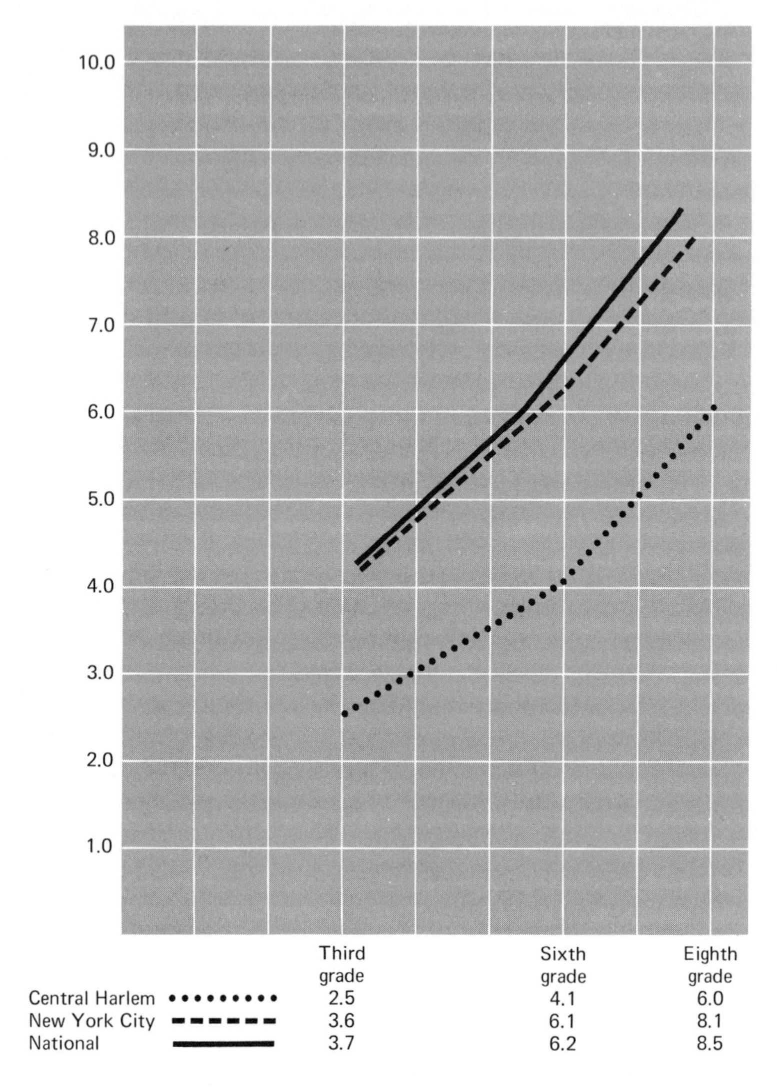

Figure 3.1 Median equivalent grades in reading comprehension for Central Harlem and New York City pupils compared to national norms.
SOURCE: Kenneth B. Clark, *Dark Ghetto* (New York: Harper & Row, 1965), p. 122.

in New York who had been admitted to more than one school in the city during their elementary-school career (*see* Table 3.12).

The effects of in-migration itself from both the rural South and from Puerto Rico is evident in Table 3.13, in a revealing study by the New York City Board of Education. The interesting conclusion from this data is that not only do in-migrant city children achieve at lower levels than others, a reasonable assumption from the quality of the

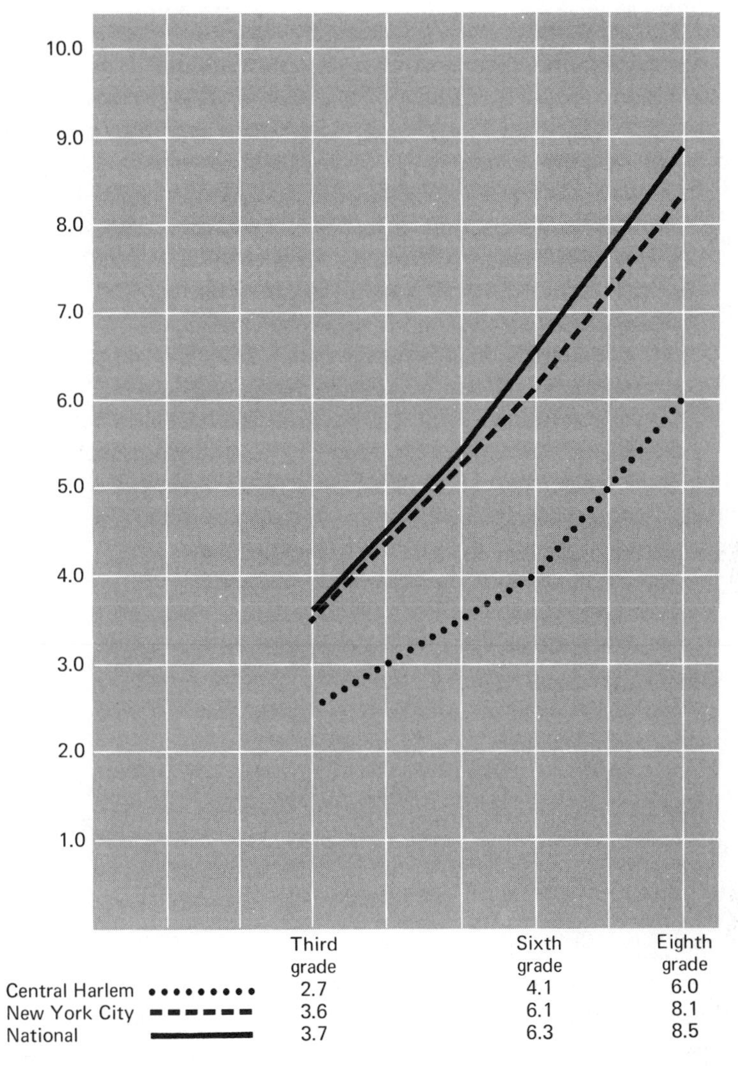

Figure 3.2 Median equivalent grades in word knowledge for Central Harlem and New York City pupils compared to national norms.
SOURCE: Kenneth B. Clark, *Dark Ghetto* (New York: Harper & Row, 1965), p. 122.

schooling which they or their parents experienced earlier, but that New York-born children tend to do less well in schools that are heavily saturated with in-migrants. Several probable explanations may be suggested for this finding; two may be true in part. First, the most heavily in-migrant schools are in the worst part of the ghetto, what the Cleveland study called the "Crisis Ghetto," and the New York-born children in these neighborhoods are thus among the most deeply disadvantaged of

Table 3.11 Number of Elementary Schools in Manhattan Showing Given Percent of Pupil Transiency by Districts,* School Year 1959-1960

Percent of transiency	Districts 1, 2, 3, 4	Districts 5, 7, 9	Districts 6, 8	Districts 10, 11	Districts 12, 13, 14	Borough total
100 and above	—	—	3	—	—	3
90–99	—	—	5	—	—	5
80–89	2	—	4	—	1	7
70–79	2	2	—	1	—	5
60–69	3	3	2	1	1	10
50–59	4	5	2	4	3	18
40–49	4	4	1	5	7	21
30–39	—	1	—	1	3	5
20–29	6	2	—	1	5	14
10–19	1	—	—	1	1	3
Total	22	17	17	14	21	91
Median	49.5	52.5	88.2	47.5	41.6	50.9

* New and discontinued organizations not included

SOURCE: Blanche Robins Kasindorf, *Pupil Transiency in the Elementary and Junior High Schools, 1959-60,* New York Board of Education Bureau of Educational Research and Statistics (March 1961), p. 3.

their group. Second, it is equally plausible that schools with high proportions of in-migrant children are so loaded with problems and pressures that the school itself is disorganized and unable to cope with them.

The probability of the latter explanation is heightened by the descriptive materials available about these schools in the inner city. For the statistics of achievement level and saturation do nothing to convey the real crisis in human relationships one often finds there; the atmosphere of despair, hostility, exhaustion, counteraccusation, misunderstanding, and mutual aggression that represents the real crisis in urban education. To communicate that atmosphere there is nothing that can adequately substitute for the reports of participants and observers, and the following excerpts represent a fair sampling of many points of view.

The slum children themselves seem to pay little attention to their schools; at least they are not very exercised about them. As the MES data in chapter 6 will show, the attitudes of those pupils in very special schools do not markedly differ from their peers in ordinary slum schools. When a sample of delinquent and predelinquent children from the Washington, D.C., schools were interviewed extensively about their lives, they did not choose to talk very much about school hours, and when they were pressed to do so, tended to produce the following kinds of responses:

Table 3.12 Mean Reading Grades and Significance of Differences in Mean Reading Grades of Disadvantaged Pupils Showing Varying Degrees of Mobility

Group	*N*	Mean grade	*SD*	*t*
Test I—Word knowledge				
Third grade				
One admission	384	3.7	1.18	4.44†
Two admissions	285	3.3	1.13	
Two admissions	285	3.3	1.13	3.33†
Three admissions	110	2.9	1.03	
Three admissions	110	2.9	1.03	1.54
Four admissions	106	2.7	0.86	
Sixth grade				
One admission	384	6.4	2.34	3.53†
Two admissions	285	5.8	2.05	
Two admissions	285	5.8	2.05	3.18†
Three admissions	110	5.1	1.62	
Three admissions	110	5.1	1.62	2.38*
Four admissions	106	4.6	1.40	
Test II—Reading				
Third grade				
One admission	384	3.5	1.15	3.75†
Two admissions	285	3.2	0.93	
Two admissions	285	3.2	0.93	3.64†
Three admissions	110	2.8	1.07	
Three admissions	110	2.8	1.07	2.31*
Four admissions	106	2.5	0.89	
Sixth grade				
One admission	384	6.3	2.24	2.94†
Two admissions	285	5.8	2.11	
Two admissions	285	5.8	2.11	3.48†
Three admissions	110	5.0	1.79	
Three admissions	110	5.0	1.79	2.73†
Four admissions	106	4.4	1.38	

* Significant at .05 level.
† Significant at .01 level.

SOURCE: Joseph Justman, "Academic Aptitude and Reading Test Scores of Disadvantaged Children Showing Varying Degrees of Mobility," *Journal of Educational Measurement* (December 1965), p. 154.

Table 3.13 Mean Reading Scores of Grade 6 Pupils in New York City Schools (schools grouped by their proportion of in-migrant pupils)

Mean reading scores and significance of difference of mean reading scores of Puerto Rican in-migrant and indigenous pupils in grade 6 in schools showing varying degrees of in-migration

Degree of in-migration	Group	*N*	Mean	*SD*	*D*	SE_D	*t*
Light	In-migrant	31	4.6	1.18	0.5	0.30	1.67
	Indigenous	51	5.1	1.36			
Moderate	In-migrant	155	4.2	1.19	0.5	0.16	3.12*
	Indigenous	152	4.7	1.54			
Heavy	In-migrant	369	4.2	1.07	0.3	0.10	3.00*
	Indigenous	272	4.5	1.36			

* Significant at .01 level.

Mean reading scores and significance of difference of mean reading scores of Negro in-migrant and indigenous pupils in grade 6 in schools showing varying degrees of in-migration

Degree of in-migration	Group	*N*	Mean	*SD*	*D*	SE_D	*t*
Light	In-migrant	42	5.1	1.23	0.5	0.28	1.78
	Indigenous	148	5.6	1.66			
Moderate	In-migrant	159	4.2	1.50	0.2	0.15	1.33
	Indigenous	594	5.0	1.69			
Heavy	In-migrant	80	5.1	1.69	0.2	0.20	1.00
	Indigenous	224	4.9	1.51			

SOURCE: L. Moriber, *School Functioning of Pupils Born in Other Areas and in New York City* (New York City Board of Education, 1962), p.92.

Yes, I like physical education and mathematics, I like that a little bit and English I like that a little bit, but the rest of them I don't like them too well. What kind of student I am in school? I don't know 'cause I don't hardly ever do no work in school. (Why?) 'Cause I don't like to. The only time I do some work is down in the workshop and physical education. Sometimes I do some work in mathematics. . .

Some of the people at school nice and some bad. If they don't like you they yell at you, and always want to get you in trouble. You don't do nothing and she say she know you did. . .

Worst thing about school is it takes me so long before you go home—that's the worst thing. You stay too many hours at school, stay there and teachers don't let you go to the bathroom sometimes, don't let you get a drink of water. Got to have a pass to go out. But some days you don't feel like doing no work, you feel tired—kinda tiredlike. . .

I don't like school. When they have plays, that's the only thing I like about it. All of us be down in our class and get together and they be singing Christmas Carols and all that. That's good. The only think I can do is arithmetic. You go in there and don't know how to spell and don't bring in your arithmetic, and if you don't bring your papers in the room, stand outside in the hall and let Mr. Ellis see you or Mr. Rogers, when the principal aint there. Stand out in the hall and the next thing if you aint got a necktie on they send you home and bring your mother back when you come, 'cause you aint got no necktie and you make a mistake and don't bring no necktie you got go home and bring your mother and you come back 'cause you be late, and then try to 'splain something to the principal or to your teacher, they never believe you, they swear that you lying and all that, and then when you do tell the truth they swear that you lying and when you lying they swear you telling the truth. And that's why I don't like school. . .[27]

Older boys who have dropped out of high school are not overwhelmingly negative. But they see themselves often as misinterpreted by the authorities and constantly nagged at:

Interviewer: What did they [teachers] do when they picked on you?

Black Dropout: Like sometimes, you know, I ain't doing nothing, they just start bugging me. They just started talking and all this trash.

I: What did they say?

BDO: Oh, like, what you doing, do your work and all that. Sometimes I can't quit talking cause I ain't been talking and it be somebody else that been talking.

I: Anything else you dislike about school?

BDO: No.

I: Why did you drop school?

BDO: I got expelled.

I: Can you tell me about that?

BDO: Well, you see, I was getting in a little bit of trouble, so one day, in the cafeteria; you know, they have teachers that be in there, so this one teacher, he thought I snuck ahead in line but I didn't, so when I got up to get my milk, he told the boy not to give it to me, and then, so I said some-

27. Paul A. Fine, *Neighbors of the President* (Contract No. OS-63-60, Department of Health, Education and Welfare, 1963), pp. 98-100, 103.

thing, so then he grab me and then, you know, we sort of tussled a little bit and then I had to go down to the principal's office and he . . . ah . . . he . . . ah, Mr. ———, the principal, he expelled me. He kicked me out.

Interviewer: Why did you leave school?

White Dropout: Got sick and tired of school.

I: Got sick and tired of school? How did you get sick and tired of school? What happened?

WDO: Oh, the teachers kept on bugging me.

I: Bugging you?

WDO: Yes.

I: How do teachers bug students? I have heard this expression time and again, but I don't understand what it is. How do teachers bug a student?

WDO: They push me around, or something like that.

I: Push you around how?

WDO: Shove me or something.

I: Where do they shove you? Who shoves you?

WDO: The teachers.

I: Why do they shove you?

WDO: I talked in class or something like that. Fooled around a couple of times.

I: Why do you think they did that?

WDO: Oh, they got mad at me, and pushed me around, so I started pushing them around.[28]

Here are some teachers speaking about the problems of these schools as they perceive them:

Another young inner-city teacher in a school which had undergone transition from an extremely good main-line school remarked, "Yes, I have my name on the transfer list. I have stayed for five years and I have had it. My parents tell me I'm becoming impossible to live with. I think it has reached the point where I am becoming emotionally disturbed. I want to do a good job, but I can't teach. The constant tension in the classroom drains my energy. I am not able to have fun with my children or have anything special for a lesson because with any permissiveness, they all go to pieces."[29]

A man who had taught for four years at a large inner-city school commented, "I'm not saying that the case is hopeless. I am saying that something

28. S.M. Miller, "Types of Dropouts: The Unemployables," in H.L. Miller and M.B. Smiley (eds.), *Education in the Metropolis* (New York: The Free Press, 1967), pp. 76-77.

29. Robert J. Havighurst, *The Public Schools of Chicago, op. cit.*, p. 159.

is going to have to be done on the home level before you can do anything in the school. Look, you get kids coming in with no paper. They can't even get up a dime to buy a pad of paper. So what do you do? You make it up to them, you supply the paper. What do you do in the situation in which there's five, six or seven kids sleeping in one room, and even more than one kid in a bed? Many of these people don't have any medical aid, as well as the fact that there's no challenge in their society for school. I had a kid in my room who was walking around with an excruciating toothache for three days. The parents had to wait a long time to get him into the County Hospital to the dentist. So what do you do? It's not that I'm making a fortune. I hate to see the kid in pain, so I took him to the dentist. The tooth had to be pulled. Here's a poor kid walking around really suffering. Can you study with a toothache?"[30]

Many of these children don't realize the worth of an education. They have no desire to improve themselves. And they don't care much about school and schoolwork as a result. That makes it very difficult to teach them. That kind of problem is particularly bad in a school like ———. That's not a very privileged school. It's very under-privileged, as a matter of fact. So we have a pretty tough element there, a bunch of bums. I might as well say it. That kind you can't teach at all. They don't want to be there at all, and so you can't do anything with them. And even many of the others—they're simply indifferent to the advantages of education. So they're indifferent, they don't care about their homework.[31]

I decided to read them a story one day. I started reading them "Puss in Boots" and they just burst out laughing. I couldn't understand what I had said that had made them burst out like that. I went back over the story and tried to find out what it might be. I couldn't see anything that would make them laugh. Later one of the other teachers asked me what had happened. She was one of the older teachers. I told her that I didn't know; that I was just reading them a story and they thought it was extremely funny. She asked me what story I read them and I told her "Puss in Boots." She said, "Oh, I should have warned you not to read that one." It seems that Puss means something else to them. It means something awful—I wouldn't even tell you what. It doesn't mean a thing to us.[32]

But other teachers, more empathetic to the children and themselves alienated from the middle-class orientation implicit in the statements above, lay the blame on the school and its staff:

30. *Ibid.*, pp. 162-163.
31. Howard S. Becker, "Social Class Variations in Teacher-Pupil Relationships," *Journal of Educational Sociology*, Vol. 25 (April 1952), pp. 462-463.
32. *Ibid.*, p. 463.

I have a vision of the system as it exists today:

At the top—tough, authoritarian, political, Irish Catholics who send their kids to parochial school and despise the teachers and the children who don't have the guts or the money to get out.

In the middle, teachers and supervisors up to principals, who come from lower class white minority backgrounds, many of which (like the Italians and the Jews) are strongly tinged with cultural masochism.

And at the bottom, the children.

The system is certainly one of the most secure and protected of all the secure and protected civil-service jobs; it is, to judge by its personnel, quite adequately paid and rewarded and vacationed and pensioned.

But it is medieval serfdom; and the serfs are willing and active participants. They complain, and dissipate their energies in complaining. They hate, and dissipate their hatred in suffering, in provoking guilt, in destroying the children around them, and then they stand over the corpses, weeping, weeping at the terrible system, this deus ex machina, this THING that did it, that did it to THEM, that did not let them succeed. They drive with a passionate and single-minded overpowering drive toward failure, and in this, at least, and overwhelmingly, they succeed.

And don't tell me that they don't fail with the middle-class kids, too, only the failure is one of mind and imagination and openness and courage, not the paper skills of math tables and reading achievement.

Alinsky says a democracy lacking in popular participation dies of paralysis. But participation requires courage and strength. The school system, lacking courage and strength, and participation, dies of paralysis every day.

Maybe what the teachers of the immigrants of fifty years ago had was not better kids (don't tell me babies out of Italy with the evil-eye and the garlic around the neck weren't less culturally deprived than the PR's today) but more courage, more self-respect, and a fair share of faith in their jobs and themselves and their children.[33]

In an effort to compensate for some of the tremendous deficiencies in the school system, I tried to institute new programs from the time I started teaching. For example, I wrote a special grammar book for my students using their language, songs and slang, and which they enjoyed more than the usual type of grammar book which constantly told them they were "wrong." I also developed a program designed to give all students with reading problems a double period of English, using very small classes and understanding, sympathetic teachers, who would take a personal interest in the students and thereby help to motivate them to do better in their studies. Along with other teachers from the school system I was chosen last year by the board of education to write a

33. Unpublished manuscript. Thanks are due Miss Gloria Channon for permission to use this excerpt.

Negro literature unit for use in all high schools. After completing the work, however, my department head told me that it would not be used in our high school because he felt that white students needed it more than ours did!

Despite all my efforts to help the students, I was informed last March that I was being transferred from the school. One official paper said, "she seems to take too much interest in the students and the community." I was terribly dismayed, not for myself but for my students, many of whom felt that school was a cold and hostile place, except for the presence of a few concerned teachers, who always seemed to be transferred soon after they came to the school.

What they need is an atmosphere of flexible discipline, warmth, and understanding. This is what I tried to achieve in my classroom. However, my success with the students only seemed to increase the ire of my associates and "superiors." The only hope for the future lies in the increased awareness of young people about what is being done to them, and the concerted efforts of community leaders, as well as the youth, to *militantly* fight the inequities that have been kept hidden from the public via meaningless diplomas and endless promises from hypocritical public officials.[34]

The education experts also differ about the extent of the problem and where the blame lies. Edgar Friedenberg, probably the most biting critic of urban school systems, sums up the case of the teacher-critics this way:

What Kohl, Kozol, Schrag, Greene and Ryan, among others, have established beyond question is that the dreadful conditions they describe are quite general. They are *not* peculiar to any one school or city . . . A second implication of these books—or rather, of the conditions described in them—is also very obvious, though it will be so repugnant to the liberal, intellectual tradition that it is hard to come right out and write it: The urban slum schools are run by awful people.

The worst categories of school personnel are brought together and reinforce each other here: tyrants whom the parents of higher-status children would not tolerate; silly and malicious teachers who would be shriveled by the sophistication with which middle-class parents would dismiss them as case studies in abnormal psychology; and timid and vulnerable beginners who are assigned to the slum schools because their own professional status is so low that the authorities assume—albeit, as these books show, with some risk—they will not dare criticize them. It seems to me important, for the sake of clarity, that a moral judgment be made. These people are not going to be improved by instruction or therapy; they do not have good intentions; and so long as they dominate the schools, the schools are not going to be improved from within. But they may possibly be improved by coercion from without. We are dealing here with people who have a lot of faith in punishment, manipulation

34. Richard Wisniewski, *New Teachers in Urban Schools* (New York: Random House, Inc., 1968), pp. 135-136.

and taking orders from above—and remedies do usually work with people who have faith in them, even when they are useless or harmful to others.[35]

To which Robert Havighurst replies:

This is such a direct and positive statement that there can hardly be any question about its meaning. It means that urban slum-school principals are bad people, generally tyrants; and classroom teachers are either silly and malicious, if they are experienced teachers, or they are timid and vulnerable beginners. This is a non-responsible statement.

This writer does not argue against the publication of these books and articles. They are important pieces of what should be a very complex picture of a complex situation. Edgar Friedenberg presents his opinions with an effective and beautiful style. Jonathan Kozol writes subjectively as a young man pioneering and reacting personally to some disturbing facts of his new experience. Herbert Kohl gives a vivid picture of the reactions of middle-grade Harlem pupils to life and to school when they are taught by a creative and freedom-loving teacher.

[But] the readers [thus] get little pieces of reality without seeing the whole complex reality. And Friedenberg's conclusions about the character of teachers in slum schools is certainly not proven by these bits of experience. The statement quoted above goes beyond non-responsibility and perhaps is irresponsible.

The responsible editors and publications may properly be expected to present a more responsible picture of the schools in the big cities. If they publish non-responsible books and articles, they should at least balance their productions with writing that is more responsible so that a reasonably careful reader may get a balanced picture. . .

The main trouble with the slum school is the family factor. Many of the vocal critics of big-city schools have a naive faith in what the school can accomplish when it is not aided by the family. Yet substantial studies of school achievement in relation to family socio-economic status show that the family environment is more important than the school in determining a child's educational achievement.

Fundamental recent studies have shown that family environment in the preschool years has more control over the child's later school achievement than any other element in the child's postnatal life. This is due to the fact that the most important steps of mental development are learned before school age from the language that the child learns in the family, the examples he sees of parents and older brothers and sisters reading and conversing, and the way his own questions and attempts at conversation are treated. . .

35. Edgar Z. Friedenberg, "Requiem for the Urban School," *Saturday Review*, Vol. 50 (November 18, 1967), p. 94.

The only result from this kind of criticism of the big-city school staff is one that we already see. The teacher's organizations become angry and defensive. They ask whether their critics have ever taught in a public school. They claim that parents and citizens are unfair to them, the hard-working teachers. They recognize that they are being made a collective scapegoat for the troubles of the city. They respond by criticizing the administration of the schools and the civic organizations that are concerned about the schools, and they demand a greater share in making decisions about the schools.

As for the administrators of the school system, they tend to become apathetic when they see scanty results from their best efforts on the one hand, and get ill-founded criticism on the other hand. . .

The tendency of some critics of the schools to lay the whole burden on the schools and the whole blame for the plight of disadvantaged youth on the schools is unfair, unrealistic and can only lead to more difficulties for the schools and for the cities. It is time for a moratorium on purely negative criticisms of the public schools.[36]

METROPOLITANISM AND THE CENTRAL CITY SCHOOLS

There are two general approaches to the school problems of the central city. One is to generate an enormous range of proposals and programs to improve their performance directly. These will be considered in detail in the second part of this book. The second approach can be dealt with appropriately here in the context of our examination of metropolitan areas and their problems.

Concern for metropolitan growth and its effect on the uneven development of school systems began at least as early as the forties among educators. The concern has focused on two major issues: the disparity in local financial resources available for schooling as affluent members of the area moved to the suburbs, taking with them a major source of tax revenue for schools; and the uneven distribution of educational needs, with growing numbers of educationally disadvantaged children concentrated in the central city, requiring greater than average educational efforts that central city governments do not have the tax resources to finance. What revenues they do command, furthermore, are increasingly subject to competition from other sectors of city service, such as welfare and the police.

There have been numerous suggestions made for dealing with these

36. Robert J. Havighurst, "It's Time for a Moratorium on Negativism," *The United Teacher* (September 4, 1968), pp. 18-19.

problems on a metropolitan basis, but political difficulties have prevented any but fragmentary results. Still, before turning to the major focus of this book, the improvement of the schools themselves, it is useful to examine briefly at least one of the current proposals for approaching urban education problems from a metropolitan perspective. Marvin Alkin's proposal is used here as an illustration.[37]

Alkin points out that the typical school reorganization plan that proceeds by unifying existing districts has little effect on the total metropolitan area; it may reduce financial inequities for small pockets of the area, but little else. "One way to achieve the objective of comparability of financial resources and educational needs among school districts," he argues, "is to reorganize school districts in such a way that they will include both segments of the central city and portions of the surrounding suburbs." Thus, since it is desirable that districts be geographically continuous, the result would be a number of districts that might resemble sectors of a circle—pie-shaped wedges—rather than concentric circles.

Such a plan would result not only in spreading financial resources more equitably but would have other positive benefits. It would force suburban residents to pay careful attention to the problems of central city schools, which they can now comfortably ignore. The news media, too, which generally focus on the central cities, might pay more attention to the suburbs.

Although such a scheme envisages some form of metropolitan tax levied on property and distributed to districts on a per-pupil basis, Alkin also considers the role of the state in his proposed financial restructuring. Some states leave the support of education almost exclusively to local government, and others retain almost complete control and supply most of the financing themselves, but the majority of states combine local and state control and financing. Approximately three-quarters of the states now use a formula called the "foundation program," in which a basic minimum is supplied each district with the assumption that districts will raise additional revenue. Such programs, however, for the most part do not provide enough support for even a minimum level of education. Indeed, says Alkin:

> . . . the level of most foundation programs is so low that there is generally a need to exceed it, and the wealthier the district, the easier the task of raising the expenditure level. Moreover, foundation programs are characterized by an additional feature—the provision of a flat grant, in which even the wealthy districts are guaranteed a minimum grant from the legislature.

37. Marvin C. Alkin, "Revenues for Education in Metropolitan Areas," in Robert J. Havighurst (ed.), (*Metropolitanism, op. cit.*), pp. 123-147.

The problem is compounded by the fact that even if state funds and local contributions could be equalized for rich and poor districts the poorer districts, with the most difficult educational problems to overcome, would still be disadvantaged, because they have only as much to spend as those districts where children learn readily. This assumes that what is necessary is not merely equality of resources but equality of results. A few states have met the issue in larger cities by introducing a "density factor" in apportioning educational funds. New York State began by adding 10 percent to the regular aid for its six largest cities, a figure that in 1965 rose to 17.5 percent.

But, as Alkin points out, there seems to be no rational basis for selecting one of these figures over the other; what is needed is an acceptable way to calculate the degree of educational need for a school district routinely, and base financial support on that. His proposal is that each state develop an "index of educational need" for each school district, based on a system of statewide testing similar to the Regents Examinations in New York or the statewide tests in California. Other data on the characteristics of each district would also be collected, including income and social class, delinquency rate, percentages of homes without a father, and so on.

Using this data, Alkin suggests that we can predict the mean achievement levels of each district and then distribute state educational funds in such a way as to provide the most assistance to those districts with the lowest predicted achievement, the least to those with highest predicted achievement. By using the predicted scores, rather than actual scores, the state would not penalize districts that reach actual achievement levels higher than those one would expect on the basis of their socioeconomic characteristics.

Since school districts are likely to reach better levels for their children than those predictable on the basis of socioeconomic characteristics by levying higher tax rates for school support, or by better utilizing their existing educational resources, the result of this scheme, says Alkin, should be to encourage efficiency among school administrators.

Such plans for metropolitan or state solution of the problems in the central city school are interesting and have long-range significance. But even Alkin concedes that the diverse governments of metropolitan areas are unlikely soon to permit the redrawing of school district lines as he suggests, nor are state legislatures very sympathetic to the idea of distributing state tax money on the basis of need. In the foreseeable future the central cities must cope with their problems using their own resources and whatever help they can get from the federal government for expensive, specialized programs.

Recommended Reading

A good introduction to the problems of urban sociology is *Cities and Society* by Paul K. Hatt and Albert J. Reiss, Jr. (New York: The Free Press, 1957). Daniel Moynihan and Nathan Glazer's *Beyond the Melting Pot* (Cambridge, Mass.: MIT Press, 1963) is a lively and interesting examination of the ethnic minorities in New York City; *Dark Ghetto* by Kenneth B. Clark (New York: Harper & Row, 1965) is the classic modern view of central Harlem and the plight of its residents; and Charles Silberman's *Crisis in Black and White* (New York: Random House, Inc., 1964) looks more generally at the urban black citizen. There are a number of illuminating autobiographical accounts by men who grew up in the urban ghetto, among them Claude Brown's *Manchild in the Promised Land* (New York: The Macmillan Company, 1965), and Piri Thomas' *Down These Mean Streets* (New York: Alfred A. Knopf, 1967).

Robert Havighurst's *The Public Schools of Chicago* (Chicago: The Board of Education of the City of Chicago, 1964) is the most complete survey available of an urban school system. There are many useful collections of pieces from the vast literature on the urban school; to cite only a few: Joan Roberts' *School Children of the Urban Slum* (New York: The Free Press, 1967); Harry Passow's *Education in Depressed Areas* (New York: Bureau of Publications, Teachers College, Columbia University, 1963) and *Education of the Disadvantaged* (New York: Holt, Rinehart and Winston, Inc., 1967); Harry Miller and Marjorie Smiley's *Education in the Metropolis* and *Policy Issues in Urban Education* (New York: The Free Press, 1967 and 1968).

An insider's view of the slum school may be found in Jonathan Kozol's *Death at an Early Age* (Boston: Houghton Mifflin Company, 1967), fairly typical of the mood of a number of books by young teachers in recent years.

4

THE FAMILY

Economic and social status and the conditions of urbanism are, in a sense, statistical artifacts and do not themselves directly influence the behavior of urban school children. The factor that mediates between these large abstractions and the individual is the structure of family life.

It is within the intimate relationships of the family that the child learns his most basic lessons: what to value and what to fear, what to expect from others and what sort of life to anticipate for himself. It is also within the family that he takes the very early crucial steps of cognitive and emotional development that either prepare him for later growth or handicap him when he is provided with opportunity for growth. The patterns of family relationships are, in turn, linked to socioeconomic status and urban environment through the backgrounds of family members and their perceptions of their life chances. Thus, as this chapter will explain in considerable detail, the poor educational backgrounds of fathers and mothers provide fewer opportunities for their children to be exposed to significant types of stimulation important for school success. The conditions of urban life for lower-class minority group youngsters also interact in a complex way with the broader patterns of life chance; they provide, for example, greater opportunities for alienation and the attraction of alternative and exciting life styles. The young narcotics addicts in the city are above average in intelligence, but the life of addiction begins so early that they seldom bother to finish school.

The family is an institution about which most people feel extremely sensitive, and it is therefore not surprising that of all the controversies in urban education examined in this book, the argument about black family structure is the most bitter and emotional. It is with the hope of providing a more objective framework for the later examination of this issue that the section on background concepts below begins with a general treatment of kinship from an anthropological point of view.

CONCEPTS: FAMILY STRUCTURE AND STIMULUS DEPRIVATION

Theoretically it is possible for a human society to provide any form for relationship between men and women ranging from complete promiscuity to strict monogamy. In fact, promiscuity, a state in which every male would be eligible to mate with every female, appears to be incompatible with any known form of human organization, and of all other theoretical forms of marriage only two are found with any great frequency: polygamy, the marriage of one man with several women, and monogamy, the marriage of one man to one woman.

Cross-cultural studies demonstrate that the only form of marriage accepted by all societies is monogamy, though some may permit and even encourage other forms at the same time. Kephart suggests that this is so because it is a system that has more to recommend it than any other:

> Under a monogamous system: (a) group members at the normal marrying age have maximal opportunity to procure a mate; (b) relatively few members are "left out" of marriage, compared to the matrimonial residue inherent in polygynous and polyandrous forms; (c) an effective method of sexual gratification is provided for both men *and* women; (d) intra-sex jealousy and quarrels, often a problem in polygynous forms of marriage are held to a minimum; (e) socio-legal factors involved in inheritance, property rights, and lineage are relatively easy to handle; (f) emotional needs of spouses—needs associated with primary group responses—are more effectively fulfilled than under any other marital form; and (g) child-rearing practices can be effectively aimed at establishing close emotional ties between parents and children.[1]

Within the system of monogamy itself, however, there are wide cultural variations in emphasis on how the family regards children and

1. William M. Kephart, *The Family, Society, and the Individual.* (Boston: Houghton Mifflin Company, 1966), p. 56.

relatives and in how much stability is sought. The American stereotype of marriage views it as a sequence of events beginning with courtship, proceeding to marriage, then to the raising of a family within a relatively self-contained *conjugal* or *nuclear* unit. Although this is the established pattern of most Western societies, a frequently found alternative is the *consanguine* system, in which marriage and family are distinct from one another. Though a couple marry, their loyalty is primarily retained by their original family and they may live with or near either the husband's or wife's family, depending on their culture's particular rule about how family descent runs. Their children are integrated into the larger kinship group, sometimes called the "extended family."

Each of these forms has both its strengths and weaknesses, and a society must pay the price in the disadvantages if it is to have the advantages of any system to which it is committed. The conjugal type gives freer rein to the individual choices of its members and permits each generation to adapt to social change much more quickly, since it is considerably more independent of the older generation. It is probable, too, that emotional satisfactions of a number of kinds are more available to children in the smaller, more cohesive nuclear family than in the extended one. But the nuclear family is also more structurally fragile, because death, illness, or desertion can have immediate and important consequences for all family members, and particularly for the children. It also has far greater difficulty taking care of the aged, who often find themselves isolated and rejected.

Within the large, urban, fast-changing societies of the West, where the conjugal family has an obvious appropriateness, its fragility has become increasingly apparent. The probability for any marriage in the United States to end in divorce has been variously calculated as one out of four to one out of five. The social causes for this contemporary instability of American marriage are well-known; many of the older functions of the family have been taken over by other agencies; the entrance of large numbers of married women into the job market make them less dependent on their husbands; moral and religious sanctions against divorce have declined. All of these forces make dissolution of marriage easier and thus permit the divorce rate to rise. More fundamentally, it is probably the structure of the conjugal family, so susceptible to inner and outer stresses, that lies at the root of the problem.

If this is so, one would expect those families subject to most social and economic stress to be most unstable, and indeed they are. Working with a random sample of divorces, Goode calculated the following "Index of Proneness to Divorce":[2]

2. William Goode, *After Divorce* (New York: The Free Press, 1956), p. 47.

Occupational Status	Index
Professional, proprietary	67.7
Clerical, sales	83.2
Skilled and foremen	74.1
Semiskilled, operatives	126.1
Unskilled	197.7

Though it has been suggested that the rising divorce rate may reflect a movement away from strict monogamy to some form of "serial polygamy," in which everyone is permitted to have more than one wife or husband so long as he does not have them all at the same time, the data in the "Index" would argue that the problem is rather one of alleviating strains associated with one's position in the social class structure.

A further reasonable supposition is that as conjugal marriage proves too fragile to take the strain of lower-class life, the family tends to reform itself closer to the model of the extended family type, which is stronger in the face of outside pressures. Thus, some observers emphasize the positive aspects of lower-class culture, which Frank Riessman describes as:

> The cooperativeness and mutual aid that mark the extended family, the avoidance of strain accompanying competitiveness and individualism; the equalitarianism, informality and humor; the freedom from self-blame and parental protection, the children's enjoyment of each other's company and lessened sibling rivalry. . .[3]

Riessman's view, however, is by no means generally accepted. Robert Havighurst replies:

> . . . there is substantial doubt that the socially disadvantaged children in our big cities have *any* positive qualities of potential value in urban society in which they are systematically better than the children of families who participate fully in the mass culture. The writer does not know of any comparative study which shows American lower-lower class children to be superior in any positive respect to American upper working class or middle class children. . .[4]

This conflict in view is one that will reverberate throughout the chapter as it examines the controversies over family environment and education.

3. Frank Riessman, "Low Income Culture: The Strengths of the Poor," *Journal of Marriage and the Family* (November 1964), p. 419.

4. Robert J. Havighurst, "Who Are the Socially Disadvantaged?", in Everett T. Keach, Jr., *et al.* (eds.), *Education and the Social Crisis* (New York: John Wiley & Sons, Inc., 1967), p. 27.

Stimulus Deprivation

Chapter 2 discussed the concept of a *culture of poverty* which arouses so much controversy because it assumes differences in fundamental values in an historical period in which our social values are undergoing critical attack. There is a less value-laden aspect to differences in family background as one looks across social class lines and an aspect that may be closer to success in school. Martin Deutsch, in his studies of lower-class child development, calls this aspect of family environment stimulus deprivation, a term that encompasses a broad range of lower- and middle-class differences in what happens to children in their early years.

It is not that the lower-class child is exposed to less stimulation in his environment so much as that the stimuli have less variety and range and are not directly related to cognitive skills that the school later requires him to develop. Thus, even the number and variety of objects surrounding the child is limited in the lower-class home to a few pieces of furniture, a minimum of cooking and eating utensils, and a limited number of toys. Not only is the average middle-class child exposed to greater variety of shapes and colors in the objects about him but his parents have sufficient income to buy toys that are in many cases designed to provide cognitive growth. Deutsch points out that lacking early experience with the process of form discrimination provided by constant manipulation of objects of a variety of shapes, the child may be handicapped when he is later confronted with the need to discriminate abstract letter forms.[5] The difference between a "C" and a "G" is a fairly subtle one, for example, and being able to tell them apart depends on a well-developed sense of form discrimination.

The ability to remember, so important a part of school skills, does not necessarily develop as the child matures, but, Deutsch argues, requires training. The middle-class child, from his earliest years, is gently prodded to recall previous events and experiences, and when he does remember, is rewarded by parental approval. The often minimal level of interaction between lower-class children and adults seldom includes these persistent attempts to develop the habit of memory, and children do not themselves spontaneously stimulate one another to recall experiences.

The amount and character of parental interaction with the child accounts for many of the important elements of stimulation in other ways. A sense of time is not transmitted as a significant part of the child's life. Ordering one's life by the clock is a relatively recent de-

5. Martin P. Deutsch, "The Disadvantaged Child and the Learning Process," in A. Harry Passow (ed.), *Education in Depressed Areas* (New York: Bureau of Publications, Teachers College, Columbia University, 1963), pp. 168-178.

velopment historically, and it is significant that the modern timepiece did not come into use until the rise of the European middle classes with their business activities. The middle-class family organizes its varied activities into an ordered schedule, and the child is early impressed with the need to fit into that schedule. Though a sense of time may have no direct relationship to learning, the school organizes itself in many essential ways by the clock, which makes it comfortable for the middle-class child and rather strange for many lower-class children.

In a more general sense the characteristic pattern of interaction between lower-class children and adults inhibits the development of one of the most important underlying relationships in the classroom, the need for the child to see the teacher as a resource, not only for information but for feedback which tells him if he is doing something correctly. The consistent interaction that characterizes middle-class children and parents features a flow of signals that tell the child when an explanation he has offered is correct or incorrect, answers his questions about why certain things are so, and supplies new words and concepts. As most parents will attest, this is a wearying process and demands time, stamina, and unexhaustible patience—resources seldom available to the low-income mother of a large family. The middle-class child gets accustomed, too, to obtaining adult approval and reward for successfully accomplishing fairly complicated cognitive tasks. The lower-class child does many tasks also, but they tend to be concrete and physical ones, and the assurance of adult reward is less often present.

Though all of these forms of early stimulation bear an obvious relationship to school experiences, the most important class difference in family stimulation is probably linguistic. The earliest cognitive training of the family consists of teaching the child to speak the language, and much of the future hinges on what precisely that language is. Bernard Shaw wrote an enchanting play many years ago, *Pygmalion,* in which an expert phonetician bet that he could pass off as high society a lower-class girl who sold flowers in the street simply by training her to speak the language correctly. One does not have to be a social scientist to recognize the extent to which we judge the social status of others by their pronunciation and syntax; people intuitively recognize these as more reliable indicators than dress or social context, which is why many upper-class people do not hesitate to potter about in ancient, frayed clothes or drive old jalopies.

The problem does not merely consist of the fact that the child brings lower-class language habits to the school which is dedicated to their eradication—with often disastrous results for the child's self-esteem—but that lower-class language is not an efficient tool for handling many of the tasks set by the curriculum. Basil Bernstein, the British linguistics expert who has studied the language of various class strata intensively, distinguishes between two forms of language: one, the *restricted,* is the language of many lower-class families; the *elaborated* is found most often in better-educated middle-class families. A restricted language is characterized by:

1. Short, grammatically simple, often unfinished sentences.
2. A repetitive use of conjunctions (so, then, because).
3. Little use of subordinate clauses to modify the dominant subject.
4. An inability to hold a formal subject through a speech sequence, resulting in poor informational communication.
5. Rigid and limited use of adjectives and adverbs.
6. Frequent use of the personal pronoun, and little use of self-reference pronoun.
7. Frequent statements that confound the reason and the conclusion to produce a categorical statement.
8. Considerable use of phrases that signal a requirement for the previous speech sequence to be reinforced: "Wouldn't it? You see? You know?"
9. Above all, it is a language of *implicit* rather than *explicit* meaning.

Because it is difficult, if not impossible, to understand complex and abstract relationships without being able to put them into clear language forms, the school difficulties of children with a restricted language are easy to understand. As Bernstein puts it:

> . . . when a child speaks he voluntarily produces changes in his field of stimuli and his subsequent behavior is modified by the nature of these changes . . . Forms of spoken language in the process of their learning initiate, generalize, and reinforce special types of relationship with the environment and thus create for the individual particular dimensions of significance.[6]

A restricted language code is particularly unable to handle abstractions adequately, and educational psychologists such as David Ausubel argue that it is primarily the lower-class child's difficulty in shifting from concrete to abstract modes of thought that leaves him further behind as he progresses through school grades.[7] Bernstein, too, has noted that the widening of the achievement gap begins at about the fourth grade, when the child encounters the concept of ratio in arithmetic, the first point at which an understanding of mathematical process

6. Basil Bernstein, "Linguistic Codes, Hesitation Phenomena and Intelligence," *Language and Speech,* Vol. 5, Part I (October-December 1962), p. 31.

7. David P. Ausubel, "The Effects of Cultural Deprivation on Learning Patterns," *Audiovisual Instruction,* Vol. 10 (January 1965), pp. 10-12.

depends on an ability to grasp an abstract concept rather than a relationship that can be concretely demonstrated.[8]

CLASS, COLOR, AND FAMILY STRUCTURE

A crucial issue for the school is the extent to which it is possible—or even if it is possible—to predict from such evident cues as social class position or skin color the existence of specific family patterns that often relate to particular kinds of cognitive or behavioral problems in the classroom. How much confidence can one have, for example, in the relationships just described between class level and the existence of particular forms of stimulation? Teachers and administrators in the urban school, in fact, do operate on the assumption that it is possible to make such predictions with some confidence; this section will examine that assumption in detail.

There is a good deal of evidence that family environment strongly influences both the growth of conceptual abilities, through the type of stimulation provided the child, and his emotional development. What is not so clear is the extent to which specific family practices can be related to social class position.

Berelson and Steiner, without reporting on the *magnitude* of the differences, summarize the state of our knowledge of behavior variations between social classes as:

> . . . lower class infants and children are subject to less parental supervision but more parental authority, to more physical punishment and less use of reasoning as a disciplinary measure, to less control of sexual and other impulses, to more freedom to express aggression (except against the parent) and to engage in violence, to earlier sex typing of behavior (i.e., to what males and females are supposed to be and do), to less development of conscience, to less stress toward achievement, to less equalitarian treatment vis a vis the parents, and to less permissive upbringing than are their middle class contemporaries.[9]

The implications of these family tendencies for later behavioral differences in school and out have been detailed by many behavioral scientists in a variety of ways. A good illustration may be found in Kobrin's analysis of differences in adaptation to the stresses of adolescence.[10]

8. Basil Bernstein, *op. cit.*, pp. 44-45.

9. Bernard Berelson and Gary A. Steiner, *Human Behavior* (New York: Harcourt, Brace & World, Inc., 1964), pp. 479-480.

10. Solomon Kobrin, "The Impact of Cultural Factors on Selected Problems of Adolescent Development in the Middle and Lower Class," *The American Journal of Orthopsychiatry,* Vol. 33 (April 1962), pp. 387-390.

His general thesis is that middle-class families are organized to foster impulse control, planning for the future, and achievement in their children for the purposes of maximizing the status of family members. Lower-class families, on the other hand, not being committed to a positive program of child training and often too harassed and despairing to care, foster the child's expression of impulse, aggressiveness, and independence.

Thus, the period of early adolescence is dealt with quite differently, according to Kobrin, by lower- and middle-class families. It is a period generally in which parent-child conflict is at a minimum and one in which there is a reasonable accommodation of the sharply different interests of adults and children. In middle-class families this period is marked by an almost relentless supervision of the young person; although he seems to have a good deal of freedom, it is a freedom that is much qualified by adult supervision through which the child is subtly conditioned to accept adult authority.

The spontaneous street life of the lower-class boy is largely unsupervised, and he is not forced to accept the same type of implicit acceptance of adult authority. As a result, when he moves into the direct struggle with the demands of adults that characterizes the later period of adolescence, he finds it difficult to keep that conflict within bounds; if the rejection of the adult is too extreme the adolescent is handicapped in assimilating the needed elements of adult identity.

In this second stage adolescents face a very uncomfortable psychological situation. They need adult models to guide them into the world of adult life, yet they will not readily accept dictation. Because they are engaged in a struggle for independence from parents, the parent is seldom acceptable as a model. Although nonparental models are nowhere very plentiful, the middle-class child is far more likely to find such an adult available than the lower-class child, and for a number of reasons. One is that the nonparental adults surrounding him (teachers, group workers, and so on) are culturally strange to the lower-class youngster, and their guidance is consequently less acceptable. As for the adults of his own class, the reduced level of interest in child training among the lower class, the fact that it is not a legitimate object of great concern makes his finding an adult model close by unlikely. As a result, Kobrin points out, lower-class adolescents tend to select models from among their next age group; and so the street culture, and with it models of delinquent behavior, is transmitted almost intact.

During this period also the child is in conflict between his need to achieve independence, to become an autonomous person, and his still influential dependency needs. The middle-class family, with a heavy investment in its children, is more protective and controlling, and far more readily accepts stages when the adolescent regresses into dependency. The lower-class family, less protective and controlling, finds it much easier to accept the phases when the child is more autonomous. So, the greatest problem of the middle-class child is establishing his independence; less recognized, perhaps, is the fact that the lower-class child has the obverse problem, that of managing his dependency needs. The aggressive, rule-breaking high-school boy may be reacting to his fear of being dependent on teachers and administrators, reacting to his refusal to recognize that in some ways dependency is useful and necessary.

Such analyses of the relation of class family structure to general behavior patterns are attractive and often persuasive; they seem to fit the facts; and there is a fair amount of evidence that such a linkage exists. Nevertheless, it should be accepted only with a good deal of cautious reservation.

In the first place the primary evidence for sharp differences in early social class child-rearing patterns is subject to some dispute. Two separate extensive investigations in the fifties emerged with findings that were different enough from each other to give rise to years of conjecture and attempts to explain the discrepancies. There is good evidence, moreover, that middle-class child-rearing practices tend to shift fairly quickly on the basis of changes in expert opinion.

Secondly, many of the studies on which the correlation between social class and personality outcomes is based have used worrisomely small samples. Nor are the findings of these studies uniformly in the same direction; a number of them do not establish any relationship between class and child behavior. Richard Wolf, for example, in a study to be examined in a later section of this chapter, found a high correlation between aspects of family environment and the IQ's of his fifth-grade subjects, but almost no correlation between the social class position of the families and IQ. McKinley found tendencies in lower-class parents to use more severe discipline with their children and for fathers to evidence more hostility toward their sons. But both of these seem to correlate just as well with the father's satisfaction with his work as with the social class.[11] To generalize, the evidence seems very clear that family environment produces consistently different kinds of behavior in children, but not very good evidence that particular social class status very consistently predicts particular family environments.

Interpretation is made even more difficult by the evidence that finds a wide variety of family styles within what is customarily considered a single class. A striking example may be found in Eleanor

11. Bernard Goldstein, *Low Income Youth in Urban Areas* (New York: Holt, Rinehart and Winston, Inc., 1967), pp. 15-16.

Pavenstedt's study of two groups of lower-class families living in the same neighborhood in an Eastern city. One group of families was at the upper end of the group, stable working class, upwardly mobile; the other was at the lower end, deprived, disorganized, "multiproblem" families. (Only a few of these subjects were black.) Observations were made during home visits in the course of two projects. Because the differences between these two groups of children are crucial to an understanding of the school's problem, and are an antidote to stereotyping by social class, Pavenstedt's descriptions are worth reproducing in detail:

. . . the children [of the stable working-class families] lacked intellectual stimulation. Our presence in their lives aroused their mothers' interest in many aspects of the children's development that otherwise would have passed unheeded. They bought toys at first resembling the developmental testing material and later the play material to which we had exposed them. . . . Details of health care, i.e., bowel management, feeding, dressing, etc., were outlined by the pediatrician on our staff, but we observed that the mothers were just as likely to heed the advice of family members and neighbors. The majority were fairly adaptable as regards toilet training; they abandoned their efforts when the child showed no readiness to respond or objected strenuously. The children of this group were overtly neglected only by a few mothers who had serious character problems and then only briefly and under stress. As infants they seldom were separated. Later the mothers usually had one evening away from home while father or another relative babysat. The families were greatly concerned for the welfare of their children . . . In most of these families they were the first concern.

Language development covered the normal range on the Gesell, Merrill-Palmer, Binet, and Wechsler intelligence tests. These mothers talked to their children from an early age. In fact, they projected adult comprehension and responses onto the infants, sometimes even the newborn. Smiling gave rise to considerable social interaction and pleasure. Response to and encouragement of vocalizations were frequent but not always present. Some mothers encouraged and welcomed motor development whereas others often unwittingly discouraged it, depending on their need to hurry the children along or to infantilize them. The same was true of education toward independence. However, all the children were feeding themselves by the time they were two and dressing themselves before they were three.

Fathers often became more involved in actually playing with the children, whereas the mothers participated only verbally while carrying on their housework. The extent to which the mothers entered into their children's fantasies was again a factor of the mothers' personality makeup. Considerable permissiveness was granted the children around coming into the parental bed at night.

The concept that children needed to be trained, to be taught to obey and conform was universal. Fear of delinquent behavior was wide-spread. There were many different methods used to instill parental standards. There was not a single home where the mother and father failed to ask themselves how they best could reach and manage their child, even though impulsivity, impatience and anger might break through at times and interfere with their plans. They never lost sight of their parental role. Except for short periods of special stress or depression, the children were carefully and affectionately supervised.

The mothers' voices often were raised. They accused themselves of yelling at the children. This was perhaps the most frequent deterrent used. Physical punishment was rejected by only a few of the parents, and spanking was sometimes administered at a surprisingly early age. There was more teasing than we had had any awareness of. Some mothers in this group were determined to control their child, particularly a son, from very early in life. Although the children sometimes bore the brunt of a parent's feelings toward another adult, a sincere effort was made to deal equitably with the child. Some mothers ruefully shared with us their awareness of such displacement of anger to the child.

As their children came of school age, parents showed more concern that they conform to the teacher's expectations than about learning per se. While teachers described mothers as cooperative and wanting to help and to do well for their children, it was often the fathers who took poor achievement more seriously and even helped their children with homework. Mothers frequently were protective, particularly of boys. In their adaptation to school, none of the children appeared to have discipline or behavior problems. In first grade some of them encountered difficulty in learning, but they managed to make sufficient improvement when pressure was brought to bear so that none of them had to repeat.

Let us turn now to the disorganized, grossly deprived, multiproblem families of our demonstration project. The women of this group, when first encountered by the writer in a reformatory, were inadequately diagnosed as schizoid personality or narcissistic character disorder. The ineffectiveness of our welfare, custodial, and protective agencies in altering their lives and those of their children lay clearly exposed.

When they were re-encountered on the obstetrical service of a city hospital and found to be unreferrable because of their failure to maintain constructive contacts with social agencies, we decided to go into their homes. We found them very suspicious and guarded but nevertheless accessible.

The anthropologist on our project called their cultural fringe—skid row, or preferred to speak of it as a protoculture since there are no values, rituals or directions.

As long as the staff consisted of only family workers, we were unable to obtain a clear picture of the children. The adults in the families were in constant crises. They completely absorbed the workers. We know only that (contrary to what one might expect) the small children were seldom overtly aggressive, or destructive, or engaged in sexual exploits. We had seen them as shadowy, underfed little waifs with meaningless smiles, seldom toilet-trained, climbing into the laps of our visitors at every opportunity and attempting to ingratiate themselves.

It took months or often a year of skillful, especially adapted casework in the homes before the parents would allow their three- and four-year olds to come into our nursery school.

When they finally allowed the teachers to pick up the children, no recognition was given either by the children or by the parents to the fact that they were leaving for the first time with people they hardly knew for a place they had seen only a few times. No goodbyes were said, no mother came to the window and no child spoke about his mother or home during the better part of two months. It gradually became clear that their separation anxiety, shared no doubt by the mothers, was so overwhelming that the thought of separation had to be completely avoided. After several months of attendance when they had begun to relate to their teacher, the theme of desertion dominated their play. By now many of the mothers, too, were bidding their children goodbye.

This shared fear of separation gives us a clue to the intensity of distrust and suspicion these families feel toward organized, i.e., middle-class society. The proposal that their children come to our nursery school aroused a fear that they would be exposing themselves to dangers from outside against which experience had shown they were powerless. Their self-image was so degraded that they expected to be criticized and punished, deprived of their privacy and even of their children.

The youngest child was usually found in his crib in a back room. Diapers were changed infrequently. As often as not, a partially full bottle was somewhere in the crib beyond the baby's reach. During our visits, crying often remained unheeded while the mother discussed her own worries and needs, or she would hold the baby with little attention to his comfort. The outstanding characteristic in these homes was that activities were impulse-determined; consistency was totally absent. The mother might stay in bed until noon while the children also were kept in bed or ran around unsupervised. Although families sometimes ate breakfast or dinner together, there was no pattern for anything. Until children had learned not to mess with food, the mothers fed them and prevented them from holding the spoon. Curiously enough, they always dressed their children, who were completely passive and expected to be dressed. Most children ran around in an undershirt and diapers until they were about two and a half years old. Then they were dressed, and only then let out to play. Once out-of-doors they received no supervision. We saw them standing around, holding onto some outdoor toy and watching other children play. Sometimes the mother called them to have something to eat or when it was getting dark. The children often came running in to ask for money to buy candy or ice cream.

We saw children crying from some injury dash into the apartment, run past mother to their bed and continue to scream there. The mothers seldom inquired about their injuries or attempted to comfort them. Ridicule was as likely to be the response. There were no toys in children's rooms; the beds left little space to play. What toys there were usually were kept on shelves beyond the children's reach.

Poor planning on the mothers' part made it necessary to wash large piles of clothes daily. The children apparently often wore each other's clothes to judge from the fit. None of the children owned anything; a recent gift might be taken away by a sibling without anyone's intervening. The parents often failed to discriminate between the children. A parent incensed by the behavior of one child, was seen dealing a blow to another child who was closer. Communication by means of words hardly existed. Directions were indefinite or hung unfinished in mid-air. Reprimands were often high-pitched and angry. The children usually were put to bed immediately after supper, regardless of their age. Although boys and girls slept in the same bed, a great issue was made of not looking at each other while undressing or bathing. As the children outgrew babyhood, the parents differentiated very little between the parent and child roles. The parents' needs were as pressing and as often indulged as were those of the children. There was strong competition for the attention of helpful adults. All this grimness was interspersed with attempts at mothering which were not maintained because of the mother's tension and lack of self-control. Many of these mothers seemed to think nothing of leaving the home for hours on end with a four- or five-year-old in charge of the babies.

Children in such an environment have to learn to cope for themselves, and these children were extraordinarily adept in certain areas. Extremely skillful at reading their cues, they focused on adults and manipulated them so as to obtain the attention, praise, food, money or whatever else they wanted. Some people thought of this as "object hunger," i.e. the longing for a person who would provide an affectionate, giving relationship. No doubt the absence of anyone sufficiently attentive to the child to allow him to relate had led to this extreme alertness. However, the element of avoiding the adult's anger and sudden impulsive reactions contributed to it as well. They recognized a drunk on the street and were careful to keep their distance. They also manipulated other children and were able to gain possession of another child's toy without raising an outcry. As soon as they were allowed out, they ran errands, usually with a slip of paper. They learned early that you obtained things for money. They soon learned to keep secrets, to cover up for their parents and to say, "Mother isn't here," or, "Mother has a headache," when she was intoxicated.

In our nursery school we had ample opportunity to observe these children. We already have mentioned the total absence of separation anxiety at first. Actually all emotions were veiled. The children masked pleasure by clowning and grimacing and showed no distress when hurt. They wore wide smiles quite inappropriately. When disappointed or angry, they would fade away. When upset or anxious, they might become paralyzed or engage in some frantic repetitive activity. Nevertheless, many of them, surprisingly well-dressed for nursery school, had a certain charm.

Many of them formed their words so poorly that it was at first almost impossible to understand them at three and four years of age. Words were used imitatively and often quite out of context. Instructions, when attended to, were at times repeated but not translated into action. Concrete demonstrations were necessary.

The children were overly obedient in many instances. They never expected their requests to be fulfilled and might wander off while the adult was engaged in helping them. They failed to discriminate between adults and would just as soon run to a stranger. They didn't know the teachers' names and there was no carryover from day to day. There was considerable pseudoindependence and self-sufficiency but no negativism or self-assertion. They were hyper-alert to sounds outside and to the gestures of adults around them.

Rivalry seemed the only determinant for the choice of a toy. It was immaturely handled and the children failed to become involved in play except briefly when an adult was right there. For a long time, however, they did not allow the teacher to be close to them. No questions were asked, no problem-solving activity engaged in. Often they would repeat the same movements indefinitely.

They usually were well-coordinated in gross motor activity but lack of concern about harm to their bodies disguised this proficiency. They suddenly fell and bruised themselves and seemed never to learn from past experience. Even in fine motor coordination they were better equipped than appeared at first. This was demonstrated as soon as they felt free enough to choose their own activity, but was much less in evidence when they had a task imposed on them. An outstanding trait was their great sense of rhythm. As with autistic children, they could be reached by music and could much more readily memorize a verse when it was set to music. They listened attentively and responded with rhythmic body movements.

The siblings seldom comforted or helped each other in trouble unless a younger sibling appealed directly to an older one. Then encouragement, praise or assistance was promptly forthcoming. A girl three and one half years old reported quite casually that when the baby cried during the night the parents wouldn't hear the infant; the girl would get milk from the refrigerator, warm it and feed the baby. From what she had observed of the child's activities at home the nursery school teacher felt this was a credible report.[12]

School professionals would do well to note Pavenstedt's conclusion that superficially "it is not easy to distinguish between these two groups of children. They come from the same neighborhood and are equally

12. Eleanor Pavenstedt, "A Comparison of the Child-rearing Environment of Upper-lower and Very Low-lower Class Families," *American Journal of Orthopsychiatry*, Vol. 35 (January 1965), pp. 92-96.

well-dressed. Yet they must be separated, for they require a totally different approach."[13]

THE CONTROVERSY OVER THE BLACK FAMILY

The issue of how much one can predict family patterns from social class status is debated—when there is any disagreement about it at all—in scholarly circles. The similar question of whether the black American family at low-income levels can be described as possessing singular characteristics that set it apart not only from middle-class family patterns but from the white lower class has developed into a great, roaring controversy that at one point spilled over into the mass media and became a public and political issue. The storm focused on a government report entitled *The Negro Family: The Case for National Action* written by Daniel Moynihan, then (1965) Assistant Secretary of Labor in the administration of Lyndon Johnson. Because the black lower-class family is so directly a concern of the urban schools, the report and the controversy surrounding it is of considerable significance to urban educators.[14]

The background for the report is of some interest and importance to later events. Moynihan wrote it, according to Rainwater and Yancey, as a reflection of his "belief that policy making in the government should make greater use of the social sciences for problem diagnosis and description."[15] It was intended as a document for circulation only among interested officials and for the use of the President. As a result of the report, and several memoranda to the presidential staff, Moynihan collaborated on the writing of a presidential address in June of 1965 on the issue of civil rights for black citizens, in which the President announced that he intended to call a White House Conference to consider answers to the problem, a conference whose goal would be "to shatter forever not only the barriers of law and public practice but the walls which bound the condition of man by the color of his skin."[16]

By the time the conference, now scaled down to a planning meeting for a later full conference, gathered in November the report, copies of which had found their way to newspapers and to members of the academic and civil rights communities, had precipitated an angry and bitter fight among those groups.

13. *Ibid.*, pp. 97-98.

14. *The Negro Family, The Case for National Action* (Washington, D.C.: U.S. Department of Labor, U.S. Government Printing Office, 1965).

15. Lee Rainwater and William L. Yancey, *The Moynihan Report and the Politics of Controversy* (Cambridge, Mass.: MIT Press, 1967), p. 4.

16. *Ibid.*, p. 3.

When the White House Conference met, its director announced to the amusement of the audience that he had been reliably informed that no such person as Daniel Patrick Moynihan existed, the report on the Negro family became one of several subjects about which civil rights leaders expressed indignation, the press searched out these rumblings and characterized them as one of the main events at the conferences, and the controversy was used to support the apparent view of some high administration figures that the conference was a "total disaster."[17]

The report itself is relatively short, crammed with statistics, and embodies a simple and direct line of argument. Moynihan finds the roots of the problem for blacks in slavery and the Reconstruction Era. The American institution of slavery was a particularly repressive one compared to other forms that developed in the same hemisphere, and its effect on the black family was especially atrocious. The slave's children could be sold; his marriage was not recognized; his wife could be violated or sold. He was permitted no religion without his master's permission, kept in ignorance, given no recognition as a human being. The slave household, as a result, tended to develop as a fatherless family, with its strength and focus in the mother.

The Reconstruction Period, with its development of social forms of repression to replace the legal ones of slavery, reinforced this family pattern. Jim Crow and other forms of humiliation and repression worked against the emergence of a strong father figure; " 'keeping the Negro in his place' can be translated as keeping the Negro male in his place: the female was not a threat to anyone."[18]

In the more recent migration to Northern cities the black male has been further penalized in the job market; work is more readily available to the woman; and again the humiliations arising out of Northern prejudice and discrimination weigh most heavily on the male ego.

The central thesis of the Moynihan report is that something must be done to stabilize black family structure:

The fundamental problem, in which (the widening gap) is most clearly the case, is that of family structure. The evidence—not final, but powerfully persuasive—is that the Negro family in the urban ghettos is crumbling. A middle class group has managed to save itself, but for vast numbers of the unskilled, poorly educated city working class the fabric of conventional social relationships has all but disintegrated. There are indications that the situation may have been arrested in the past few years, but the general post-war trend is unmistakable. So long as this situation persists, the cycle of poverty and disadvantage will continue to repeat itself.[19]

17. *Ibid.*, p. 5.
18. *Ibid.*, p. 62.
19. Moynihan, *op. cit.*, no page number.

The case for family deterioration is based on a number of measures. First, the instability of marriage itself, compared with white separation and divorce rates, as shown in Table 4.1. Thus, the percentage of dissolved marriages reaches a striking high of almost 25 percent in urban places. While the percentage of female-headed families has been dropping among whites since 1940, it has been rising among blacks.

Table 4.1 Percent Distribution of Ever-Married Females with Husbands Absent or Divorced, Rural-Urban, 1960

	Urban		Rural nonfarm		Rural farm	
	Nonwhite	White	Nonwhite	White	Nonwhite	White
Total, husbands absent or divorced	22.9	7.9	14.7	5.7	9.6	3.0
Total, husbands absent	17.3	3.9	12.6	3.6	8.6	2.0
Separated	12.7	1.8	7.8	1.2	5.6	0.5
Husbands absent for other reasons	4.6	2.1	4.8	2.4	3.0	1.5
Total, divorced	5.6	4.0	2.1	2.1	1.0	1.0

SOURCE: *U.S. Census of Population, 1960, Nonwhite Population by Race* PC(2) 1c, table 9, pp. 9-10, in *The Negro Family: The Case for National Action* (Washington, D.C.: U.S. Department of Labor, 1965), p. 6.

Second, the nonwhite illegitimacy rate is eight times that of the white. In the District of Columbia, notes Moynihan, the rate grew from 21.8 percent in 1950 to 29.5 percent in 1964. Overall, nearly one-quarter of black births are now illegitimate.[20]

A combination of these factors has led to a "startling increase" in welfare dependency among nonwhites. "The majority of Negro children receive public assistance under the AFDC program [Aid to Families with Dependent Children] at one point or another in their childhood."[21] Moynihan finds particularly alarming the fact that in 1964, as shown in Fig. 4.1, the number of AFDC cases sharply increased at the same time that the nonwhite unemployment rate declined, though in previous years the direction of these indices had paralleled one another.

The report goes on to discuss "the tangle of pathology" in the black community (a phrase borrowed from Kenneth Clark, who used it in a

20. *Ibid.*, p. 10.
21. *Ibid.*, p. 12.

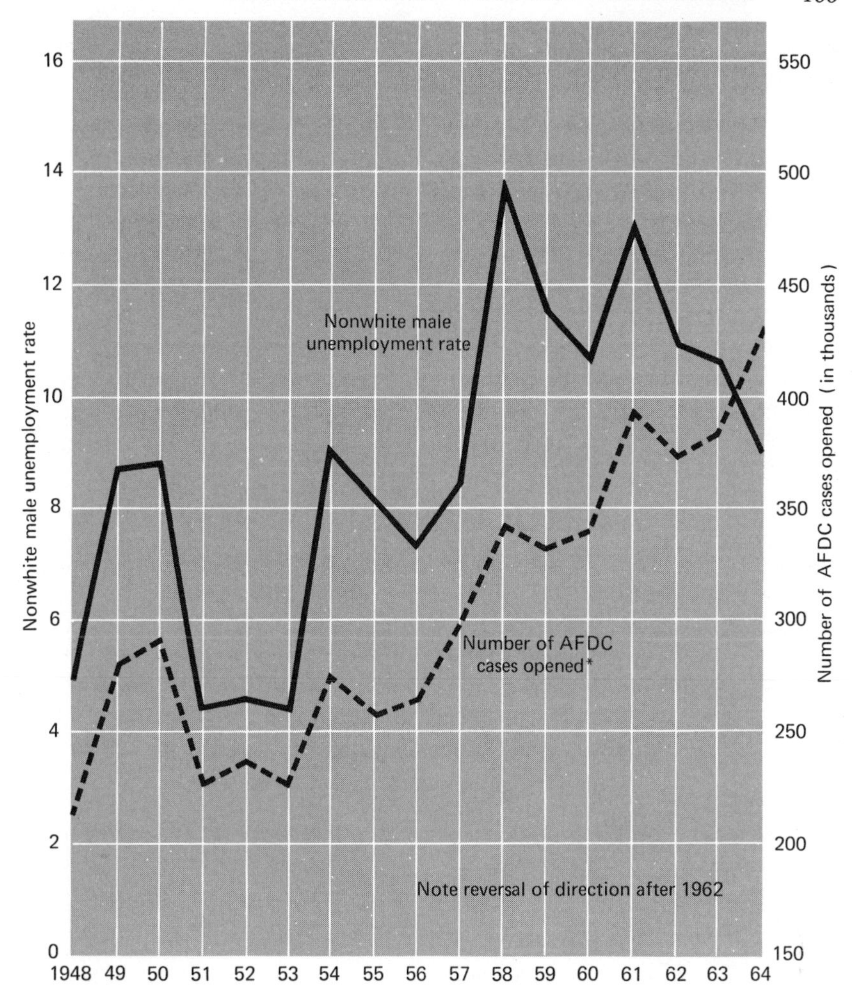

Figure 4.1 Cases opened under ADFC compared with unemployment rate for nonwhite males. *does not include cases opened under program, which commenced in some states in 1961, of assistance to children whose fathers are present but unemployed.

SOURCE: *The Negro Family: The Case for National Action* (Washington, D.C.: Department of Labor, U.S. Government Printing Office, 1965), p. 13.

report on conditions in Harlem), which Moynihan relates clearly to the weakness of family structure, noting:

There is, presumably, no special reason why a society in which males are dominant in family relationships is to be preferred to a matriarchal arrangement. However, it is clearly a disadvantage for a minority group to be operating on one principle, while the great majority of the population, and the one with the most advantages to begin with, is operating on another. This is the present situation of the Negro. Ours is a society which presumes male leadership in private and public affairs. The arrangements of society facilitate such leadership and reward it.[22]

The symptoms of family pathology which he stresses are:

1. The continuing pattern of matriarchy, as indicated by the poorer performance in school and lower rates of persistence in school of the black male as compared to the female, as well as the better position established by the female in white-collar and professional fields of employment (*see* Chapter 1 of this text for confirmatory data).

2. The influence on the boy of the absence of the father is particularly emphasized. "White children without fathers at least perceive all about them the pattern of men working. Negro children without fathers flounder—and fail." School enrollment in the upper grades, for example, seems clearly related to the presence of parents, as in Table 4.2.

Table 4.2 Percent of Nonwhite Males Enrolled in School, by Age and Presence of Parents, 1960

Age	Both parents present	One parent present	Neither parent present
5 years	41.7	44.2	34.3
6 years	79.3	78.7	73.8
7 to 9 years	96.1	95.3	93.9
10 to 13 years	96.2	95.5	93.0
14 and 15 years	91.8	89.9	85.0
16 and 17 years	78.0	72.7	63.2
18 and 19 years	46.5	40.0	32.3

SOURCE: *1960 Census, School Enrollment* PC(2) 5a, table 3, p. 24, in *The Negro Family: The Case for National Action* (Washington, D.C.: U.S. Department of Labor, 1965), p. 37.

3. Poverty, failure, and isolation has resulted in a disastrously high rate of delinquency and crime among black youth. Admitting that crime data is undoubtedly biased against blacks, who are arraigned much more casually than are whites, Moynihan nevertheless doubts that differences as large as those in Tables 4.3 and 4.4 can be accounted for by this factor.

Rates of juvenile delinquency and narcotics addiction are similarly cited to demonstrate the personality effects of being reared in a disorganized home without a father.

As Rainwater and Yancey sum it up:

22. *Ibid.*, p. 29.

Moynihan, then, saw a vicious cycle operating. Negro men have no stable place in the economic system; as a result, they cannot be strong husbands and fathers. Therefore Negro families break up, and women must assume the task of rearing children without male assistance; often the woman must assume the task of bringing in income also. Since the children do not grow up in a stable home, and so learn that they cannot look forward to a stable life, they are not able to accomplish in school, leave school early, and therefore are in a very poor position to qualify for jobs that will produce a decent family income; and the cycle starts again.[23]

Table 4.3 Number of City Arrests in 1963*

	White	Negro
Offenses charged, total	24,805	35,520
Murder and nonnegligent manslaughter	1662	2593
Forcible rape	3199	3570
Aggravated assault	19,944	29,357

* In 2892 cities with population over 2500

SOURCE: *Crime in the United States,* Federal Bureau of Investigation, 1963, table 31, p. 117, in *The Negro Family: The Case for National Action* (Washington, D.C.: U.S. Department of Labor, 1965), p. 38.

Table 4.4 Number of Arrests in 1963

	White	Negro
Offences charged, total	31,988	38,549
Murder and nonnegligent manslaughter	2288	2948
Forcible rape	4402	3935
Aggravated assault	25,298	31,666

SOURCE: *Crime in the United States,* Federal Bureau of Investigation, 1963, table 25, p. 111, in *The Negro Family: The Case for National Action* (Washington, D.C.: U.S. Department of Labor, 1965), p. 39.

Having defined the problem, Moynihan does not explicitly propose the solution except in stating what he sees as the essential direction for national policy:

In a word, a national effort towards the problem of Negro Americans must be directed towards the question of family structure. The object should be to strengthen the Negro family so as to enable it to raise and support its members as do other families. After that, how this group of Americans chooses to

23. Rainwater and Yancey, *op. cit.,* p. 6.

run its affairs, take advantage of its opportunities, or fail to do so, is none of the nation's business.[24]

The attacks on the report came from many sources: the academic community, government officials, churchmen, and civil rights leaders. Their criticisms overlapped, however, so that one can summarize them best by disregarding the source:

1. Much of the early flood of criticism was based not on a careful reading of the report itself but on newspaper coverage of it. Before copies were generally available the report had been leaked to some newsmen, who picked up sensational implications and exaggerated them, as the mass media are likely to do in most circumstances. Many of these accounts gave the impression that the report viewed the problem as due exclusively to family instability, ignoring Moynihan's major thesis of a cycle of causation in which discrimination played a dominant role. Civil rights sympathizers feared that the data in the report, though widely known by social scientists and others involved in the problem, would be seized on by racists to justify their view of the black as depraved and brutish.

There was specifically a lively apprehension that the report's alarm about the illegitimacy rate would be picked up and used against the black and, indeed, much of the early attack on the report was based on an outraged reaction to the data on illegitimacy. This fear had some foundation from an already existing body of opinion; even so thoughtful and civilized a journalist as Theodore White had, in his *The Making of the President 1964,* indulged in a savage tirade against black illegitimacy in big cities as "the biological potential of the despairing Negro for upsetting the entire course of American urban civilization."[25] More generally, there was a feeling that singling out the black family as a special problem was itself a form of racism on Moynihan's part, that he was putting the blame for the black condition on this minority alone and thus absolving the white society that had created the problem.

Rainwater and Yancey persuasively argue that this type of criticism was an unfortunate result of the context of the report rather than of the material itself. If Moynihan had known that the report would become a public document, the tone in which it was written would in all probability have been quite different. The leakage to the newspapers before the report itself was available to responsible and interested persons, in their view, caused much of the later difficulty.

2. A good deal of the criticism of the report focused on the question

24. Moynihan, *op. cit.,* pp. 47-48.

25. Theodore H. White, *The Making of the President 1964* (New York: New American Library of World Literature, Inc., 1965), p. 275.

of where one considers the roots of the problem to be. In adopting the view of black historians that black family instability can be traced to its situation under slavery Moynihan unwittingly aroused the ire of many civil rights militants who had recently come to see this view as, in their words, a "copout" for the present white society, a way of saying that current discrimination is not doing the damage. Furthermore, there must be considerable question about this historical thesis when one notes that these same problems of family instability are found among mountain whites recently arrived in urban areas.

The report does, in fact, make much of job discrimination as a source for family instability, and in a version that Moynihan prepared for the scholarly journal *Daedalus,* he made unemployment the central issue. It is possible, without straining, to see both the historical and contemporary forces as important, and, indeed, some black militants also perceive the historical influence as primary.

In a recent book by two black psychiatrists, *Black Rage,* for example, Moynihan is dismissed as "simplistic" because his report assumes that overcoming employment discrimination will solve the problem. On the basis of their clinical experience the authors argue that the psychological damage resulting from slavery and the persisting institutionalization of attitudes toward the black man are the crucial element:

> The problem is a latter-day version of the problem faced by the slave family. How does one build a family, make it strong, and breed from it strong men and women when the institutional structures of the nation make it impossible for the family to serve its primary purpose—the protection of its members? The Negro family is weak and relatively ineffective because the United States sets its hand against black people and by the strength of wealth, size, and number *prevents* black families from protecting their members.[26]

3. Most of the academic attack on the Moynihan report consists of variations on this same theme of oversimplification. Moynihan, it was claimed, had overlooked the great range of family structures within black culture, even within the lower class itself. Government social scientists pointed out that his alarm over the data on fatherless families and illegitimacy was unwarranted. The increase in female-headed families, they demonstrated (see Table 4.5), had been gradual from 1949 to 1959, and from 1960 to 1964 showed no net rise at all. (By 1965 it was 24.9 percent.) Over a period of fifteen years, then, the increase was only about one-third of a percentage point a year.

Similarly, the same critics pointed out that the number of illegit-

26. William H. Grier and Price M. Cobbs, *Black Rage* (New York: Basic Books, Inc., 1968), p. 84.

imate births rose between 1954 and 1964 from 176,600 to 276,000, which, they conceded, is a tremendous number. But, "in terms of people's behavior, the only relevant index of increase in illegitimacy is *rate,* that is, the number of births out of wedlock per one thousand unmarried women of childbearing age."[27] In the latter part of the period under consideration that rate has oscillated within a two-point spread and, in effect, is at a plateau.

The major issue here, clearly, is not whether there is a problem but whether things are getting worse and should be considered critical. Another attack on the sophistication of Moynihan's data leads to the same question: What happens if one compares the indices of family instability not merely between blacks and whites generally but between comparable income levels within each group? An example of what does happen to the percentages is shown for female-headed families in Figure 4.2. The general conclusion from such analyses seems to be that though there are differences by color they are less important than differences between higher and lower income levels.

Table 4.5 Families Headed by a Woman as Percent of All Families by Color—Selected Periods, 1949-1964

	Families Headed by a Woman as Percent of Total	
Year	White	Nonwhite
1964	8.8	23.4
1963	8.6	23.3
1962	8.6	23.2
1961	8.9	21.6
1960	8.7	22.4
1959	8.4	23.6
1958	8.6	22.4
1957	8.9	21.9
1956	8.8	20.5
1955	9.0	20.7
1954	8.3	19.2
1953	8.4	18.1
1952	9.2	17.9
1950	8.4	19.1
1949	8.8	18.8

SOURCE: Lee Rainwater and William L. Yancey, *The Moynihan Report and the Politics of Controversy* (Cambridge, Mass.: MIT Press, 1967), p. 348.

27. Elizabeth Herzog, "Is There a Breakdown of the Negro Family?", *Social Work* (January 1966), reprinted in Rainwater and Yancey, *op. cit.,* p. 348.

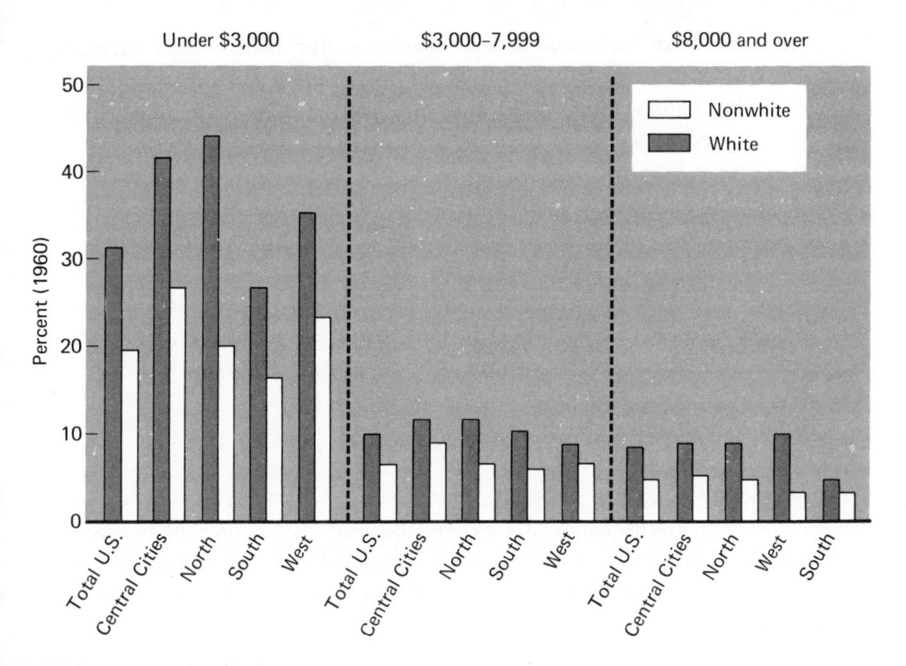

Figure 4.2 White and nonwhite families with female heads, by region.
SOURCE: Lee Rainwater and William L. Yancey, *The Moynihan Report and the Politics of Controversy* (Cambridge, Mass.: MIT Press, 1967), p. 322.

How *much* illegitimacy or family instability makes a social crisis and how much more influential income is than race is, of course, a matter for individual determination. But the consequences of any particular judgment makes a considerable difference in social strategy generally, as Rainwater and Yancey point out:

> . . . by demonstrating that differences between Negroes and whites are largely accounted for by differences in income, one demonstrates that the attack should be on poverty not race. . . . One is not far from saying that color makes no difference and that it is the economic position that is the sole determinant. Simply because one factor accounts for a greater amount of the difference does not mean that the other factor should be forgotten. The results of these statements is that we will begin to forget that color does make a difference in American society . . . Color does make a difference—not only discrimination but also culture makes a difference.[28]

4. Finally, one of the most fundamental points of attack on the report took the view that Moynihan assumed middle-class family structure was the only viable one and was somehow sacred. Floyd McKissick, then director of CORE, a militant civil rights group, put it bluntly:

28. *Ibid.*, p. 183.

My major criticism of the report is that it assumes that middle class values are the correct ones for everyone in America. Just because Moynihan believes in the middle class values doesn't mean that they are the best for everyone. Moynihan thinks everyone should have a family structure like his own.[29]

A more sophisticated version of this criticism was voiced by a number of intellectuals who realized that the report specifically noted the existence of variations in family structure (*see* page 135). What Moynihan failed to see, they argued, was that the symptoms of family instability he stressed were not so much pathological but realistic social adaptations to the special situation confronting the black family in this society.

As Herbert Gans puts it:

However much the picture of family life painted in that report may grate on middle-class moral sensibilities, it may well be that instability, illegitimacy and matriarchy are the most positive adaptations possible to the economic conditions which Negroes must endure, and will only change with the removal of those conditions.[30]

He proceeds to point out that family breakdown occurs for many different reasons, and does not necessarily produce pathological reactions among children. Further, variations in family styles have different meanings for different groups. Illegitimacy is not punished among the lower class as it is in the middle class; illegitimate children are as welcome as legitimate ones, and consequently are unlikely to suffer pathological consequences.

Illegitimacy and the bearing of children generally have a different meaning in this population than in the middle class one. Adolescent Negro girls often invite pregnancy because having children is their way of becoming adults, and of making sure that they will have a family in which they can play the dominant role for which they have been trained by their culture. If having children offers them a reason for living in the same way that sexual prowess does for Negro men, then alternate rewards and sources of hope must be available before illegitimacy can either be judged by middle class standards, or programs developed to do away with it.[31]

The authors of *Black Rage* make the same general point in discussing the black pattern of mothering:

29. *Ibid.*, p. 200.

30. Herbert J. Gans, "The Negro Family: Reflections on the Moynihan Report," *Commonweal* (October 15, 1965), p. 48.

31. *Ibid.*, p. 50.

[The mother] interprets the society to the children and takes as her task the shaping of their character to meet the world as she knows it. This is every mother's task. But the black mother has a more ominous message for her child and feels more urgently the need to get the message across. The child must know that the white world is dangerous and that if he does not understand its rules it may kill him . . . She must produce and shape and mold a unique type of man. She must intuitively cut off and blunt his masculine assertiveness and aggression lest these put the boy's life in jeopardy . . . As a result, black men develop considerable hostility toward black women as the inhibiting instruments of an oppressive system.[32]

The general thesis that black family structure constitutes a reasonable response to the situation, and does not necessarily produce pathology, has been particularly elaborated on the issue of fatherlessness. Because Moynihan's assumption in the report seems to be that this is the crucial factor making for delinquency, school difficulty, and violence, the criticism on this score strikes at the heart of his argument.

Indeed, the relationship between most social pathology and growing up in a fatherless household seems on the surface a very strong one, but on analysis somewhat tenuous. That is, when a group of fatherless boys is compared to a group of boys from intact families, one often finds higher rates of one form or another of social deviance. But if one then also examines the quality of the adult-child relationship, regardless of family structure, the relationship tends to disappear.

To illustrate, a study of 255 boys over a period of five years looked intensively at the effects of parental absence and found generally that emotional pathology occurred only among those fatherless boys whose mothers themselves tended to be deviant or rejecting.[33] The findings on antisocial behavior are particularly critical for the present issue. Direct observations of the boys permitted grouping them into those who belonged to delinquent gangs (or used the gangs as a reference group for their own behavior) and those who did not. As Tables 4.6 and 4.7 indicate, it was the presence of family conflict rather than fatherlessness that seemed to make the difference. Another measure of deviancy, convictions for felonies, appears to demonstrate a relationship with fatherlessness.

But the authors cite several findings that point out that the absence of a generally stable home environment *rather than the specific absence of the father* is the important factor: Boys reared in a conflicted *but intact* home were just as likely to become criminals as fatherless boys;

32. Grier and Cobbs, *op. cit.*, p. 61.

33. Joan McCord, William McCord, and Emily Thurber, "Some Effects of Paternal Absence on Male Children," *Journal of Abnormal Psychology*, Vol. 64 (1962), pp. 361-369.

Table 4.6 Relation between Home Conditions and Using Delinquent Groups as Reference Groups

Home condition	Percent
Broken homes (N 55)	20
Conflictful homes (N 30)	43
Tranquil homes (N 120)	18

SOURCE: Joan McCord et al., "Some Effects of Paternal Absence on Male Children," *Journal of Abnormal Psychology,* Vol. 64 (1962), p. 367.

Table 4.7 The Proportion of Boys Who Became Criminals from Different Home Conditions

Home condition	Percent
Broken homes	36
Conflictful homes	40
Tranquil homes	22

SOURCE: Joan McCord et al., "Some Effects of Paternal Absence on Male Children," *Journal of Abnormal Psychology,* Vol. 64 (1962), p. 367.

the criminal rate among boys who had some kind of parent substitute was identical to that of father-absent boys; none of the thirteen father-absent boys cared for by warm, nondeviant mothers, whose fathers had not been deviant, became criminals.

These findings led the authors to reexamine the data of the famous Glueck study of juvenile delinquency. Recomputing their figures, and breaking down the "broken home" boys into those who did and those who did not have parent substitutes, they found that the data no longer supports the theory that broken homes are related to delinquency. "Among their 500 delinquents, 72 were from broken homes without parent substitutes. In contrast, 230 of the delinquents, compared to 60 of the nondelinquents, has substitute parents."[34]

The connections between social class, ethnicity, and family structure then clearly are not amenable to easy generalization or to reliable stereotype. It is tempting to conclude either that the contradictions make it possible to dismiss these relationships as unproven or to shrug them off as statistical niggles that do not affect the general thesis that class and ethnic factors produce very different family structures.

Either of these options is untenable for educators and teachers who must work with families in lower-class urban neighborhoods. The somewhat imperfect present state of our knowledge requires instead the ex-

34. *Ibid.,* p. 494, footnote.

ercise of one of the most difficult of all human abilities—that of living with and using ambiguity. It is useful to know that the probability is greater of finding certain patterns of family environment among the children of a lower-class black neighborhood than in children of another part of the city. That probability is better than chance (which is what social scientists need to assert a real difference), but it is far from certainty. It is crucial, on the other hand, to realize that for any particular child from any particular family there exists a reasonably good probability of his not conforming to the general pattern. This is a difficult state of mind to maintain, but certainly within the capability of well-trained professionals.

FAMILY ENVIRONMENT AND SCHOOL SUCCESS

However unreliable the relationship between social class position and particular family climates, the evidence is very strong for a clear connection between how the child is treated in the family and his later success in school and life, though even this relationship is not without its ambiguities. Assuming that success in school is in great measure a combined result of intelligence and a drive to succeed, this section looks at how these two key characteristics correlate with elements of family environment.

MEASURED INTELLIGENCE

One needs to be deliberately specific in discussing intelligence in this context; a long and elaborate argument would be required in order to assert that the IQ test "really" measures intelligence. It is only necessary here to note that it is generally agreed that abilities measured by such a test as the Stanford-Binet are mainly those demanded for successful performance in today's schools.

In view of the previously cited absence of any very strong correlation between schooling and social mobility, it is interesting to note that IQ apparently plays a substantial role in mobility, *regardless of schooling.* The findings of one American study were that "the proportion of actual mobility that may be imputed to disparities between the intelligence of sons and the occupational status of their fathers was estimated to be 40 percent."[35] Confirming evidence may be seen in Table 4.8, from

35. C.A. Anderson, J.C. Brown, and M.J. Bowman, "Intelligence and Occupational Mobility," *The Journal of Political Economy,* Vol. 40 (1952), pp. 218-239, quoted in Seymour M. Lipset and Reinhard Bendix, *Social Mobility in Industrial Society* (Berkeley: University of California Press, 1964), p. 234.

a study in Sweden. Note that among those of working-class origin with IQ's among the upper third (above 119), about 80 percent had moved upward in social class position; furthermore, of those in the upper class who had IQ's *below* the upper third, only 16 percent remained in the upper class. Even considering that this data is uncorrected for differences in schooling between fathers and sons, the evidence points to a considerable effect of intelligence on mobility.

Table 4.8 Relationship between IQ and Social Mobility among Stockholm Men Aged 24 in 1949 (percentages)

	Father's social class and son's IQ								
	Upper-class father			Middle-class father			Lower-class father		
	Under 105	105-118	119+	Under 105	105-118	119+	Under 105	105-118	119+
Upper	6	17	68	2	4	35	—	1	10
Middle	89	79	31	55	76	59	37	55	70
Lower	6	3	1	43	21	6	63	44	20
Number of respondents	18	70	164	112	222	288	395	445	183

SOURCE: Seymour M. Lipset and Reinhard Bendix, *Social Mobility in Industrial Society* (Berkeley: University of California Press, 1964), p. 233.

The most important determinant of IQ appears to be social class position itself; note the two-thirds of upper-class boys and only one-fifth of lower-class boys in the upper third of distribution in the Swedish sample. It is impossible to tell how much of the difference is due to a possible chance distribution of "native" intelligence and how much to abilities stressed in middle-class environment. There is one family characteristic, however, that correlates with IQ even when social class is held constant, and that is family size.

A longitudinal study in Scotland by Nisbet and Entwistle found sizeable differences in IQ for children from families of various numbers, favoring the small families.[36] Significantly, the effect is greater for those IQ tests in which verbal skill is most important, though it shows up for nonverbal tests as well, as indicated in Tables 4.9 and 4.10. As is evident from the latter table, though the upper two classes produce higher-scoring children and also have smaller families, there is a relation between test scores and family size within each of the social class

36. J.D. Nisbet and N.J. Entwistle, "Intelligence and Family Size," *British Journal of Educational Psychology,* Vol. 37 (June 1967), pp. 188-193.

Table 4.9 Mean Scores on English Test at Age 12 by Family Size and by Social Class (Sexes Separately)

Social class (sex)		I and II		III (Nonmanual)		III (Manual)		IV and V	
		B	G	B	G	B	G	B	G
	1	111.1	110.8	106.6	108.4*	102.9	107.4	102.2	104.8
	2	110.1	110.8	103.9	109.5	100.9	103.3	94.7	98.4
Family size	3	106.9	107.1	102.5	104.9	98.9	102.4	96.4	97.1
	4	105.7	112.0	96.4	104.3	98.1	96.7	96.8	94.2
	5	105.9*	107.5*	89.0*	105.4*	95.6	95.4	90.1	95.9
	6+	97.9*	117.0*	99.0*	112.0*	95.0	90.3	90.7	89.8
Total N for each social class		228	218	198	165	689	625	361	384

* Indicates N for subgroup is less than 20.

SOURCE: J. D. Nisbet and N. J. Entwistle, "Intelligence and Family Size," *British Journal of Educational Psychology,* Vol. 37 (June 1967), p. 191.

Table 4.10 Mean Scores on Nonverbal Test at Age 11 by Family Size and by Social Class (Sexes Separately)

Social class (sex)		I and II		III (Nonmanual)		III (Manual)		IV and V	
		B	G	B	G	B	G	B	G
	1	108.2	107.8	107.0	105.7	100.4	102.2	98.5	102.8
	2	110.4	108.6	103.1	107.0	102.7	103.6	97.1	99.2
Family size	3	107.9	108.6	104.8	106.7	100.0	101.8	98.8	98.9
	4	105.7	114.3	93.6	101.3	99.8	98.1	98.7	94.2
	5	103.1*	102.9*	101.0*	107.0*	95.9	98.7	92.6	96.9
	6+	105.4*	108.7*	102.0*	104.5*	95.3	90.4	92.3	90.9
Total *N* for each social class		228	218	198	165	689	625	361	384

* Indicates *N* for subgroup is less than 20.

SOURCE: J. D. Nisbet and N. J. Entwistle, "Intelligence and Family Size," *British Journal of Educational Psychology,* Vol. 37 (June 1967), p. 191.

groupings. The relation is just not another aspect of the differences between social classes.

These findings are in accord with most of the studies of social mobility in the West, all of which indicate that upwardly mobile and better-educated children from lower status groups are likely to come from small families. Reflecting on these studies Lipset and Bendix remark:

> It can be argued that "small family" is simply a spurious variable which "intervenes" between the motivation and education of the parents and the motivation and education of the offspring; that it is the better educated and mobility-motivated parents from the lower strata who tend to restrict the number of their children, that these are also the parents who motivate their children to advance and would do so whatever the size of their family. Although there is an element of truth in this, research data indicate that the size of the family itself has a number of dynamic consequences which affect social mobility and should therefore be considered as an "independent variable."[37]

These effects of family size can be summarized as follows:

1. If family income is limited, the family with fewer children can obviously better afford to feed, clothe, and educate them; limited resources can be more effectively channeled. This is particularly so in the provision of education, even where there are free public high schools, since the cost of keeping the child off the labor market can be prohibitive for families with many children to support.

2. The small family increases the involvement of children with adults. Lipset and Bendix summarize an extensive body of research that supports the view that stimulation for achievement in children may result from early and long-continued association with adults and their values, rather than with other children. Studies of highly successful persons tend to show, for example, that they are likely to be only children, oldest children, or children with longer than average distance between themselves and the next oldest child. Gifted children are likely to come from families that kept them isolated from other children. Available evidence also indicates that the degree of adult contact may be the most important single factor in linguistic development.

THE ROLE OF GENETICS IN IQ

Any consideration such as the foregoing of the influence of environment on measured IQ must be tempered by the assertion of some experts that the major determinant of what we call intelligence is inheritance. In a recent article Arthur Jensen argues that the gap between both lower class and middle class and black and white IQ levels cannot be closed by educational efforts because those differences are to

37. Lipset and Bendix, *op. cit.*, p. 241.

a great extent due to genetics. His case, much more persuasively argued and far better buttressed with evidence than previous attempts to argue for genetic differences between blacks and whites will undoubtedly create as great a controversy as Moynihan's report. It is summarized below:[38]

1. Whatever intelligence *really* is, it is for all practical purposes whatever the IQ test measures. What most IQ tests measure in common is a factor that Spearman called *g*: the ability to see relationships, to sense similarities among different stimuli and differences among similar stimuli. "Fluid" intelligence is closest to *g*, less dependent on experience and education; "crystallized" intelligence depends considerably on organized knowledge and intellectual skills.

2. Since psychologists looked for measures of social competence or superiority in devising the IQ, they inevitably arrived at qualities that correlate with high status and recognized occupational prestige. If we were a hunting culture the IQ might have embodied measures of speed and visual acuity. It is not surprising then that estimates of the intelligence required for a given occupational level correlate very highly with the prestige that the general public accords to that occupation. Nor is it surprising that some studies find correlations as high as .71 between IQ and later occupational status.*

3. IQ, though not fixed, argues Jensen, is due more to inheritance than to environment. He defines the issue this way:

> The legitimate question is not whether the characteristic is due to heredity or environment, but what proportion of population variation in the characteristic is attributable to genotypic variation . . . and what proportion is attributable to non-genetic or environmental variation in the population. . .[39]

After an extensive review of available genetic studies of IQ, of parents and offspring, foster parents and adopted children, other kinship correlations, identical twins reared together and apart, and the effects of inbreeding on IQ, Jensen concludes that about 75 percent of variations in IQ is explained by inheritance, 25 percent by environmental factors.

4. Furthermore, he argues, the evidence on environmental influence suggests that much of it is restricted to prenatal variables such as

* In contrast with the very moderate relation between years of schooling and occupational status cited earlier. IQ and years of schooling obviously themselves overlap, and the issue of whether IQ operates directly or indirectly through education is too technical to handle here.

38. Arthur R. Jensen, "How Much Can We Boost IQ and Scholastic Achievement?", *Harvard Educational Review*, Vol. 39 (Winter 1969), pp. 1-123.

39. *Ibid.*, p. 42.

the mother's nutrition or to the very early period of life itself. How then explain the cases of sudden spurts in IQ when a child is switched from conditions of great deprivation to a normal environment, or the increases in IQ in intensive early childhood programs such as Head Start? His answers: a. "Below a certain threshold of environmental adequacy, deprivation can have a markedly depressing effect on intelligence. But above this threshold environmental variations cause relatively small differences in intelligence."[39] Only a small proportion of the urban population we think of as disadvantaged are below that threshold, but we can expect IQ spurts only for the *severely* deprived. b. Most of the preschool improvement in IQ (seldom greater than 10 points) he attributes to a greater familiarity with the tasks of the test or to a statistical phenomenon, "regression to the mean." When a group close to one of the extremes of a distribution is tested, then is retested at a later time, the mean of the group will tend to move toward the natural mean of the entire population (the IQ population mean is 100). Jensen reviews the literature on compensatory education (*see* chapter 6 in this book) and finds little evidence of any program that succeeded in raising group IQ's more than one could expect as a result of these phenomena.

5. Jensen's most controversial conclusion is that not only is there a sizeable inheritance factor in social class variations in IQ but also in black-white differences; theoretically this should be so because high rates of intermarriage create a "genetic pool." The evidence he cites is varied: black-white differences in IQ at all social class levels, when social amenities are presumably relatively equal; the higher group IQ's of American Indians living in worse environments than blacks; the strikingly different physiological patterns of black and white infants; the sheer magnitude of group IQ differences between blacks and whites, which he argues is unlikely to result from purely environmental influences.

6. Since the relation between both class and race and academic *achievement* is much less than that between class, race, and IQ, Jensen concludes that we are mistaken in trying to improve the ability of disadvantaged groups (individuals are another matter) to master tasks in ways that require *g* functioning. Many of these tasks and the competencies relevant to them can be learned associatively, by rote and practice, without a thorough grasp of the relationships involved. The trouble, he argues, is that we insist that all children learn *why* 1 plus 1 equals 2 before we let them go on to learn that 2 plus 2 equals 4. In this general conclusion, at least, he echoes some educational sociologists who also suggest that the aims, curricula, and methods of schools in lower socioeconomic areas be completely revamped to fit the characteristics and needs of lower-class youth more closely.

39. *Ibid.*, p. 60.

THE CRITICS REPLY

In a later issue of the same journal that carried Jensen's essay, seven psychologists and educators responded to an invitation to comment on Jensen's thesis. It is difficult to summarize their diverse and often complex criticisms, but the major lines of disagreement can be indicated; the interested reader will find it a challenging and rewarding experience to consult the pieces themselves.

1. Most of the critics tend to accept Jensen's estimate that 75 percent of IQ can be explained by genetic background. But they provide several more optimistic interpretations of this general finding. Thus, Cronbach notes that even if the IQ test were perfect, one could expect a fairly sizeable error in estimating the theoretical IQ of a number of people of the same genotype.

> Hence, persons having the same genes are distributed over an IQ range of more than 25 points. With run-of-the-statistics cases and within the range of present environments, the individual who draws an environment fitted to his genotype develops an IQ some 6 points better than the expected IQ for that genotype, and 12 or more points better than does one who is unlucky in the draw. If an effect of this size could be brought under control and applied population-wide, it would surely be economically and culturally beneficial.[40]

A second major counterinterpretation refers to Jensen's own analogy to the heritability of height. There is general agreement that height is largely genetically determined; yet, as several critics point out, the average height of people in some countries has steadily increased.

> E^2 [Jensen's symbol for the effect of environment in his general equation] tells us how much the variance would be reduced if the environment were held constant. It does not directly tell us how much improvement in IQ to expect from a given change in the environment. In particular, it offers no guidance as to the consequences of a new environmental influence. For example, conventional heritability measures for height show a value of nearly 1. Yet, because of unidentified environmental influences, the mean height in the United States and Japan has risen by a spectacular amount. Another kind of illustration is provided by the discovery of a cure for a hereditary disease. In such cases, any information on prior heritability may become irrelevant. . .[41]

40. Lee J. Cronbach, "Heredity, Environment, and Educational Policy," *Harvard Educational Review,* Vol. 39, No. 2 (Spring 1969), pp. 343-344.

41. James F. Crow, "Genetic Theories and Influences: Comments on the Value of Diversity," *Harvard Educational Review,* Vol. 39, No. 2 (Spring 1969), pp. 306-307.

2. There is considerable disagreement with Jensen's view of the importance and stability of the IQ test as a measure of *g*, and with his interpretation of longitudinal change in IQ. Thus, Hunt notes that if about half the variations in IQ at age seventeen can be explained by age four and five, it is just as reasonable to emphasize the importance of the amount that is available to be changed by environment as it is to point out that part of later variations may be fixed.[42]

3. Several writers point to a variety of studies with contrary findings, which Jensen neglected to review, and suggest that he has generally ignored a wide area of evidence outside the field of genetics, from the animal laboratories and from social psychology. Hunt and Cronbach in particular cite a number of studies that argue for the great plasticity of the organism as it interacts with environment.[43]

4. Perhaps the weakest point of attack is on Jensen's claim that compensatory education efforts have largely failed. Weak, because many of the critics disputing it appear to believe that the claim is based only on the ineffectiveness of summer Head Start programs, apparently unaware of the large number of evaluations of much longer and more intensive programs.[44] The critics themselves are in disagreement about the *long term* effects of preschool instruction or enrichment; as Bereiter notes about some of them: "Most likely such programs, operating blindly in this regard, could do no more than teach early what would be learned later anyway, so that IQs eventually return to their expected levels."[45] Most of those who argue for the importance of the environment, however, base their cases on the *timing* of these programs; enrichment must begin almost as soon as the child is born. Since this thesis has not yet been adequately tested, the possibility of early environmental intervention as an answer to Jensen must await empirical proof.

ACHIEVEMENT MOTIVATION

Evidence on family characteristics that relate to aspiration for social mobility has already been discussed in chapter 2 of this book. A fascinating series of investigations that bear more directly on aspiration for success in school performance generally confirm the earlier conclusions. These studies have used McClelland's measure of *achievement need* to examine the possibility that some family environments are more

42. J. McV. Hunt, "Has Compensatory Education Failed? Has It Been Attempted?", *Harvard Educational Review,* Vol. 39, No. 2 (Spring 1969), pp. 278-300.
43. Hunt, *op. cit.,* pp. 288-293.
44. For example, Hunt, *op. cit.,* p. 296.
45. Carl Bereiter, "The Future of Individual Differences," *Harvard Educational Review,* Vol. 39, No. 2 (Spring 1969), p. 316.

likely to produce children with a greater drive to achieve than others. McClelland found an apparently reliable method for measuring this type of drive by asking people to invent stories about a series of pictures presented to them. Here is a description of one such picture as an illustration of the method and two different stories in response to it:

A boy about eighteen years old is sitting at his desk in an occupied classroom. A book lies open before him but he is not looking at it. The boy rests his forehead on one hand as he gazes pensively out toward the viewer.

A story that contains a good deal of what McClelland calls "achievement imagery" was obtained from one student as follows:

1. This chap is doing some heavy meditating. He is a sophomore and has reached an intellectual crisis. He cannot make up his mind. He is troubled and worried.

2. He is trying to reconcile the philosophies of Descartes and Thomas Aquinas—and at his tender age of eighteen. He has read several books on philosophy and feels the weight of the world on his shoulders.

3. He wants to present a clearcut synthesis of these two conflicting philosophies, to satisfy his ego and to gain academic recognition from his professor.

4. He will screw himself up royally. Too inexperienced and uninformed, he has tackled too great a problem. He will give up in despair, go down to the G———, and drown his sorrows in a bucket of beer.

Now, here is another story that shows a low level of achievement imagery:

1. The boy in the checkered shirt whose name is Ed is in a classroom. He is supposed to be listening to the teacher.

2. Ed has been troubled by his father's drunkenness and his maltreatment of Ed's mother. He thinks of this often and worries about it.

3. Ed is thinking of leaving home for a while in the hope that this will shock his parents into getting along.

4. He will leave home but will only meet further disillusionment away from home.[46]

In a revealing study of need achievement in relation to family experience Winterbottom obtained scores for a small group of boys aged eight to ten, having them tell stories in response to verbal cues rather

46. J.W. Atkinson (ed.), *Motives in Fantasy, Action, and Society* (Princeton, N.J.: D. Van Nostrand Company, Inc., 1958), p. 697.

than pictures.[47] She also interviewed the boys' mothers, asking questions about how they thought children ought to be raised, particularly in regard to a number of types of child behavior which all parents require their children to master. For example: to stand up for his own rights with other children, to know his way around his part of the city, to be willing to try new things on his own without depending on his mother for help, to be able to eat alone without help in cutting and handling food, and so forth.

After dividing the boys into high-achievement and low-achievement scorers, Winterbottom was able to look at differences in maternal expectation between the two groups. On many of the items mothers of high-achievers reported expecting mastery of the task at markedly earlier ages than did mothers of low-achievers. Significantly, the tasks on which they differed did not involve the physical caretaking of motherhood; mothers of high-scoring sons were not particularly concerned with unloading the duties of tying shoelaces or cutting meat or buttoning coats. Their concern was that the boys be willing to move out on their own into new experiences, to acquire skills and to explore the environment by themselves. This maternal attitude toward the development of their sons Winterbottom calls *early independence training.*

There were two other important differences between the two groups of mothers. One was that the mothers of low-scoring sons believed in more restrictions on behavior: "not to fight with children to get his own way." Second, by a ratio of two-to-one, mothers of high-scorers were more likely to reward their sons' achievements or signs of mastery with physical manifestations such as hugging and kissing.

These results, of course, merely indicate the attitudes of the mothers, how they think they *should* behave. That the attitudes probably reflect real behavior is suggested in another study by Rosen and D'Andrade.[48] These investigators visited forty homes, twenty of which included a son who had tested high on achievement need, the other twenty with a son who had tested low. They set a task for the boy—that of building a tower from a set of irregularly shaped blocks—and made it further difficult by blindfolding him and permitting him to use only one hand. The parents were asked to watch him, and although they could not physically intervene were told that they could offer any verbal help they wished.

While the boy worked, the parents urged him on, gave him directions, shouted or groaned at his progress. But there was a difference be-

47. Marion R. Winterbottom, "The Relation of Need for Achievement to Learning Experiences in Independence and Mastery," in J.S. Atkinson (ed.), *Motives in Fantasy, Action and Society* (Princeton, N.J.: D. Van Nostrand Company, Inc., 1958), chapter 33.

48. B.C. Rosen and R.C. D'Andrade, "The Psychosocial Origin of Achievement Motivation," *Sociometry,* Vol. 22 (1959), pp. 185-218.

tween the parents of high- and low-scorers. The former worked up a lot of tension over the task, were hopeful and encouraging, and when it went well the mothers in particular rewarded the boys with great warmth and physical affection. The fathers of the low-scorers were distinctive in a tendency to give specific directions, to make decisions for the boys, and react with irritation when things went badly.

Some caution is required in interpreting these results, despite the high correlation in these and other studies between achievement motivation and early independence training. As Roger Brown notes:

> It is unlikely that any particular expectation or set of expectations can create high achievement motivation. A mother who read Winterbottom's results and decided to produce a highly motivated son by expecting her son to "know his way around the city," "do well in competition," "and make his own friends" before he was eight years old might be disappointed by the results. Motive creation cannot be that simple.[49]

Brown suggests that it is the total maternal role, the whole home atmosphere that is probably the important causal factor. Thus, early independence training happens to be one of the ways a particular kind of mother behaves toward her sons, but it may not ultimately be the significant thing about her.

Whatever its status as an independent cause for achievement, however, independence training appears also to be linked specifically to scholastic motivation. A study by Elder found this positive relationship in adolescents in both middle- and lower-class families. A similar relationship held between independence training and actual achievement as measured by grade averages. Of the differences that remained between the social classes in his sample Elder notes:

> The residual social class effect may be partially explained by differences between middle and lower class values. Although parental independence training may stimulate the desire to achieve, the objects and activities in which this motivation is invested and toward which it is directed are likely to be consonant with the values of the child and his parents. The lower class child may, as a result of his parents' training, have a need to achieve, but not in a middle class institution such as the public school.[50]

It is important to note, with regard to the earlier discussion of the discrepancy between social class position and family environments, that

49. Roger Brown, *Social Psychology* (New York: The Free Press, 1965), p. 448.

50. Glenn H. Elder, Jr., *Adolescent Achievement and Mobility Aspirations* (Chapel Hill: University of North Carolina, Institute for Research in Social Science, 1962), quoted in Bernard Goldstein, *op. cit.*, p. 54.

of the three variables in Elder's study—*class, parental education,* and *independence training*—the last of these accounted for the greatest proportion of the differences in academic motivation and that social class accounted for the least proportion.

This lack of connection is confirmed by several other studies of family environment that have a bearing on school achievement. The first was Richard Wolf's investigation using a random sample of fifth-graders from a school system representing urban, rural, and suburban schools.[51] (It is probably significant that lower-class children were under-represented in his sample.) Wolf compared intelligence test scores of the children with an elaborate series of ratings of home environment made on the basis of interviews with mothers. The scales measured the amount of parental urging toward achievement, parental stress on language development, and the parents' provisions for learning in the home. The multiple correlation between IQ and the thirteen scales that made up these clusters of factors is very high — .69.

Among all of the scales, those that best predicted IQ were measures of the parents' expectations of the child's intellectual growth, the mother's information about his intellectual development, the opportunities provided for enlarging his vocabulary, the extent to which the parents gave the child assistance in learning. When the scale measures are regrouped into an Index of Educational Environment, the correlation between that index and school grades turns out to be .80. In this sample at least almost two-thirds of the variations in academic achievement are explained by family environment.*

The surprising finding, in confirmation of Elder's study, is that the relationship between educational environment of the home and social class is very small. If there had been a better representation of lower-lower children in the sample, to be sure, that correlation might have been increased; but it is unlikely that the increase would have been sub-

* Though this finding appears to contradict Jensen's thesis of the primacy of the genetic variable directly, the contradiction may be more apparent than real. The overlap between parental IQ and home environment is undoubtedly considerable. Perhaps the only evidence available on what happens to the relationship between home environment and IQ when the genetic variable is at a minimum is a study by Burks. To test the influence of environment alone, Burks worked with a group of adopted children who had been placed in homes by agencies which did not try to match children's real parents with their adoptive parents. Under these conditions in which environment is separated from its interrelation with inheritance, Burks obtained a correlation of only .42 between environmental ratings and the children's IQ.[52]

51. Richard M. Wolf, *The Identification and Measurement of Environmental Process Variables Related to Intelligence* (Ph.D. Dissertation, University of Chicago, 1964).

52. B.S. Burks, "The Relative Influence of Nature and Nurture upon Mental Development: A Comparative Study of Foster Parent-Foster Child Resemblance and True Parent-True Child Resemblance," *Yearbook of the National Society for the Study of Education* (1928), pp. 219-316.

stantial. We will return to this puzzling aspect of the data at the end of this chapter.

The general picture is clear, and may usefully be conceptualized in Fantini and Weinstein's terms:[53] Families provide an early *hidden curriculum* which in some cases constitutes an effective set of learning experiences consonant with the later demands of the school and in other cases does not. The extraordinary importance of this preschool curriculum can best be understood by considering the results of Bloom's careful review of longitudinal studies of intellectual development, from which he concluded that 50 percent of the variation in cognitive ability at the age of eighteen can be explained by abilities already manifest at the age of four.[54]

ETHNICITY AND ACHIEVEMENT

Whatever the merits of Moynihan's thesis that the black family be singled out as a special phenomenon, there is a small body of interesting evidence for a claim that ethnicity influences cognitive development related to schooling, quite apart from social class.

In one ingeniously conceived study the investigator compared two groups of boys from a Brooklyn Jewish neighborhood. Though the groups live close to one another and are of the same middle-class composition, their ethnic backgrounds differ historically. One is Ashkenazi, the European Jew whose tradition emphasizes the importance of scholarship and learning; the other is Sephardic, whose tradition puts stress on commercial and financial success. When the average IQ's of the groups on entering school are compared, one finds a substantial and significant difference. The families representing the Ashkenazi tradition apparently provide the kind of environment in which verbal performance is rewarded and in which the child is urged to achieve in that area, enabling him to do much better on the IQ test.[55]

A recent study that has become a classic proved beyond doubt, on a much broader scale, that ethnic family background influences the pattern of cognitive abilities.[56] The investigation by Lesser, Fifer, and Clark selected four groups of first-grade children: Chinese, black, Jew-

53. Mario Fantini and Gerald Weinstein, *The Disadvantaged* (New York: Harper & Row, 1968), chapter 2.

54. Benjamin S. Bloom, *Stability and Change in Human Characteristics* (New York: John Wiley & Sons, Inc., 1964).

55. Morris Gross, *Learning Readiness in Two Jewish Groups* (New York: Center for Urban Education, 1968).

56. Gerald Lesser, Gordon Fifer, and Donald H. Clark, *Mental Abilities of Children in Different Social and Cultural Groups* (Washington, D.C.: U.S. Office of Education, Cooperative Research Project No. 1635, 1964).

ish, and Puerto Rican—each composed of equal numbers of girls and boys. To insure that any test differences reflected real differences in ability rather than differences in the familiarity of test materials, special tests were constructed that presupposed only experiences that are common and familiar within all the various social classes and ethnic groups in New York City.

The abilities tested were verbal, reasoning, numerical, and spacial. To free the situation as much as possible from bias, the children were

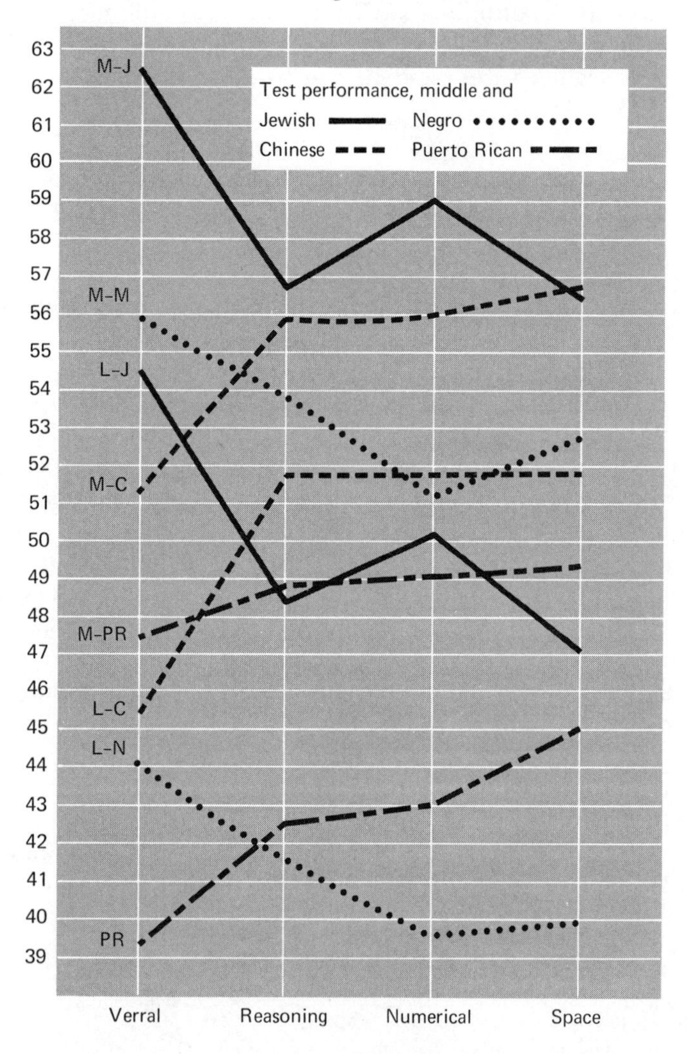

Figure 4.3 Performance on tests of four mental abilities by children of different cultural and social class backgrounds.

SOURCE: Gerald Lesser, *et. al., Mental Abilities of Children in Different Social and Cultural Groups,* U.S. Office of Education, Cooperative Research Project No. 1635 (1964).

tested by trained psychologists of their own ethnic background, to permit the administration to be done in the child's primary language, in English, or the most effective combination of the languages for any particular child. The major results of the study are shown in Figure 4.3.

To a surprisingly consistent degree each of the ethnic groups demonstrate a *pattern* of abilities that is very much the same regardless of social class position. Social class does make a difference in the *level* at which the ability is manifested, but not in the pattern. Ethnicity not only influences the pattern but also the level of the abilities.

The interactions between the two factors of class and ethnicity are summarized by the investigators in this way:

> a. On each mental ability scale, social class position produces more of a difference in the mental abilities of the Negro children than for the other groups. That is, middle-class Negro children are more different in the level of mental abilities from the lower-class Negroes than, for example, the middle-class Chinese are from the lower-class Chinese.
>
> b. On each mental ability scale, the scores of the middle-class children from the various ethnic groups resemble each other to a greater extent than do the scores of the lower-class children from the various ethnic groups. That is, the middle-class Chinese, Jewish, Negro and Puerto Rican children are more alike in their mental ability scores than are the lower-class Chinese, Jewish, Negro and Puerto Rican children.[57]

It has long been assumed that the aspirations of lower-class black parents for their children were consonant with these findings as to their specially handicapped position in relation to mental abilities, that they were lower than normal even for lower-class parents. In fact, the opposite seems to be the case. A number of investigations have recently shown that a majority of black parents, at least those above the very lowest poverty level, have higher academic ambitions for their sons than do even middle-class parents; they report wanting their sons to have a college education, and many wish to see them enter the professions. That these aspirations communicate themselves to the children is confirmed by other surveys of comparative aspirations among children.

Irwin Katz suggests that these aspirations are the source for much anxiety in school for the lower-class black child.[58] They are so high in relation to the real amount of effort that lower-class parents devote to their children's educational needs, and so unrealistic in view of the existing academic retardation, that it is difficult to see them as other

57. *Ibid.*, pp. 132-133.

58. Irwin Katz, "Academic Motivation and Equal Educational Opportunity," *Harvard Educational Review*, Vol. 38, No. 1 (Winter 1968), pp. 57-65.

than wishful fantasies. In Katz' view, however, the aspirations do get communicated as parental expectations that the child is supposed to fulfill. As such, they tend to make the child overcritical of his own efforts and, since the ability to meet significant expectations creates anxiety, overanxious in the academic situation.

Values and goals have been internalized, but not

> . . . the behavioral mechanism requisite for attaining them. The disjunction of cognitions and behaviors is not difficult to understand, for verbal attitudes are relatively easy to acquire through mere imitation of verbalizations observed in adult or peer models. If the attitudes expressed are the "correct" ones, i.e., held by socializing agents . . . they will tend to get reinforced either directly or vicariously. But performing the behaviors that are instrumental for attaining the goals is a more difficult feat than the acquisition of verbal attitudes about the goal, especially when there are no models of competency to imitate, and when achievement strivings are not socially recognized and reinforced.[59]

Thus, the reason that one finds black high-school students expressing *higher* aspirations than whites, Katz speculates, is that they are substituting verbal expressions of achievement for the achievement behavior they are unable to act out. But since the high verbal aspiration highlights the gap between what is expected and what is achieved, "as the Negro student falls increasingly behind in his school work, the expression of high verbal standards contributes to a growing demoralization."[60]

SOME REFLECTIONS ON THE RELATION BETWEEN FAMILY AND EDUCATION

We might summarize the evidence described in this chapter, contradictions and all, in the following statement:

1. There is a clear, consistent, and fairly high relationship between social class position and both measured intelligence and school achievement.

2. There is a consistent and probably greater relationship between particular family environments and both intelligence and school achievements, notably those that include parental urging to do well coupled with consistent help that realistically prepares the child for the types of intellectual and linguistic performance required in school.

3. Parental urging by itself, and underlying parental aspirations,

59. *Ibid.*, pp. 63-64.
60. *Ibid.*, p. 64.

do not appear to operate very consistently, as witness the case of the lower-class black family. Aspirations must be accompanied by parental attention—note the consistently positive factor of smaller families—and be directed to *academic* achievement instead of some other success goal.

4. Despite items 1 and 2 above, which would lead one to assume that social class status should clearly differentiate among types of family environment, since both class and environment predict academic achievement, the correlation of these two variables is not a consistent one, appearing in some studies and only weakly, if at all, in others.

One explanation of the anomaly is in the sample variation among different studies. It is perfectly possible to find a sample of lower-class children almost all of whom are in the stable working class and whose family environments do not greatly differ in range from that of a sample of middle-class children, particularly if these latter do not come from upper-middle professional families. Wolf's study of family educational process variables, for example, used a sample that admittedly underrepresented lower-lower-class families.

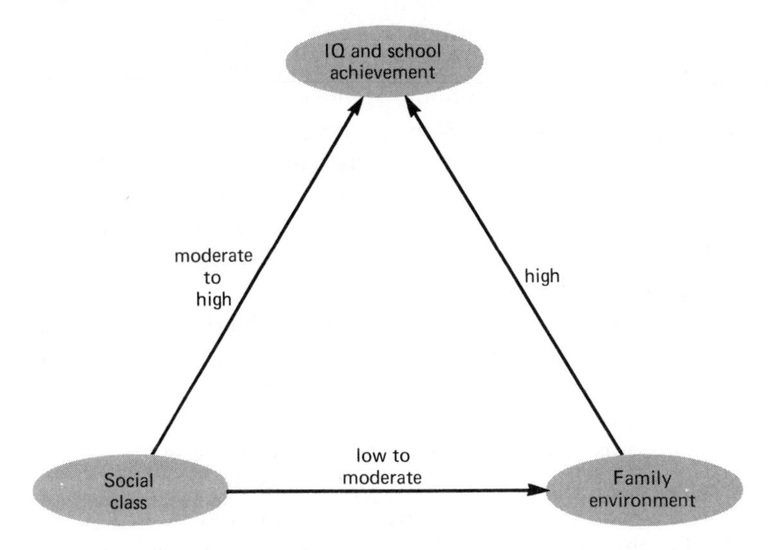

Figure 4.4 General relationship between social class, family environment, and achievement.

Another possibility is that we are simply dealing with a good deal of overlap between two causal variables (*see* Figure 4.4). If 20–25 percent of the variations in intelligence and school grades can be explained by social class, a good deal remains to be accounted for. Suppose that there are sizeable numbers of families technically designated as lower class that provide helpful environments for their children, because the parents happen to be better educated than their station would predict or for any number of other possible reasons. Then the relationship between family environment and school achievement would be larger than that between social class and school achievement because *some* of this latter relation depends on differences in family environment. So, the prediction on the basis of family environment includes some of the already explained variation due to social class. The variability of the third relationship, between family environment and social class, is probably due to differences in sampling; higher when representative numbers of lower-lower-class children are included, lower when they are omitted.

To return to the earlier discussion of teacher predictions: The further away one gets within the lower class generally from the absolute bottom of the social scale, the riskier it becomes to predict a particular kind of family environment for a lower-class child, and consequently how well he may do in school. If ethnic factors are involved, using aspiration as a cue to school achievement becomes particularly unreliable on the present evidence.

Finally, one must at least consider the possibility of increasing the lower-class family's *skills* for providing help to their children in school, since aspiration without know-how seems of little use. It is difficult to assess the degree to which such a program might be useful. There are several modest plans aimed at training parents to establish the most positive home environments for school achievement, though the evidence for their success is purely anecdotal. There is more rigorous evidence for the possibility of helping parents to provide their children with a better self-concept as achievers (*see* chapter 5).

But it is unlikely that intervention at the family level can crucially affect the environment of those homes which account for the most difficult problems of the urban schools, as a recent controlled study of the multiproblem family demonstrates.[61]

The study was done in New York State in a nonurban county and gave special, intensive service for thirty-one months by a team of highly trained social workers to fifty multiproblem families. An equal number of similar families were used as a control and were given normal public assistance service. The families were assessed both before and after the experiment on a number of variables that are relevant to the issues examined in this chapter: family relationships, individual behavior, care and training of children, social activities, economic practices, household practices, health conditions, and relation to worker and community resources.

61. "Casework Found No Poverty Cure," *New York Times* (September 19, 1968), p. 55.

The major finding was that while the demonstration group attained a slightly better degree of family functioning, its progress was not sufficiently greater than the control group's to be significant. Indeed, "a subsidiary finding indicated that the more often the problem family saw its caseworker, the less progress it showed," a result that was understandably termed "unsettling" by the director of the agency which conducted the study.

It is unsettling from the viewpoint of the school as well. If almost three years of consistent effort by trained social workers fails to change the environment of this kind of family, the school is unlikely to do much better. Whether it can succeed with the children themselves is a question for later chapters.

A final cautionary note on the entire question of the family influence on school success is appropriate before we leave the issue. Other factors in the slum environment may also relate to school achievement, though the relationship has been little investigated and is not well understood. A recent report of a careful piece of research on neighborhood gang membership described an unusually clearcut finding: Not one of the actual gang members in good standing were reading at or above grade level in school; those boys who were on the fringes of the group or who had been rejected by the gang for one reason or another showed a much more normal distribution of reading scores and many of them were reading at or above grade level.[62] The influence of the peer group may well turn out to be of sizeable importance, and may explain some of the contradictions in the relationship between family environment alone and school achievement.

Recommended Reading

The classic historical study of the black family is Edward Franklin Frazier's *The Negro Family in the United States* (Chicago: University of Chicago Press, 1966). The Moynihan Report, *The Negro Family: The Case for National Action* (Washington, D.C.: U.S. Department of Labor, 1965), is included intact in Lee Rainwater and William L. Yancey's *The Moynihan Report and the Politics of Controversy* (Cambridge, Mass.: MIT Press, 1967), a fascinating analysis of the public uproar described in this chapter. A recent study by Salvador Minuchin and others, *Families of the Slums* (New York: Basic Books, Inc., 1968), pro-

62. William Labov and Clarence Robins, "A Note on the Relation of Reading Failure to Peer Group Status in Urban Ghettos," *The Record,* Vol. 70, No. 5 (February 1969), pp. 395-406.

vides transcriptions of taped interviews with slum families and analyzes them from a psychoanalytic orientation; *Black Rage* by William Grier and Price Cobbs (New York: Basic Books, Inc., 1968) brings the same orientation to the black family in particular.

Bernard Goldstein's *Low Income Youth in Urban Areas* (New York: Holt, Rinehart and Winston, Inc., 1967), is a valuable review of the research literature on urban youth organized around a developmental viewpoint. Benjamin Bloom's much cited *Stability and Change in Human Characteristics* (New York: John Wiley & Sons, Inc., 1964), is a different kind of review and analysis of the longitudinal research on cognitive development, and brings the school's contribution into much needed perspective.

5

A PSYCHOLOGICAL ASIDE: PREJUDICE, SELF-CONCEPT, AND THE SELF-FULFILLING PROPHECY

While this book focuses on the *social* foundations of urban education, it is difficult to separate the psychological factors bearing on the problems of the urban school, though these deserve a treatment easily as lengthy. When necessary, in preceding chapters, we have dealt, often summarily, with data and concepts that are primarily psychological, where their relationship to the social and economic processes under discussion clearly had to be considered.

At this point, having surveyed the socioeconomic hypotheses advanced to explain the high rate of academic retardation in urban schools, we pause to take account of a widely accepted explanation that emphasizes the psychological nature of the problem. Though it is difficult to do it complete justice in such a brief compass, this chapter can at least outline the basic assumptions made, the conceptual framework, and the types of evidence used to support a point of view.

Briefly the argument runs as follows: Growing up in a deeply prejudiced society, the minority group youngster, and particularly the black child, acquires a damaged view of his own person and of his capacity. The cognitive lacks in his early environment could easily be overcome by the school, if its personnel were not so deeply prejudiced that they expect only minimal performance from the child. Feeling inferior from the beginning, the child accepts this negative evaluation of himself on some level, but on another responds either with hostility to the teachers and administrators who scorn him or turns the hostility inward and depreciates himself. In either case it is unlikely that he will be in a frame of mind to learn.

CONCEPTS: PREJUDICE AND SELF-CONCEPT

The word prejudice derives originally from a Latin noun, *praejudicium,* and has, like many Latin root words, undergone a considerable change in meaning since classical times. To the ancients *praejudicium* meant a precedent, in fact, a judgment based on previous decisions and experiences. Later, the term in English acquired the meaning of judgment formed before due examination and consideration of the facts; in other words, a premature or hasty judgment. Finally, the term acquired its present emotional flavor of favoring or not favoring which accompanies such a hasty judgment.[1] The new English dictionary offers a definition which has the virtue of being both brief and including the positive as well as the negative aspects: "A feeling favorable or unfavorable toward a person or thing prior to or not based on actual experience." Gordon Allport in *The Nature of Prejudice* offers the following definition: "An avertive or hostile attitude toward a person who belongs to a group simply because he belongs to that group and is therefore presumed to have the objectionable qualities ascribed to the group."[2] Although prejudice is an important concept in social science and represents part of a generally important social problem in American life, we are specifically concerned with the assumption that prejudice, along with teacher expectation, contributes to a lowered self-concept for minority group and disadvantaged youngsters, and that this in turn leads to inferior performance in the school. Later in the chapter we will evaluate research relating to this performance. Let us now look briefly at some theories concerning the source or causes of prejudice in human beings, since these are basic to our consideration of possible programs for identifying and reducing prejudice among school personnel.[3]

One theory traces prejudices directly to cultural patterns found in society. It suggests that much prejudice is based on conformity with certain cultural norms which support prejudice. For example, this theory might account for patterns of prejudice toward blacks in the American South. These negative feelings and attitudes are an important part of the social values of the "Southern way of life." It might also account for the German attitude toward Jews during the rise of Nazism. There is some evidence that many Germans participated in the persecution and the extermination of Jews not out of any violent feeling of anti-Semitism but rather out of acceptance of the general social values of German society, in fact out of thoroughgoing social conformity.

1. *The New English Dictionary,* Sir James A.H. Murray (ed.), Vol. 7, Part II, (New York: Oxford University Press, 1909), p. 1275.

2. Gordon W. Allport, *The Nature of Prejudice,* abridged (New York: Anchor Books, 1958), p. 8.

3. *Ibid.,* chapter 13.

A second theory looks for the source of prejudice in the economic relationship between human groups. One particular interpretation, which might be called the "exploitation" theory, has gained importance in recent years and has even been adopted by some black power groups as central to prejudice in American society. This theory, summarized by Cox, is as follows: "Race prejudice is a social attitude propagated among the public by an exploiting class for the purpose of stigmatizing some group as inferior so that the exploitation of either the group itself or its resources may both be justified."[4] It is certainly true that economic exploitation and racial prejudice have frequently been, and at the present time are, closely related. On the other hand, it is not clear, for example, that Jews have been historically the victims of any special amount of economic exploitation in the United States, while anti-Semitism has generally existed in American society.

Since prejudice is a psychological condition or attitude, it is quite appropriate that several specifically psychological theories have been developed as to its basis.

The *frustration-aggression theory* traces frustration in modern society to a number of causes. It may be the result of a constitutional illness or physical condition. It may come from family relations, from other sources nearby in the community, or from political events rather far removed from the individual. One common human response to all of these frustrations is to direct them on to some other target. This psychological device is called *displacement*. The familiar cartoon progression of the boss "chewing out" the office worker, the worker going home and yelling at his wife, the wife scolding her child, and the child kicking the cat perfectly illustrates the frustration-aggression theory. (It should be noted that not all frustration is manifested in the form of aggression.)

In connection with this theory we must look at one of the most common and widely used concepts relating to prejudice and discrimination, that of the *scapegoat*. The term scapegoat originated in the Old Testament. On the day of atonement a live goat was chosen, then a high priest laid both his hands on the goat's head and confessed over it the iniquities of the children of Israel. The sins of the Israelites were thus symbolically transferred to the beast, who was taken out into the wilderness and let go. The Israelites apparently felt purged and for the time being guiltless. Today the idea of a scapegoat still involves three stages: guilt, which generates frustration, which in turn generates aggression. Aggression becomes displaced on relatively defenseless "goats." Blaming and stereotyping are then used to rationalize displaced hostility.

This sequence may be accepted as reasonably valid, provided certain qualifications are kept in mind. First, frustration as we have noted above does not always lead to aggression. Second, aggression itself is not

4. O.C. Cox, *Caste, Class and Race* (New York: Doubleday & Company, Inc., 1948), p. 393.

always displaced; that is, under certain conditions it may be directed against one's self rather than against others. Third, displacement does not, as the theory may seem to suggest, necessarily relieve the feeling of frustration, or may do so for only a short period of time. One other important consideration, which has notable implications for programs designed to eliminate or reduce prejudice, is that the source of frustration is likely to have absolutely nothing to do with the object or the group upon which the aggression is displaced. According to this theory, prejudice is completely irrational.

Another psychological concept important in explaining prejudice is *projection,* defined by Freud as the tendency to attribute falsely to other people motives or traits which are our own but which are too painful for us to admit consciously. The Nazi accusation that Jews were sadistic is perhaps the clearest illustration of the projection theory. There is virtually no sadism in Jewish culture and tradition. But the conspicuous pleasure many Nazis took in torturing Jews and others showed that sadism was in fact an approved Nazi policy.[5]

A third important psychological theory is the *authoritarian personality.*[6] This hypothesis holds that prejudice is one attitude which characterizes a particular personality type. Through appropriate psychological tests and clinical interviews certain individuals can be identified as prejudiced. Those people who hate blacks are also likely to have contempt for Jews or Puerto Ricans or Russians. In addition to holding prejudiced attitudes toward a great variety of minority groups, the "authoritarian personality" also tends to possess the following characteristics:

1. ambivalence toward parents
2. a feeling of hostility, which as adults they seem to be unwilling or unable to express
3. *moralism*—a tendency to take rigidly moralistic views, including strict insistence on good manners, conventions, strong emphasis on conventional virtues
4. *dichotomization*—the tendency to divide people especially into only two groups: we and they, the weak and the strong, the good and the bad
5. *a need for definiteness*—the apparent fear of saying, "I don't know"; requiring definite and specific answers and information, especially when presented with unfamiliar situations
6. *externalization* or the tendency to believe that things happen

5. Rudolph M. Loewenstein, *Christians and Jews* (New York: International Universities Press, Inc., 1951), p. 45.

6. T.W. Adorno, Elsie Frendel-Brunswik, Daniel J. Levenson, and R. Nevitt Sanford, *The Authoritarian Personality* (New York: Harper & Row, 1950).

"out there," with no control over one's own destiny. This person believes, for example, that "although many people may scoff, it may be shown that astrology can explain a lot of things."

7. *institutionalism*—the desire to have order and, especially, social order. In institutional memberships—such as lodges, churches, or the nation—the prejudiced personality finds a defense against the disquiet of his personal life.

8. *nationalism*—which brings with it a close link between patriotism of a certain type and prejudice. (A study of an American suburban middle-class community by Frankel-Brunswick is particularly revealing of this relationship. It was established that the higher the degree of nationalism, that is, of an identification between one's self and the policies of the nation, the higher the degree of anti-Semitism.)

9. *authoritarianism*—the preference for order and particularly a vertical arrangement of power.

This last characteristic represents an extremely important dimension of the prejudiced personality. He seems uncomfortable living in a democracy and feels that what America needs is "more discipline." He may choose to have an orderly, authoritative powerful society. He tends to see American society in terms of power, that is, he identifies some people as having a great deal of power, others as having little power, and still others as having no power.

The evidence for most of these psychological mechanisms is primarily clinical in nature, and some social psychologists have been wary of the leap from individual structure to social structure. The concept of an authoritarian personality in particular has recently come under attack because it correlates so closely with educational attainment.[7] But, it is important to keep in mind that there is nothing mutually exclusive about any of these theories. It is not necessary to select one and to argue that it alone is the source of all prejudice. In fact, prejudice, as it exists in American society, seems likely to have multiple causes. Depending upon the individual, his social and cultural position, several theories may be necessary to explain racial attitudes in America. The theory which explains the white Southern middle-class attitude toward blacks would not be adequate to explain the prejudice of the white skilled worker in a Northern city.

Self-Concept

Human personality is a complicated and complex construct in the behavioral sciences, and psychologists disagree about its definition. Most

7. Roger Brown, *Social Psychology* (New York: The Free Press, 1965), chapter 10.

authorities would accept the idea that a central part of any definition is the individual's conception of himself. We could also say that in terms of motivation (whatever impels an individual to act or not act), a very significant role is played in this determination by what the individual thinks about himself. A self-concept need not be accurate in any objective sense. We find youngsters with good academic ability who perceive themselves as not being able to do school work. A very attractive girl may consider herself plain. The source of this self-concept, whether accurate or not, is external; it is learned. The forces that contribute to the development of self-concept are for the most part the institutions which we have been considering in other chapters: the family, the peer group, other significant adults in the child's life, the culture in which the child grows up, and the school. Through interaction with these institutions, individuals develop differing concepts of themselves. This concept of the self is always in terms of degrees of adequacy. Many psychologists define adequacy as one of the fundamental human needs. Jersild expresses it this way: "The needs associated with a person's idea and appraisal of himself include both desires for enhancing his self esteem and also striving to preserve the integrity and consistency of his self."[8]

In looking at the relationship of self-concept, aspiration, and achievement in school we will be particularly concerned with racial minorities and disadvantaged groups. We might expect to find that prejudice, discrimination, and a different kind of expectation would have some effect on the self-concept of minority and disadvantaged youngsters. Gordon Allport asks:

> What would happen to your own personality if you heard over and over again that you were lazy, a simple child of nature, expected to steal, and had inferior blood? Suppose this opinion were forced on you by the majority of your fellow citizens. And suppose nothing you could do would change this opinion, because you happen to have black skin.[9]

The general assumption (clearly illustrated by this quotation) in much recent educational writing is that lower-class and minority group youngsters have a lower self-concept than white and middle-class youngsters. A recent study by Anthony and Louise Soares of the University of Bridgeport challenges this general assumption. In comparing the self-concept or "self perception" of 514 urban elementary school children, half from a disadvantaged school, half from an advantaged one, they discovered that "not only did the disadvantaged group indicate positive self perceptions, it also had higher self perceptions than the advantaged

8. Arthur J. Jersild, "Emotional Development," in L. Carmichael (ed.), *Manual of Child Psychology*, 2d ed. (New York: John Wiley & Sons, Inc., 1954), p. 837.

9. Allport, *op. cit.*, p. 142.

group."[10] These results are more readily understood when one notes that all the children involved attend neighborhood schools. In other words, disadvantaged children are exposed only to other disadvantaged people in school as well as at home and in their neighborhoods. As a corollary, the Coleman Report postulated that when black pupils became part of an integrated school system, their self-concepts diminished. Advantaged children, however, associate only with other advantaged persons in school and at home. The ensuing associations and challenges for the disadvantaged have an effect upon the level of aspiration they hold for themselves and which others have of them. Since they are functioning according to expectations by teachers and parents, they are satisfied with themselves. Hence a positive self-concept and reflected self.

"On the other hand the advantaged child may be more pressured than he should be by his parents and other adults. If he does not measure up to their expectations the result may be lower self esteem and lower (even though positive) self perceptions."[11]

What seems to be involved in the findings of this study is a distinction between a *general* self-concept or self-perception, in which disadvantaged youngsters may come off reasonably well, at least when they are in segregated schools, and a *self-concept of achievement,* that is, self measured against the standards and expectations of the school as a middle-class institution. It is important to realize that the studies reported later in this chapter, although they do not necessarily use this wording, are really dealing with self-concept of achievement and not the more general self-perception identified by Soares and Soares. The following examples illustrate self-concept in relation to school and aspiration.

Jonathan Kozol, a former teacher in a predominantly black public school in Boston, provides an illustration of the consequences of these attitudes about the self. Due to overcrowding, Kozol's regular class was one of many meeting in a section of the chaotic assembly hall.

It was not their fault. They had done nothing to deserve substitute teachers. And it was not their fault now if they could not hear my words clearly since it also was true that I could barely hear theirs. Yet the way that they dealt with this dilemma, at least on the level at which I could observe it, was to blame not the school but themselves. Not one of these children would say to me, "Mr. Kozol, it's too noisy." Not one of them would say, "Mr. Kozol, what's going on here?" "This is a crazy place to learn." This instead is what I heard.

"Mr. Kozol, I'm trying as hard as I can but I just can't hear a word that you say." "Mr. Kozol, please don't be angry. It's so hard. I couldn't hear you." "Mr.

10. Anthony T. Soares and Louise M. Soares, "Self-Perceptions of Culturally Disadvantaged Children," *American Educational Research Journal,* Vol. 6, No. 1 (January 1969), pp. 31-45.

11. *Ibid.,* p. 42.

Kozol, please would you read it to me one more time." You could not escape the absolute assumption that this mess was not only their own fault, but something to be ashamed of. It was a triumph of pedagogic brain washing. The place was ugly, noisy, rotten. Yet the children before me found it natural and automatic to accept as normal, the school's structural inadequacies and to incorporate them as it were right into themselves. As if perhaps the rotting timbers might not be objective calamities but self condemning configurations of their own making. As if the frenzied noise and overcrowding were a condition and an indictment not of the school building itself but rather of their own inadequate mentalities or of their own incapacitated souls.[12]

The following is a young adolescent Puerto Rican boy discussing his own future.

I think about what I should do when I get out of school and I just don't know. The people in my neighborhood, in Harlem, and downtown, they're all doing it wrong. If one tries to get out the rest laughs. Like they say that they tried and couldn't do it and you're not going to do it either. Then this guy feels, well, maybe I can't do it, and he comes back into the slum. You figure, you know, they failed, man. I might as well give up. I mean even someone like Adam Clayton. Okay. Maybe he studied as a child, I guess to be a congressman. It doesn't matter how much money you got. You got to be doing your stuff. But maybe that money his father had helped him. Because maybe his father gave him special things, you know, private schools, things like that. Or maybe he never once had even to go to a slum area.

And that's the thing that give a feeling of inferior. It tells a person that no matter how hard they try to get out, that's the whole thing right there. I mean a rich person wouldn't have to go around mugging people or robbing them. The trouble really is down at Harlem because Harlem is a place where you don't get anything of anything. That's where like you used to live when you didn't have nothing. Until you get something you'll never get out of that place. . . . Me? I'm Puerto Rican. Colored. And I'm not going to turn my back on that. But if you ask me if I could say, which would you rather be, well, I mean you've got to face it, I mean anybody would. If you asked me which I'd rather be, well, man, I'd rather be white.[13]

THE SCHOOL AND SELF-CONCEPT

Brookover, Paterson, and Thomas conducted a study which looked directly at the relationship between the self-concept of ability and actual

12. Jonathan Kozol, *Death at an Early Age* (New York: Bantam Books, Inc., 1968), pp. 60-61.

13. Charlotte Leon Mayerson (ed.), *Two Blocks Apart* (New York: Avon Books, 1966), pp. 104, 105, 107.

school achievement.[14] The sample consisted of 1050 seventh-grade students in four public junior high schools. Standard measures of intelligence, the California Test of Mental Maturity, and interviews were used to collect the data. The investigators concluded that self-concept of ability is significantly related to achievement at the .57 level. The student's self-concept of ability is also positively related to the image he perceives others to have of him. Parents were rated by nearly all the subjects as particularly important in their lives and concerned about how well they do in school. Finally, students who aspire or expect to go to college have significantly higher self-concepts of ability than students with low educational aspirations. Unfortunately, no conclusions can be drawn about racial differences and self-concept, since this study included no nonwhite students in the sample population. It is important to note here that this study does not attempt to indicate what the causal relationship is between self-concept and achievement. Indeed, it is probably far more complex than a direct one, with variables such as confidence, ability, work habits, interest, and others intervening between the concept of self and actual achievement levels.

Other factors besides achievement are clearly important. Wylie tested the hypotheses that more modest self-estimates of ability would occur in girls as compared to boys, in blacks as compared to whites, and in children whose fathers are in lower-level occupations as compared to those whose fathers are in higher-level occupations.[15] The study was conducted in a small industrial Pennsylvania city and the sample consisted of 823 boys and girls in grades seven, eight, and nine. The IQ scores from the SRA Primary Mental Abilities Test were used as an estimate of individual differences in ability; and three kinds of self-estimates of ability were obtained from the children who were tested in their home rooms. Father's occupation was taken from the school records and rated on the Hollingshead-Redlich scale.

All three hypotheses were supported by this study. That is, girls, blacks, and children whose fathers were in the lower-level occupations tended to have more modest self-estimates of ability. These hypotheses were supported when holding constant such factors as age, school attendance, and IQ.

The role of the teacher as a factor in both self-concept and achievement is important. A study by Davidson and Lang examined the relationship between children's perceptions of their teacher's feeling toward them as related to their own self-perception, school achievement, and

14. Wilbur B. Brookover, Ann Paterson, and Shailer Thomas, "Self-Concept of Ability and School Achievement," Cooperative Research Project No. 845 (East Lansing, Mich.: Office of Research and Publications, Michigan State University, 1962).

15. Ruth S. Wylie, "Children's Estimates of Their Schoolwork Ability as a Function of Sex, Race and Socioeconomic Level," *Journal of Personality,* Vol. 31 (June 1963), pp. 204-224.

behavior.[16] The study involved the testing of three hypotheses. First, the experimenters believed they would find a positive correlation between the children's perception of their teacher's feelings toward them and the children's perceptions of themselves. They predicted that the more favorable the child's perception of himself, the more positive will be his perception of his teacher's feelings toward him. Secondly, they assumed that they would find a positive relationship between the student's favorable perception of teachers' feelings and good academic achievement. Thirdly, they posited a positive relationship between the student's favorable perception of teachers' feelings and desirable classroom behavior. The instrument used was a checklist of thirty-five words judged by a panel of teachers and junior high school principals as favorable or unfavorable. Words included such concepts as a nuisance (unfavorable), unafraid (u), cheerful (favorable), a leader (f), unhappy (u). The subjects included in this study were 89 boys and 114 girls attending fourth, fifth, and sixth grades in a New York City public school. Children were distributed in ten different classrooms and represented a wide range in socioeconomic status. It proved possible for the experimenters to divide the youngsters into three distinct groups on the basis of their father's and/or mother's occupation. The upper group of 63 children came from families of professional people, white-collar workers, and businessmen; the middle group of 57 children had parents who were skilled workers, policemen, firemen; and the low group contained 83 children of semiskilled, unskilled, and a number of unemployed parents.

The checklist of trait names was administered twice to the children. At first the children were instructed to respond in terms of "My teacher thinks I am ————." The teachers, nine women and one man, rated their pupils on academic achievement on a four-point scale: very good, adequate, below average, and very bad. They were also asked to rate each child on ten behavioral or personality characteristics. A weight of plus one was assigned to each of four traits judged to be desirable: eager, obedient, cooperative, assertive. A weight of minus one was given to the characteristics judged to be undesirable: disorderly, destructive, hostile, defiant, unfriendly, troublesome. The findings of the study supported the original hypotheses.

1. Children's perception of their teacher's feelings toward them was correlated positively and significantly with their own self-perception. The child with the more favorable self-image was the one who more

16. Helen H. Davidson and Gerhard Lang, "Children's Perceptions of Their Teachers' Feelings toward Them Related to Self-Perception, School Achievement and Behavior," *Journal of Experimental Education,* Vol. 29 (December 1960), pp. 107-118.

likely than not perceived his teacher's feelings toward him more favorably.

2. The more positive the children's perception of their teacher's feelings, the better was their academic achievement and the more desirable their classroom behavior as rated by the teachers.

3. Children in the upper and middle social class groups perceived their teacher's feelings toward them more favorably than did the children in the lower social class group.

4. Not surprisingly, social class position was also found to be positively related to achievement in school.

Further statistical analysis of the data collected in this study revealed that the social class variable plays an important part in the way a child perceives his teacher's feelings toward him, *regardless of his achievement in school.* Similarly, within each social class group there is a close relationship between the level of academic achievement and the child's judgment about the teacher's feelings toward him. These results are important because they indicate that both social class position and academic achievement operate independently in affecting the way a child will perceive his teacher's feelings toward him. The implications of this study are important for teachers, since they suggest that students view with importance teachers' attitudes toward them; and, the students' perception of attitudes in school are closely related to both their academic achievement and social class position.

At least equally important for the urban disadvantaged youngster as regards achievement is his aspiration—what he wants and expects both educationally and occupationally. Gottlieb looked directly at the aspirations and expectations of white and black students composed by social class and by region.[17] The researcher used as his sample four groups of adolescent youngsters:

1. students from two black segregated high schools, one rural and one urban

2. students from a white segregated high school from each of the above two communities

3. a twenty-five percent random sample of black and white students in an interracial high school in a newly industrialized Midwestern community

4. a twenty-five percent random sample of black students in an all black high school in a Northern metropolis

Gottlieb found that for both Southern and Northern white students

17. David Gottlieb, "Goal Aspirations and Goal Fulfillments: Differences between Deprived and Affluent American Adolescents," *American Journal of Orthopsychiatry*, Vol. 34 (October 1964), pp. 934-941.

the lower the class background the lower the mobility aspirations. Among black youth, however, he found that more than 80 percent at each class level expressed a desire for college, although black males from Southern segregated schools were more likely to do so than those from Northern schools. At the same time he found that black youth from each social class and type of school were less likely than comparable whites to select occupational fields requiring graduate or professional training. Gottlieb found that among his white respondents there was a declining discrepancy between college-going aspirations and expectations at each higher status level.

Among black students at each status level, however, at least 20 percent of those aspiring to college did not actually expect to go. "Negro students at the southern segregated schools are more likely than those in the northern schools to match expectations with aspirations. The greatest discrepancy is found among Negro youth in the northern interracial high schools."[18] It seems likely that this discrepancy, which represents a significant gap between what Northern urban black youth want and what they actually expect to get may be an important factor in the recent civil disorders.

Another perspective on the difference between aspiration and expectation is offered by Weiner and Murray who discuss the difference between the reality and the ideal of certain goals.[19] When a middle-class parent is asked whether his child is going to college and when a lower-class parent is asked the same question, the authors suggest that the "yes" which the investigator is likely to get from both parents mean rather different things. To the middle-class parent it means "yes, it is sure. Obviously my child will get into college as I got into college, and so on." The lower-class parent, on the other hand, answers "yes" as a wish, not as a fact.

In a study which these authors conducted in a Westchester community comparing the occupational goals of middle-class and lower-class children it was discovered that most parents and children of both groups listed a professional occupation as the goal. When the lower socioeconomic children were asked how far they expected to go in school, 52 percent reported that they would continue their education through college, and 33 percent through high school. The curriculum in which these students were enrolled was checked. Only 37 percent were taking college preparatory courses. This compares to the middle-class group, 95 percent of whom said they intended to go on through college, and 100 percent of whom were enrolled in a college preparatory course.

18. *Ibid.*, p. 936.

19. Max Weiner and Walter Murray, "Another Look at the Culturally Deprived and Their Levels of Aspiration," *Journal of Educational Sociology*, Vol. 36 (March 1963), pp. 319-321.

Sociologist Bernard Rosen has examined the differences in motivation, values, and aspirations of six racial and ethnic groups.[20] He found that blacks as an ethnic group had educational aspirations comparable to those of Jews, Greeks, and white Protestants, and higher than those of the Italians and French-Canadians. Vocational aspirations of blacks were, Rosen discovered, the lowest of any of the six ethnic groups. Social class and ethnicity were found to interact in influencing the aspirations of youngsters in this study, but neither one by itself could predict an individual score. Ethnic differences in educational and vocational aspirations persisted when social class was discounted. However, some of the differences between ethnic groups in aspirations, Rosen believes, were probably a function of their class composition. Rosen's findings, and particularly his distinction between educational and occupational aspirations, are similar to the real and ideal aspirations of Weiner and Murray. It seems reasonable to assume that the occupational aspirations represent the realistic assessment on the part of black youngsters of their life chances, while educational aspirations are likely to be the result of widely held and apparently deeply embedded values attached to education in American society.

The results of these studies certainly indicate the difficulty of analyzing and doing research on terms as difficult to define as self-concept and aspiration. They do, however, indicate that self-concept is an important factor in school achievement; and that expectation, or in Weiner's and Murray's term, reality goals, are related in some way to the different performance of lower-class and nonwhite youngsters.

THE SCHOOL AS SELF-FULFILLING PROPHET

One conclusion from much of the preceding account of self-concept and achievement might easily be that the school acts as a relatively neutral arena for the interaction of the two variables. It provides an opportunity to achieve for those children who view themselves as achievers; it may heighten the self-concept of some by rewarding those who achieve. Some psychologists have recently suggested that far from playing a passive role the school actively and directly intervenes by imposing its own view of some children's chances to achieve successfully. The crucial mechanism for the intervention is the self-fulfilling prophecy.

Several decades ago a noted American sociologist, W.I. Thomas, made the following statement: "If men define situations as real, they

20. Bernard C. Rosen, "The Achievement Syndrome: A Psychocultural Dimension of Social Stratification," *American Sociological Review*, Vol. 21 (April 1956), pp. 203-211.

are real in their consequences."[21] There is nothing very mysterious about this prediction, and in a general way we know it to be true about ordinary life. Sociologist Robert Merton provides an illuminating illustration from the economic sphere.[22] He suggests that the failure of the American banking system in the 1930s was due in large part to self-fulfilling prophecy. Before banks failed, they were in fact solvent institutions. Their solvency was known to the board of directors, to presidents, officers, and many workers in the banks. To their depositors, who were concerned about the general economic collapse of the society and saw the banks as one more institution which seemed likely to fail, the definition of this economic reality was quite different. They began, then, with a definition of reality which was false. However, as they proceeded to withdraw their money from banks all over the country, their behavior and action soon produced what they had erroneously believed to be true, the failure of the banks. Their expectation and prophecy quite clearly caused the collapse.

On a more local level William Whyte in his famous *Street Corner Society* observed that among the group of young men he was studying, certain expectations pertained as to bowling skills.[23] Whyte discovered that the group knew how well each man was expected to bowl and that this expectation seemed to influence his performance significantly. The group knew that one of the members would not be bowling well when they played that night. Indeed, he did not, even though on the previous night he had bowled exceedingly well. Whyte concluded that somehow the expectation of the group communicated itself to the bowler and influenced his score.

Perhaps the operation of the self-fulfilling prophecy in our social life may most importantly be seen in the area of race relations. We begin with a view on the part of many white citizens that blacks are inferior. It is important to remember that this definition is accepted as actual reality. Although not intended by whites to effect black inferiority, it is simply accepted as a fact. But flowing from such a definition are a number of very serious consequences. Whites, particularly those in powerful positions in many parts of American society, allocate to blacks a lesser share in privileges and opportunities, since they believe blacks to be inferior. Given fewer privileges and opportunities, based on an assumption of black inferiority, tends to produce visible evidence of that inferiority. Whites observe blacks in menial jobs, with limited

21. W.I. Thomas, "The Relation of Research to the Social Process," in *Essays on Research in the Social Sciences* (Washington, D.C.: The Brookings Institution, 1931), p. 189.

22. Robert K. Merton, *Social Theory and Social Structure* (New York: The Free Press, 1957), pp. 421-436.

23. W.F. Whyte, *Street Corner Society* (Chicago: University of Chicago Press, 1943).

education, poor housing, and having a variety of health problems. From this it is extremely easy to conclude that blacks *are* inferior. The fact of having made the definition creates the conditions under which the prophecy is realized.

The reader should keep in mind that there is nothing apparent in the concept of the self-fulfilling prophecy that forces it to move in a negative direction only. The following story illustrates the positive influence of the self-fulfilling prophecy.

James Sweeney taught industrial management and psychiatry at Tulane University where he was responsible for the operation of the bio-medical computer center. It was Sweeney's expectation that he could make even a poorly educated Negro into a computer operator. The poorly educated Negro chosen was George Johnson, former hospital porter who became janitor at the computer center. In the morning he swept and cleaned; in the afternoon he learned about computers. He was learning a great deal about computers when the word circulated that to be a computer operator one had to earn a certain score on an I.Q. test. Johnson took the test which showed that he should not even be able to learn to type, much less operate a computer. But Sweeney was not convinced. He went to the administration and threatened, "No Johnson, no Sweeney." Both stayed. Sweeney still runs the computer center and Johnson now runs the main computer room, in which position he is responsible for the training of new employees.[24]

The question that concerns us is to what extent and in what way the self-fulfilling prophecy affects the learning of disadvantaged youngsters in urban schools. Later in the chapter we will look specifically at the evidence available on this question. At this point, however, it seems important to state that for most education writers and researchers there is an underlying assumption that the self-fulfilling prophecy is operating. Martin Deutsch, Burton Clark, Frank Riessman, William Kvaraceus, and Kenneth Clark all agree that children classed as disadvantaged are expected by their teachers to be unable to learn. The following transcription of comments by a first-year teacher shows the self-fulfilling prophecy being manifested in the school.

Mrs. Jones explained about the environmental problems that these children have. Some of them never see a newspaper. Some of them have never been on the subway. The parents are so busy having parties and things that they have no time for their children. They can't even take them to a museum or anything. It's very important that teachers stress books. Mrs. Jones tells her class that if anyone asks what you want for Christmas, you can say a book. She told

24. Robert Rosenthal and Lenore Jacobson, *Pygmalion in the Classroom* (New York: Holt, Rinehart and Winston, Inc., 1968), pp. 3-4.

me that she had a 6-1 class last year and it was absolutely amazing how many children never even saw a newspaper. They can't read Spanish either. So she said that the educational problem lies with the parents. They are the ones who have to be educated. It's just a shame that the children have to suffer. I guess this problem will take an awful lot to straighten out. I guess it won't take one day or even a year. It will take time. . . .

Robert did every bit of work ever assigned. He caught on very very quickly to all phases of work, besides doing his work well, quickly, efficiently and neatly. Even though on the reading readiness he only scored in the 50th percentile, I felt he really stood out and I also felt that once you're in a "1" class, unless you really don't belong, you have a better chance. For some reason the "1" class on the grade is really the only class that you would term a good class. . . .

I believe my school is a pretty good school. It isn't in the best neighborhood. There are many, many problems in my school, but on the whole I think that the teachers and administrators work together and I do believe that they are doing the best they can with the problems that are around. You have to remember that in a school such as ours the children are not as ready and willing to learn as in school in middle class neighborhoods.[25]

Another illustration of school attitudes is a guidance counselor's response to a question about the lack of motivation in central Harlem school pupils.

"The children have a poor self image and unrealistic aspirations. If you ask them what they want to be they say 'a doctor,' or something like that." When asked what would you say to a child who wanted to be a doctor she replied, "I would present the situation to him as it really is. Show him how little possibility he has for that. I would tell him about the related fields, technicians, etc."[26]

Malcolm X, assassinated black Muslim leader, describes his own school experience.

. . . the topmost scholastic standing, I remember, kept shifting between me, a girl named Audrey Slaugh, and a boy named Jimmy Cotton. . . . One day, just about when those of us who had passed were about to move up to 8-A, from which we would enter high school the next year, something happened which was to become the first major turning point of my life.

Somehow, I happened to be alone in the classroom with Mr. Ostrowski, my English teacher. He was a tall, rather reddish-white man and he had a thick mustache. I had gotten some of my best marks under him, and he had always made me feel that he liked me. He was, as I have mentioned a natural-born

25. Estelle Fuchs, *Teachers Talk* (New York: Anchor Books, 1969), pp. 171-179.
26. Kenneth B. Clark, *Dark Ghetto* (New York: Harper & Row, 1965), p. 133.

"advisor," about what you ought to read, to do, or think—about any and everything. . . .

I know that he probably meant well in what he happened to advise me that day. I doubt that he meant any harm. It was just in his nature as an American white man. I was one of his top students, one of the school's top students—but all he could see for me was the kind of future "in your place" that almost all white people see for black people.

He told me, "Malcolm, you ought to be thinking about a career. Have you been giving it thought?"

The truth is, I hadn't. I never have figured out why I told him, "Well, yes, sir, I've been thinking I'd like to be a lawyer." Lansing, (Mich.) certainly had no Negro lawyers—or doctors either—in those days, to hold up an image I might have aspired to. All I really knew for certain was that a lawyer didn't wash dishes, as I was doing.

Mr. Ostrowski looked surprised, I remember, and leaned back in his chair and clasped his hands behind his head. He kind of half-smiled and said, "Malcolm, one of life's first needs is for us to be realistic. Don't misunderstand me, now. We all here like you, you know that. But you've got to be realistic about being a nigger. A lawyer—that's no realistic goal for a nigger. You need to think about something you *can* be. You're good with your hands—making things. Everybody admires your carpentry shop work. Why don't you plan on carpentry? People like you as a person—you'd get all kinds of work."

What made it really begin to disturb me was Mr. Ostrowski's advice to others in my class—all of them white. Most of them had told him they were planning to become farmers, like their parents—to one day take over their family farms. But those who wanted to strike out on their own, to try something new, he had encouraged. Some, mostly girls, wanted to be teachers. A few wanted other professions, such as one boy who wanted to become a county agent; another, a veterinarian; and one girl wanted to be a nurse. They all reported that Mr. Ostrowski had encouraged whatever they had wanted. Yet nearly none of them had earned marks equal to mine.

It was a surprising thing that I had never thought of it that way before, but I realized that whatever I wasn't, I *was* smarter than nearly all of those white kids. But apparently I was still not intelligent enough, in their eyes, to become whatever *I* wanted to be.

It was then that I began to change—inside.[27]

Perhaps the most articulate and outspoken critic of the education that is provided for disadvantaged youngsters in urban areas is Kenneth B. Clark, Professor of Social Psychology at City College. In two volumes, *Dark Ghetto* and *Youth in the Ghetto, a Study of Youth Opportunities in Central Harlem,* Clark outlines his charge that the main cause for the

27. Malcolm X, *The Autobiography of Malcolm X* (New York: Grove Press, Inc., 1966), pp. 35-37.

failure of black youngsters to perform equally with white youngsters in public schools is the educators' "self-fulfilling prophecy."[28] In addition to quoting illustrative material such as that above, Clark offers in evidence certain educational programs which have achieved success and which he believes prove that the self-fulfilling prophecy is an extremely significant reason for the failure of disadvantaged nonwhite youngsters. Before presenting his case, Clark makes the following statement:

> Given no evidence to the contrary the assumption can be made that cultural and economic backgrounds of pupils do not constitute a barrier to the type of learning which can reasonably be expected of normal children in the elementary grades—however much of a barrier such backgrounds are in respect to social problems such as delinquency, emotional stability, and the like. Only when it is permitted to be a barrier does it become a cumulative, deteriorating force.[29]

The first study which Clark cites to support this statement is a crash program of remedial reading started in 1955 and continuing through the summer of 1964 at the Northside Center for Child Development in New York.[30] The program involved daily and intensive remedial reading for youngsters who were retarded in public schools. One month of daily instruction, Clark states, can produce a reading gain on an average of almost one school year. He reports that children with the least retardation made the most advances. Those with IQ's above 110 gained more than two years of reading achievement. But even the most retarded gained at least five months. Clark points out that this group of students was economically inferior and behind in reading, but that nothing was done to change their "cultural deprivation." The only difference was that they were being taught to read by individuals who believed that they could learn and who related to them with warmth and acceptance. A follow-up study showed that they retained the gains made in the summer but unfortunately did not advance any further once back in their regular public schools.

What can we say about this as proof for the existence and importance of the self-fulfilling prophecy? Unfortunately not very much. Too many questions are left unanswered about the youngsters involved in the program. For example, how did their social and economic backgrounds, their "cultural deprivation" compare with other youngsters in the Harlem community? Since it was a volunteer program, what motivational factors were involved? Why did they volunteer? And how did they differ from those equally retarded who did not volunteer? Clark's sug-

28. Clark, *op. cit.;* and Kenneth B. Clark, *Youth in the Ghetto* (New York: Harlem Youth Opportunities Unlimited, Inc., 1964).
29. Clark, *Dark Ghetto, op. cit.,* pp. 139-140.
30. *Ibid.,* pp. 140-141.

gestion based on this experience, namely that the public schools should significantly change their curriculum in the early grades and concentrate great blocks of time on reading, is probably an excellent one. However, this experience does not prove the crucial significance of the self-fulfilling prophecy.

Professor Clark next turns to an historical case to support his contention that cultural deprivation cannot account for discrepancies in learning between black and white youngsters. He notes that children attending Harlem schools in the 1920s and 1930s had average academic ability, close to and almost equal to white norms. He suggests that Professor Otto Klineberg's study of the performance of black children migrating from the South to the North and of those already in Northern schools during the thirties could be used as evidence that during those decades the discrepancy between norms of white students and those of black students was minimal compared with the present gap. It would be difficult to argue, Professor Clark continues, that blacks were less culturally deprived at that time than they were in the 1950s. Here again he has raised an interesting point, but not one that "proves" that cultural deprivation is not a factor nor that expectation is the primary factor resulting in the widening gap between white and nonwhite metropolitan students. One would need to know the racial distribution of youngsters in the Harlem schools in the 1920s or 1930s, as well as have more information about their economic disadvantage compared with white pupils' economic disadvantage in New York City public schools at that time.

This historical argument depends on one strange concept, that is, that teachers in the New York City public schools in the twenties had equal expectations for their black and white students. This, at a period when social psychology textbooks (at least until Klineberg's study became widely known) were stating that blacks were in fact genetically less intelligent than whites.[31] Nevertheless this general topic, the history of the widening gap between black and white performance, is one which is important and seems worthy of further research.

Coming back to the present, Professor Clark offers as an example of changed performance without changed level in cultural deprivation the experience of Junior High School #43, located on the edge of Harlem. This school, a rather typical lower-class junior high school in New York City, was selected to participate in the pilot demonstration guidance program. The results after three years were rather startling. For example, six times as many students went to college (25 percent as compared with the earlier figure of 4 percent); the dropout rate fell one-half from 50 percent to 25 percent; 81 percent were judged to have

31. *Ibid.*, p. 141.

greater intelligence than their earlier IQ and achievement scores would have predicted. In the eleventh grade the average IQ scores went up by nine points. In the two-and-a-half years between tests, from the fall of seventh grade to the spring of ninth grade, the average student gained 4.3 years in reading scores, compared with 1.7 years during an earlier similar period. Professor Clark suggests that there was nothing very revolutionary about the educational methods introduced in this pilot program and that the miracle was due to an "implementation of the belief that children can learn." The emphasis on discipline in the school was toned down. Teachers were evaluated more on their teaching skill than on discipline. There was better communication between the administration and teachers. It is true that additional professional personnel were added to the school in the form of guidance counselors and some special teachers; but as far as Clark's argument concerning this radical improvement in learning is concerned, it is quite true that no attempt was made to change the cultural deprivational level of the students of J.H.S. #43 fundamentally.

The Banneker Project in St. Louis, Missouri, is another case which Professor Clark uses to illustrate his position. The Banneker school district is one of five elementary school groups in the city and has the largest proportion of black students. The neighborhood is characterized by old housing, high crime rate, and high unemployment. Ten thousand out of the sixteen thousand children in the Banneker district are black. In 1957 St. Louis public schools inaugurated a three-track system of ability grouping based upon standardized IQ and achievement scores. These scores for students in the Banneker district showed that 7 percent had track one (the highest) scores whereas 47 percent went into track three. Scores in all academic areas were consistently below grade level, with an IQ median of 90.5 with over 12 percent below IQ 79. The district director, Dr. Samuel Shepherd, inaugurated a program designed to upgrade the performance of these youngsters. The concentration was on the attitude of the teachers and school administrators. No secret was made of the low scores of the Banneker district children, but these scores, rather than being explained away as due to cultural deprivation, were used to stimulate improvement. The teachers were asked, for example, to ignore IQ scores and treat all children as if they had superior ability. Scores by school were made public and compared, and actual competition was set up between schools in the district. Shepherd himself made numerous visits to classrooms in an attempt to motivate his principals and teachers.

It is important to note that in this program no drastic change was made in the curriculum, in instructional techniques, or in the basic underprivileged social situation of the children and their families. What Shepherd attempted to change was the attitude and perspectives of the teachers and school administrators. As a result of this intensive yet inexpensive program children assigned to track one increased from 7 percent to 22 percent; track three, the lowest, fell from 47.1 percent to 10.9 percent. IQ was raised approximately 10 points. Again Clark hammers home that this remarkable improvement in learning included no change in factors of cultural deprivation. What was changed was the attitude and expectations of teachers and school administrators.

What can be said about these last two illustrations in support of Clark's argument? They are clearly the strongest of the cases he offers. They show that learning can be improved dramatically without wiping out slums, desegregating all racially imbalanced schools, or mounting a massive program of home-and-family and parent-and-community education.

Unfortunately we must make note of the further development of these two programs. Junior High School #43, primarily because of its success, was expanded and developed into the Higher Horizons program of the New York City Board of Education. In this broadened form the final analysis made by the Board of Education itself was that Higher Horizons was a failure.[32] The success of the Banneker district schools in St. Louis has also faded. As reported in *Racial Isolation in the Public Schools,* a report published by the United States Commission on Civil Rights, the Banneker schools' relative position in comparison to primarily white schools in St. Louis is not better than other black schools.[33] The gains that were made during the first three years of the program have not been maintained.

The apparent inability of Higher Horizons and the Banneker Project to hold increases made in the initial years suggest the influence of a variable that has importance for all innovative educational programs, the so-called "Hawthorne effect" which takes its name from the Hawthorne plant of the Western Electric Company just ouside of Chicago where the phenomenon first came to the attention of social scientists.

This plant was the scene of an intensive series of experiments primarily investigating the effects of working conditions on employees' performances. As the experimenters began introducing changes into the control work group they made a remarkable discovery: Under certain conditions it was apparently of little importance what change was introduced into the working situation. The level of illumination under which work was done, for example, was at first considerably increased,

32. J. Wayne Wrightstone *et al., Evaluation of Higher Horizons Programs for Underprivileged Children* (New York City: Board of Education, 1964).

33. A Report of the United States Commission on Civil Rights, *Racial Isolation in the Public Schools* (Washington, D.C.: U.S. Commission on Civil Rights, 1967), pp. 120-122.

then gradually decreased. But under all gradations of illumination, work levels either increased or stayed the same. This was not at all what the experimenters had expected. Clearly an unknown factor was involved.

Based on the Hawthorne experience, behavioral scientists have developed the theory that this increased performance, regardless of changes in work conditions, was in actuality a reaction to the experimental situation itself, not to the particular or specific variables introduced by investigators, the experimental group, in other words, responding to the very fact that they were an experimental group and had been selected out of all other workers in the factory.

The implications are extremely significant for research in all areas of behavioral science, and particularly in education. It means that some innovative programs in education may succeed initially not because of particular changes in techniques, methodology, or attitudes but because students realize something new, exciting, and different is going on. When the program is no longer new, exciting, or different, a fading effect may take over, such as that which was noted in the Banneker district and in Higher Horizons programs.

One other kind of evidence offered by Professor Clark must be considered here. In *Youth in the Ghetto* he provides an analysis of IQ and performance scores of youngsters in central Harlem's elementary schools. Through statistical analysis of these scores Professor Clark shows that "the ranking of central Harlem schools in terms of the performance of sixth grade pupils is more accurately predicted by changes occurring between the third and sixth grades than by the actual performances of pupils in an earlier stage in their educational progress."[34] Professor Clark goes on to say that "from this, one can infer that the source of educational problems of Harlem's youth lies in processes which occur during the time they are in school, rather then in processes prior to their entrance into school."[35] Here again one may say that the conclusion calls for serious consideration by educators, but it is not proven that teacher attitude and expectation or that schools alone are the source of the educational deterioration and failure of nonwhite youth. The influence of home and community does, after all, continue after the children enter school.

None of the evidence offered by Professor Clark in support of the crucial role teacher expectation and attitude play in educating the disadvantaged is based on experimental study focused directly on that theory. He has been forced to draw conclusions concerning the effect of attitude from innovative programs and statistics not specifically created for dealing with this point.

34. Clark, *Youth in the Ghetto, op. cit.*, p. 211.
35. *Ibid.*, p. 212.

Let us now examine a study designed to measure the effect of teacher attitude and expectation on school performance, *Pygmalion in the Classroom, Teacher Expectation and Pupils' Intellectual Development,* by Robert Rosenthal and Leonore Jacobson.[36] This study was conducted in a public elementary school, which the authors call Oak School, located in an older section of a medium-sized American city. It is primarily lower and working class in student population. The fathers are mostly unskilled and skilled workers. Many of the children, the authors report, are from broken homes where mothers work and/or the family receives welfare funds. About one-sixth of the school's population of 650 students consist of Mexican children, the only minority group in the school. Enrollment is not stable. Transfers in and out number as high as 200 or 30 percent during an academic year. Oak School follows the district policy of ability-grouping its children. Grouping is based primarily on reading performance with three levels for each grade, one through six, termed fast, medium, and slow tracks. The authors point out that though children at Oak School are not assigned to these tracks on the basis of IQ scores but rather on reading, there is nevertheless a substantial difference in the average IQ's of the three tracks. There were twenty teachers at Oak School during the time of the experiment, two of whom were male. From year to year teachers tended to be assigned to the same grade level, but there was a fairly regular rotation of track assignment within each grade level.

The actual research procedure at Oak School began with the administration of a test entitled "The Harvard Test of Instructive Acquisition." Each teacher received a copy of the following explanations.

Study of Inflected Acquisition (Harvard–National Science Foundation)

All children show hills, plateaus, and valleys in their scholastic progress. The study being conducted at Harvard with the support of the National Science Foundation is interested in those children who show an unusual forward spurt of academic progress. These spurts can and do occur at any level of academic functioning. When these spurts occur in children who have not been functioning too well academically it is familiarly referred to as late blooming.

As a part of our study we are further validating a test which predicts the likelihood that a child will show an inflection point or spurt within the near future. This test which will be administered in your school will allow us to predict which youngsters are most likely to show an academic spurt. The top 20%, approximately, of the scores on this test will probably be found at

36. Rosenthal and Jacobson, *op. cit.*

various levels of academic functioning. The development of the test for predicting inflections or "spurts" is not yet such that every one of the top 20% will show the spurt or "blooming" effect. But, the top 20% of the children *will* show a more significant inflection or spurt in their learning within the next year or less than will the remaining 80% of the children.

Because of the experimental nature of the tests, basic principles of test construction do not permit us to discuss the test or the test scores either with the parents or the children themselves.

Upon completion of this study, participating districts will be advised of the results.[37]

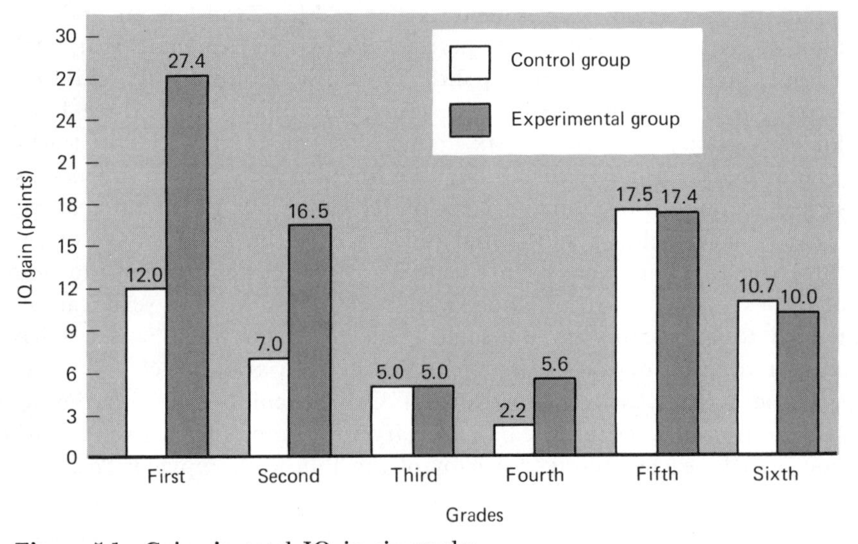

Figure 5.1 Gains in total IQ in six grades.
SOURCE: Robert Rosenthal and Lenore Jacobson, *Pygmalion in the Classroom* (New York: Holt, Rinehart and Winston, Inc., 1968), p. 75.

In fact, the test of Inflected Acquisitions was a standardized, relatively nonverbal test of intelligence, Flanigan's Tests of General Ability (TOGA). This test was first administered in the spring of 1964. At the end of the summer, just before school began, 20 percent of the children of Oak School were designated as academic spurters and their names were given to teachers in September. In point of fact this 20 percent of the "special" children had been selected *"by random"* from the student population. This, then, was the situation: Teachers had been told to expect increased performance from certain youngsters on the basis of a misrepresented test. The students identified as those likely to improve their performances were actually selected at random from the school population.

37. *Ibid.*, p. 66.

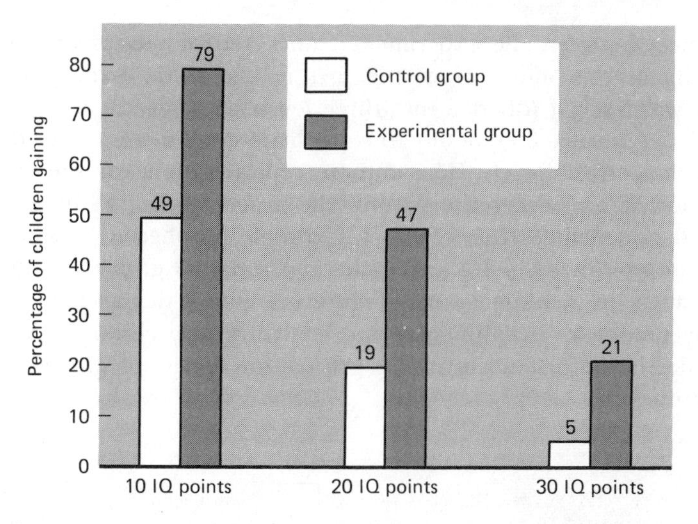

Figure 5.2 Percentages of first- and second-graders gaining 10, 20, or 30 total IQ points.

SOURCE: Robert Rosenthal and Lenore Jacobson, *Pygmalion in the Classroom* (New York: Holt, Rinehart and Winston, Inc., 1968), p. 76.

What were the results? In the school year of the experiment, 1964-1965, the undesignated control group children gained over 8 IQ points; while the experimental group children, the "special" children, gained over 12. The difference in gains could be ascribed to chance in only two out of one hundred times (*see* Figures 5.1 and 5.2 and Table 5.1). One can see from the figures and table the most dramatic effects of increased teacher expectation were in the first and second grades. The

Table 5.1 Mean Gain in Total IQ after One Year by Experimental- and Control-Group Children in Each of Six Grades

	Control		Experimental		Expectancy advantage	
Grade	*N*	Gain	*N*	Gain	IQ points	One-tail $p < .05$*
1	48	+12.0	7	+27.4	+15.4	.002
2	47	+ 7.0	12	+16.5	+ 9.5	.02
3	40	+ 5.0	14	+ 5.0	− 0.0	
4	49	+ 2.2	12	+ 5.6	+ 3.4	
5	26	+17.5 (−)	9	+17.4 (+)	− 0.0	
6	45	+10.7	11	+10.0	− 0.7	
Total	255	+ 8.42	65	+12.22	+ 3.80	.02

* Mean square within treatments within classrooms = 164.24.

SOURCE: Robert Rosenthal and Lenore Jacobson, *Pygmalion in the Classroom* (New York: Holt, Rinehart and Winston, Inc., 1968), p. 75.

differences between the experimental and control groups decrease dramatically as one moves from the first to the sixth grade. Since Oak School was tracked (divided into three levels of academic ability), it was possible to see whether or not the predictions of success were different across these track levels. The authors report: "None of the statistical tests showed any difference among the three tracks in the extent to which they benefited from teachers' favorable prophecies."[38] In addition to the improvement in IQ scores, the experimental group also increased significantly in reading grades. Figure 5.3 shows the average gains in reading grades by experimental and control group children. Again the difference is significant and much greater for the lower grades than for higher ones.

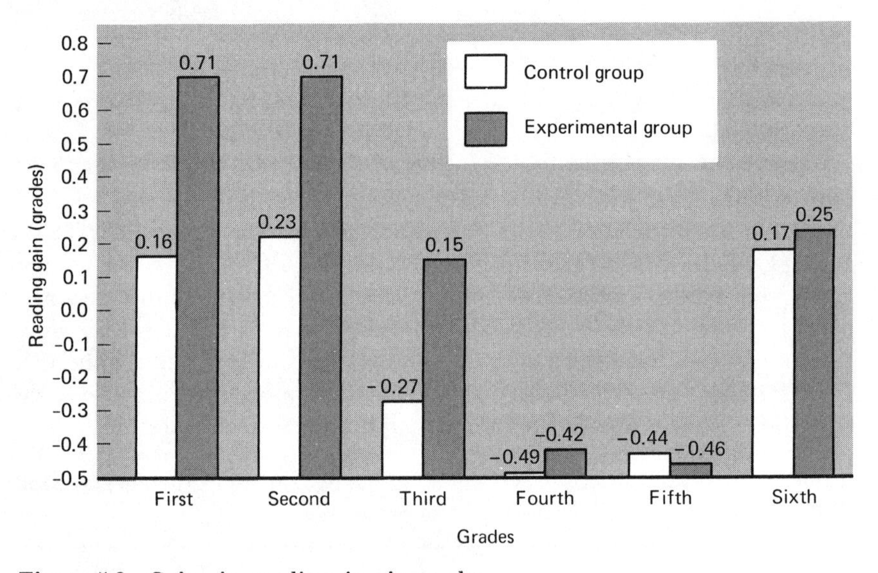

Figure 5.3 Gains in reading in six grades.
SOURCE: Robert Rosenthal and Lenore Jacobson, *Pygmalion in the Classroom* (New York: Holt, Rinehart and Winston, Inc., 1968), p. 100.

How do the authors of the study account for these differences? How does teacher expectation really translate itself into increased performance? The authors believe that there is a kind of covert communication between teacher and pupil about which we know very little scientifically. They suggest that experimenters working with animal subjects which were expected to do well judged that they treated these subjects in a more pleasant, friendly, enthusiastic fashion. Perhaps, the authors continue, teachers also treated their pupils in a more pleasant,

38. *Ibid.,* p. 78.

friendly, and enthusiastic fashion when they expected superior performance. It is possible also that more classroom attention was given to children whom teachers had tabbed as "spurters." More recitation time might have been allotted for the special children to show the competence that was expected of them. *Pygmalion in the Classroom* unfortunately does not deal directly with this problem of interaction. Rosenthal and Jacobson conclude their speculations by pointing out that although a great deal has been written about teacher influence, very few investigators have systematically observed the processes by which teachers *do* influence.

In evaluating *Pygmalion in the Classroom* it should first be noted that this study represents the most complete attempt yet made to demonstrate the influence of teacher attitude and expectation on the performance of youngsters in school. There are, however, several reservations which must be noted. The first concerns reports of two other studies similar in intent and to some extent similar in structure to the Oak School experiment where the results are quite different. The authors report a study conducted in two Midwestern schools which in their judgment was similar enough in design to the Oak School for results to be compared. "No expectancy advantage was found for either boys or girls as measured by total IQ or verbal IQ. For reasoning IQ, however, the results were opposite to those found at Oak School."[39] One possible reason for the difference in results might be that the two Midwestern schools, unlike Oak School, drew their pupils from a substantial middle-class community in which there was not a large proportion of minority group members.

Another, similar study at the Crest School showed gains for the experimental group children, but the magnitude of the effect was not large, and statistically significant only in the case of reasoning IQ.[40]

Another study by Pitt involved a sample of pupils comprising 165 fifth-grade boys: one-third of their IQ's were reported to teachers accurately; one-third were reported 10 points higher, and one-third 10 points lower. At the end of the school year the children of these three groups were compared on school grades, achievement tests, teacher ratings, and pupil self-ratings. Pitt found essentially no effects on the objective tests of achievement of the arbitrarily raised or lower IQ's.[41] Rosenthal and Jacobson suggest that this result might be due to the teachers knowing their children for seven or eight weeks before being given the IQ scores. The judgment or expectation on the part of the teacher had already been established for her pupils.

Another and more serious criticism of the tests used in the Rosen-

39. *Ibid.*, p. 96.
40. *Ibid.*, p. 96.
41. *Ibid.*, pp. 57-58.

thal-Jacobson study has been made by Professor Robert Thorndike.[42] Thorndike's criticism centers on the fact that TOGA (Tests of General Ability), the basic instrument used, shows a mean of 58 on the subtest of reasoning for the first grade. Thorndike points out that to obtain a mean of IQ 58 would require an average raw score of 2 out of 28, when chance alone should have produced a score of 5 or 6. Thorndike does not indicate whether he believes this startling result is due to a faulty test or bad administration. But in any event he argues it casts serious doubt on results: "When the clock strikes 13, doubt is cast not only on the last stroke but also on all that has gone before."[43]

The other general question which should be raised about *Pygmalion in the Classroom* is why the differences between the gains of the experimental over the control group diminished so drastically as one moved from grade one to grade six. The authors suggest several possible interpretations of this decrease. First, younger children are generally regarded by educators as more malleable, less fixed, and more capable of change. The conditions of the experiment then were most effective with younger children, simply because the younger child is easier to change. Another possible factor involves the reputation which youngsters build up after a number of years in the school. Children in the first and second grades have not had time to be judged quite so thoroughly as youngsters in the fourth, fifth, and sixth grades. Another consideration might be that teachers in the early years are more effective than teachers in the later grades. Two administrators who were familiar with the teachers in the Oak School rated them on overall effectiveness and *did* rate teachers in the first, second, and third grades significantly higher than teachers in the fourth, fifth, and sixth grades.

One last question about *Pygmalion in the Classroom* may be raised about the typical nature of the Oak Street school. As noted above, the control group not selected for a spurt in performance showed an increase of 8 IQ points. No explanation is offered for this improvement, although it is very atypical for lower-class or slum schools. A more typical pattern is for IQ and performance scores to decline over the years, creating the "cumulative deficit" reported by Martin Deutsch.[44] Although the Oak School study represents a considerable improvement in focus and sophistication over other kinds of evidence available on the relationship of teacher attitude and expectation to academic performance, no single study in any field can be said to prove conclusively the existence or nature of such a relationship. What educators may

42. Robert L. Thorndike, *"Pygmalion in the Classroom,"* in *The Record,* Vol. 70, No. 8 (May 1969), pp. 805-807.

43. *Ibid.,* p. 807.

44. Martin P. Deutsch, "The Disadvantaged Child and the Learning Process," in A. Harry Passow (ed.), *Education in Depressed Areas* (New York: Bureau of Publications, Teachers College, Columbia University, 1963), pp. 163-179.

hopefully look forward to are further studies, improved and refined methodologically, focusing on different kinds of students in a variety of school situations, so that gradually a considerable body of evidence may be built up about this important relationship.

Although making changes in the school climate to support a more positive self-concept and better achievement for disadvantaged urban youngsters may be the most difficult aspect of education to effect, a number of general possibilities are open. Gordon Allport suggests three approaches appropriate for dealing with prejudice in a school setting.[45]

1. *Formal educational methods.* Almost every suggestion for improving the training of teachers over the past decade has included considerably more work in the sociology of minority groups, cultural anthropology, and courses in human relations. The assumption is clearly that by providing the urban teacher with more knowledge about the minority group and lower-class youngsters she will encounter in her work, her attitudes and expectations may be changed. Given the increased racial and socioeconomic segregation in urban areas of the United States, many middle- and lower-middle-class white students will have had little contact with minority group and lower-class children. This book, for example, hopes to provide prospective teachers with more information and understanding about students in the urban classroom.

Considering some of the irrational sources of prejudice discussed earlier in this chapter, it seems unlikely that an individual with strongly held prejudices will have his or her attitude fundamentally changed by an informational program. What seems more likely is that the educational approach may help retard the development of strongly prejudiced attitudes, particularly those which might develop from the initial culture shock of a middle-class teacher entering and working in a lower-class school.

2. *Contact and acquaintance programs.* The contact approach has also become a standard part of proposed revisions for teacher-education programs. Almost all of them include increased student-teacher participation in community activities, and in some cases actual residence in the community, designed to develop a much more profound awareness of the community which surrounds the lower-class school:

To be maximumly effective contact and acquaintance programs should lead to a sense of equality. Social status should occur in ordinary purposeful pursuits, avoid artificiality, and if possible enjoy the sanction of the community in which they occur. The deeper and more genuine the association the greater its effect. While it may help somewhat to place members of different ethnic groups side

45. Allport, *op. cit.*, pp. 448-456.

by side on a job, the gain is greater if these members regard themselves as part of a team.[46]

This quotation from Allport points to difficulties with programs for increased contact between prospective teachers and the residents of poor urban communities. It would be difficult to develop a sense of equality in social status between a prospective teacher and a poor uneducated parent in an urban ghetto. The avoidance of artificiality, too, presents some problem, since in almost all cases prospective teachers will not live in urban slum communities. Although contacts between teachers, prospective teachers, and the lower-class community are certainly to be encouraged, one should not expect from them dramatic and fundamental changes in the attitudes and expectations of teachers.

3. *Group retraining methods.* Perhaps this is the most hopeful program for changing attitudes and dealing with prejudice. Its applications to teachers and educators are quite obvious. Since this type of program can be carried out in the school and in the community, and since it can involve a number of teachers from the same school, its impact and effect on education might well be significant.

In recent years there has been a flood of specific proposals or actual programs to work on the problem of improving the self-concept of the minority group child from both the child's and the teacher's point of view. Some of the more promising of them are reviewed below.

ENHANCING THE CHILD'S SELF-IMAGE

Professor Jeanne Grambs clearly outlines the need when she says:

The Negro child from earliest school entry through graduation from high school needs continued opportunities to see himself and his racial group in a realistically positive light. He needs to understand what color and race mean. He needs to learn about those of his race and other disadvantaged groups who have succeeded. And he needs to clarify his understanding of his own group history and current group situations.[47]

There are clear implications here for the curriculum of the ghetto school; some attempts have already been made to introduce more meaningful and pertinent material into the urban school curriculum. Many of these are discussed in chapter 7.

46. *Ibid.*, p. 454.

47. Jean D. Grambs, "The Self-Concept: Basis for Reeducation of Negro Youth," in William C. Kvaraceus *et al.*, *Negro Self-Concept* (New York: McGraw-Hill, Inc., 1965), p. 21.

The curriculum approach may not necessarily represent an attack on the problem of self-concept directly. Given some of the evidence presented earlier in this chapter, which established the relationship between achievement and self-concept, it may be more effective to work directly on achievement, to provide material and to train teachers in ways which will increase directly the academic achievement of black youngsters. Success in school is likely to increase one's own concept about what one is able to do. Other educators suggest that first the self-concept must be dealt with before increased academic performance may be expected. Since the causal relationship between performance in school and self-concept is not at all clearly established, it may well be that we have here the classic chicken-and-egg argument.

In their book, *The Disadvantaged: Challenge to Education,* Fantini and Weinstein argue that the self-concept of black youngsters may be affected by increasing significantly the degree of student participation in school.[48] They point to evidence from the civil rights movement involving young black children in the South who seemed to develop considerably improved self-images through participation.

1. *Action involvement.* The children were placed in action roles through marches, demonstrations, going to jail, and even being beaten or molested by the police.
2. *Sense of power in numbers.* They belonged to a massive power movement and those in traditional power roles (white political structure) were forced to bargain and compromise. Children were acting on rather than being acted upon.
3. *Creative expression of discontent.* For a people who have had to keep so much resentment and frustration to themselves, the movement provided an outlet with support and channels through which discontent could be utilized for bettering existing conditions.
4. *Recognition.* They see themselves through the news media as heroes, as people who are battling to right a wrong, and who are being celebrated.
5. *Clarity of goals.* Almost every child interviewed was able to articulate the immediate and the long-term goal of the movement. "I want my mom to get paid the same as whites for the same work." "I want to be able to vote." "I don't want my children to be in the same mess." "Freedom: better jobs and better homes."[49]

They go on to conclude that "the objects and positive self concept and participation in a democratic society can be reached through a

48. Mario D. Fantini and Gerald Weinstein, *The Disadvantaged* (New York: Harper & Row, 1968).
49. *Ibid.,* p. 355.

school process which utilizes social action."[50] It should be pointed out that such a program introducing social action into the school curriculum would require a considerable degree of flexibility on the part of both teachers and school administrators. It needs to be pointed out that the assumption underlying the question is whether urban schooling can be made as exciting as civil rights activities, whether the excitement and involvement outlined can in fact be translated to the school setting and made an integral part of the learning process. The "learning is fun" concept is not widely supported by the psychology of learning. Nevertheless, in certain curriculum areas and for certain kinds of school projects or school-community projects, Fantini and Weinstein's suggestions may be helpful.

David and Pearl Ausabel discuss two structural changes in schools which they believe would play an important part in enhancing ego development (self-concept).[51] Desegregation, they admit, would be no panacea for problems of ego development or self-concept, and initially in some areas there might well be increased personality problems for black youngsters. In spite of these transitional problems they feel:

> . . . a desegregated school offers the Negro child his first taste of social equality and his first experience of first class citizenship. He can enjoy the stimulating effect of competition with white children and can use them as realistic yardsticks in measuring his own worth and changes for academic and vocational success. Under these circumstances educational achievement no longer seems so pointless and aspirations for higher occupational status in the wide culture acquire more substance.

Rather strangely, however, after making this strong statement, the Ausabels come out against "artificial attempts to end de facto school desegregation." They view it as not only impractical to transport youngsters from one school district to another but also as victimizing certain white children and thereby increasing racial tension. They conclude rather lamely by suggesting that "it seems more reasonable to work for the elimination of this type of school segregation by directly attacking its underlying cause and that is neighborhood segregation."[52]

Robert Coles, a psychiatrist who has studied black children both in the South and the North, disagrees.

> In general, what I have found is that children bussed across a northern city do quite well in school and manage increasingly well with their white classmates.

50. *Ibid.*, pp. 355, 356.

51. David P. Ausabel and Pearl Ausabel, "Ego Development among Segregated Negro Children," in A. Harry Passow (ed.), *Education in Depressed Areas* (New York: Bureau of Publications, Teachers College, Columbia University, 1963), pp. 109-141.

52. *Ibid.*, p. 131.

Like their southern counterparts these Negro children make do astonishingly well in schools clearly better than the ones they have left. They become leaders in both their families and their neighborhoods, sources of information about the "white world," children who "have been there," and return daily with stories to tell and examples to inspire. Academically some of these children have not only managed well but were found to be far brighter than anyone before had realized.

Others had needed to receive tutoring help from college students. The majority have done new and difficult work on their own and passed their tests well enough to get promoted and become better educated. "To tell the truth I think my Jean is talking a little white these days. Her accent I mean." Whether there is any glory in that particular achievement Jean and her mother feel more as her mother says it "at home" with the rest of the American people.

A portion of the rest of the American people feel more at home with Jean too. I have watched white children show these Negro children fear, distrust, suspicion and occasional outright nastiness. On the whole they were at first silent and guarded. But in a short time increasingly friendly and forgetful of racial distinctions. Friendships have been made and in general an atmosphere of mutual respect holds between the two groups of children. As one teacher put it, correcting my way of talking, "They are not two groups. Just one. Children at school here. I wouldn't have thought it so easy if it hadn't happened. I suppose after it happens it's easier than before. It's easier to solve a real problem than worry about one and be afraid of one that might happen."[53]

The Ausabels' second suggestion for enhancing ego development involves the whole problem of community action and community involvement in the school—written before the rapid growth of the black power movement in the United States and before specific attempts had been made to install programs of decentralization. They urge "the support of parents and of the Negro community at large, that must be enlisted if we hope to make permanent progress in the education of Negro children."[54] The relationship between the urban slum school and its community is analyzed in chapter 11. It is clearly the underlying assumption of both the black power advocates and more moderate leaders in black communities that school decentralization and/or community control will in fact lead directly to increased self-concept and enhanced ego development for black youngsters.

On the face of it these developments may seem to promise some success. However, since no urban school system has as yet been decentralized, there is really no evidence to support or contradict this contention.

53. Robert Coles, "When Northern Schools Desegregate," in Meyer Weinberg (ed.), *Integrated Education* (Beverly Hills, Calif.: Glencoe Press, 1968), p. 260.
54. Ausabel, *op. cit.*, p. 131.

CHANGING TEACHER ATTITUDES

Although we cannot describe or predict very accurately the nature of the relationship between teacher expectation and student performance it seems reasonable to assume it exists. This being the case, what can educators do to develop favorable and positive expectations toward disadvantaged youngsters? It must be admitted immediately that attitude change is extremely difficult to effect, especially in adults. Research in this area shows that although deep-set attitudes, beliefs, and expectations may be changed, the change requires considerable patience, time, and effort. Perhaps the most widely used techniques for attempting change of attitude is "human relations training" for teachers.

This training—offered under a variety of titles such as intergroup relations, human relations, group dynamics, or sensitivity training—is characterized by an attempt to open up, to explore, and eventually to change attitudes and expectations which will in turn lead to a future change in classroom behavior. There is evidence that this approach can be successful, particularly in intensive situations. The human-relations technique has been notably less successful with teachers in less-intensive situations, such as ordinary summer sessions or late afternoon or evening courses during the school year.

As an aid in evaluating the human-relations approach, we will examine one training program involving classroom teachers of the urban disadvantaged which was judged to be successful.

In the summer of 1965 at Hunter College in New York City an intensive six-week summer program was offered to forty-five elementary-school teachers from urban slum neighborhoods.[55] Funded by the U.S. Office of Education as one of seventy-five training institutes, the focus was directly on elementary teaching. The program was divided into four discrete blocks of time designed to accomplish specific purposes.

The first of these blocks was composed of a series of sensitivity-training sessions in the form of "T" groups, a learning device developed over the past fifteen years by the National Training Laboratory. These training sessions were set up as an unstructured series of discussions in which a skilled trainer helped the participants understand and deal with their own developing interactions and their accompanying feelings. The assumption was clearly that teachers who would understand and interpret their own interactions and feelings in a group such as this could presumably in the future translate this understanding in the classroom setting.

The second major block of time consisted of a teaching practicum

55. Harry L. Miller, "Human Relations Institute for Teachers of Disadvantaged Children," in Bruce W. Tuckman and John L. O'Brien (eds.), *Preparing to Teach the Disadvantaged* (New York: The Free Press, 1969), pp. 243-256.

in which the participants worked under supervision with a group of children recruited for the summer from a nearby elementary school. The second time block was divided into input sessions preceding the actual work with children and devoted to examining available curriculum materials, conferring with visiting specialists and attending staff lectures on curriculum and teaching methods for the disadvantaged child; and planning sessions for a period of four weeks, working with children from disadvantaged areas, testing new materials and approaches. The sessions were held in the morning, one day a week, concentrating on a particular aspect of the task. Each participant was also asked to keep a diary describing his or her experiences with the children, making notes on progress and results of any experimentation with materials and methods. The practicum clearly allowed these students to practice insights gained in the T groups, as they developed their relationships with the children.

The third block of time, a series of lecture discussions, was devoted to research and theory available on the social, cultural, and psychological roots of problems in the disadvantaged child's schooling. These sessions were based on assigned reading in a specially organized library of books and journal articles through which students were encouraged to browse. On several occasions visiting specialists were invited to speak on a specific body of experimental research.

The fourth block of work focused on the relationship between the slum school and its community. Sessions were held at the college with visiting community experts discussing neighborhood problems, while others were held in Harlem and Bedford-Stuyvesant in New York City where the students visited a variety of social centers and talked with local residents.

The forty-five participants in this summer institute were chosen from over seven hundred applications. Selections were made on a variety of criteria. Each applicant was first given a rating representing weighted scores based on teaching experience, academic record, principal's recommendation, the interest expressed by the principal in making use of the teacher's institute experience, and a statement by the applicant about how he or she intended to use this experience. The original intention had been to select at least two teachers from the same school on the assumption that this team would support one another in changing practices in the school during the next academic year. However, using the composite scores mentioned above, it proved impossible to form such teams. The eventual selection included only eight two-person teams and one five-member team from the school in which the practicum was to be conducted.

The available evidence, both subjective and objective, suggests that this particular human-relations training institute succeeded in at least its immediate purpose, although there was no follow-up study available to ascertain whether or not the training made a difference in classroom behavior. Two objective measures before and after the institute assessed the impact of the T-group experience. An instrument was administered which was composed of a series of incidents involving minority group members from which the respondent was to select a statement he thought would most accurately describe the feelings of the person involved. Comparing the before and after scores, there was a clear trend in the desired direction, but the scores on the pretest were so high that the change was not statistically significant (which means that although the trend was in the right direction, it is quite likely that the change was due to chance). This probably points to a high level of awareness on the part of urban teachers in matters of race relations. Indeed, the evaluator reports that several members of the group confessed during the institute that they had not recorded their real judgment on this initial instrument.

The second objective instrument used attempted to measure changes in two variables: willingness to be open about one's own feelings with pupils, colleagues, and superiors; and willingness to give other persons in these categories feedback about one's own feelings about them. In both variables of openness and feedback the results were in the desired direction and were statistically significant at the 5 percent level. (This means that the probability of the observed change being due to chance was less than 5 percent.)

Subjective evidence supported the conclusion from this data. Individual comments by participants indicated that they found the experiences during the institute powerful and awakening. The most frequently heard complaint about the institute on the part of both staff and students was, however, that there was simply not enough time available to accomplish objectives. At the end of the institute the participants were asked to reevaluate a questionnaire which they had completed during the first week, and indicate whether they would now add to, delete, or change the original emphasis of any of their statements. The alterations showed an overwhelming trend toward recognizing the need for sensitivity and understanding. Changes included "more sensitivity," "understanding of the culture," "know one's self better," "accept the child as he is," "understand how the child learns." Another noticeable trend was reflected in responses which moved into the area of what the school, and particularly the teacher, could do about the achievement problem. This represented a change from the belief that the problems lie completely outside the school in the child's community and culture. The amendments included such statements as "teachers should have faith in the potential of a child," "handicaps should be a challenge," "schools should provide more relevant and meaningful materials in the curriculum." There was also a considerable shift in the direction of differentiating among disadvantaged children as a group and a rejection of stereotyping. One participant, for example, deleted his original comment that "they are not appreciative of what the school tries to do for them." He made a marginal note: "That's patronizing."

The evaluation of this six-week institute concluded with a set of recommendations for training programs with a human-relations focus.

SOME RECOMMENDATIONS FOR INSTITUTES WITH A HUMAN-RELATIONS FOCUS

Viewed as a whole the outcomes of this institute would encourage an emphasis on human relations training in summer programs for teachers of the disadvantaged with the following changes made in the pattern described.

A. Radically changed recruiting procedure by restricting participants to four or five schools with sympathetic and interested principals from which teams of eight to ten teachers could be recruited and to include some supervisors. This recruiting procedure would radically change the design of human relations training in addition to other changes which seem appropriate. The T groups would now be "family groups" and would address themselves to school problems where they are relevant as well as to personal growth and self understanding.

B. The training period should exclusively occupy the first ten days or two weeks of the institute and take place in a residential setting. Two weeks is preferable for it would permit some work on the conditions for creativity.

C. The second two weeks should focus on two activities: input or theory, research and precept; and intensive planning sessions in small groups for the coming classroom sessions, using visiting experts for periods of from two to three days, not only to make presentations but to sit in with planning groups and help them to develop ideas for experimental procedures and demonstration lessons.

D. A third two-week period in a practicum in classrooms during the morning and review groups during the afternoon. Ideally a group of regular summer elementary schools which are relatively close to one another should be made available for this period with the staff teachers prepared for the two-week invasion. If the institute participants work in teams of four, ten or eleven regular classes will be all that is required. One might be able to arrange these in two or three schools. The supervisory staff should not have too great difficulty covering that number of classes regularly.

E. A three or four day additional period for general evaluation and reporting would be useful, bringing the total time for the institute to about six and a half weeks, slightly longer than the one described. The budget would not be markedly higher if one could obtain the necessary staff only for the period when the need for special talents is indicated.[56]

Recommended Reading

The classic and still valid survey of prejudice is Gordon Allport's *The Nature of Prejudice* (New York: Anchor Books, 1958), available in a slightly abridged edition. Kenneth B. Clark's *Prejudice and Your Child* (Boston: The Beacon Press, 1963) is a useful survey of the impact of racial prejudice.

The Autobiography of Malcolm X (New York: Grove Press, Inc., 1966) offers an excellent case history of a radically changed self-image. *Two Blocks Apart* (New York: Avon Books, 1966) provides an interesting contrast of self-perception from a lower-class Puerto Rican and a middle-class Irish youth growing up in New York City. *Negro Self-Concept* by William Kvaraceus *et al.* (New York: McGraw-Hill, Inc., 1965), is a useful collection of educational thinking on the problems of minority group self-concept. Mario Fantini and Gerald Weinstein in *The Disadvantaged: Challenge to Education,* chapter 10 (New York: Harper & Row, 1968), describe ways in which a relevant curriculum can lead to improved self-concept and better learning. *Racial Isolation in the Public Schools* (A Report of the United States Commission on Civil Rights, Washington, D.C., 1967) deals critically with educational programs that have so far attempted to raise minority group youngsters' self-concepts.

A good general survey on the problems of minority groups is provided by Milton Barron in *Minorities in a Changing World* (New York: Alfred A. Knopf, 1967).

56. *Ibid.,* pp. 255-256.

PART II

The Schools and Their Communities

6

CURRICULUM AND THE URBAN SCHOOL

Up to this point we have looked primarily at the influence on levels of school achievement of factors that, in the main, are not under the control of the educational institution. We have seen how massive social determinants—such as class and ethnicity, migration and urban milieu—affect family environment and self-concept in ways that appear to account for a very considerable part of the academic retardation of lower-class city children and particularly black ghetto children. In this chapter we turn to a concentration on what the school itself can do to modify the results of these social forces; this is the concern of the remainder of the book.

One might well ask, after reading the preceding chapters, whether such powerful forces *can* be modified by a single institution, particularly if it is a relatively weak one. Family environment generally, and self-concept among black children in particular, appear to account for so considerable a proportion of the variation in school achievement that only a minor portion is left out. There are several more optimistic views of the situation that one can take. One is that even accepting the upper limit of family influence on school achievement of, say, two-thirds, there is still a third of the variation in achievement to be accounted for.

An even more hopeful position may be stated in this way: Family and personal factors correlate so well with school success primarily because the school does little to change the odds for those children who come to it with background handicaps. If it made a strenuous effort to compensate for those deficiencies, instead of routinely accepting them, the picture would change.

This chapter and succeeding ones will examine this possibility in detail, in a review of the influence on urban school achievement of curriculum, teaching, administration and organization of the school, school population mixture, and school-community relations; assessing the programs for change in these areas as well as the yet-to-be tried proposals for change.

CONCEPTS: CURRICULUM

What the term *curriculum* actually stands for varies with the user. Some educators have recently contended that it includes everything the school does that influences its sought-after outcomes: materials, teaching, extracurricular activities, administration, and even architecture. But to take such an all-inclusive view does not preclude the necessity of looking at separate aspects of the schools, if only for the sake of clarity, and little seems to be gained by considering them all together.

For present purposes, curriculum is treated as the instructional objectives of the school, the ways in which these outcomes are allocated in specific sequences, and learning materials provided to aid in their achievement. Both administration and methods of instruction will be reserved for later treatment, though it is not always easy to find a clear dividing line between teaching and curriculum.

The aims of the American public school are partly the result of a long historical development that has left significant residues in the present curriculum. The early and prolonged domination of education by Protestant churches, so prominent in the settlement of the country, is still visible in the moral tone of some education objectives and in the stress on character development in the schools. So the schools have always been blamed for any presumed lack of virtue among the youth of any generation.

As the domination of the church declined, generally after the Revolution, and the secular national state was established, the school was increasingly influenced by the business community that was becoming more powerful in society generally. The shift occasioned no conflict because leaders of organized religion saw businessmen as their natural allies. They shared the set of values that Max Weber called the "Protestant Ethic," which still profoundly influences the aims of the school. That ethic consists primarily of the values that were earlier described as those of the lower middle class: success, social mobility, the moral virtue of work, individualism, responsibility, and respect for authority.

Business influence on the school, which began in earnest in the last third of the 19th century, resulted not only in a stress on training the young in these values, so consonant with the needs of business and industrial organizations, it was also instrumental in a curriculum shift toward more vocational training and the development of white-collar skills increasingly necessary to the business enterprise.

In this century the federal government has become powerful enough to influence the form of the curriculum of an educational system that is constitutionally subject only to the authority of the states. The national interest, for example, or at least one view of the national interest, dictated in the fifties an increased emphasis on mathematics and science to enable the nation to compete with the Soviet Union. Whether the schools succeeded in imbuing youth with a proper spirit of patriotism has also been a recurrent issue in 20th century education. And few social studies teachers risk presenting the "other side" of international disputes to which the United States has been a party.

In a sense, to describe these forces as influences on the public school curriculum is to mistake the case; they represent major changes in the shape of the society as a whole; and as our society is, so are the schools. A society whose mainstream still respects the moral values of the Protestant Ethic, is strongly nationalistic, and puts a premium on the material progress that is based on a prospering economy will naturally use a tax-supported school system to support these values. The arguments about whether or not the public school should seek *these* general outcomes, however, occur primarily between members of the public and the more sophisticated schoolmen who perceive that the society itself is undergoing change and that the schools must follow suit.

Among educators the main curriculum conflict is put in somewhat different terms. There have been varying ideas about what outcomes the school should emphasize during the past century, but the majority of them are variants of two major positions. Since it is these two that provide the foundation for the clearest conflict over what the curriculum of the urban school should be, the discussion at this point will ignore some minor but important differences between the variations and present a simplified version of the conflict. To avoid the risk of confusion with systematic philosophical analysis, the positions will be described as *rationalist* and *developmental.*

The rationalist view, although surely the more conservative of the two, is by no means an enemy of change; it does, however, recognize that the question of what is taught in the school must take account of the present shape of the society and of the variety of forces moving in it. Any rational curriculum must find an accommodation between three often different demands: the needs of the individual child, the needs of the community and of the larger society, and the requirements of academic tradition. No one argues about whether the elementary school should teach reading (except, perhaps, Paul Goodman), because in this instance all three demands agree—the child needs to read if he is to become a productive and participating member of his society; a highly developed technical society needs literate workers; and, without the ability to read, most of the accumulated knowledge of the past is unavailable. The cases of history, foreign languages, or even geometry are not similarly clearcut.

The rationalist assumes that the human animal and his social institutions tend to have a great deal of stability and drag, despite the appearance of very rapid change. Much of what seems to be change may turn out to be trivial fad; even in the world of fashion, where the pace of change appears to be dizzying, he might point out that there are only three basic dress shapes that have reappeared throughout history. Despite environmental variations, the games of power, love, war, authority, status, and other basics of human life recur in relatively familiar patterns, though in fresh outward guise, in each generation.

This view has several important consequences for curriculum development. First, if the most fundamentally important things do not change very much, the experienced elder has the right and, indeed, the responsibility of deciding what the young person most needs to learn. Youths should certainly be permitted to make individual choices where it is reasonable for them to do so—their own vocational and career preferences, for example, the pursuit of any special interest in a particular discipline, and the like. But, because adults know the society into which youths must move, have better information about the problems they will confront, and have already mastered some part of the heritage of the past, they ought certainly to do a wiser job of selecting the desired outcomes of schooling.

Second, the accumulated experience of the past is an invaluable resource for understanding present problems and present situations. So, an uninformed observer of a clash between the presidential and congressional branches of the government may ridicule a system in which no one seems to have enough power to get some important end accomplished. The rationalist would point out that the framers of the Constitution had considered a wide variety of political structures and had decided that, given the disputatious nature of men generally, it was best not to give any one source of authority too much power. The ability of many to block the desires of some may be frustrating, but such a situation was, they were persuaded, less harmful than one in which it was easy for the representative of one particular interest to sweep away all opposition.

Past experience with recurrent problems of man often seems of little use to the young, who tend to see all problems as fresh and new; for them only the present seems very meaningful. The rationalist, realizing this, does not hesitate to build curricula about subject matter and materials that are of no immediate interest to the learner. In his view there is no substitute for knowledge if one is to form judgments or come to decisions about any important matter. To understand the stories on the front page of a day's edition of the *New York Times* requires some background in political history, geography, the structure of government, labor laws, and the principles of ethics and economics. So, for example, the child may not understand why it will be important to know about far-away countries, but the adult can, and he should induce the student to learn geography.

Within this general framework a number of significantly different curriculum viewpoints may be found. Some stress the further importance of acquiring basic intellectual skills necessary to utilize knowledge: the processes of rational thought, problem-solving abilities, critical analysis, and so forth. Others focus on the need to prepare youth for vocational or professional life. In any case, the assumptions are that the school must prepare the young for productive and participating life in the society in which they will find themselves, and that the school has a rather good idea of what they will need in order to live the good life in that society.

A similarly extreme version of the *developmental* view would start with individual needs, paying little attention to either the needs of society or the demands of academic tradition. The total growth of the child, not merely his intellectual development, is the major consideration; and since no individual grows as any other, one must begin with the individual child and understand how he sees the world, what his particular interests and needs are, what stimulation he needs to grow in his particular way.

A significantly different perspective on man and his social environment is fundamental to this perspective. Instead of explaining the recurrent problems of the race as due to the nature of the human animal himself, the developmentalist is likely to perceive them as the result of consistently bad social arrangements. War is caused by the desire of the few in social authority who want wealth or power, not by any fundamental aggressiveness in man. There is abundant evidence from the study of primitive cultures that in a society which underplays aggression, hostility, and competition men live in harmonious cooperation.

A structured curriculum that prepares the child to live in the present social order, then, is destructive in a number of ways. First, it teaches him to adapt to an environment that is essentially dehumanizing, that is likely to prevent the growth of his truly human capabilities for love and cooperative behavior and demand that he be competitive and work toward goals imposed on him by the society rather than those which he finds meaningful. One special emphasis within the developmental perspective suggests that the school's role is to prepare youth to *reconstruct* the social order.

Second, a structured curriculum impedes the child's growth generally by restricting his self-determination. The developmental view sees as the end product of growth the greatest possible realization of the unique self, the emergence of all that is latent and potential in any person, the flowering of his emotional and intellectual capacities. Such a self-realizing individual is not only capable of richly satisfying relationships with other people but of deciding what he wants to do with his life, what is important to him. He is able to resist social pressures and thus can play a creative social role as well, helping to move the society to restructure itself in more human terms.

To impose the will of others on the child in regard to what he must learn is clearly the worst preparation for this person. What one learns becomes a part of oneself; to insist that a child learn something because an adult thinks it is important, though it does not interest him, is to deny the child the right to determine what his self shall become. It forces him to form himself in the adult's image rather than as his own unique person.

The developmental curriculum, then, is less a curriculum than a prescription for a series of experiences in which the child is helped to understand himself and his relations with others, and in which he can grope toward a continuing and growing definition of selfhood. As he does so, he is enabled to make his own decisions about what he wants to do, how he wishes to relate to the larger society and to his own future. The characteristics of such a curriculum, though not its content, are relatively easy to deduce from its assumptions. It is highly individualized and varied; it begins at all times with the immediate interests and problems of the child; and the desired outcomes are perceived in terms of psychological processes and states rather than in specified behaviors or intellectual abilities.

Though the rationalist view can accommodate itself fairly easily to the public-school institution that resulted from an historical development described earlier, the developmental position is strongly at odds with such a system. It becomes relevant to the education of the city slum child, as we shall see, only at the point at which one begins to consider the total reconstruction of the city school as it now exists.

CURRICULUM EXPERIMENTATION AND THE HAWTHORNE EFFECT

Most of the funds provided for urban schools in the last decade for the specific purpose of improving the academic retardation of lower-class minority youngsters have been used for curriculum changes: giving very young children special kinds of preparatory experiences, or emphasizing one part of the curriculum over another, or developing new curriculum materials. Much of the remainder of this chapter will consist of assessments of one or another such experimental variation. An understanding of some major pitfalls in all experiments with school populations is essential for any judgment of the results of those experiments; particularly important is a grasp of the possible influence of the experimental conditions themselves.

Innovations in education are particularly susceptible to the Hawthorne effect (described in the preceding chapter) because children are very sensitive to variations in the amount of attention being paid to them. For example: Several years ago there was much public stir about the effectiveness of the "talking typewriter" in teaching disadvantaged children to read. The device consists of a special typewriter connected to a computer that is programmed to interact with the child. The child, on instruction, types a word; the machine can type a response either telling him that he is correct or providing the necessary correction. David Rosenhan repeated the early experiments with only one change. All of the adults involved were instructed not to pay much attention to the children as they worked with the machine, to treat the entire situation matter-of-factly. There were, this time, no newspaper photographers popping flashbulbs, no reporters interviewing the children, no proudly beaming adults watching. Under these conditions the children made no greater progress than they might be expected to have made in the average classroom.[1]

As we examine the curriculum ferment in the urban school the general issue of methodology and the particular influence of the Hawthorne effect will play an important role in the assessment.

THE EFFECT OF THE SCHOOL ON THE ACHIEVEMENT OF THE DISADVANTAGED CHILD

Before proceeding to examine curriculum innovation for the urban school an important general question must be confronted directly: Do any aspects of the school itself have much of a chance of influencing achievement, given the powerful predictive force of social class and family environment?

In the minds of the general public such a question seems nonsensical; the layman assumes (an assumption unfortunately shared by some professional educators) that any positive change in a school characteristic will automatically better the achievement level of the students. Lay

1. David L. Rosenhan, "Cultural Deprivation and Learning" (paper presented at the Annual Meeting of the American Educational Research Association, February 12, 1968, mimeo).

judgments of the effectiveness of a school system are likely to be based on any visible or dramatic feature of the schools. But the effect on pupil achievement level of any particular school characteristic is, in reality, not very well understood; several major studies have attempted to answer this question—with ambiguous results. One set of answers comes from the nationwide sample of schools represented in Project Talent, described earlier; another set from a survey conducted by James Coleman for the U.S. Office of Education was intended to give definitive data on the extent to which we provide equal educational opportunity. Because the Coleman study has aroused a wide-ranging controversy, this section will focus on its findings, with some reference to other relevant data that either support or contradict it.[2]

Coleman's sample of schools is representative of the range of schools nationally, though a number of them failed to return his detailed questionnaires. It has been argued that these losses from the sample seriously affect the conclusions of the study, but Coleman is probably correct in saying that since the nonrespondents did not differ substantially from those schools that returned questionnaires the data is representative of the whole population of schools.

The basic idea of the study was to examine the "inputs" the school provides in the form of curriculum, facilities, teaching, pupil recruitment, and so on and compare them with the "outputs" of the system in the form of achievement differences. As Moynihan puts it, "in effect, the Coleman study was intended to prove beyond further question two central theses of the reform establishment: first that school facilities available to minorities were shockingly unequal; and second, that this accounted for unequal outcomes."[3] In fact, as chapter 9 will show, it did not find the first of these to be very strikingly true; as for the second, the data seem to indicate that nothing about the school program itself has a very great effect on the achievement of pupils. To summarize:

1. For both white and minority group children facilities and curriculum had least effect on achievement; teacher quality has a somewhat greater influence, but not very much greater; the educational background of fellow students had the most influence (*see* chapter 9 for a discussion of this last finding).

2. Differences in any of these aspects of the school are more influential for black children than they are for whites; that is, it makes less difference if a white child attends a school with good facilities and good teachers than it does for his black counterpart.

2. James Coleman, *Equality of Educational Opportunity* (Washington, D.C.: U.S. Department of Health, Education and Welfare, U.S. Government Printing Office, 1966).

3. Daniel P. Moynihan, "Sources of Resistance to the Coleman Report," *Harvard Educational Review,* Vol. 38, No. 1 (Winter 1968), p. 26.

The general conclusion of the report was not to dispute earlier findings of a relationship between school inputs and achievement results but to suggest that its influence was much less great than most people assumed. To accept the findings as valid one would have to conclude, with Coleman, that equality of educational opportunity means much more than merely providing the same resources; it requires substantially *greater* efforts for those who come to school educationally handicapped.

A number of educators have refused, however, to accept the findings as presented. Their criticisms of the report are varied and in many cases technical:

1. The survey was forced to use a number of indirect measures that substitute for direct observation or measurement. Forty-five measures were used, for example, that described the school itself, but there was no direct measure of such a variable as teacher quality; it had to be inferred from a variety of indirect data such as the teacher's estimate of the quality of the college he attended, his years of experience, his highest degree received, and his score on a verbal test. Pupils were asked whether they had an encyclopedia at home, which was used as one way of inferring parental interest in the education of their children. Such indirect measures introduce a good deal of uncertainty into any final interpretation of results.

2. A major attack has been mounted on the way Coleman analyzed his data. (The Appendix provides an example of the multiple regression analysis he used.) He began his analysis by first computing the correlation between socioeconomic status and achievement, then held the first factor constant while looking at the influence of school inputs. When the social background is controlled first, the school resources add very little predictive power to the analysis. Samuel Bowles has shown that if you control for school resources first, then look at what is contributed by social background, you get radically different results than if school resources are not so controlled. The amount of variation in achievement scores of twelfth grade black students that is explained by "teachers' verbal ability" more than doubles if one runs the analysis that way. Bowles explains why:

Both approaches, however, give misleading results. Let me try to explain why this is so. Assume that we want to predict the weight of children on the basis of knowledge of both their age and their height. Because heights and ages of children are closely associated, we can predict a child's weight if we know only his age nearly as well as when we know both his height and his age. If we can read the analysis the other way around, i.e., first controlled for height and then investigated the additional predictive power associated with the variable age, the result would be of course reversed. We would find very little additional predictive power associated with age.

A similar statistical difficulty arises in the Coleman analysis because the level of resources devoted to the child's education and the child's own social background are not independent. When we control for the social class of the student, we implicitly control also for some part of the variation in school resources. . . By choosing to control first for social-background factors, the authors of the report inadvertently biased its analysis against finding school resources to be an important determinant of scholastic achievement.[4]

A reanalysis of the Coleman data currently underway should provide us with a new view of the influence of school resources, though it is likely, as Bowles points out, to be an overestimate in the opposite direction and should be interpreted cautiously.

3. The weakness of the school's influence found by Coleman is further attacked on the basis that it contradicts earlier studies of the relation between school factors and achievement. In fact, the findings of Project Talent, in comparing school characteristics and student achievement in the five largest cities, tend to support Coleman, because the relationships turned out to be contradictory. Thus, in this study, per-pupil expenditures were indeed more important for low-income students than for others; the correlations are .46 and .07 respectively. Teacher experience is also significant; the correlation between English achievement and teacher experience is .55 among low-income students, and only .16 for middle-income students.[5]

But, other common-sense assumptions, as Goldstein's survey points out, are not supported by this data:

Low income students, for example, do *better* (in English achievement) the larger the class sizes ($r = .54$); the *larger* the senior class ($r = .71$); the *fewer* the study halls provided ($r = -.48$); the *fewer* the books in the library ($r = -.12$); the *lower* the starting salaries for teachers ($r = -.13$); the *more* students on double schedules ($r = .16$); the higher the dropout rate ($r = .20$); and the *lower* the participation of parents in PTA ($r = -.32$).

In nearly all those cases, the findings for higher income students are the the reverse, or are that the variable makes no difference. . . We do not suggest that these correlations are to be taken seriously as indications of what does and what does not make for academic achievement among low- and middle-income students; only that, manifestly, we have not begun to understand the factors that do.[6]

4. Samuel Bowles, "Towards Equality of Educational Opportunity?", *Harvard Educational Review,* Vol. 38, No. 1 (Winter 1968), pp. 92-93.

5. Bernard Goldstein, *Low Income Youth in Urban Areas* (New York: Holt, Rinehart and Winston, Inc., 1967), p. 43.

6. *Ibid.,* pp. 43-44.

Nevertheless, other critics have pointed out that a number of studies fairly consistently find that per-pupil expenditure and teacher experience, to take only two factors, have substantial effects on achievement. The results of Samuel Goodman's New York State study based on the records of 70,000 pupils in a representative sample of schools in the state are shown in Table 6.1. Even with the usual high relation between socioeconomic status and achievement, several school factors have significant associations with achievement. Henry Dyer cites additional data from several other studies, but not all of it substantiates his thesis that such important factors as teacher experience and per-pupil expenditure really make a difference.[7] One of those he describes, the Mollenkopf and Melville study of one hundred schools, found the influence of teacher experience to be negligible, and the other did not specifically analyze for these school factors.

Table 6.1 Correlations of Certain School Factors with Pupil Achievement and Socioeconomic Status

Variable	Correlation with composite achievement score at grade 7: Raw correlation	Correlation with composite achievement score at grade 7: Partial correlation (SES partialled out)
Teacher experience	.56	,37
Per-pupil expenditure	.51	.31
Special staff per 1000 pupils	.24	.12
Classroom atmosphere*	.24	.23
Socioeconomic status of parents	.61	—

* "Classroom atmosphere" is a measure of the degree to which a school is rated "subject-centered" vs. "child-centered," the ratings being based on an instrument known as *The Growing Edge* by P. R. Mort *et al.* (New York: Metropolitan Study Council, 1957).

SOURCE: Henry R. Dyer, "School Factors and Equal Educational Opportunity," *Harvard Educational Review,* Vol. 38, No. 1 (Winter 1968), p. 43.

One of Dyer's major criticisms of the Coleman study, however, must be taken seriously. He points out that Coleman measured school achievement by testing verbal ability at various school levels; since this ability is difficult to change radically, he argues that "Coleman's analysis probably makes for an underestimate of the importance of factors that school systems do in fact control."[8] In support of this view he cites Shaycroft's

7. Henry R. Dyer, "School Factors and Equal Educational Opportunity," *Harvard Educational Review,* Vol. 38, No. 1 (Winter 1968), pp. 38-56.
8. *Ibid.,* p. 46.

longitudinal study of some of the Project Talent data that uses achievement in actual curriculum areas such as literature, mathematics, art, accounting, mechanics, and electricity. Not only do students show substantial growth in these subjects through the course of their schooling but, with socioeconomic status controlled, students in some schools learn more or improve their ability more than in other schools.

Although Dyer and his fellow critics can hardly be said to have made an overwhelming case for the faultiness of Coleman's conclusions, it is a strong enough one to merit serious consideration of the question: "Suppose the Coleman study underestimates the effectiveness of school characteristics in influencing pupil effectiveness, what are the implications?"

Oddly enough, two of the severest critics of the Coleman findings answer that objection rather pessimistically. After his devastating attack on the statistical methodology of the study, Bowles remarks:

> The same evidence mentioned earlier suggests that were we merely to raise the quality of the teaching resources devoted to the education of Negroes to the level of that currently devoted to whites, we would significantly improve Negro achievement. Nevertheless, we would reduce the gap in Negro and white verbal achievement at grade 12 by only a little more than a quarter.[9]

Dyer answers it in a very interesting way. Since it is probable that the actual correlations between measures of school characteristics and achievement are too low, he argues that it might be useful to take a very lenient view of their significance. He proceeds by disregarding the socioeconomic status correction factor and then looking through the raw correlations between school characteristics and achievement. He accepts as significant *any* school characteristic that correlated .20 or better with any one or more of the three achievement measures—reading, mathematics, and general information—in any one of the eight ethnic categories at either grade 6 or grade 9. In his words: "This may seem like an excessively lenient acceptance criterion, but in view of the probable amount of noise in the basic data, a considerable amount of leniency is needed if one is to identify any school variables at all that might be worth speculating about."[10]

The procedure turned out to be very useful, as Tables 6.2 and 6.3 indicate. For one thing, it is clear that school characteristics make considerably more difference for some of the minority group youngsters than they do for the white majority. Fourteen items have an influence on Puerto Rican achievement, for example, and only two of them for the Northern white group.

9. Bowles, *op. cit.,* p. 95.
10. Dyer, *op. cit.,* p. 50.

Table 6.2 Correlates of Pupil Achievement* (grades 6 and 9)

School characteristics†	*Groups of Pupils* Mexican-Americans	Puerto Ricans	Indian-Americans	Oriental-Americans	Negroes North	Negroes South	Whites North	Whites South	Total
Student body characteristics									
Proportion of pupils with encyclopedia in the home	X	X	X	X		X			5
Proportion of school's graduates in college		X							1
Proportion in college prep curriculum	X	X	X	X		X		X	6
Average attendance as percentage of enrollment	X	X							2
Proportion of pupils who are white	X	X	X						3
Average number of white pupils in preceding year	X	X	X						3
Mean nonverbal test score	X	X	X	X	X	X	X	X	8
Mean verbal test score	X	X	X	X	X	X	X	X	8
Proportion of pupils who think teacher expects their best work	X	X							2
Proportion of pupils whose mothers went to college			X					X	2

Table 6.2 Correlates of Pupil Achievement*(*continued*)

School characteristics†	Groups of Pupils								
	Mexican-Americans	Puerto Ricans	Indian-Americans	Oriental-Americans	Negroes North	Negroes South	Whites North	Whites South	Total
Characteristics of instructional personnel									
Teacher's estimate of quality of own college	X	X		X					3
Teacher's verbal score	X	X	X	X		X			5
Teacher's race	X	X	X	X					4
Teacher's preference for teaching middle class	X		X						2
Teacher's attitude toward integration	X	X	X						3
Teacher's salary		X		X		X			3
Finances and program									
Per-pupil expenditure				X					1
Comprehensiveness of curriculum				X	X				2
Mathematics offering	X		X						2
Totals	14	14	12	10	3	6	2	4	

* Based on data in the *Supplemental Appendix to the Survey on Equality of Education Opportunity* (Washington, D.C.: Office of Education, 1966).

† An *X* in any column indicates that the school characteristic in question correlates 0.2 or higher with one or more achievement test variables at either grade 6 or grade 9 or both.

SOURCE: Henry R. Dyer, "School Factors and Equal Educational Opportunity," *Harvard Educational Review,* Vol. 38, No. 1 (Winter 1968), p. 49.

Table 6.3 Noncorrelates of Pupil Achievement (grades 6 and 9)

Student body characteristics
Number of twelfth-grade pupils
Pupil mobility (transfers in and out)
Average hours pupils spend on homework
Proportion of pupils who read over 16 books the preceding summer
Teacher's perception of quality of student body
Proportion of students whose mothers expect their best work
Characteristics of instructional personnel
Teacher's socioeconomic status
Teacher's experience
Teacher's localism
Teacher's highest degree received
Teacher's absences
Amount of teacher turnover
Availability of guidance counselors
Pupil-teacher ratio
Program, facilities, other
Extracurricular offerings
Tracking
Movement between tracks
Accelerated curriculum
Policy on promotion of slow learners
Foreign language offering
Number of days in session
Length of school day
Number of science labs
Volumes per pupil in school library
School location (urban-rural)
Teacher's perception of quality of school

SOURCE: Henry R. Dyer, "School Factors and Equal Educational Opportunity," *Harvard Educational Review,* Vol. 38, No. 1 (Winter 1968), p. 50.

A second striking feature of the table of influential characteristics is that most of the items have to do with the characteristics of the *people* who are in the school, both pupils and teachers. Dyer's conclusions are:

A comparison of these functional items with the non-functional items in Table III suggests that closing the educational gap between the white majority and the colored minorities is going to require more social and educational imagination and sustained effort than has hitherto been typical of most school systems.

It is fairly obvious that the school characteristics that turn out to be non-functional are the *easy-to-change* characteristics. As a consequence, over the next decade or two, educators will no doubt be having to fight off pressures from without and temptations from within to try to achieve instant improvement by pouring money and effort into the easy-to-change non-functioning features of school systems (the paper credentials, the readily purchasable gimmicks) at the expense of the hard-to-change features that in the long run are more likely to make a real difference in what children become.[11]

This tough-minded conclusion is very considerably substantiated by a critical examination of the efforts at compensatory education, to which we now turn.

COMPENSATORY PROGRAMS FOR THE DISADVANTAGED CHILD

By the last half of the decade of the fifties the population changes in the central cities, combined with the growing strength of the civil rights movement, turned national attention to the urban schools' difficulties. In the early years of the sixties a great many academic conferences were held and reports written about what must be done. During this period the term "compensatory education" was coined, its meaning clearly implying a diagnosis as well as a remedy for the problem. If the lower-class child, and particularly the lower-class black child, did not do well in school because of environmentally induced deficits in training and language, then the school must compensate for these deficits with special programs aimed at overcoming them specifically.

By the middle of the decade, spurred by substantial federal grants, a large number of compensatory programs went into effect in many of the urban school systems throughout the country. By this writing, although few of these projects have been rigorously evaluated, enough of them have reported results in some form of systematic assessment to provide evidence on which to base a tentative conclusion of their effectiveness.

First, a review of the most common features of these efforts to compensate, as they emerge from wide-ranging surveys:[12]

Reading and language development. This constitutes perhaps the major emphasis in most programs and includes the use of specially trained reading teachers; the extension of time devoted to reading in-

11. *Ibid.*, p. 51.

12. Edmund S. Gordon and Doxey A. Wilkerson, *Compensatory Education for the Disadvantaged* (New York: College Entrance Examination Board, 1966).

struction; the development of special materials presumed to be of interest to the disadvantaged child; and, for those youngsters who do not speak English, special methods and materials for developing bilingualism.

Several innovations of more than common interest are worth noting. One of these is the use of a special alphabet to teach reading, the Initial Teaching Alphabet (ITA). It assumes that much of the difficulty in learning to read, particularly with children who lack verbal backgrounds, is because the English language is confusingly complex, with a number of sounds that are written in different ways—the "u" sound in "you" and "yew," for example. In ITA any symbol is sounded in one and only one way; once a child has learned to read, he seldom finds it difficult to make the shift from ITA to the ordinary alphabet.

A great deal of money has been devoted to the effort of making reading materials less alien for the minority group child. One of the most widespread early criticisms of the urban ghetto school had been that reader illustrations gave the black child little opportunity to identify. Almost without exception they pictured white, blond children who lived in suburban homes or in the country, occasionally visiting granddaddy's farm. Not only were they offensively and misleadingly one-sided racially—implying the nonexistence of anyone with brown, black, or yellow skin—but they presented a remarkably innocuous image of life, devoid of trouble, fear, passion, pain, or reality. Many new reading series have since appeared, of widely varying quality; some of them, unhappily, have merely colored the skins of a few of the children without much other change, but there are some very good new readers as well.

Changes in teacher allocation. A wide variety of practices have been developed to deploy teaching resources more effectively, among them team teaching and the ungraded class. The first of these, by assigning two or three or four teachers to a class, permits a more flexible use of teacher time and encourages individualized or small-group instruction for children needing special help, while other members of the teaching team are supervising activities appropriate for a large group.

The ungraded primary school is an innovation suggested for elementary schools generally; it has been adapted for compensatory education programs because it promises to avoid many of the problems faced by retarded children. In such a system the first two or three grades are considered as a block of years undivided by separate grade levels; the child progresses toward mastery of required skills and knowledge at his own pace. For each subject he works with a group of other children at his own level of mastery. Thus, the wide variations in ability among these children is taken into account without the stigma of "being left behind a grade" or of having to compete against unfair odds.

Recognition of minority contributions. New curriculum materials have been developed that emphasize the contribution minority groups have made to American life and that describe their cultures. The most notable area of such development is in black history and culture; some urban high schools have introduced courses in black literature as well. The movement is not without its problems; some historians fear that in the attempt to redress the prejudiced treatment of the black role in American history, found in most school textbooks, equally bad history will be written, distorting the black image in the opposite direction. There is some question, too, about the usefulness of treating the role of the black as a separate subject. Far better, some social-studies experts argue, is an approach that would include the description of that role fairly and in perspective as part of general history texts and courses.

Field trips and guest speakers have also been used to help the minority group child see that there are roles that he can play other than those for which the society at large stereotypes him.

Extracurricular innovations. These include a wide variety of efforts to extend the influence of the school into nonschool time. New York City has long provided an All-Day Neighborhood program for selected children in a number of schools. An extension of the school program, combined with supervised recreation is offered for children who need it throughout the afternoon. Neighborhood study centers, staffed with volunteer tutors, have appeared in many city slum sections; these often operate on Saturdays as well and increasingly extend their activities into the summer months.

Parental involvement. Almost all large programs of compensatory education recognize the need to involve parents in the project. Visits by teachers and other project staff to the homes of pupils are encouraged, and a wide variety of methods developed to bring the parents into the school for informal activities. Some schools now have "parents' rooms," where mothers can drop in for sewing or cooking lessons or for a chat with neighbors.

The "new careers" movement (*see* chapter 1) has provided opportunity for many special programs to hire members of the school community, often parents of the children in the school, as extra resources to perform helping roles. They may be employed as teacher aides in the classroom or as family aides, acting as liaison between the school and other parents. Many schools now employ professionals, too, who spend all of their time working on parent and community problems, explaining school goals to parents and helping teachers understand the community.

Teacher recruitment and training. The variety of special programs in this area are described in the next chapter.

Guidance. Almost every project school has instituted special guidance and counseling services or increased already existing ones. Observers note a change in the traditional definition of the guidance role from one that emphasizes the special-problems child or the misfit toward giving services to all the children in project schools. Counselors not only provide vocational information on a more intensive basis than before but also are using group counseling techniques aimed at improving the children's self-image and school motivation.

All of these compensatory devices have been employed in a number of mixtures in both preschool programs like Head Start and in the regular school program. The following section considers at length their effectiveness in several cases where many devices have been used together within total programs. But even if a program of that kind were to be successful, it would be impossible to tell what part of the compensatory effort was responsible for success. Because such information is of obvious strategical importance, it is useful to consider the evidence that exists on the isolated effectiveness of several of these approaches.

One would suppose from the proven influence of family environment that working with parents and with the community should have a substantial impact on the achievement of the child. Most programs that have worked with parents, however, have not evaluated that effort in any controlled sense. There is some evidence from the experimental work of Brookover, cited in Chapter 5 on the achievement self-concept, that training parents to relate in specific ways to their sons as achievers is far more effective than anything the school is apparently able to do. It is important to note, though, that Brookover's experiment involved a fairly prolonged, structured series of training sessions for the parents, a situation unlikely to hold the really multiproblem families.

The relative failure of school counseling in that experiment is not surprising, in view of the previous evidence from a variety of experimental studies that counseling is of little empirical value either in reducing dropouts or raising achievement levels. A good recent example is the latest report of a five-year program, called Project Able, instituted in a number of New York City high schools. These schools were permitted additional counseling staff and the services of psychologists and social workers. At the end of four years an evaluation found no measurable effect in the way students were selecting courses, in course loads, in term averages, in attendance, or in dropout rates.[13]

Such findings are puzzling and subject to several different interpretations. One possibility is that although counseling helps people feel better about their problems, it is not powerful enough in the school setting to influence a change in behavior. Another is that our measure-

13. Joseph Reswick, *The Effectiveness of Full-time and Coordinated Guidance Services in the High School* (Project Able 4th Report, New York City Board of Education, January 1966, mimeo).

ments are too rough to pick up the real differences in attitudes that actually occur. A third possibility is that the evidence accurately indicates that school counseling simply is not at all helpful to children, a conclusion that most educators are reluctant to adopt in view of the anecdotal evidence from counselors and counselees that it *has* helped.

In another area of compensatory programming, the development of new reading materials, the same conflict between positive anecdotal evidence of preference or of improved achievement and little or no *measurable* gains is fairly common also. One of the earliest series of multiracial preprimers was developed and put into use by the Detroit public schools. The stories included both black and white characters and were designed specifically to develop correct speech patterns.

The primers were used experimentally in twelve classes of first-graders, in twelve different schools; six of these classes used the City Schools material, the others a Standard Series.[14] Scores on word recognition and oral reading tests were not significantly different between control and experimental groups, though children who used the City Schools texts had a higher number of perfect word recognition scores and made fewer errors in oral reading. After classroom instruction had been completed with the primers, a sample of the children were asked to choose from a pile of both types of readers the book they would be most interested in reading again, and a significant majority chose one of the City Schools stories.

So, though the children were clearly more interested in the new readers, the absence of any real overall difference in word skill achievement is not very encouraging evidence of effectiveness. Since the twelve classes were not equated in any way at the beginning, it is difficult to interpret the findings at all; any observed differences might be due to the presence of different kinds of children in some of the classes.

Reading material intended for disadvantaged children at the high-school or junior high-school level presents even greater difficulty for evaluation. Controlling such factors as teaching and reading ability is harder to do, and one has the added problem of what measurement to use to determine effectiveness. For example, a set of junior high readers for literature classes has been developed on the assumption that black youngsters will be interested in reading stories and poems which centrally reflect themes in their own lives: coping with difficult circumstances, striving, and so on.[15] Some tests of the texts show increased reading skills among youngsters who used them in the classroom; others do not. But those who designed the anthologies are not at all sure that improvement in reading skill is the most important result to be achieved in any event;

14. Gertrude Whipple, *Appraisal of the City Schools Reading Program* (Detroit Public Schools, November 1963, offset).

15. *The Project English Series* (New York: The Macmillan Company, 1967).

appreciation of the role of literature in giving one insight into personal problems and an increased interest in reading generally might be much more important. For this particular series there is a considerable amount of anecdotal evidence that these latter aims are realized for many children, whatever doubt there may be about improvement in reading skills.

Though difficult to generalize, it is probably fair to say that many of the newly developed reading texts and anthologies that deliberately seek to be multiracial, or closer to the child's experience, or easier for him to identify with are successful in being more interesting for the slum child. It is impossible to say with any assurance at all that any of them result directly in a marked improvement in tested reading levels.

AN EVALUATION OF COMPENSATORY EDUCATION PROGRAMS

Thousands of compensatory programs have been established across the country in the last half of the sixties, but it is impossible to generalize about their success. Most of them have not even been reported in the available literature, and those that have are seldom accompanied by the results of a satisfactory evaluation effort.

As a substitute for a broad review of compensatory programs, then, this section will focus on three major projects: Head Start; a Quincy, Illinois, school program; and New York City's More Effective School project. The first of these is a national program, the second an intensive effort in a moderate-sized city, the third is a somewhat less intensive program in the nation's largest city.

One of the earliest programs of the agency that Congress created to fight poverty, the Office of Economic Opportunity, Head Start was an immediate popular success. It was much influenced by the work of Martin Deutsch and others during the late fifties and early sixties in applying the fundamental idea of compensatory education in the most direct possible fashion—compensate for early deficiencies *before* the child gets to school in special preschool programs.[16] Though such an attempt would sooner or later have been made in any event, the OEC's early start on it can in some measure be attributed to the fact that Congress had instructed that agency to conduct no educational programs during regular school hours for children in school.

Head Start was much more than nursery school training for disadvantaged children. Originally, at least, it included medical and dental treatment (many of the children, it turned out, had never been seen by

16. Martin P. Deutsch, "The Disadvantaged Child and the Learning Process," in A. Harry Passow (ed.) *Education in Depressed Areas* (New York: Bureau of Publications, Teachers College, Columbia University, 1963), pp. 168-178.

a doctor or a dentist), social work intervention if necessary to help the family, and strenuous attempts to bridge the gap between the school program and the community. Much use was made of "indigenous" aides, women who lived in the poverty areas who were hired by the program to serve as liaison with the families of the children or in the classroom as teacher aides. It was in the best educational sense a program for the whole child.

The curriculum of Head Start was developed by early childhood experts to conform to the best of modern preschool practice, particularly shaped to provide an environment that stressed experiences assumed to be lacking in the lower-class home and neighborhood—free play with a great variety of materials of different shapes, colors, and textures; an emphasis on verbal experiences of many types—listening to stories read by the teacher, having the child talk into a tape recorder and listen to his own voice, becoming familiar with the shapes of the letters of the alphabet, and so on.

Head Start was so successful that popular accounts of the first summer programs gave the impression that the problem of the disadvantaged school child had once and for all been solved. Many of the children in the summer preschools made astonishing gains over the period of a few months in measured verbal skills and even in IQ; *group* averages in many cases were impressively higher than on pretests. Experts were more cautious, but even they were enthusiastic, as in this report from an observer of the early trials:

Fortunately, the majority of teachers did capitalize on the small group and did make the transition to preschool type of curriculum. Activities included art, stories, science activities, creative play and visits to various community facilities. These programs were designed to stimulate children's thinking—but, in contrast to situations mentioned earlier, the curriculum was geared to the interests and abilities appropriate to the children of this age.

I feel much of the success of the program was due to the factor of class size. For years educators have asked for small groups and Head Start has demonstrated the value of such class size. The most consistent comment from teachers was in terms of class size and their feeling that substantial gains were possible since they could provide each child with maximum individualized instruction. Whether or not communities will ultimately bear the high cost of small group instruction is another matter. However, this may be the price we must pay for earlier deprivation.

I also believe that the program will ultimately affect the entire educational field in another way. Everywhere I went, school administrators were discussing ways to extend school downward. . .[17]

17. Keith Osborn, "Project Head Start—An Assessment," in Harry L. Miller (ed.), *Education for the Disadvantaged* (New York: The Free Press, 1967), p. 135.

But even as the first Head Starters entered school some educators began to have doubts about the lasting nature of the summer gains. Annie Butler, in an article prophetically entitled "Will Head Start Be a False Start?", warned that the schools would have to change if the preschool progress were to be maintained:

It has been predicted that Head Start and other preschool education programs will result in some of the most revolutionary developments in elementary education this country has ever known. A tremendous corps of teachers has been helped to understand concepts of child development which are important in working with young children, including the deprived; further, they have had experience in planning programs for them. If we now forget what has been learned this summer and expect Head Start children to "adjust" to existing school programs, these children will have made a "false start." If these children really are to have a head start, changes will have to be provided by many schools.[18]

Within a few years, though Head Start programs in many instances had been lengthened to extend through the entire school year, controlled studies that took the place of earlier informal observation confirmed fears of a regression in gains made in preschool experiences once the child enrolled in school. The amount of regression varied, depending probably on the original degree of retardation in the particular group of children and on the quality of the program, but it almost always occurred.

It is easy, however, to overemphasize the regression phenomenon. A look at an example of a carefully run program that has been rigorously evaluated will provide a balanced view of what preschooling can do at best:[19]

The Perry Preschool Project is an experiment with replications to assess the impact of a cognitive program upon the educability of functionally retarded, culturally deprived, Negro, preschool children. The program consists of a cognitively oriented morning preschool, afternoon home visits to involve mothers in the educative process and group meetings for the parents of the children in the program.

At the end of the second year of operation, the Project arrived at a stage where some data began to give hints of possible outcomes. Three groups, or waves, were involved by June, 1964: Wave 0 who started as four-year-olds in September, 1962, Wave I who started as three-year-olds in September, 1962,

18. Annie L. Butler, "Will Head Start Be a False Start?", *Childhood Education* (November 1965), p. 166.

19. David P. Weikart *et al., Perry Preschool Project Progress Report* (Ypsilanti Public Schools, June 1964, mimeo), reprinted in Harry L. Miller, *op. cit.,* pp. 138-140.

and Wave 2 who started as three-year-olds in September, 1963. The findings on the various waves are summarized below.

Wave 0. The only group to enter the project as four-year-olds, the Wave 0 experimental group demonstrated a first-year intellectual spurt as measured by the Stanford-Binet. As with the Leiter and the Peabody, however, the difference between the control and experimental groups on the Binet was not statistically significant after two years (one year in preschool and one year in kindergarten). While only one of the subscales of the Illinois Test yielded a significantly higher mean, the general trend was in favor of the experimental group, particularly on the more complex subscales. The Gates Reading Readiness Tests also showed that the experimental group was generally superior to the control group. The two Gates subtests on which statistical significance was found were the more complex ones.

Perhaps the most important finding was that the experimental group appeared significantly better than the control group in the eyes of the kindergarten teachers in interest in subject matter, initiative, use of the teacher, level of imagination, and level of verbal communication. While the standardized test data on Wave 0 do not prove the superiority of the experimental group in intelligence, the academic tools and attitudes with which this group left kindergarten suggest that these children will probably continue to excel the control group in first grade.

Wave 1. The Wave 0 Stanford-Binet IQ pattern was repeated by Wave 1, the first group to complete two years of pre-school. Following the first-year spurt, the experimental group did not differ significantly from its control by the end of the second year. Neither did the Leiter show the experimental group to be significantly superior at the end of the second year. The Peabody, however, demonstrated a marked superiority of the experimental group. This encouraging finding was supported by the Illinois Test on which the experimental group performed better than the control particularly on complex subscales, reaching statistical significance on two sub-scales.

The failures of the cognitively oriented preschool to improve on first-year gains on the Stanford-Binet is cause for concern.

Wave 2. Data for this wave are limited to the first year in pre-school. The expected first-year spurt as measured by the Stanford Binet is dramatically evident. The Peabody results followed the identical pattern found in Wave 1, and the Leiter also recorded a first-year growth spurt. Wave 2 can be said to have had an educational environment which is different in two ways from the one provided for the previous waves. First, the teachers had had a year of experience in evolving specific techniques to work with three-year-olds. Second, the Wave 2 children had the benefit of learning from four-year-old children who had had a year of preschool at age three. All the waves arriving after Wave 2 will continue to have the same kind of environment as the one from which Wave 2 appears to have benefited.

Despite the moderate successes of this kind of carefully planned and taught preschool program, the results of more routinely undertaken and larger scale attempts most often are negative; control groups usually catch up with the preschoolers within a year or two, and the early spurt in growth subsides.[20]

The length of time the child spends in the program, surprisingly, does not appear to affect the results, as a very careful study of children who were involved for three different periods of time shows.[21] Some of the wide variation in results, however, may be due to differences in family attitudes; one study that paid attention to that variable reports that children from families who voluntarily enrolled did significantly better than those who had to be persuaded to send their children.[22]

Experts have advanced a variety of explanations for the disappointing long-range effects of the preschool programs. A popular one is that as the program was extended to large numbers of children, the impact of the program was "watered down"; efforts were less intensive, teachers less well trained, classes larger. The "watering down" explanation, often given when an experimental program fails after it is instituted more widely, does not in this instance seem very plausible. There is little evidence that even the intensive programs managed to maintain gain rates of more than moderate size over a long period; it is very likely, too, that the dramatic experimental gains in early periods can be explained as a Hawthorne effect.

There is some evidence for the possibility that preschool training simply does not have any lasting effect for children of any background, whatever their degree of cognitive retardation. A longitudinal study of a large number of Toronto children found that by the end of four years in school the earlier advantage shown by children who attended some form of preschool disappeared; to put it perhaps more accurately, what seems to happen is that the children without such training manage to catch up after some years of schooling.[23]

The response from experts to the disappointment of earlier hopes that an answer had been found for the learning retardation of the

20. *See,* for example, M.A. Krider and M. Petsche, "An Evaluation of Head Start Preschool Enrichment Programs as They Affect the Intellectual Ability and Social Adjustment and the Achievement Level of Five Year Old Children Enrolled in Lincoln, Nebraska" (Nebraska University, 1967); S.B. Chorost, *An Evaluation of the Effects of a Summer Head Start Program* (Staten Island, New York: Walcoff Research Center, June 1967).

21. *A Study of the Full-Year 1966 Head Start Program* (Washington, D.C.: Planning Research Corporation, 1967).

22. Douglas Holmes *et al., An Evaluation of Differences among Different Classes of Head Start Participants* (Associated YM-YWHA's of Greater New York, 1966).

23. Judith A. Palmer, *The Effects of Junior Kindergarten on Achievement* (Toronto Board of Education, 1966).

disadvantaged child took several forms. One was to argue that most of the Head Start programs were based on early childhood theories that work very well for middle-class nursery schools but are inappropriate for children who are seriously retarded linguistically. At the University of Illinois Bereiter and Engelmann began experimenting with a highly structured program, far from the relaxed, playful atmosphere advocated by early childhood experts. It is noteworthy that the most successful of the groups in the Perry Preschool Project cited earlier were subjected to the kind of experience proposed by Bereiter and Engelmann:

To summarize other findings from the three waves taken together, the instructional method found to be effective is "verbal bombardment," which means that the teacher maintains a steady stream of questions and comments to draw the child's attention to aspects of his environment. The "bombardment" does not necessarily demand answers on the part of the children. It is continued in rewarding the child for good performance, in disciplining him, and in presenting academic material, and the complexity of the language is increased as the child's verbal ability develops. It is this "bombardment" that seems to produce dramatic growth in intelligence.[24]

Here is a description of what happened in one of the University of Illinois classes:

Presentation	Reasons
Teacher: (presents picture of rifle) This is a ————.	She begins with no verbal explanation. Lengthy verbal preambles do not make learning easier or the material more meaningful to naïve children. They simply bore the child or entertain him in a passive nonproductive manner.
Child B: Gun	
Teacher: Good. It is a gun.	She would have favored the word *rifle* instead of *gun*, but since *gun* is correct and since the response was apparently the product of thinking, she uses *gun* and she praises the child.
Teacher: Let's all say it. This is a gun. Again. This is a gun.	The children seem uninterested. Learning will not proceed smoothly unless the teacher can secure the children's interest. Many motivating devices are

24. Weikart, *op. cit.,* p. 140.

possible, but the teacher prefers one that will favor the members of the class who are paying attention.

Teacher: Let's say it one more time. This is an alligator.

Child D: It ain't neither.

This device would not be recommended if the children had only a tenuous grasp of the concept. The teacher feels reasonably sure, however, that every child in the class knows what a gun is. The task, therefore, is a test of their attention not their knowledge.

Teacher: That's what I said. I said, "This is a bulldog."

All the children are interested now. They are aware of the sham battle of wits and they enjoy it, because they understand that they usually win.

Children (A, B, C, D, E): No, no. It ain't no bulldog. That a *gun.*

The children are laughing at the teacher. She pretends to be hurt.

Teacher: Well, what did I say?

She has ordered the task so that the proof hinges on what was said. The children who attended to the presentation are the only ones who are in a position to apply the coup de grace.

Children: You say that a bulldog.

The teacher apparently wilts, as the children laugh.

Teacher: You're just too smart for me. You listen so big that I can't get away with a thing.

The moral: knowledge is strength. If one thinks and remembers, he can even "outsmart" his teacher. (Moral 2: Even teachers are wrong sometimes.)

Teacher: Okay. I'll start again. This is a gun. Is that right?

The children are attentive. Perhaps they are motivated out of a desire to catch the teacher in another mistake, but they are definitely motivated. So the teacher proceeds quickly. The common error beginning teachers make is to win children over and then feel obliged to talk to them at length. This technique is poor.

Teacher: This is a weapon. This is a gun. This is a weapon.

Child D: No it ain't no weapon.

The teacher realizes that she has made a strategic mistake. She has set the children up to catch her errors. Now when she tries to present a new name the children suppose that she is still carrying on the game. She realizes that she should have introduced the object as a weapon and not as a gun in the first place. She introduced the gun statement first because she felt it would be better to acknowledge the object by the familiar name before introducing the class name.

Teacher: (presents pictures of knife, cannon, pistol) This is a weapon. This is a weapon. These are weapons. Say it with me. This is a weapon. These are weapons. Let's hear that last one again. Make it buzz. These are weaponszzz.

She does not argue with Child D because she feels that little would be gained, and time would be lost. Instead, she resorts to a familiar presentation pattern that has been used in connection with labels. The use of this presentation, she feels, will demonstrate to the children that she is serious, that the game is over.

Teacher: (Refers to knife) This weapon is a ————. Who knows?

Child E: A knife.

Teacher: Yes, a knife. Let's say it. This weapon is a knife. Again. This weapon is a knife.

She beats the children to the punch. Before they could raise the objection that the first picture did not depict a weapon but a knife, the teacher presented a full acknowledgment in one statement. She demonstrated that it is, in fact, a weapon. At the same time, she allowed the children to show off their knowledge about the knife.

Teacher: (Refers to cannon) This weapon is a ————. Who knows?

She phrases her questions so that the children can answer with a single word. Yet, her questions are phrased so that the single-word answer completes the statement "This weapon is a ————." She reinforces the statement even when she wishes to move fast.

Child C: Battle.

Teacher: That's pretty good. You use this thing in a battle, but it's called a cannon. This weapon is a *cannon*. Say it, everybody. This weapon is a cannon.

She wants the child to know that she approves of the manner in which he is thinking, but that his answer is wrong. She rates his answer as a reasonable one, but follows with a clear correction.

Teacher: Is this a *battle*? . . . No, this is *not* a battle. This weapon is a ————. Come on, tell me.

When a child makes a mistake of this kind, his mistake may be picked up by the other children, and will often be repeated by the child who made it. She therefore labors the identification of the cannon.

Children A and D: Cannon.

The teacher notices that Child B is not

Child B: (Mumble)

forming statements but is trying to imitate the sounds made by Child A and Child D.

Teacher: Boy, I'm really proud of A and D. Do you hear the way they are talking up? And are they ever thinking! I'm really proud of them.

The old adage about catching flies with honey applies to the classroom situation. The teacher could have put Child B on the carpet, which would have taken time and might have disgraced him for only a momentary lapse. If he persists, she will be forced into more direct means, but, for now, she selected the band-wagon motivating technique.

Children A, C, D, E.: Me too. Me too.

Teacher: Okay, just keep it up. Here we go. (Refers to pictures) This is a weapon. This is a weapon.

She reviews the new statement before introducing the new task.

Child A: I got a cannon at . . . (stops talking as teacher holds outstretched hands only a few inches in front of child's face).

The summary should be conducted at a fast pace, so that the pieces are brought together and the children know where they are. Interruptions at this point are costly. The child is discouraged when the teacher's hand is placed close to his face—a useful technique.

Teacher: Here's the rule: (claps rhythmically) If you use it to hurt somebody, then it's a weapon. Again, If you use it to hurt somebody, then it's a weapon. Say it with me. If you use it to hurt somebody, then it's a weapon. One more time. If you use it to hurt somebody, then it's a weapon.

The teacher drills this rule until the children learn it. They have learned in connection with other rules that the teacher will expect them to use the rule in the next set of tasks. They also know that she thinks rules of this kind are important—so important that she will not relent until this one has been learned (assuming that the rule is not beyond them).[25]

In a long-range study of the effects of these methods, Karnes has tentatively found that the more highly structured nursery school gets better results, though she suggests that even these higher gains are unlikely to be maintained without further intervention once the child has entered school.[26]

25. Carl Bereiter and Siegfried Engelmann, *Teaching Disadvantaged Children in the Preschool* (Englewood Cliffs, N.J.: Prentice-Hall, Inc., 1966), pp. 105-108

26. Merle B. Karnes, *A Research Program to Determine the Effects of Various Preschool Intervention Programs* (University of Illinois, Institute for Research in Exceptional Children, 1968).

Another response has been to abandon the hope that very much can be gained at the preschool level, suggesting that we must turn our attention to a reformation of the school itself. In a vigorous attack on what he calls the "preschool mythology," Frank Riessman argued that what we are doing is attempting to prepare children for presently inadequate educational systems; "the emphasis is not on changing educational institutions but on changing these youngsters to fit into existing programs."[27]

There is evidence, he claims, that disadvantaged children come to school eager to learn and curious, a curiosity that is soon dampened by their teachers and the general school environment. Since it is now clear that preschool programs cannot offset this discouragement, the school itself must be restructured. The author points out that there are a number of experimental findings that show disadvantaged school-aged youngsters *can* learn, given the right situation and sufficient motivation, and that we have available many new educational techniques—such as team teaching, programmed instruction, role playing, and so on—which fit the learning styles of the lower-class child much better than present methods.

Other educators, too, have turned their attention to the school itself, and there is available by now some hard evidence on attempts to bring significant amounts of compensatory intervention into the school program. Since the passage of the 1965 Elementary and Secondary Education Act, there has been a tremendous number of fragmented compensatory efforts in most urban schools, but they have been difficult to evaluate, even where the will to do so existed, because of the great number of variables operating in the school situation. Only recently have there been any careful assessments of what might be called "total compensatory" programs at the elementary-school level.

THE QUINCY EXPERIMENT

Quincy, Illinois, a city of 45,000 people, has a sizeable population of socially disadvantaged youth and provides a good case study in what a compensatory program can accomplish in a middle-sized city. In 1955 Gordon Liddle directed a program aimed at helping slow-learning high-school students there, but follow-up data indicated that not only had the special program failed to improve academic achievement, it did little for later work adjustment.[28] Concluding that this effort had been "too

27. Frank Riessman, "The New Preschool Mythology: Child-Centered Radicalism," *American Child* (Spring 1966), p. 19.

28. Gordon P. Liddle, "An Experimental Program for Slow Learning Adolescents," *Educational Leadership* (December 1965).

little and too late," Liddle turned to the primary grades. A five-year project was begun in 1961 in four elementary schools in the underprivileged area of the city.[29]

The children who were in kindergarten during one school year, plus those who joined them during the first half of first grade, constituted a control group. The experimental group included all those who entered kindergarten during the following year, plus those who joined the classes during first grade. The children were pretested with both the standard IQ test and the Peabody Picture Vocabulary Test, as well as a self-concept instrument and a number of achievement measures. Although one would expect that groups selected so arbitrarily would be very much the same, pretest results indicated superior standing for the control group on the performance part of the IQ test and on the Peabody. These differences were statistically controlled in the final analysis, however.

An interpretation of those results depends on having a clear picture of the program developed for the experimental group, a summary of which follows:

Enrichment experiences. During the four project years teachers and staff conducted over a hundred field trips to forty different sites around which teachers developed a number of lessons. Children drew pictures, wrote about the experience, produced primitive TV programs about them, did bulletin board displays using Polaroid pictures. Several mothers accompanied the group, and when a child's father worked at the place being visited, an attempt was made to have him serve as the group's guide.

The children were exposed to a program designed to help them become more careful listeners, beginning with sound discrimination exercises using ordinary sounds as well as orchestral instruments.

A variety of role-playing situations was developed to capitalize on the children's more physical pattern of communication. The staff found also that puppetry was useful in increasing verbal expressiveness, and the children acted out stories with puppets they made themselves. One class put on a show for their parents that was so successful it was repeated for all four schools and also at a PTA meeting.

Special science and language classes were organized for some of the groups. One of the project staff consultants started a class in Spanish during a third-grade study of Mexico, from which evolved a Mexican Christmas Fiesta carried out for parents by the children. Another school had a volunteer conducting French classes.

During kindergarten the children were introduced to the public library; they took many field trips there to get acquainted with the

29. Gordon P. Liddle *et al.*, *Educational Improvement for the Disadvantaged in an Elementary Setting* (Springfield, Ill.: Charles C Thomas, 1967).

staff and to watch puppet shows. They were given library cards in the first grade, and during the summer months were taken to the library as part of a summer reading program. During the second grade they were assigned to Girl Scout volunteers in a program that emphasized regular trips to the library.

Other enrichment activities included a creative mix of film showings, providing the children with magazines on a regular basis, a special art program, attendance at professional concerts, and a garden project. All this was supplemented by six-week reading programs during the summers, to which a one-week day camp experience was added.

There was enrichment for teachers too. The project sent teachers to study other programs for the disadvantaged in Milwaukee, Detroit, St. Louis, and Chicago; and the project staff worked closely with any teacher who expressed an interest in experimenting with teaching techniques.

Parental participation. The Quincy project is notable for the intensity with which it worked with parents of the experimental group children. Each parent was interviewed by a staff family worker, the first in a series of both formal and informal contacts with project parents. The staff person served as an interpretive liaison with the school and with the child's teacher and also as a contact with a number of social agencies that might help to solve family problems.

Teachers were encouraged to make home visits. To avoid encroaching on her personal time, project staff substituted in classrooms, thus freeing the teacher to visit during school hours. A two-hour training workshop was instituted to help teachers make these contacts more effective. Yet only six of twenty-two teachers who participated in the project over the years chose to make home visits.

The project slowly built up very impressive attendance records at parent meetings, which were held bimonthly. Meetings were informal, with coffee served during rather than after meetings; people sat around a table instead of in rows; baby sitters were furnished; and family workers urged parents to attend.

At two of the schools parents decided to improve the kindergarten classrooms and mothers made curtains and painted furniture while fathers built a playhouse for the children. At one school the family worker helped organize a family trip to the St. Louis zoo, and in later years the group took a number of one-day excursions.

In all, sixty-three parent meetings were conducted by the staff during the four project years. In the final year attendance exceeded 50 percent in all four schools, and with the aim of maintaining some contact with those parents who did not participate, a monthly newsletter was established in every school. Each issue summarized what had gone on at the parents' meeting, notified parents of forthcoming field trips, reproduced brief essays by parents on such topics as "How much help should parents give with homework" or "What one parent thinks of home visits by the teacher."

Results. Although the staff was disappointed in their inability to persuade either principals or teachers that significant curriculum change was desirable, it is obvious that they were able to develop a truly saturation compensatory program for the experimental group. No one can doubt that during the project years the school program was a better one or that individual families received needed help in a number of ways.

But, what of the major question of the effect of compensatory programming on measurable school achievement? The results turn out to be surprisingly meager. As Table 6.4 shows, the experimental group (after taking account of its initial disadvantage by the use of covariance techniques) did significantly better on the Wechsler Verbal test and on the total Wechsler score, but not on the other major intellectual measures. And, despite the statistical significance, it is clear from raw scores that the group differences are not very meaningful. Scores on the self-concept instrument showed the same statistically significant but very small absolute difference in favor of the experimental group (a mean of 27.6 versus 26.4 for the controls). The third-grade Iowa Achievement Tests showed no group differences.

It is encouraging, however, that in confirmation of the Coleman study findings those pupils suffering the greatest degree of cultural

Table 6.4 Analysis of Covariance, Summary Table

Test	Mean group IQ		Significance level (percents)
	Experimental	Control	
WISC verbal			
Pre	90.1	92.5	
Post	93.3	92.5	5
WISC performance			
Pre	94.7	98.1	
Post	99.5	100.2	N.S.
WISC total			
Pre	91.6	95.9	
Post	94.7	95.9	5
Peabody			
Pre	91.7	97.8	
Post	92.8	95.8	N.S.

SOURCE: Gordon P. Liddle *et al.*, *Educational Improvement for the Disadvantaged in an Elementary Setting* (Springfield, Ill.: Charles C Thomas, 1967), p. 77.

handicap showed the greatest gains over the controls, as Table 6.5 indicates.

Table 6.5 Scores on the Wechsler by Degree of Cultural Handicap

Degree of handicap	Mean pretest	Mean posttest	Mean change	Number of pupils
Experimental group				
Considerable	86.9	92.2	5.3*	68
Moderate	92.2	94.0	1.8	38
Little or none	102.8	107.8	5.0	28
Control group				
Considerable	88.1	90.1	2.0	63
Moderate	92.4	93.3	.9	46
Little or none	104.9	104.7	—.2	49

* Prepost difference significant at the 5 percent level of confidence.

SOURCE: Gordon P. Liddle *et al., Educational Improvement for the Disadvantaged in an Elementary Setting* (Springfield, Ill.: Charles C Thomas, 1967), pp. 78.

NEW YORK CITY'S MES PROGRAM

In 1964 a planning committee for more effective schools (MES), established by the city's superintendent of schools, submitted a report recommending policy guidelines for producing more effective education for children of the city's slum areas. The recommendations involved basic changes in four aspects: pupils and curriculum, personnel, school plant and organization, and community relations; and included such specifics as selecting schools for the program to maximize integration, setting a maximum class size of twenty-two, providing teacher specialists, grouping classes heterogeneously, instituting team teaching, and emphasizing positive school-community relations.

The program was established in 1964 in ten schools; in 1965 eleven additional schools were designated for the experiment. In the evaluation data cited below[30] the first group is referred to as "Old ME schools," the second group as "New ME schools." At this writing the program has been subjected to four different assessments at various points in its history and a fifth is underway. The fourth evaluation study is reported here; the Old MES had then been in operation for three years, the New MES for two.

The data for this study were gathered primarily through observational visits of a team of two educational experts who (1) rated the quality of class functioning in visits to classes that were selected randomly as well as to classes selected by the principal; (2) interviewed

30. David J. Fox, *Expansion of the More Effective School Program* (Center for Urban Education, September 1967, mimeo).

staff to obtain their appraisals of the school's effectiveness; (3) arranged to have the children fill out simple rating instruments that measured their perceptions of themselves and of the school; (4) obtained data on arithmetic and reading test scores throughout the period under study. A total of 300 classes in the middle grades were observed, plus another 68 early childhood classes visited by specialists in that field. Similar data was collected for a group of control schools.

The findings were contradictory in ways that educational experimenters find relatively common:

1. There was considerable variation in effectiveness from school to school, suggesting that a fruitful direction for follow-up research is to examine the reasons for the differences. Although a possible assumption is that a special combination of school factors accounts for the greater effectiveness of some schools, it is, of course, equally plausible that the explanation lies in different characteristics of the student bodies.

2. As perceived by the staff the climate of the experimental schools was enthusiastic, hopeful, and interested. The parents were enthusiastic, and even the observers, in their overall ratings of the schools, agreed that they were places to which they would willingly send their own children.

3. Despite considerable administrative and organizational change, however, there was little curriculum innovation of instructional adaptation to smaller classes. The report notes:

> Observers noted that a majority of lessons they saw could have been taught to larger classes with no loss of effectiveness. When asked about changes in "method of instruction," administrators and teachers alike pointed to the small class and the use of specialists and cluster teachers which we would consider administrative changes rather than changes in method of instruction. All levels of staff noted that the basic weakness of the program, or their major disappointment with it, centered about the functioning of teachers, which they attributed to inexperience and lack of preparation. All of these comments combined to a general agreement that in the absence of specific preparation, teachers have not revised techniques of instruction to obtain the presumed instructional advantages of the small class and the availability of specialized instruction. In view of this, the lack of academic progress is not surprising.[31]

4. Both in comparison with the control schools and in general progress within the ME schools, the children showed little overall difference in attitudes or achievement. Because the focus of this book is on the academic retardation of large city slum children, the data on this point is worth a more detailed look.

31. *Ibid.*, p. 122.

First, the children's functioning in the classroom was rated on the basis of an assessment of five observable behaviors: verbal fluency of those children who participated, their interest and enthusiasm, the amount of overall participation, the proportion of children volunteering, and the number of children who raised spontaneous questions. Measures of the first four of these variables showed no difference between ME and control children. On the fifth, ME children were significantly better, but the absolute number of children who raised spontaneous questions was, in any case, very small.

Second, children's perception of their class was measured by having them respond to twenty statements about it, for example, "Everyone can do a good job if he tries" and "Good class, except for one or two children." The results are shown in Table 6.6, where ME children's per-

Table 6.6 Item Response Patterns for *My Class* by Type of School*

Statement	Type of School			
	MES	Control	OE Sending	OE Receiving
Everyone can do a good job if he tries	92	93	95	94
Good class, except for one or two children	85	83	82	82
Do interesting things in class	77	83	78	82
Can have a good time in class	74	72	78	74
Not hard to make friends	71	67	70	71
Children in class happy when you do something for them	72	64	66	72
Everyone in class has a chance to show what he can do	64	68	65	74
Don't need better classroom to do best work	59	62	56	60
Everyone in this class wants to work hard	52	45	52	61
Feel that they do belong in this class	51	39	49	48
Everyone is trying to keep classroom nice	47	40	43	53
Children in class are not pretty mean	45	38	44	57
Children do want to try new things	45	33	44	47
Do have things needed to do best work	43	30	39	40
Everyone in class is polite	38	31	38	48
A lot of children like to do things together	34	32	32	38
Not many children in class are unfair	32	28	30	38
Everyone in class minds his own business	26	22	25	33
You can trust almost anyone in this class	23	16	22	31

* Figures cited are percentage giving positive response.

SOURCE: David J. Fox, *Expansion of the More Effective School Program* (Center for Urban Education, September 1967, mimeo), p. 47.

ceptions are compared not only to control school children but to responses from a previous study of open enrollment that had used the same instrument. "Sending schools" are those from which the children in that earlier study were bussed; "OE receiving" children were those who participated in the bussing program and who were rating the middle-class schools in which they were enrolled. The ME children show slightly more positive perceptions than controls, but are no more positive than the broader sample of children in sending schools.

Third, the findings on both arithmetic and reading achievement are open to some variable interpretation. Table 6.7 shows arithmetic test results over a two- and three-year period respectively for both Old and New ME schools. The initial gains (in terms of decreasing retardation) of the third-graders in the Old ME schools during the first two years of the project are reversed during the third year; in the case of those who were fourth-graders at the beginning of the project, initial gains were retained, but no further ones made. In the case of the New ME schools, the fourth-graders seem to have made a gain in the first year, then just held their own; for the fifth-graders the program appears to have had no impact at all.

Much the same pattern of early performance increase, then decline during the third year of the program, emerges for reading scores, as the longitudinal data in Table 6.8 indicates. This table examines the progress of those children who had been in the Old ME schools for the full three years, providing the program with its best chance to show effectiveness. Clearly, three full years of MES did not have any effect on the increasing retardation of the second- and third-graders, though it did have some initial effect on the children who began the program in grade four.

The report concludes that there is no consistent effect on achievement that can be demonstrated for the ME schools, and suggests that early gains for some groups probably are due to a Hawthorne effect. It does, however, note that for some children in particular ME schools were indeed more effective, thus perhaps explaining why the program as a whole did not materially affect average achievement levels. Table 6.9 presents reading scores separately for children who had never attended any other school *and* who had a full three years of ME schooling, compared to those who had the full program but had a history of school mobility, and to those who had less than the full three years and a history of mobility. The comparison consistently favors those with a consecutive educational history and full MES, though even these remain behind the norm by half a year. The larger differences between the two groups that share a history of school disruption suggest that MES does make some difference.

Table 6.7 Longitudinal Study in Arithmetic Achievement, Old and New MES

Grade	Date of test	Number of children	Median	Norm at testing	Comparison with norm	NET Change		
						By May 1966	During 1966-1967	By March 1967
Old MES								
3	Oct. 1964	628	2.6	3.1	–.5			
4	May 1966	628	4.5	4.8	–.3	+.2	–.4	–.2
5	Mar. 1967	531	4.9	5.6	–.7			
4	Oct. 1964	656	3.0	4.1	–1.1			
5	May 1966	656	5.1	5.8	–.7	+.4	0	+.4
6	Mar. 1967	408*	5.9	6.6	–.7			
New MES								
4	Oct. 1965	741	3.1	4.2	–1.1			
4	May 1966	741	4.2	4.8	–.6	+.5	0	+.5
5	Mar. 1967	383	5.0	5.6	–.6			
5	Oct. 1965	694	4.0	5.2	–1.2			
5	May 1966	694	4.5	5.8	–1.3	–.1	+.1	0
6	Mar. 1967	102*	5.4	6.6	–1.2			

* The attrition here reflects the fact that few ME schools have a sixth grade.

SOURCE: David J. Fox, *Expansion of the More Effective School Program* (Center for Urban Education, September 1967, mimeo), p. 40.

Table 6.8 Longitudinal Analysis of Progress in Reading, MES, October 1964 through April 1967, Median Reading Grade

Grade	Number	Date of test	Median grade	Norm at testing	Comparison with norm	NET Change		
						By May 1966	During 1966–1967	By Apr. 1967
2	784	Oct. 1964	1.8	2.1	—.3			
3	784	May 1966	3.7	3.8	—.1	+.2	—.6	—.4
4	744	Apr. 1967	4.0	4.7	—.7			
3	759	Oct. 1964	2.7	3.1	—.4			
4	759	May 1966	4.2	4.8	—.6	—.2	—.3	—.5
5	697	Apr. 1967	4.8	5.7	—.9			
4	567	Oct. 1964	3.2	4.1	—.9			
5	567	May 1966	5.2	5.8	—.6	+.3	—.3	0
6	395	Apr. 1967	5.8	6.7	—.9			

SOURCE: David J. Fox, *Expansion of the More Effective School Program* (Center for Urban Education, September 1967, mimeo), p. 60.

Table 6.9 Comparison of Reading Levels for Children with Different Educational Histories by Grade, Old ME Schools Only

Current grade	Gp.	Education	MES	Median	Q3	Q1	IQR	Norm
4	1	Unbroken	Full	4.1	4.9	3.4	1.5	
	2	Broken	Full	3.9	4.6	3.2	1.4	4.7
	3	Broken	Partial	3.6	4.3	3.1	1.2	
5	1	Unbroken	Full	4.9	6.0	4.1	1.9	
	2	Broken	Full	4.7	5.7	3.9	1.8	5.7
	3	Broken	Partial	4.4	5.4	3.7	1.7	
6	1	Unbroken	Full	5.9	8.7	4.8	3.9	
	2	Broken	Full	5.6	7.3	4.4	2.9	6.7
	3	Broken	Partial	5.0	7.0	4.0	3.0	

SOURCE: David J. Fox, *Expansion of the More Effective School Program* (Center for Urban Education, September 1967, mimeo), p. 67.

This important finding is confirmed by a later study of MES by Forlano, who separated for examination those children who had an unbroken record in MES, comparing their reading scores with a matched sample of other slum school children. A year after the Fox study these children were reading almost at the level of national norms. For this most stable group of children, then, the schools are more effective.[32]

The report itself has been subjected to much the same criticism that the Coleman study received. It is significant that much of the criticism has been initiated by New York's United Federation of Teachers, which had been involved in the early recommendation for the program and had zealously cooperated in its implementation. The union had attacked the city school system for many years for what it claimed was inadequate school facilities, focusing particularly on its reluctance to reduce class size, which, despite overwhelming research evidence to the contrary, the union saw as crucial to academic achievement. Since the heart of the MES reorganization was reduction of class rolls to about twenty or less, the union refused to believe that no substantial gains resulted. Furthermore, the conclusion of the evaluator, David Fox of City College of New York, that the lack of consistent gains could be attributed to teachers' inability to take advantage of the freedom to experiment and innovate would obviously be unacceptable to an organization devoted to the interest and reputations of the teachers involved.

Much of the criticism, consequently, is so colored by defensiveness that it is difficult to treat it seriously. Fox is accused, for example, of recommending that MES be discontinued on the basis of only a few years of operation, of not giving the program a chance.[33] In fact, Fox carefully points out:

> . . . we have tried to keep in mind that the program being evaluated originally came into existence a few months after the publication of the report recommending it, and had been in existence only two years when we began our study in the fall of 1966. Indeed, in reading this report, the reader should understand that this evaluation belongs to the family of short-term evaluations conducted in the early years of a new program. Such evaluations cannot be considered definitive studies of a program's worth, but rather short-term evaluations that have their place in identifying the initial impact of a program, providing evidence of its potential strengths and weaknesses, and providing a basis for predicting its ultimate effect.[34]

32. George Forlano and Jack Abramson, *Measuring Pupil Growth in Reading in the More Effective Schools* (New York: Board of Education of the City of New York, April 1968).

33. Sidney Schwager, "An Analysis of the Evaluation of the MES Program Conducted by the Center for Urban Education," *Urban Review*, Vol. 2, No. 6 (May 1968), pp. 18-23.

34. Fox, *op. cit.*, p. 3.

Table 6.10 Profiles of Median School Achievement in Reading across Three Years of MES, by Grade, Type of School, Fall and Spring

Grade	Type of school	Oct. 1964	Oct. 1965	Oct. 1966	May 1965	May 1966	April 1967	Projected May 1967
2	Old MES	1.8	1.9	1.8	2.4	2.8	2.6	2.7
	New MES	x	1.6	1.8	x	2.4	2.6	2.7
3	Old MES	2.6	2.6	2.5	3.4	3.7	3.5	3.6
	New MES	x	2.4	2.4	x	3.4	3.4	3.5
4	Old MES	3.0	3.4	3.3	4.1	4.2	3.9	4.0
	New MES	x	3.2	3.2	x	3.7	4.0	4.1
5	Old MES	4.0	4.4	3.8	5.1	5.2	4.5	4.6
	New MES	x	4.1	3.7	x	4.5	4.6	4.7
6	Old MES	4.9	5.1	5.1	6.1	6.1	5.5	5.6
	New MES	x	4.6	4.6	x	5.3	5.5	5.6

SOURCE: David J. Fox, *Expansion of the More Effective School Program* (Center for Urban Education, September 1967, mimeo), p. 59.

Nor does the report at any point recommend discontinuance of the program.

More serious are the questions raised about the adequacy of measurement. The important class observation, for example, used a series of rating scales that asked for judgments on such general variables as "pupil interest and enthusiasms," without carefully defining what behavior was to be included in this category. Furthermore, in assessing the reliability of his observers, Fox simply calculated the percentage of times his team members agreed with one another within one rating scale point, instead of calculating the more rigorous correlation coefficients.

Most of the purely methodological criticisms have to do with this observational area of the study; there is little doubt that the measurement standards used were not as rigorous as the study's importance should have dictated. The critics somewhat vitiate their argument on this score, however, by enthusiastically accepting *some* of the data obtained with the same unreliable measures which they argue makes other data unacceptable. Most of the observational data is very favorable to MES, some is not; one cannot accept the evidence that teachers are better, that discipline is good, and that lessons are planned with greater relevance to the child's experience, and reject evidence from the same source that teachers were not making use of smaller class size.

The core of the argument lies in the interpretation of achievement data. Here, the critics build a case for the genuine effectiveness of MES by charging that the norms used by the study are national norms rather than those based on achievement of New York's slum school population, and that the data itself reveals that MES children did make greater gains than either control school children or the general population of slum school children. Since the current educational crisis concerns the question of whether ghetto children can be helped to do as well academically as the average white mainstream child, and not whether they can do better than their own group, the first of these arguments is not very persuasive. The second is worth a careful look by all interested persons and is a matter for individual judgment.[35] The report itself records a number of instances in which MES children did comparatively better, but in almost all *overall* instances these differences are small.

It is true that the longitudinal comparisons in the study of progress from grade to grade do not restrict the comparison only to those children present throughout the entire time period; it is also true that the reading test employed is not sensitive to very poor reading performances and consequently may overestimate the reading levels of the presumably

35. *See Urban Review,* Vol. 2, No. 6 (May 1968), for several analyses.

less competent control schools. Both of these possible sources of error must modify the degree of confidence one can have in the final assessment. But, as Fox points out in answering his critics, the most crucial evidence for the ME schools' lack of significant impact does not involve either a comparison with the controls or a consideration of longitudinal achievement by some group of pupils but rather an overall improvement of the schools' record in raising achievement levels. And, as Table 6.10 shows, the schools have not become measurably more effective during a three-year period in doing so.

No one can question that for some pupils, during some periods of time and in some of the schools, measurable progress was made in reducing academic retardation, but the dispute ultimately resolves into a question of whether the gains are of sufficient scope to justify the necessary expenditure.

COST/BENEFIT ANALYSIS AND COMPENSATORY EDUCATION

The MES controversy thus expands to a much broader consideration. New York City's ME program required a doubling of the city's normal expenditure per pupil, from about $450 to $900, an additional $10 million per year for 2 percent of its schools. The Head Start program, of course, runs into hundreds of millions a year on a national scale, and even so modest a project as the Quincy experiment with four elementary schools required a total of twelve professional staff years.

Do the modest and inconsistent gains shown by all three programs, which are thoroughly representative of compensatory program results generally, justify the expenditures? Or, in the terms of cost/benefit analysis popularized by an influential Secretary of Defense, are the benefits achieved by this particular line of attack on academic retardation in the urban slum school sufficient for us to allocate resources at this level as a matter of policy?

Many would argue that this kind of analysis is irrelevant to social policy, that the kind of reasoning that makes sense when applied to a decision about the design one should select for a military plane hardly does so when applied to matters of education. It would be difficult to calculate the benefits deriving from these programs, they suggest, even if only a minority of the children involved were helped. From this point of view the values of our society look topsy-turvy when the social benefits of a new military plane justify billions in cost but the relatively small cost of special educational programs for underprivileged children is questioned because educators have not triumphantly succeeded in wiping out the problem.

As attractive as this view appears to be for most educators, it obscures the very real advantages of a cost/benefit approach, which requires a critical look at the actual payoff for social programs and some hard evidence for the relative effectiveness of alternative solutions. In this case it would force us to examine the social benefits of concentrating on raising the academic achievement levels of lower-class minorities; if the ultimate aim is to insure everyone a good chance at a stable and adequately rewarding occupation, the cost of trying to achieve it through educational intervention may be far greater than subsidizing employers to expand their employment and training opportunities. Even if the benefits of greater success in school should appear large enough to justify very sizeable costs, it might turn out that some strategy quite different from compensatory approaches is more effective in justifying much bigger costs, on the same principle that some people use in buying expensive clothes because they are likely to wear better and last longer.

The professional reaction to the limited success of even the best of compensatory education efforts has been varied. One group of educators takes the stand that the resources we have thrown into compensating for the handicaps of social background have been so piddling that we can hardly expect to have dented the problem. If we require unequal resources to produce similar results for children of unequal backgrounds, who is to say *how* unequal the resources must be? There are currently underway experiments requiring four times the normal expenditure per pupil, the results of which should provide some analysis of that comparison.

Other experts have abandoned the idea of compensatory education in favor of a search of alternatives, whether or not they happen to be more costly. Although the search has not yet hardened into actual, going projects, it is possible to see at this point the directions in which the field of urban education is likely to move in the immediate future.

ALTERNATIVES TO COMPENSATION

By far the most extreme proposal, one that has been argued hardest by Christopher Jencks, is that we simply do away with the publicly supported school system.[36] The grounds for doing so are as simple and direct as the proposal itself: The urban public system, through a

36. Christopher Jencks, "Is The Public School Obsolete?", *The Public Interest* (Winter 1968), pp. 18-27.

bureaucratic hardening of the arteries, has amply demonstrated that it is incapable of dealing adequately with the learning needs of lower class and ethnic minority children, and it is too cumbersome and hard to move to offer much hope that it can change itself into an institution that can do the required job.

If the system were abandoned, and all parents given an educational allowance for their children, they would at least have free choice in selecting schooling. The assumption of the argument is that in a free-market situation, people will spend their money in ways that maximize the achievement of their own self-interests. Jencks has elaborated the idea by suggesting that in such a situation a vast array of private schools will spring up, whose continued existence will depend on their proven ability to help children learn; if a parent is unsatisfied with his child's program, he need merely enroll him in another school. Experimentation with ways of improving the achievement of socially retarded children will be widespread, as schools compete with one another for pupils, instead of being bogged down in red tape.

The general idea is an attractive one for a number of reasons. Although no government officials have publicly sanctioned it, the substitution of private schooling for public responsibility must surely be a seductive alternative for urban politicians under constant attack for the performance of public schools. In a society that appears to be swinging back to an affirmation of the virtues of private competition, after a generation of emphasizing governmental repsonsibility for the public welfare (Congress is even now seriously considering a recommendation to make the postal service an autonomous corporation), the suggestion seems hopefully progressive rather than conservative. The competition of private firms for the consumer's dollar has led to increasing affluence and an unparalleled array of choice for the society at large; why should it not do the same for education?

The plan rests, however, on a number of questionable assumptions. The prospect of a possible profit would no doubt attract a number of corporations currently looking for ways of diversifying their operations, as the market for programmed instruction devices has already attracted them. But the efficiency of private industry, and their admirable tendency to allocate resources to research and development to a far greater extent than any government-controlled enterprise, has not yet been shown to be effective in education. The teaching machines themselves are creatively engineered, but the learning materials that go in them, the "software," have been disappointing. The Office of Economic Opportunity put up for contract to private corporations the operation of a number of Job Corps centers; the results of this were discussed in chapter 1.

Furthermore, to the extent that private industry does enter a field of schooling organized as a free market, the result is likely to be a substitution of one large-scale bureaucracy for another, a private for a public one. The tendency in the American economy is toward amalgamation, in order to take advantage of economies of scale; and it is very doubtful that Jencks' vision of a large number of small, independent, competing schools would be realized, as more efficient organizations created larger and larger school chains.

To the degree that small independent schools were established, it is likely that they would be run by those people who already possess the credentials that the state would surely insist on requiring, the principals and teachers who now operate within the public school system. It seems unlikely that they would do a better job under those circumstances than they now do.

NARROWING THE FOCUS: HAVIGHURST'S PROPOSAL FOR ALIENATED YOUTH

At the opposite extreme of the alternatives proposed is the suggestion that, without attempting large-scale reforms in the school as presently constituted, we identify the specific group of children for whom the school program seems irrelevant, and concentrate on them as a separate problem.

Robert Havighurst and Lindley Stiles suggest that the major problem involves about 15 percent of American youngsters whom they call "the alienated."[37] They come mostly from families that are on the bottom of the social scale in whatever community they live, whose adaptation to this circumstance and to their family environment takes the form of socially deviant behavior and lack of interest in school. In a community like Kansas City, where there are few blacks, their names are English, Scotch, Irish, German; in New York or Chicago the youngsters are black or Puerto Rican; in Los Angeles, Mexican or Indian.

Most lower-class children, the authors have pointed out, do well enough in school. These particular youths represent a special case; and, because in large central cities they constitute a considerably greater proportion than the national average of 15 percent, the school problems they create become the problems of the entire system. Havighurst and Stiles propose a large-scale systematic program aimed at keeping them in school by making school more relevant, and moving them gradually into a satisfactory occupational life.

The boys of this group in particular have not found a viable route

37. Robert J. Havighurst and Lindley J. Stiles, "A National Policy for Alienated Youth," *Phi Delta Kappan,* Vol. XLII, No. 7 (April 1961), pp. 283-291.

to competent adulthood. A generation or two ago boys who found school a continual failure experience had other routes available; there were many unskilled jobs for young people that provided a toehold on the occupational ladder. School dropouts could become farm hands, elevator operators, messenger boys, or factory workers; and acquire skills on the job and experience that enabled them to move on to better jobs or at least to establish stable positions in some organization. In 1920 more than half of the boys aged fourteen to seventeen were employed half- or fulltime. Since then farm jobs have steadily decreased, as have unskilled factory jobs. Automation and improved communication systems have caused the virtual disappearance of such occupations as messenger and elevator operator.

Havighurst and Stiles propose the creation of a new route to adulthood for alienated boys, organized within the public school program and with the following characteristics:

1. The program will begin at age thirteen or fourteen and continue through age eighteen, though some may graduate a few years earlier.
2. It will emphasize job disciplines such as working cooperatively with others, taking orders, punctuality, responsibility.
3. It will directly lead to stable, adult jobs.
4. It will consist mainly of a program of work experience, plus study at an intellectual level appropriate for those boys.

The authors of the proposal describe the program as involving three major stages. In the first, students will work in groups under supervision for part of the day in situations largely outside the labor market: in parks, playgrounds, beaches, or at similar community maintenance jobs; or doing simple clerical work such as envelope stuffing in sheltered workshops in the school on contract jobs.

In the second stage the boys would work parttime on an individual basis with employers in private industry or in the public sector, with the school maintaining fairly close supervision during this time. Finally, the boys would be placed in fulltime jobs and aided for a time by guidance and supervision from the school.

The corollary school program suggested would emphasize practical learning geared to the work done by students, with some academic activities on relatively low abstraction levels and a considerable use of audiovisual aids.

For many, the major dilemma posed by proposals such as this is the apparently irrevocable commitment to a particular occupational level at so early an age. Havighurst and Stiles suggest that identifying alienated boys at the age of thirteen is a relatively simple matter: One looks for those exhibiting signs of "aggressive maladjustment," presumably meaning early difficulties with the police or school disciplinary authorities, and a record of school academic failure. If one considers it likely that any substantial number of such boys may be late bloomers or might undergo some sort of adolescent awakening to the value of schooling after the age of thirteen, such a program seems altogether too confining. Some observers see the likelihood of such a change as so remote that the possible benefits for both the boys and society in a well-organized work experience program outweigh the distasteful necessity of imposing a particular type of future on the group as a whole.

RECONSTRUCTING THE SCHOOL

Between the radical alternative of destroying the public system as an institution and a narrow focus on the most troublesome group of alienated pupils are a number of proposals for making fundamental changes in the structure of the public school. Compensatory education merely intensifies already existing programs or adds special features to the on-going structure of activities. The very modest gains of such compensatory efforts, it is suggested, may mean that for minority group youngsters and perhaps for all children the school as presently organized needs a thorough overhaul.

Proposals for doing so are varied; New York City is beginning experimental work with at least three different approaches. For the sake of clarity we present below only two models of school reconstruction: one that might be proposed by a rationalist in education; the second an existing proposal that fits into the developmental approach as described earlier.

A RATIONALIST VIEW

As a basis for school reconstruction one might well adopt the approach to learning mastery recently elaborated by Benjamin Bloom which, although it is a general statement, has great relevance for the schooling of the socially disadvantaged.[38] We class it as "rationalist" because it accepts the present learning goals of the school as given.

Bloom begins his argument by criticizing the basic expectations of most teachers that for any given course of instruction about a third of the students will do well, will master the skill or the material; about a third will learn a good deal, but not enough to be regarded as good

38. Benjamin S. Bloom, "Learning for Mastery," *Evaluation Comment,* Vol. 1, No. 2 (Center for the Study of Evaluation of Instructional Programs, University of California at Los Angeles, May 1968, unpaged).

students; and a third will fail or "just get by." In justification of such an attitude, when the teacher tests a class he distributes the results on a normal curve and assigns appropriate grades. The explanation is that aptitude for any particular learning task is normally distributed, and if the same instruction is provided, the end result will be a normal distribution of achievement. Generally speaking, the correlation between aptitude and achievement can be expected to be high, about .70 or higher.

Bloom's suggestion for mastery learning is based on the different assumption that students' aptitudes are normally distributed, but if the type of instruction and the time devoted to a particular task is made appropriate to levels of aptitude, the majority should be able to achieve mastery:

Most students (perhaps over 90%) can master what we have to teach them, and it is the task of instruction to find the means which will enable our students to master the subject under consideration. Our basic task is to determine what we mean by mastery of the subject and to search for the methods and materials which will enable the largest proportion of our students to attain such mastery.[39]

For this purpose, a substitute definition of aptitude is needed, and it has been proposed by John Carroll as: *the amount of time required by the learner to attain mastery of a learning task.* Bloom is convinced by his study of aptitude distributions that there is a considerable difference between an approximately 5 percent of students who have some special talent for a subject and the remainder of the population; there may be another 5 percent at the bottom of the aptitude distribution who have just as special disabilities (as in the case of dyslexic students in reading classes). But for the 90 percent in between:

We believe [as does Carroll] that aptitudes are predictive of rate of learning rather than the level (or complexity) of learning that is possible. Thus, we are expressing a view that, given sufficient time (and appropriate types of help) 95 percent of students (the top 5 percent plus the next 90 percent) can learn a subject up to a high level of mastery. We are convinced that the grade of A as an index of mastery of a subject can, under appropriate conditions, be achieved by up to 95 percent of the students in a class.[40]

The abandonment of the normal curve of achievement can be justified on several grounds, Bloom argues. Though it may be appropriate in a society that can use only a limited number of highly educated per-

39. *Ibid.*, p. 1.
40. *Ibid.*, p. 4.

sons, as a means of identifying those with the greatest talent, a society such as ours, that requires an increasingly skilled labor force, must find ways of increasing the proportion of the well-educated of any age group. Secondly, the normal curve is an appropriate statement of chance activity, of randomness; but educators are engaged in purposeful activity, and the distribution of achievement should be very different from the normal curve.

An ideal strategy for learning mastery, presumably, would be to supply a tutor for each student. In the absence of such an expensive ideal, some form of the ungraded school would be necessary, with children grouped according to their instructional needs. Bloom stresses the importance of getting students concerned with levels of performance instead of with grades. In one informal experiment he permitted the instructor to work normally (on the assumption that teaching behavior is the most difficult of the variables to change in the situation), but provided extensive feedback on progress to the students and the teacher. Where supplementary instruction for some seemed necessary, that also was supplied.

Bloom suggests that mastery has far-reaching consequences for the individual and his view of the world:

> The student desires some control over his environment, and mastery of a subject gives him some feeling of control over a part of his environment. Interest in a subject is both a cause of mastery of the subject as well as a result of mastery. Motivation for further learning is one of the more important consequences of mastery. At a deeper level is the student's self-concept. Each person searches for positive recognition of his worth and he comes to view himself as adequate in those areas where he receives assurance of his competence or success . . . Mastery and its public recognition provide the necessary reassurance and reinforcement to help the student view himself as adequate.[41]

It is interesting to speculate on what a ghetto elementary school based on such principles would look like. It would probably contain at least the following elements:

1. Children would enter at the age of three for several years of nursery and kindergarten activities designed to provide time enough for the development of readiness and symbolic mastery which is later required. This period might also be used for intensive diagnostic work on each child, to determine subsequent individual treatment.

2. It is likely that some children would be diagnosed as disturbed emotionally or as having special disabilities. The former might be assigned to residential centers in which school work is conducted as part

41. *Ibid.*, p. 11.

of a therapeutic environment and where teachers with special training work with counseling and psychiatric staffs. The latter might be assigned to corrective classes or provided some form of individual therapy.

3. The standard classroom would disappear, and with it the routinely organized work day for the teacher. A tentative estimate of the capacity of each child would determine his placement in a particular learning environment, how much time he would spend in school daily, and the kind of teacher to whom he would be assigned. Some children would spend most of the day in a one-to-one tutoring situation, possibly using college student volunteers or community aides under the supervision of a skilled teacher. Others might work in small groups of three or four, sometimes with a teacher, at other periods working together on assignments. Still others might do very well in a normal-sized classroom group.

4. Whatever the situation, the focus would be on performance levels attained in moving toward a set of learning goals fixed for each individual or group. Bloom suggests breaking such goals down into small blocks of subgoals that can be evaluated every two weeks or so. The results of the testing can then be fed back to both teachers and pupils as guides for further work. As a consequence, one or another group might have its schedule lengthened or an individual child might be shifted into a different setting more appropriate to his pace.

Such a program, obviously, would result in the graduation of children with mastery over different levels of work in different learning areas. But all will have mastered *some* skills, which assumes that the school must agree on a priority among all the goals that it considers important. At the elementary level this is not a very difficult task; most rationalist-oriented educators would agree that if one cannot do everything, then a mastery of language and number skills is more important than learning about Indians and Thanksgiving. The problem is more complicated at the secondary-school level. Is science more important than history? Literature more important than mathematics? Such a determination may have to be based on a complex of factors, including the young person's aptitudes and interests as well as the possible direction of his later work life.

A DEVELOPMENTAL VIEW

Although it reorganizes the basic pattern of school life, the rationalist proposal leaves the most fundamental aspect of the school untouched, the goal of cognitive development. A revision of that goal itself is where the developmental educator begins. The model presented here is the one elaborated by Mario Fantini and Gerald Weinstein, who have provided a more detailed plan for school reconstruction than appears anywhere in the literature.[42]

Their basic premise is that the school system as it exists not only fails with disadvantaged youth but fails in crucial ways to serve middle-class youngsters who apparently do well in it. In a society in rapid change, say Fantini and Weinstein, the school goes through the same motions, teaching the same sterile bodies of knowledge to children who must grow up to live in a society where the realities have little to do with what they learned in school.

What, for instance, does the white middle-class child experience in his modern suburban school that is relevant to the problems he will confront in modern society? In a lily-white school population with a curriculum that ignores the history and current plight of his black fellow citizens, he is unlikely to understand the racial crisis that confronts the society. He is cut off by his milieu from any appreciation of what it means to live in poverty, what central city urbanism means, how others unlike himself feel about life, and, indeed, how *he* feels about himself and life. His school sets him the task of acquiring bodies of knowledge that serve to accredit him for college entrance, but that are largely meaningless to him at the time and of little use to him in the future, should he ever remember them.

The problem of relevance is even more serious for the schools of the central city, Fantini and Weinstein argue, because of the special conditions of urbanism. Their analysis of the urban condition is related to a number of what they consider fundamental human issues:

> Human beings have a combination of personal issues with which they continually attempt to deal in some satisfactory manner. Many of these issues are common enough to be designated as a pattern—a "human issue". . . . These human issues can generally be grouped into issues revolving around safety, security, or survival, which include most of the physical needs—food, clothing, shelter, health—as well as the emotional needs for safety and security. A separate grouping can be made of those issues dealing with psychosocial needs of love, recognition, status, affiliation, and potency, agency or effect. In addition, a third grouping may be made: one dealing with aesthetic, knowledge seeking, spiritual and self-actualizing issues . . . we intend to deal with the middle range of issues described, the psychosocial group, and to limit even those to the issues of identity, connectedness or affiliation, and power . . .[43]

What are the realities of urban life as they affect these last three human

42. Mario Fantini and Gerald Weinstein, *Making Urban Schools Work* (New York: Holt, Rinehart and Winston, Inc., 1968).

43. *Ibid.*, p. 4.

needs? The density of the central city, they argue, results inevitably in a loss of identity for those who live in it, as daily life becomes mechanized and depersonalized. These two qualities are also dramatically evident in the urban school, with its large classes, routinization, and recordkeeping.

The large-scale bureaucratization of most of the institutions with which the urban-dweller must deal leads to feelings of apathy and powerlessness. And so it is in the urban school: "The verdict rendered most often is that in reality the client is at the service of the institution. Thus 'You can't fight City Hall' has become 'You can't fight the Board of Education.' "[44]

The great diversity of peoples, attitudes, values, and habits in the large city, though it may provide some with exciting possibilities of growth and experience, is threatening to most people, say Fantini and Weinstein, because physical and psychological boundaries keep people apart and alienated from one another. In the urban school:

> Many of the processes established by the school are intended to stamp out diversity both cultural and individual, so that the urban school actually alienates diverse pupils and keeps them disconnected from the school. Until recently, for example, it was illegal in New York for a teacher in a school to speak in Spanish to Spanish-speaking pupils except in foreign language classes.[45]

If these are the social realities of urbanism, and if the school is supposed to play a role in helping people to cope with them, it must change in very fundamental ways. Since we cannot very easily change the traditional educational objectives of the school, one alternative is to bring social realities into the curriculum as one way of improving basic skills and standard academic achievement. Fantini and Weinstein fear that if one tried to "slip in" social realities through this back-door process, neither the skill areas nor the social realities would be well-served. They propose instead that the school stress social realities as content in their own right, "content that has intrinsic value because it is integrally related to the learner, to his personal concerns, and to the needs of an open, self-renewing society."[46]

Their model for the urban school, then, has four different sets of objectives. "A" objectives are those presently legitimate aims of the school, including proficiency in the symbolic manipulations involved in reading and mathematics, the acquisition of knowledge and important concepts, and familiarity with modes of inquiry. A second set, "B" ob-

44. *Ibid.,* p. 8.
45. *Ibid.,* p. 9.
46. *Ibid.,* p. 16.

jectives, have to do with teaching children how to cope with their powerlessness, learning the skills of negotiating with adults, of getting what they want, of organizing, of taking constructive social action. "C" objectives have to do with increasing self-awareness and the discovery of strengths and talents of which students may not be aware. Finally, "D" objectives deal with the interpersonal skills popularized in the adult culture as "sensitivity training," the ability to develop meaningful and open interactions with others.

Fantini and Weinstein envision a "three-tiered" curriculum embodying skills and knowledge development in the first, personal talent and interest identification in the second, and the social action and exploration-of-self objectives as the third tier.

In the first tier activities of the traditional kind will continue, with the modification that wherever other less-traditional objectives can be served, they should be; if foreign languages are taught, for example, Spanish or an African dialect or some other language should be substituted for the traditional options, where these others are more relevant. Tier two allows for the exploration of interests and the development of individual creativity, including vocational interest. It might include any activity from learning to play a musical instrument to working on a research project, from producing a movie to an annual career-objective analysis for each student.

As the most unfamiliar of the objectives, tier three is given the most elaborate development by the plan. It "must consistently provide a simultaneous range of experience from the personalogical (intrapersonal) to the sociological (interpersonal) domains. The issues of identity, power, and connectedness pervade both domains and everything in between them." Some sample activities suggested for this tier:

> The development of feelings of power within the self through such devices as the "action program"—selecting a series of fairly easily achieved activities that a person has always wanted to do but has somehow avoided doing.
>
> The use of available social-studies programs that teach children to analyze interactions among people in real-life situations, including perhaps their own classrooms.
>
> A continual emphasis on the feelings of the students, not only in special training situations but in the activities involved in the first two tiers.

The schedule for such a school is reproduced in Figure 6.1. Fantini and Weinstein clearly do not expect that everything can be done within the regular school day; skill centers staffed by counselors would operate outside the classroom, and analogous interest centers would also be es-

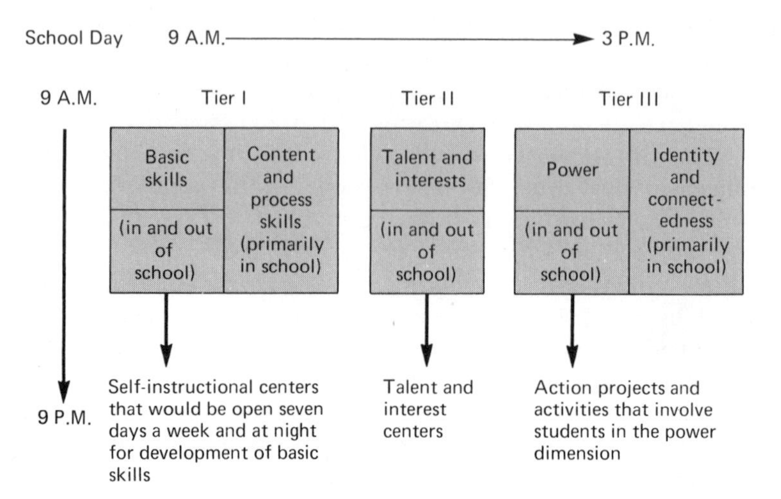

Figure 6.1 Proposed schedule and organization of Fantini and Weinstein's three-tier school.

SOURCE: Mario Fantini and Gerald Weinstein, *Making Urban Schools Work* (New York: Holt, Rinehart and Winston, Inc., 1968), p. 45.

tablished. The involvement of parents in all three levels of activity in the afternoon and evening would contribute to a stronger relationship between school and community.

The reader may find it useful to compare the costs and problems of implementation inherent in each of the two reconstruction models described here. One major difference that does not clearly emerge from the descriptions should be noted here; the rationalist scheme assumes that an improved self-concept is most likely to result from a sense of actual mastery of a skill or a body of knowledge. The developmental plan sees such a result as unlikely, because the source of feelings of inadequacy are so deeply involved in social arrangements and in attitudes that create a sense of both personal and social powerlessness.

Although individual value commitments, as well as differing cost/benefit judgments, are likely to lead to varying estimates of the worth of these two approaches to school reconstruction, both are likely to get some sort of a genuine trial in the coming decade. And, whatever one's personal judgment, it is important that both be given a chance to prove their worth; whatever the results, we are likely to learn a great deal about the educational process.

Recommended Reading

The most complete survey of compensatory education programs is Edmond Gordon's and Doxey Wilkerson's *Compensatory Education for the Disadvantaged* (New York: College Entrance Examination Board, 1966). Every education professional should be familiar with Coleman's study summarized in *Equality of Educational Opportunity* (Washington, D.C.: U.S. Department of Health, Education and Welfare, U.S. Government Printing Office, 1966), and with some of the body of critical comment on it, the best example of which is the Winter 1968 issue of the *Harvard Educational Review* (Vol. 38, No. 1). The education journals during the years 1967 and 1968 carried on a lively controversy over the question of whether integration or compensatory education is the key to the academic achievement problems of ghetto schools; the *Education Index* (New York: The H.W. Wilson Company) for those years will direct the student to relevant articles.

Teachers and students in education will be interested in looking at examples of the special materials developed for urban schools. Sample pages from a number of these may be found in S.M. Smiley's and H.L. Miller's *Policy Issues in Urban Education* (New York: The Free Press, 1968); examples from the following series may be found in most education libraries: Bank Street Readers (New York: The Macmillan Company), Gateway English anthologies (New York: The Macmillan Company), Great Cities Readers (Chicago: Follett Publishing Co.), Turner-Livingston Reading Series (Chicago: Follett Publishing Co.).

In addition to the short monograph outlining Mario Fantini's and Gerald Weinstein's proposals for school reconstruction, the same authors have published a more extensive critique and proposal called *The Disadvantaged* (New York: Harper & Row, 1968).

7

CLASSROOM DYNAMICS AND THE TEACHER

This chapter considers one of the most sensitive and poorly understood aspects of urban education; sensitive because it touches on arguments over the competence and attitudes of large numbers of professionals in the school, poorly understood because of the lack of any hard evidence for widely held beliefs about the role that the teacher is supposed to play in solving the problems of the urban school.

Most teachers themselves agree with the general public and with the majority of professional educators that the most important element in the educational process is the quality of teaching. Unfortunately, there is little agreement on the criteria for judging that quality. Despite the calm certainty with which teacher trainers and school administrators produce ratings of any teacher's classroom performance, innumerable attempts to achieve agreement among expert judges have largely failed; one of the current tendencies among some measurement experts involved in these attempts is to give up the quest for a reliable measure of quality.

Assuming that, even if we cannot measure differences in teaching performance, such differences must exist, how can one explain the absence of any consistent impact by teaching on the performance of pupils? As the data cited in the preceding chapter indicates, some large-scale studies show at least a moderate correlation between teacher experience and pupil achievement; but the Coleman study did not support that relationship. Any skill should improve with years of practice, and common sense, as well as the accumulated wisdom of the field, suggests that children should learn more from an experienced teacher. If common sense should, in this instance, prove incorrect (as Stuart Chase observed, it is that infallible sense that tells us the earth is flat), it is not simple to explain the discrepancy.

A possible explanation for moderate correlations between teacher experience and pupil achievement cited by Dyer in the preceding chapter, is that middle-class suburban schools probably have the most experienced teachers, for reasons to be discussed later; and because children in those schools also perform at higher levels, one should expect to find a correlation between teacher experience and pupil achievement, though it has little to do with the actual impact of the teacher himself. But Coleman's very extensive sample included a wide variety of schools and should have produced the same effect.

As an alternative to such speculation, one may adopt the attitude of some professional teacher trainers that easily measured aspects of teaching such as experience, quality of training, or the verbal skill of the teacher have little to do with the impact of teaching, particularly for the slum school child. The educational literature of the sixties contains hundreds of accounts of particular teachers producing astonishing results with groups of previously slow and retarded slum children. Although the majority of these are written by the teacher himself, and must consequently be accepted with some reservation, they suggest that a special rapport between teacher and children, some quality of relationship may be necessary to attain normal academic achievement in our slum schools.

This, at least, seems to be the majority opinion of teacher trainers, who agree with Kenneth Clark (*see* chapter 5) that teacher attitude and expectation are the key. An interview survey of twenty-five highly experienced professionals involved in training teachers for urban schools resulted in very substantial agreement on the image of the *effective* slum school teacher:

She should see the necessity of, and be interested in building on the children's own interests, in finding out or trying out new approaches to motivate and instruct, and in varying instructional approaches to fit individual learning styles.

She should avoid generalizing without modification about the community, the family, and other background factors related to the children, and must not perceive them as alien or different from herself.

She should have a high tolerance level for individual deviations in behavior, distinguish between children's behavior and the children as persons, be interested in how they feel, and be without feelings of threat in response to what they say or do.

She should be interested in developing success experiences for the children, be concerned about enhancing their feelings of worth, and interested in giving them freedom to make mistakes.

She should expect the children to be able to achieve normally, and feel that the school has a responsibility for adapting to *their* special backgrounds and needs.[1]

The difficulty with such general prescriptions for teacher character and attitudes is that they pose severe problems of either identification or training. No one has yet demonstrated a proven ability to predict such characteristics reliably from a written instrument or an interview, and though such workshop techniques as those described in chapter 5 appear to be successful in producing moderate atttiude change in some teachers, they are prohibitively expensive on any large scale. A crucial consideration for any strategy devised to improve teaching quality for the urban school is the magnitude of the task. In New York City alone —even if one had a magic formula for producing sensitive, accepting, loving teachers—it would be necessary to apply it to 25,000 individual teachers, about half of the instructional staff of the system.

TEACHER BEHAVIOR IN THE CLASSROOM

Fortunately, there is currently developing a body of research on classroom dynamics, based on close observation of teacher-pupil interactions, that is beginning to yield much sharper definitions of apparently desirable teacher behavior. The more clearly we can define those behaviors, the easier the training task will become. And, also fortunately, most of the research now available has been done in the urban school classroom and is directly relevant to the present discussion. The examples cited below were chosen to reflect the variety of conceptual frameworks with which researchers are approaching the analysis of classroom interaction and thus the types of generalizations that are beginning to emerge.

Louis Smith and William Geoffrey have adopted what might be called a systems analysis of classroom events.[2] In what is undoubtedly the most intensive study of a single classroom, Smith observed Geoffrey's seventh-grade class every day for a semester. His field records included a longhand account of the behavior of teacher and pupils and others who happened to come into the room; a set of summary observations and interpretations dictated each day into a tape recorder; and relevant documents, such as samples of the children's work, sociometric tests, notes from parents, and the like.

1. Project TRUE, Hunter College, New York, unpublished research.
2. Louis M. Smith and William Geoffrey, *Complexities of an Urban Classroom* (New York: Holt, Rinehart and Winston, Inc., 1968).

Geoffrey is an experienced teacher, well-organized, brisk, in command of his class, who leavens his management with humor and banter. Here is an excerpt from Smith's notes from one of the first days of the term that gives a good picture of Geoffrey's style:[3]

8.38. Observer comes in after yard duty. He receives a big "Hello, Mr. Smith" from Sandy. Geoffrey in. Banter begins over shop schedule. His comment about somebody not doing his job brings all the monitors (paper, chalk, date) into action. He corrects a schedule and takes attendance. Everyone but Lenny is present.

8:45 After paper is passed and pencils are sharpened, Geoffrey starts with "Name at top; number from 1 to 10 . . ." Raises question with Dick. "Are you going to make that your permanent seat?" "Yes sir." He starts spelling test (pop test?). "No. 1, Handsome. You are lucky to have such a handsome teacher." Geoffrey grins, everyone smiles . . . "No. 2, Warehouse. The Hawaiian Co. stores sugar in the warehouse across the street . . . Warehouse. No. 3, Coconut . . . No. 4, Gentlemen."

8:48. Messenger arrives. While handling the interruption, Geoffrey apparently suspects that someone is chewing gum. "I don't have any gum chewers in here?" Sarah says, "No, wax . . . " Everyone smiles. He generalizes rule to wax, paper clips, paper and tar.

Continues through list with humor, local items, maxims of behavior. 5. Iceberg . . . 6. Throughout. Study throughout the day . . . 7. Midnight. No one up after midnight . . . 8. Backward. There is not a backward student in this room. 9. However. However, there are some students who don't work as hard as they should. 10. Therefore. Therefore, I shall do my best to see that all of you work as hard as you can.

The analysis of the early days focuses on the development of pupil roles and how Geoffrey manages these during the process of establishing control. The authors analyze the way in which the teacher not only sets rules openly but indirectly builds a belief system for the pupils. Figure 7.1 represents one sequence of events involving giving the role of "assignment monitor" to a girl named Molly, and later substituting another child in the role.

At time 1 the teacher announces what being an assignment monitor requires—good attendance and good handwriting. At time 2 Molly volunteers, and there is the beginning belief system that persons must be adequate to the task. At time 3 Molly misspells a word in writing the assignment on the board; though spelling ability was not originally specified for the job, the authors suggest that this creates dissonance for both teacher and class—at times 4 and 5. That is, the belief that pupils

3. *Ibid.*, p. 72.

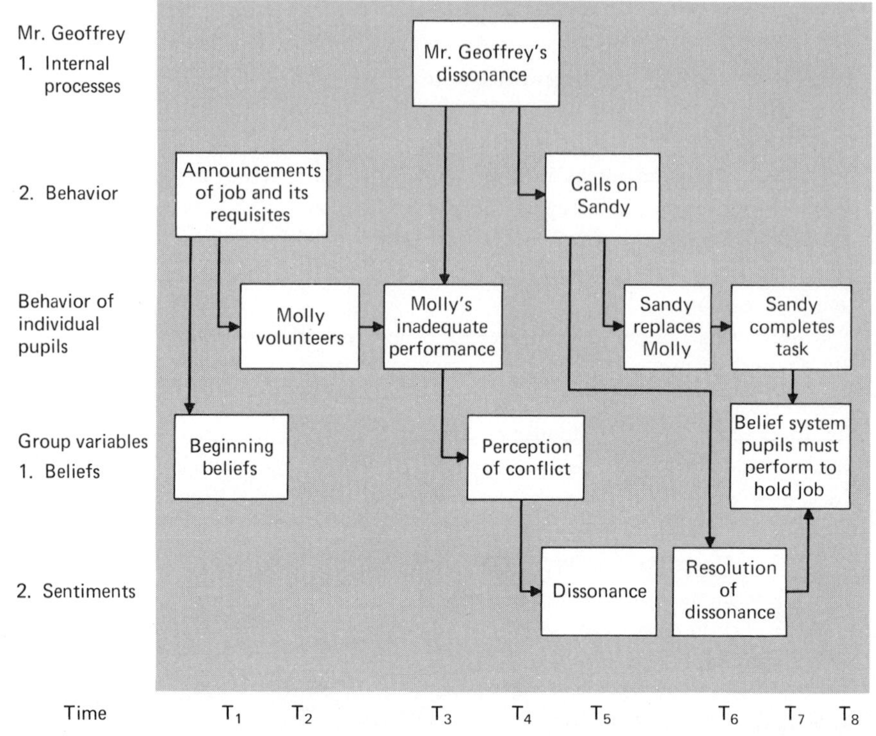

Figure 7.1 A process analysis of the development of monitor roles and belief systems.

SOURCE: Louis M. Smith and William Geoffrey, *Complexities of an Urban Classroom* (New York: Holt, Rinehart and Winston, Inc., 1968), p. 49.

must be adequate in order to have a monitor's role conflicts with the manifest fact that Molly is not doing adequately. This leads to the teacher's relieving Molly of the assignment, followed at times 7 and 8 by "the stabilizing of the belief that there is such a role as assignment monitor and that it must be carried out by someone adequate to its demands." Each of the boxes in the figure indicates what is going on during the episode at one of the levels indicated along the left line of the chart.

Out of this kind of analysis the authors conclude that Geoffrey moves very directly and in many ways to build a belief system among the pupils that consists of two major tenets: learning should be going on all the time and learning is work.

The following illustrations connect several improbable areas; first, in developing the monitor roles, one pupil raised the question about messengers. Geoffrey's response was, "Leave that open for anyone who gets his work done." Second, in discussing promotions, he said, "That's not all, the most important thing is doing your own work for me. Some of the assignments are difficult. Let's have no nonsense on not doing work . . . Do your best and do it regularly." Third, on Friday morning, the first full day, he commented, "You've had a nice vacation, now it's time to get to work . . ." and finally on Friday afternoon he commented, "School is business. Come back on Monday ready to work."

The immediate alternatives that seem open to the teacher are that academic activities are fun (gamelike), interesting (intrinsically attractive), important (for a variety of purposes), difficult or easy, and so forth. Sketching out the possible consequences of these points of view, while hazardous, also seems enlightening. It raises the basic question of the immediate consequences of pupils who have an apathetic if not hostile attitude toward school. Presenting the "reality" of academic activity joins the issue directly rather than masking it by presenting a conception different from that held by the pupils. The congruence suggests, for the immediate moment, understanding and communication. For the long term, however, this suggests that little change or possibility of change will occur. . . .[4]

As for the teacher's initial role, it appeared to be to get the children to move toward another aspect of pupils' belief system, that "the teacher gives directions and the pupils follow them." Geoffrey accomplished this by what the authors call "grooving the children," which consists primarily of giving dozens of orders involving a number of trivial actions, and of using the word "permission" over and over again. The authors point out that whatever the long-term consequences for the development of pupil creativity there may be in this process its immediate result is more efficiency and less need for teacher explanations and pleas.

They point out that the development of this system, as Geoffrey managed it, had the following advantages:

1) the requests themselves were individually quite insignificant; 2) they dealt mostly with activities in which teachers are expected to be involved; 3) they were asked of everyone; consequently to refuse would be to cast oneself in a special light; 4) the situations were cloaked with individual attention, warmth, and humor; 5) they often involved activities such as getting up and moving about, which was a pleasurable alternative to being seated for a long period of time; and 6) many of the requests involved volunteering and special, favorable attention.[5]

The summary model for this operation is shown in Figure 7.2, indicating the source of Geoffrey's own norms, as well as part of the reason for the pupils' ready compliance.

4. *Ibid.*, p. 51.
5. *Ibid.*, p. 68.

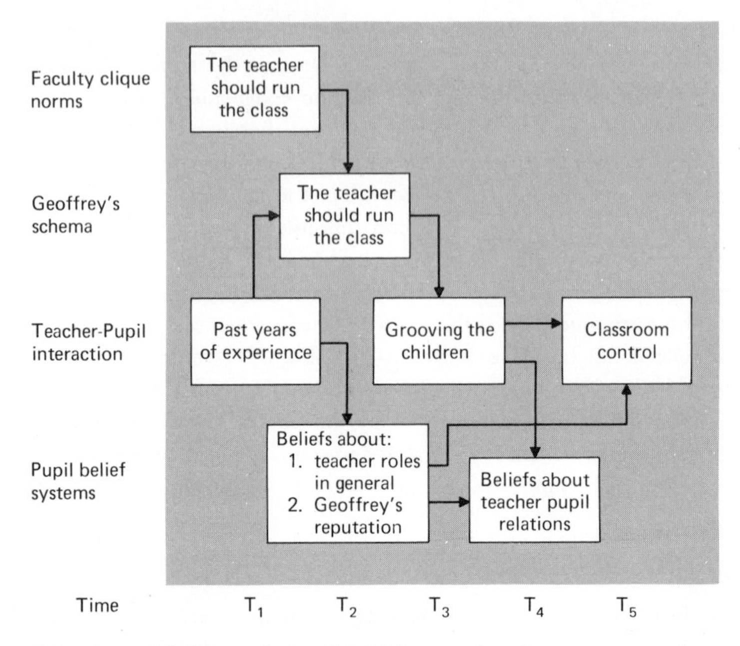

Figure 7.2 A model for analysis of initial steps in classroom control.
SOURCE: Louis M. Smith and William Geoffrey, *Complexities of an Urban Classroom* (New York: Holt, Rinehart and Winston, Inc., 1968), p. 69.

The analysis goes on to develop within this framework a complex and interesting theory of teaching that any instructor should find rewarding to consider. Of immediate interest is the insight that the approach provides into one of the major problems of slum school social structure: the establishment of classroom control and habits of work.

For a direct contrast to this smooth development of class beliefs and norms by an experienced and competent teacher, we turn next to a different type of analysis, a purely anthropological one.[6] This one is a second-grade class in a New York ghetto school; the principal himself warned the observational team that it was one of his "wild" classes. It contains twenty-four children who, said the administrator, are either non-English speaking or "seriously disturbed." It is taught by a middle-aged woman who is not yet licensed or certified, the kind of "permanent substitute" teacher who often turns up in the urban school classroom. Several observers spent a day with the class, and a condensed account of their observation follows.

During the first ten minutes Mrs. Auslander, the teacher, inspects the children's hands and leads them in a morning song about washing their hands. She then begins a drill on the days of the week. During the drill:

6. G. Alexander Moore, Jr., *Realities of the Urban Classroom* (New York: Doubleday & Company, Inc., 1967).

. . . several children are noisily running around the room hitting one another. Others sit in a stupor, apparently quite unaware of their surroundings. In the space of the first ten minutes, the teacher has already used physical force in an attempt to control the children . . . She frequently addresses her noisy, restless class, saying, "When I have everyone's attention and your hands are folded, then I will listen to what you're trying to say." Since this never happens, she never really listens to any of the children during the morning, yet many of them do seem to want to say something to her.

She suddenly turns upon a child who was quietly looking at a book. "Why are you playing with your book?"

Some children in another part of the room then begin to write, the teacher calls out, "We're talking. We're not writing now." Meantime, a few children do give her the proper names of the days; however, most of the class is not paying any attention.[7]

The teacher begins an exercise involving writing the "morning news" on the board, and then assigns the class the task of copying the sentences about the weather and what they had done the previous day into their notebooks.

Now, at 10:05, Mrs. Auslander walks around the room to see if the children are indeed copying the work from the board in their notebooks. Frequently she approaches a child and asks "Where is your book?" If the child does not answer, she repeats her question until he or she does. In one case, she repeated it a good six times, each time raising her voice more until she was shouting.

Some children are not copying because they do not have pencils, so she tries to persuade other children to lend them one. "George, will you lend a pencil to Lucille?" she asks. George has a small pencil case from which he removes a pencil to lend to Lucille. "What a nice boy you are," she commends George.

While she was looking for a pencil for Lucille, Mrs. Auslander remarked to the observer what a problem she has because the children forget or lose pencils. The observer offered a pencil for Lucille, but Mrs. Auslander protested, saying without lowering her speaking voice,"You'll never get it back." After George has lent his pencil to Lucille, Mrs. Auslander comments aloud to the observer, "You know, George *could* be a very *good* boy."[8]

The general sense of disorder is increasing slowly. The teacher tries to engage the children in a discussion of how many days there are in the months; during it, children go in and out with a pass. The teacher declares that no one else can leave, then reverses her decision and permits other children to go; tries to impress them with the rule that boys

7. *Ibid.*, pp. 53-54.
8. *Ibid.*, p. 55.

and girls take their turn at the pass; tells a boy to take his suit jacket off and threatens to report him to the principal if he doesn't obey. At 10:19:

Mrs. Auslander is telling Carol, a Negro girl, "Get up and stand in the corner and face the wall. Put your hands on your head." The girl obeys, standing in the corner at the back of the room, and immediately begins to cry. In a moment she takes her hands off her head and stops crying.

A boy who has been given the pass flourishes it. As he leaves the room, he pauses at the door and salutes the class. Once he is gone, the teacher goes to the door and, taking out her key, locks the door from the inside. Some older boys are passing in the hall. They stop at the door, look into the classroom and make faces through the window.

Mrs. Auslander is standing alongside the boy that she had earlier forced to remove his jacket: "Would you like to stay in Mr. Selby's office all day?" Carol is sucking her thumb in the corner. Disorder reigns.[9]

The children begin to come over to the observer and show her their notebooks. A Negro boy with crossed eyes is standing in front of the observer. His name is Allen. Beginning to look at the pages of his notebook, the observer asks him, "May I look at your book?" He nods eagerly. On the first page there is a note written by the teacher. "Allen has exposed himself in school today. He has many kinds of problems. Take this note home to your mother and have her sign it." A signature below this shows that his mother has read it.

A second entry is her reply. "I beat Allen at home for having done this but Allen says he didn't do it but that another boy has done it to him." The second page bears yet another note from Mrs. Auslander in ink, as her first had been. "Allen did expose himself but I do not want to make an issue of it." All these notes are in the ordinary pages of Allen's class notebook, an article he carries around with him and uses daily.[10]

By this time the observer notes that the teacher seems to be spending most of her time pushing or pinching the children. Carol has left the corner, and the teacher threatens to hit her if she does not go back. Carol returns and starts sucking her thumb again. Frequent fights are now breaking out among the children, and the teacher makes an effort to keep them quiet by trying to get them to do physical exercises. A few children join her, but most remain seated, while others are running around the room.

Angel, an Hispano boy, is becoming particularly obstreperous. He runs around the room and pushes some of the children . . . Two or three times earlier in

9. *Ibid.*, pp. 57-58.
10. *Ibid.*, p. 59.

the morning the teacher has threatened him with being sent to Mr. Selby's office . . . At 11:00 A.M. she makes good her threat, marching out of the room saying, "I'm going to get John." As soon as she is out the door, the noise in the room drops. Attention seems to be centered on the door. Three or four children ooh and ah. One child says, "Here he comes." Mrs. Auslander enters, accompanied by a tall, slender Negro boy from an older grade. They approach Angel, the small Hispano boy, who is in his seat, clutching his desk for dear life and bawling loudly. The teacher tries to pry him loose but without success. She turns to her companion, "John, would you take him, please." Angel is wailing louder all the time, and babbles, "Leave me alone. Leave me alone." He clings to his desk but John succeeds in prying him loose and drags him screaming from the room. His screams can be heard echoing down the hall.[11]

Mrs. Auslander then tries to go through a list of words from one of the readers. She tells the children to copy the words, which some do in the midst of a rain of reprimands from her. The teacher pulls one child by the ear over to the wastebasket to make him spit out some gum, sends several other children to the corner.

At 11:50 the children line up for lunch amid continual fighting. The teacher leads them down several flights of stairs on the way to the cafeteria.

The noise has been sufficient so that a man teacher comes out of a room to see what is going on. He reenters and closes his door with a bang. The children have started out ahead of the teacher and, as they go downstairs, she asks to pass between the two lines in order to get to the head of the class. The children separate and make a passageway for her along the double line. As she goes down the staircase, several children raise their feet as if to kick her.[12]

In commenting on this slice of classroom life Moore suggests it is crucial to note that Mrs. Auslander regards this as a "discipline class," though such a term is not used by any of the administrators or teachers who have mentioned the group. Since she lacks training, and has been assigned the worst class in the grade, one would suppose that Mrs. Auslander would make use of the many resources available in the school. But, in fact, she has never accepted any of the suggestions offered by the teacher trainer, never referred a single student to the guidance counselor, nor sought help from the remedial reading teacher. Having begun with the perception that her role was to discipline the children, she ignores her role as teacher.

11. *Ibid.*, p. 61.
12. *Ibid.*, pp. 63-64.

Moore goes on to analyze this situation from a number of angles, the most interesting of which involves an explanation of the authority structure of the group, using a set of terms that Irving Goffman earlier applied to the staff-patient relationships in a mental hospital.

Since the most conspicuous aspect of the group was an absence of mannerly behavior, Goffman analyzes good manners in those terms; *deference* is the appreciation one individual shows to another; *demeanor* is an aspect of a person's "ceremonial" bearing that communicates to others the message that he is worthy of respect and can be trusted not to do something dangerous.

The rules of deference in most societies permit a person with greater authority to take some liberties with those subordinate to him; he has the right to invade "the metaphorical boundary around the self" of the subordinate. But he cannot press too far, because even though superior in status, he owes his subordinates a measure of deference. In anthropological terms, certain "avoidance rituals" specify what he must *not* do; "presentational rituals" specify what he *should* do. Mrs. Auslander violates both of these. She invades the children's ideal images of themselves repeatedly by commenting negatively about them to the observer and by writing a note about past shameful behavior of one child in his notebook, not a private place. Presentation rituals consist of salutations, compliments, invitations, and minor services, of which there is almost a total lack in the foregoing account; her one compliment to George is later taken back in the comment to the observer: "George *could* be a very good boy." When properly done, touch can be taken as a friendly salutation; but here it is always an invasion of the self, and usually painful.

Her own demeanor cannot command deference in return from the children, for Mrs. Auslander never listens to them and seldom acknowledges their answers to questions she herself has asked; her general air is one of worried harassment. This being so, Moore speculates about why the children are not more openly aggressive with her.

Note that they are not. They are not violating her sacred self in the same way that she violates theirs. The closest they come is by performing what Goffman calls a "ceremonial profanation," which is the practice of defiling the recipient but in such a way and from such an angle that he retains the right to act as if he had not received the profaning message." Thus, when Mrs. Auslander passes through the double file of children in the hall, many of them ceremonially pretend to kick her behind her back. . . . When Allen does his boxing dance step every time Mrs. Auslander approaches him, he is not offending her but defending himself. He is marking very clearly and quite explicitly the boundaries of his "ideal self" which he expects, quite reasonably, that she is going to invade.[13]

13. *Ibid.*, pp. 77-78

Mrs. Auslander's definition of the class as a "discipline class," then, has resulted in continuously punitive behavior that is tantamount to a declaration of war on the children. And they fight back defensively.

When teacher trainers talk vaguely about the need for teachers to "respect" children as individuals, it is these factors of deference and demeanor that they probably mean to communicate. But, although there is a lesson here for all teachers, it is very doubtful that any amount of training could change Mrs. Auslander into a good teacher; we shall later consider the question of why such a thoroughly incompetent and harmful teacher is not immediately removed from her position.

Our third, and final, example of analytic approaches to classroom dynamics is one that employs a framework adopted from social psychology rather than anthropology, closer to Smith and Geoffrey's than to Moore's. Joan Roberts, working with the same mass of observation data that Moore used, explains the behavior of the children primarily in the terminology of group structure:

> In any group, people either formally or informally decide the answers to such questions as, who has power to control whom; who communicates to whom about what; who is preferred and who is rejected; who fulfills which functions needed in the group. Answers to these questions create stable structure for the group . . .[14]

Roberts notes that group structure arises partly from the need to do a task more efficiently by dividing labor into differentiated parts. Most people find it pleasurable to work together cooperatively on a task; much of the recent research on industrial productivity indicates that workers are often more productive when they are permitted to work as members of a team and to make social interaction a part of the task.

But in the urban slum classroom, the formal group structure emphasizes instead a model in which individuals are isolated from one another and in which the only legitimate interaction is with the leader. This is true of middle-class schoolrooms also, to be sure, but Roberts argues that middle-class children are far more accepting than lower-class ones of a situation in which social interaction is suppressed; they can more readily accept the teacher as a model and they behave less motorically.

Using class observation protocols for examples, Roberts describes the variety of reactions to the restricted interaction of the slum classroom, which can be categorized as either apathetic or aggressive.

14. Joan Roberts, *Group Behavior in Urban Classrooms* (New York: Hunter College, 1968), p. 142.

Apathy is seen in a number of covert rejection techniques that include *sleeping* or appearing to sleep:

The teacher shushes the class and instructs them to read silently about the beginning of the war in their books. By this time another girl is resting her head on the desk.

In the course of the conversations going on among the children, it becomes perfectly apparent that the students who rested their heads on their desks in the earlier social studies class have regained their energies and are talking with vivacity to their friends.[15]

Claiming physical disabilities:

A number of students complain in the course of the period of physical disabilities when they are admonished by the teacher for not paying attention. For example, one girl explains, "There is something in my eye."[16]

Staring out the window:

One girl is sitting and looking out the window. There is a big piece of construction going on across the street from the school and she seems to be observing it.[17]

Reading:

Two boys are out of it. One is gazing out the window. Another is reading comic books.

By this time V———— has an art book which she is busy reading rather than paying attention to the lesson. Another child is sitting in a seat with her legs stretched out on another desk.[18]

Other common ways of opposing the wishes of authority consist of doodling, doing homework, drawing, making necklaces out of chewing-gum wrappers. Typically, the teachers in these classes must provide the answers to their own questions and enforce attention to any material that they outline on the board.

The second type of class reaction is open and active resistance to authority, some of which has already been detailed at length in Mrs. Auslander's class. Roberts notes the following techniques:

Mockery:

When the younger teacher plays the song, Ava Maria, on the piano, some of the students sing the melody satirically. They continue this after class is over

15. *Ibid.*, p. 146.
16. *Ibid.*, p. 147.
17. *Ibid.*, p. 147.
18. *Ibid.*, p. 148.

while en route to the next class, singing the song with the same style of mockery which closed the music period.[19]

Derision:

The teacher starts by asking, "What does the word future mean?" At this point there is laughter as Dr. ————, the reading specialist, enters the room from the front door to get some materials at the back. The laughter, though suppressed, is directed toward this teacher whom the students do not particularly like.[20]

Fighting:

There are two students close to me who are attempting to sit in the same seat. They begin arguing over who the seat belongs to. . . . Some of the boys are clowning around. One of them kicks the student ahead of them while he is working. This is a big joke among the fellows and the noise level is rather high.[21]

Talking:

The students are very noisy and many are up and walking around and talking with each other and doing other things.

About six or seven students are sitting in their seats and not taking part at all. Within these two groups there are about three or four who are doing most of the talking.

The children from the beginning to the end of the period are engaged in their own individual social relationships in spite of shushing by the younger teacher and guidance by the older teacher.[22]

Roberts cites observations from a number of shop and music classes in which children are allowed to interact or to work together and where they appear to be enjoying the work and each other. She describes one exceptional ninth-grade mathematics class in which the students are permitted to communicate with one another while doing problems; the atmosphere is loud, lively, but work-oriented.

The general point of her analysis is most dramatically conveyed by a statement from Ashton-Warner, a British teacher of Maori children in New Zealand.

From long sitting, watching, and pondering (all so unprofessional) I have found out the worst enemies to what we call teaching are two. The first is the children's

19. *Ibid.*, p. 158.
20. *Ibid.*, p. 158.
21. *Ibid.*, p. 159.
22. *Ibid.*, pp. 159-160.

interest in each other. It plays the very devil with orthodox methods. If only they'd stop talking to each other, playing with each other, fighting with each other and loving each other. This unseemly and unlawful communication! In self-defense I've got to use the damn thing. So I harness the communication since I can't control it, and base my method on it. They read in pairs, sentence and sentence aloud. There's no time for either to get bored. Each checks the other's mistakes and hurries him up if he's too slow, since after all his own turn depends on it. They teach each other all their work in pairs, sitting cross-legged knee to knee on the mat, or on their tables, arguing with, correcting, abusing or smiling at each other. And between them all the time is this togetherness, so that learning is so mixed up with relationship that it becomes part of it. What an unsung creative medium is relationship.

The other trouble with this New Race is their desire to make things. If only they'd sit like the white children with their hands still and wait until they're told to do something and told how to do it. The way they draw bombers and make them with anything and roar around the room with them. Noise, noise, noise, yes. But if you don't like noise, don't be a teacher. Because children are noisy animals. . . But it's a natural noise and therefore bearable. True, there is an occasional howl of rage, a shout of accusation, soprano crying and the sound of something falling, but there is also a voice raised in joy, someone singing and the break, break, break of laughter. In any case, it's all expulsion of energy and as such a help. I let anything come . . . within safety; *but I use it.*[23]

WORK AND CONSIDERATION STRUCTURES

These examples of observational data and the conceptual structures brought to bear on understanding them represent the exciting beginnings of a thoroughgoing theory of classroom behavior in the urban school. They confirm already well-established findings from the study of other types of groups at work, notably that two elements must be present for productivity: a *work structure,* some stable way of initiating activity—organizing, planning, setting standards, and so forth—and a *considerations structure,* ways for the participants to get social and personal satisfaction from the situation. If the teacher, as leader, cannot supply the second of these structures, the children will find informal ways of getting some personal gratification by antiwork behavior.

The preceding accounts suggest that, as Geoffrey demonstrated, it is possible for a skilled and experienced teacher to supply both needs of the classroom group; but on the other hand, his class does not sound as difficult as the one Mrs. Auslander confronted. It is possible that, as

23. Sylvia Ashton-Warner, *Teacher* (New York: Simon and Schuster, Inc., 1963), pp. 103-104.

Roberts argues, the New York classes, lower on the socioeconomic scale, have a greater need for the gratification of social needs, and even Geoffrey's skill might not be sufficient to maintain the pattern of teacher-pupil interaction that characterized his style.

On a more general level this data also contributes to an understanding of a long-standing conflict over teaching styles. The philosophical differences basic to the curriculum viewpoints described in the preceding chapter have their analogues in two separate ideals of the teaching role. One of these, most appropriate to the rationalist position on curriculum, might most accurately be called the *taskmaster* role; the second, appropriate to the developmental curriculum, emphasizes the *motivator* role of the teacher.

The taskmaster image is the traditional one of the instructor: He decides on instructional aims, plans a sequence of steps through which the learner must move toward mastery, and organizes classroom activities in the most efficient way possible for the attainment of the desired cognitive behaviors. As motivator, on the other hand, the teacher is attentive primarily to the interests of the individual child and to his patterns of development. Because "the whole child" is in the classroom, the teacher must be concerned with his emotional state as well as his cognitive growth.

It is clear that the taskmaster concentrates on the work structure of the classroom, as the motivator does on the consideration structure. But it is instructive that after several generations of attack on the taskmaster role by progressive educators and the concentration of most teacher-training institutions on the motivator role the most common teaching style is still that of the taskmaster. Its persistence may in part be explained by the fact that the motivator role makes far more complex demands on the teacher, and that the neophyte's experience has largely been with taskmasters throughout his own school career. But it is possible also that the first years of teaching persuade most instructors that without a good deal of organizing and planning on their parts, children do not achieve very many of the school's objectives. The good taskmaster often learns to supply just enough consideration structure to keep the children involved in the task; and if he does not, the chances are that there is enough external pressure on the child from the family and from the situation itself to provide sufficient motivation for at least minimum achievement. But the good motivator, paying primary attention to personal and social needs, may well find himself with a happy and harmonious group of children learning a number of things that have little to do with stated school objectives.

Although most teachers use both of these roles to varying degrees, it is easy to guess why the drift toward emphasis on the taskmaster role is so persistent. There appears to be a growing number of young teachers on the urban scene who have found a way of resisting such a drift simply by rejecting, out of hand, the cognitive objectives of the traditional school for the urban poor. Here, for example, is a statement by a young teacher enthusiastically involved in one of the community-control experiments in New York City:

An even more fundamental obstacle is built into the very nature of the project. Our experiment will be evaluated in terms of the established conventional criteria: reading scores, discipline, standardized achievement tests, etc., some of which measure what they are intended to measure for *middle class children*. We have a problem when these criteria fail to measure the extent to which a child has been educated, when they simply test rote memorization, stifling of initiative and training in sitting through standardized examinations. Unleashed creativity, or a critical outlook, for example, would probably lower a child's scores on these exams, rather than raise them.

If the conventional criteria measure the wrong things, their effect is harmful to our students, yet they will determine to a great extent whether or not we will ever be free to develop our own yardsticks. In effect, we must miseducate the children before we will be allowed to educate them.[24]

This somewhat ingenuous statement fails to consider such questions as how one can develop a critical outlook without a good deal of knowledge about whatever it is one criticizes, and consequently how one gets children to acquire that knowledge; but it is, however attackable, an increasingly popular view of teaching in the urban slum school. Thus, in the cyclical fashion by which American educational ideas tend to develop, the motivator role is due in the immediate future for another testing.

PROBLEMS OF STAFFING THE URBAN SCHOOLS

If the kind of teacher most needed in the slum school is defined only as one who is sympathetic to and interested in the children of the slums, the task of staffing the schools would be relatively simple. But if one accepts the objectives of the school as it now exists, and the need to prepare lower-class children for some role in an increasingly technological society, the instructional and interpersonal skills necessary for teachers are obviously very complex. The difficulties involved in obtaining large numbers of such teachers are formidable, and are anatomized below.

24. Charles S. Isaacs, "A JHS 271 Teacher Tells It Like He Sees It," *New York Times Magazine* (November 24, 1968), pp. 53 and 54.

TURNOVER AND THE URBAN TEACHER CAREER CYCLE

The typical urban school system has significantly different proportions of younger and less-experienced teachers on the staff of lower-class schools than on any other class level, as we noted in chapter 2. The Chicago data in Table 7.1 indicates that very substantial variations in experience levels exist even between working-class schools and the slum school. Moreover, in the systems that hire teachers without full qualifications (data is available for Chicago, New York City, and Detroit), slum schools have greater proportions of less-well-trained teachers.

The reasons for these variations are simple. Because assignment to schools in lower-class neighborhoods and ghetto areas is widely considered less desirable, teachers just entering the profession and consequently without much power to indicate an assignment preference are offered positions where most of the vacancies exist. And most of the vacancies are in the slum school because its turnover rate is higher than any other, as the Herriot and St. John study cited in Chapter 2 indicated. Table 7.2 gives more precise illustrative data from Chicago; transfer requests out of slum schools are two-and-a-half times the number of those in middle-class schools. Some estimates put it as high as ten times greater.[25]

In a study of the Chicago teacher's career line, Howard Becker found that she typically begins in a less-desirable school, then takes one of two paths.[26] One of these consists of an adjustment to the situation, a resigned acceptance of professional problems with which she either does or does not learn to cope adequately. The alternative path is a restless transfer from one school to another searching for the best possible combination of tractable children and satisfactory administration.

Becker reports that perception of the problems the teachers are likely to encounter vary directly with the social class composition of the school. Their ideal is the child who responds well to discipline and is consequently easiest to manage. The slum child is viewed as uncontrollable, as well as morally unacceptable in a variety of ways, from his physical cleanliness to his sexual mores. The upper-middle-class child, on the other hand, though easy to teach, is viewed as spoiled and as not showing sufficient respect for his elders. The lower-middle- and upper-working class child seems to these teachers most ideal in response to discipline as well as in morality.

25. A.O. Boykin, *Demographic Factors Associated with Intrasystem Teacher Mobility in an Urban School System* (Ph.D. Dissertation, University of Illinois, 1964).

26. Howard S. Becker, "Social Class Variations in the Teacher-Pupil Relationship," *Journal of Educational Sociology,* Vol. 25 (April 1952), pp. 451-465.

Table 7.1 Characteristics of Teachers Related to Socioeconomic Area of School (percentages, unless otherwise stated)

	Upper or middle class	Mixed middle and working class	Stable working class	Lower class or slum	Total
		A. Elementary schools			
Sex					
Male	10	9	12	19	14
Female	90	91	88	81	86
Age					
20-25	3	9	13	19	14
26-30	7	11	15	21	16
31-40	19	23	22	32	27
41-50	26	21	18	15	18
51-65	45	34	30	13	24
66+	1	1	2	1	1
Experience by year					
1	2	5	7	11	8
2	3	4	7	12	8
3-5	6	12	16	26	19
6-15	31	36	32	36	35
16+	58	44	38	16	31
Number	264	1537	912	2409	5122
Percent of total	5	30	18	47	100
		B. High schools			
Sex					
Male	47	44	54	52	47
Female	53	56	46	48	53
Age					
20-25	14	16	17	23	18
26-30	18	15	22	21	18
31-40	23	22	23	28	24
41-50	12	17	14	12	15
51-65	31	26	21	15	23
66+	2	3	3	2	3

Table 7.1 Characteristics of Teachers (*continued*)

	Upper or middle class	Mixed middle and working class	Stable working class	Lower class or slum	Total
		B. High schools			
Experience by year					
1	5	7	11	11	9
2	5	8	11	14	10
3-5	19	20	23	29	22
6-15	35	31	28	31	31
16+	36	34	27	16	29
Number	242	1187	391	504	2328
Percent of total	10	51	17	22	100

SOURCE: Robert J. Havighurst, *The Public Schools of Chicago* (Chicago: The Board of Education of the City of Chicago, 1964), pp. 342-343.

But, to conclude that those who leave the slum school do so because they are less professionally oriented than those who stay, or that those who stay are more altruistic or dedicated is unlikely in view of the evidence presented in a study by William Wayson.

Table 7.2 Why Teachers Have Requested Transfers (percent of regular classroom teachers)

	Elementary	High school
Percent with name on transfer list	12	8
Socioeconomic area of school		
Upper or middle class	6	6
Mixed middle and working class	9	6
Stable working class	12	9
Lower class or slum	15	11
Number	616	164
Reasons given for requesting transfers		
Personal convenience	34	27
Professional advancement	15	17
Dissatisfaction with principal	15	20
Other professional dissatisfaction	16	21
Dissatisfaction with pupils and/or community	16	12
Operation of system	4	2

SOURCE: Robert J. Havighurst, *The Public Schools of Chicago* (Chicago: The Board of Education of the City of Chicago, 1964), p. 346.

Table 7.3 Types of Motives Expressed by Each Subgroup (percentages)

Type of motive (as ranked by total sample)	Percentage of teachers giving one or more responses classified in type			
	White		Negro	
	Stayer (n-27)	Leaver (n-16)	Stayer (n-15)	Leaver (n-4)*
1. Personal esteem	58†	19	33	25
2. Missionary zeal	33	31	33	25
3. Professional autonomy	37	13	27	25
4. Inertia	37†	6	13	25
5. Constraints	4	6	40††	75
6. Group belongingness	7	25	27	0
7. Accommodating principal	22†	0	13	25
8. Professional appraisal	7	38**	0	25
9. Altruism	22†	0	7	0
10. Despotism	7	13	0	0
11. Unclassified	0	6	0	0

* Negro leavers were too few in number to compare. They are shown only as a matter of interest.
** Leavers exceeded white and Negro stayers, significant at .05 level.
† White stayers exceeded white leavers, significant at .05 level.
†† Negro stayers exceeded white stayers at .05 level and white leavers at .10 level.

SOURCE: William W. Wayson, "Expressed Motives of Teachers in Slum Schools," *Urban Education,* Vol. 1, No. 4 (1965), p. 230.

Wayson studied a sample of sixty-two woman teachers in a Midwestern city. Forty-two of these had been in their present assignment for five or more years, and intended to stay; twenty were transferring from their lower-class schools.[27] Table 7.3 gives the proportions of teachers in each category who expressed one or another of the reasons listed for staying in the school as long as they had. The researcher interprets his findings as follows:

Two-thirds of the white teachers who had remained in the slum school indicated that they either feared making a change (inertia) or enjoyed freedom from interference by parents or the scrutiny of superiors (autonomy). Several of these respondents expressed other reasons for remaining in the school, but it appeared that their staying was due to these two factors and that other satisfactions were secondary. The autonomy in the slum school did not seem to stimulate efforts to change the curriculum or to improve the learning situation. Rather,

27. William W. Wayson, "Expressed Motives of Teachers in Slum Schools," *Urban Education,* Vol. 1, No. 4 (1965), pp. 223-238.

the type of autonomy sought by these respondents resulted in their withdrawal from the community and reliance upon bureaucratic defenses against pressures from outside the school.

Pupils were the most important referent group for stayers. Nearly sixty per cent of the white stayers and one-third of the Negro stayers expressed the motive to be personally liked and appreciated by their pupils. Stayers who sought personal esteem stayed in the school because they receive warm, affectionate, highly personalized responses from pupils. They doubted that schools in better neighborhoods would afford them such esteem or would afford close personal relationships with pupils.

Closely related to the desire for personal esteem were the altruistic responses given by one-fifth of the white stayers (but none of the leavers). Altruists spoke more of contributing to the personal needs of the pupil than of his contributions to teachers. Altruistic teachers seemed to fulfill their own felt needs through beneficent and maternal ministry of their pupils.

About one-fifth of the white stayers expressed an attachment to an accommodating principal who created an organization and interacted with teachers in ways that maximized their comfort and convenience. He was generous with materials and supplies, and he restrained disobedient children or belligerent parents. These reasons for staying seemed related to the motives categorized as inertia and autonomy.

Nearly forty percent of the white leavers said that they gained most satisfaction from having the principal or a supervisor give them a positive professional appraisal. They gained little satisfaction from interacting with pupils. Although leavers recognized the bureaucratic attractions of the school, those attractions were not sufficient to make leavers want to remain there.

Almost equal percentages (about one-third) of stayers and leavers, white and Negro, expressed missionary zeal. They stressed ethical relationships to other persons, "the good life," occupational mobility, or religion. Stayers tended to generalize from their successful converts feeling that even one success was worth all their efforts. Leavers tended to be frustrated by the relative infrequency with which they succeeded in their missions. Stayers felt successful when former pupils demonstrated adherence to the values espoused by the teacher. Leavers, generally younger than stayers, had not had many former pupils return to see them. Leavers sought more immediate evidence of having been successful. Responses from which these data are drawn indicated that missionary zeal is not sufficient motive to keep a teacher in the slum school and that those missionaries who stayed revised downward their aspirations in the mission field.

About one-fourth of the white leavers and a similar percentage of the Negro stayers expressed satisfaction in being affiliated with the faculty in the school. Young leavers sought belongingness as a tangible mark of professional status and were not strongly attached to the group. Negro teachers, on the other hand, seemed to gain personal status from membership in clearly defined, cohesive friendship groups that persisted even outside school.

In most other comparisons the motives expressed by Negro teachers were like those expressed by white stayers. Negroes much more than whites felt constrained to remain in the slum school.[28]

Thus, the leavers seemed to be mainly dissatisfied because the academic achievement of their pupils was below standard; and the leavers are academically oriented. Wayson categorizes them as: *climbers,* those for whom teaching was not a central part of their self-concept and for whom the opinions of superiors was important; and *threatened bureaucrats,* those whose security was threatened by an influx of pupils who differed from the ones they had been teaching or by a change in principals.

The stayers he categorizes as either: *bureaucrats,* for whom the security of the known environment or a satisfying principal was most important; and the *big sisters,* who developed highly personalized relationships with some of their pupils.

Considering both the high turnover rates created by some of these attitudes and the low level of instructional performance created by others, the administration of the central city slum school obviously faces severe problems of staffing.

As Wayson's findings suggest, there is an inevitable tendency to overlook poor teaching performance in the interests of keeping classrooms staffed with "warm bodies," if nothing else. But this is not the only reason for the retention of not merely mediocre but actively harmful teachers; there is, in addition, the influence of bureaucratic structure with its emphasis on staff tenure.

Civil service job protection, basically intended to attach the loyalty of the bureaucratic official to the organization and thus promote stability and efficiency, also, in the long run, protects the inefficient and the incompetent. Some of the teachers who stay in the slum school (it is impossible to estimate what proportion) adapt to the situation by developing a punitive and hostile style with the children. Presumably, the opportunity for continual indulgence in such behavior gratifies some deeper needs of their own, or they would not stay. Even should the administration decide that its staffing concerns do not justify retaining them, the problems in dismissing them are almost unsurmountable. The administration must present a considerable body of incontrovertible evidence at a series of hearings, and even should this succeed, the teacher still has recourse to appeals to civil service commissions and courts that, in general, tend to view civil service tenure provisions as sacred. Thus, in New York City, with a staff of close to 60,000 teachers, less than a dozen have been dismissed over the past five years, a truly amazing figure.

28. *Ibid.,* pp. 231-232.

Table 7.4 Significant Problems Reported by More than One-Third of 287 Classroom Teachers as Occurring Most Frequently and Being Most Serious

Problem statement	Percentage reported by frequency	Rank order by frequency	Percentage reported by severity	Rank order by severity	Occurring in frequency and severity
	1	2	3	4	5
1. Lack of appropriate reading materials in the home	73.9	1	72.1	1	X
2. Working with children with reading difficulties	67.6	2	67.6	2	X
3. Dealing with children who have limited vocabulary and speech patterns	60.6	3	63.8	3	X
4. Inability of children to express in writing what they can express orally	57.5	4	57.5	9	X
5. Dealing with children who don't listen to, remember, and follow instructions (tests, homework, etc.)	55.8	5	59.6	6	X
6. Finding time for individual instruction	51.2	6	59.9	5	X
7. Lack of materials in the home available to children for doing their homework or school work (e.g., pencil, paper)	49.5	7	51.2	15	X
8. Dealing with children who have limited or unsatisfactory experiences outside school	48.8	8	56.4	10	X
9. Dealing with parents not interested in their children's classwork	46.3	9	61.3	4	X
10. Helping a child who comes from a disruptive or broken home	46.0	10	58.9	7	X
11. Helping a child with social adjustment problems	39.0	11	47.4	18	X

Table 7.4 Significant Problems (*continued*)

	Percentage reported by frequency	Rank order by frequency	Percentage reported by severity	Rank order by severity	Occurring in frequency and severity
12. Having difficulty contacting parents and/or scheduling conferences	38.7	12	53.3	13	X
13. Children coming to school without proper food or sleep	38.7	13	57.8	8	X
14. Helping children keep track of their school supplies and personal possessions	38.3	14			
15. Dealing with children not motivated to work	36.6	15	52.3	14	X
16. Getting students to do homework and classwork properly	36.2	16	40.4	28	X
17. Finding methods for teaching children who are immature, lacking experience, or who have low ability	36.2	17	49.8	16	X
18. Helping children work independently	36.2	18			
19. Finding satisfactory methods of disciplining children	35.2	19	42.5	24	X
20. Dealing with a constantly disruptive child	35.2	20	54.7	11	X
21. Dealing with children who do not care if they receive poor grades	35.2	21	54.0	12	X
22. Dealing with classroom interruptions and disruptions of the normal schedule	34.5	22			
23. Dealing with children who want attention and will do anything to get it	34.1	23	49.5	17	X
24. Getting children to do their own work	33.4	24	34.1	42	X

SOURCE: Donald Cruickshank and James Leonard, *The Identification and Analysis of Perceived Problems of Teachers in Inner City Schools* (Occasional Paper No. 1, NDEA, National Institute for Advanced Study in Teaching Disadvantaged Youth, 1967), pp. 5-6.

The growing strength of teacher unionism in larger cities over the past decade, whatever benefits it may have brought to the profession generally, has on the whole worsened the problem. Trade unions are in the business of defending members against management and not of insuring the development of the most competent staffs, which is, in any sensible view, a management interest. Some union leaders, who recognize the severity of the problem, argue, at least in private, that they would welcome a more vigorous attack on the part of administration against incompetent teachers. The union must defend them, they say, but if an administrator is forceful enough in insisting on his prerogatives he would win often enough. Whatever the merits of this argument, it is certainly undeniable that urban school administrators for a variety of reasons seldom press hard for dismissal of slum school teachers who should not, by anyone's standards, be in a classroom.

COPING WITH THE SPECIAL DEMANDS OF THE SLUM SCHOOL

Although the picture of the urban teacher that emerges in the discussion above seems a fairly grim one, it is far too easy to make the teacher a convenient scapegoat for all the problems of the inner city school. There is not, in the first instance, a reasonable basis for demanding that any very large group of fairly ordinary persons—exhibiting a normally wide range of talents, attitudes, personalities, and human strengths and weaknesses—should turn out to be dedicated, altruistic, superbly competent in the face of a difficult task, and endowed with the mental stability and psychological acuity of experienced psychiatrists. It would be a very considerable miracle if they did.

There is a widespread tendency, in the second place, to depreciate the severity of the problems that the slum classroom presents for any teacher. The often-unstated premise of many of the savage critiques of slum school staffs is that if a teacher had genuine sympathy and skill, she would not complain about problems that probably are brought about by her own stereotyped perception.

Studies of teachers' perceptions of the conditions they encounter in the slum school, however, suggest that there is a reality basis for these difficulties, or they would not be agreed on in such large numbers. The most careful and the broadest survey of urban teachers' problems was done by Donald Cruikshank and James Leonard for the National Institute for Advanced Study in Teaching Disadvantaged Youth, and included data from twelve of the largest cities.[29] The authors began by

29. Donald Cruikshank and James Leonard, *The Identification and Analysis of Perceived Problems of Teachers in Inner City Schools* (Occasional Paper No. 1, NDEA, National Institute for Advanced Study in Teaching Disadvantaged Youth, 1967).

asking a number of teachers to describe the school incident which caused them the greatest concern for ten successive days; each of these incidents was rated by them in terms of its normal occurrence, its complexity, its solvability, and the degree to which it upset them. These critical incidents were synthesized into a Teacher Problem Inventory Instrument, which was filled out by all the teachers in the participating schools (N-287). Table 7.4 records those items that were reported by at least a third of the teachers as occurring most often and as being most severe.

It is hardly surprising that a setting in which the problems listed are perceived by so many teachers as frequent and severe should lead to widespread frustration and dissatisfaction. That this picture filters back to teachers in training probably accounts for the substantial number of college students in teacher-preparation programs who are doubtful about accepting an assignment in a slum school. Table 7.5 gives a picture of how a sample of New York City teacher-education students responded to the prospect of such an assignment; these students were aware of the fact that, whether they liked it or not, their initial assignment was very likely to be to a slum school, which makes the sizeable proportion of those exhibiting some resistance even more significant.

Table 7.5 Student answers to: "If your first teaching assignment were in a special service school (one with children of low socioeconomic level, high proportion of families on relief, lower than average reading achievement, and so forth), which one of the following statements comes closest to expressing how you would feel about it?"

Response	Percentage
Comes close to being exactly what I wish for	3.8
There are lots of drawbacks, but on the whole I would find it acceptable	57.7
It's not the worst thing that could happen, but I would not be pleased	21.2
I would accept, but plan to transfer as soon as I could	15.4
I would not accept, but try to find a teaching post outside the city	1.9

SOURCE: Harry L. Miller, *The Effect of Information on Student Beliefs about the Slum School* (Hunter College, Project TRUE, 1963), p. 8.

CLASS AND ETHNIC DIFFERENCES

Much of the preceding discussion of staffing problems can be summed up as an indirect result of social class variation between teachers and pupils, as a clash of life styles and moralities. If so, as time goes on, in the absence of any radical change in the way schools are run, the situation is likely to grow worse. The two converging trends are the growing concentration of lower-class populations in central city schools and the increasingly middle-class composition of the teaching profession. One must be careful to distinguish between different levels of social class origin, however. Though college attendance in itself is a good guarantee of acceptance of middle-class norms, future teachers seem to develop different attitudes toward the slum school and their willingness to teach in one. In at least one study students from families at the lowest end of the class scale are markedly more positive on both counts.[30]

But, as our social class chapter pointed out, schools in lower SES areas have a higher proportion of teachers coming from working- and lower-middle-class families, which may be significant. Edgar Friedenberg argues that as a result, the urban school has become a classic case of institutional *ressentiment*.[31] The term denotes a climate consisting of a pervasive sense of irritability and ill-humor, a petty preoccupation with rules and forms rather than with persons and what is happening to them, and disapproval of any free expression of human impulsiveness and liveliness. If it is the dominant tone of any institution, it is attributed to the presence in authority of large numbers of upwardly mobile persons who still remain at low levels of status relative to upper-middles and upper-class members of the institution.

The explanation goes this way: The school is staffed by people who, in striving to improve their social status, were forced to repress their own impulses and creative self-expressiveness in order to obtain credentials necessary for positions in middle-class institutions. Once in these positions, however, they learn that the rewards in social deference, in authority, and in economic comfort that they expected turn out to be far fewer than they had anticipated. Their chronic disappointment and bitterness give rise to the typical climate of the institutions in which they predominate, and account for the repression of any form of exuberance or creative difference in others which they forfeited for themselves.

For anyone familiar with the pervading atmosphere of many urban schools, this seems a persuasive explanation. It seems particularly applicable to those large city systems in which the schools have been dominated by an ethnic group in the course of its social struggle upward, as is the case with the Irish in Boston and the Jews in New York City. The social class bitterness of groups that have not quite yet "made

30. Harry L. Miller, "The Relation of Social Class to Slum School Attitudes among Education Students in an Urban College," *Journal of Teacher Education*, Vol. 19, No. 4 (Winter 1968), pp. 416-424.

31. Edgar Z. Friedenberg, Hilary A. Gold, and Carl Nordstrom, *Society's Children* (New York: Random House, Inc., 1967).

it" seems aggravated by a resentment based on having been the prime target for prejudice and discrimination in the past. A prevalent attitude among these groups seems to be: "We had it just as bad as the Negroes and the Puerto Ricans and made it on our own; what right do they have to special treatment?"

One crucial question that arises is whether this kind of climate, assuming it is common, accounts for achievement differences. There is no evidence that it does; indeed the evidence is in the other direction, as in the cases of experimental schools in which a sympathetic climate was clearly achieved as cited in Chapter 6.

Another crucial question is, where does the black teacher fit within these patterns? As an upwardly mobile minority group person is he not as subject to *ressentiment* as any other? In the absence of any direct study of this intriguing and important question, one can only speculate on the basis of some fragmentary and indirect evidence.

Informal and anecdotal reports from administrators and teacher supervisors seem mainly to confirm the possibility that many black teachers treat lower-class black pupils with as much if not more hostility and repression as their white counterparts. This suggests that in addition to the forces of *ressentiment* there is in operation the familiar mechanism of self-hatred that has been found among many oppressed minority groups; they take over some of the prejudices of the dominant society that discriminates against them. Thus, it is interesting that in the recent New York City community control struggle, described in the final chapter, when the local community school board dismissed over a hundred teachers, a good number of them were blacks.

On the other hand, David Gottlieb's study of teacher stereotypes and of their black pupils found significant group differences between white and black teachers. Gottlieb presented his subjects with a list of adjectives and asked the teachers to check those that applied to the children.[32] Table 7.6 presents his findings; black teachers are clearly more favorable and less stereotyped about pupils than their white colleagues.

Whatever the current state of things, the attitudes of black teachers is probably undergoing very rapid change as this is written. The middle-class black is being caught up in the tide of change in urban ghettos, and his militancy and group identification seem to most observers to be rising faster than among his lower-class brothers. The rapid rise in the number of black college students in Northern colleges, most of them exceedingly militant and race-conscious and slated to enter teaching careers, will change the present picture even more drastically. It is

32. David Gottlieb, "Teaching and Students: The Views of Negro and White Teachers," *Sociology of Education*, Vol. 37 (Summer 1964), pp. 345-353.

Table 7.6 Teachers' Race and Their Perceptions of Students

Adjectives	White percent	Negro percent	Percent differences
Ambitious	20	36	16
Athletic	25	13	12
Calm	8	19	11
Cautious	10	6	4
Cooperative	35	61	26
Cultured	2	10	8
Dominant	2	—	2
Easy going	35	29	6
Energetic	33	48	15
Forceful	8	3	5
Fun loving	45	74	29
Good looking	16	16	—
Happy	31	65	34
Hard driving	6	10	4
High strung	39	3	36
Idealistic	6	10	4
Impetuous	33	13	20
Intellectual	2	3	1
Lazy	53	19	34
High brow	14	6	8
Methodical	—	6	6
Middle brow	4	19	15
Moody	33	13	20
Obliging	37	26	11
Outgoing	33	19	14
Poised	6	6	—
Quiet	8	13	5
Rebellious	35	13	22
Reserved	6	3	3
Shy	12	21	9
Sophisticated	—	3	3
Talkative	59	6	53
Witty	—	8	8
N =	(51)	(35)	

SOURCE: David Gottlieb, "Teaching and Students: The Views of Negro and White Teachers," *Sociology of Education,* Vol. 37 (Summer 1964), p. 352.

likely that in the next generation the schools of the largest cities will witness another ethnic takeover, this time by blacks and, to a lesser extent, Puerto Ricans. In that event, the staffing problems of the central city schools may take on a totally different aspect.

IMMEDIATE ANSWERS: COMMUNITY TEACHER AIDES AND THE IMPROVEMENT OF TRAINING

One of the most promising proposals for dealing with the special problems of the slum school is to provide auxiliary personnel, themselves members of the lower-class community, who will help the teacher. There are a sizeable number of possible advantages in the employment of such auxiliaries in the classroom:

The child benefits by having an adult present from his own social background, to interpret his needs and his behavior; the children who need individual attention are more likely to get it, if the aide is deployed for occasional tutoring or small group instruction.

The teacher has a chance to play a more professional role by delegating routine clerical tasks to the auxiliary, and should thereby improve her status not only in her own eyes but in general.

The auxiliary has gained a job that is meaningful, relatively well-paid, and one that opens up the opportunity for a career; most such "new careers" programs provide for training and certification along a career ladder that ultimately leads to full licensing as a teacher.

The school administrator gets some relief from the shortage of fully-qualified professionals, and a pipeline into the community.

Because the auxiliaries either are or will become parents, a long-range positive influence on family life may accrue as they learn, both in training and in practice, some basic principles of child development.

In the present early stages of the program, a number of difficulties have arisen, which must be solved if the potential of the idea is to come anywhere near being realized. The professionals involved—including teachers, supervisors, and administrators—have been concerned with the possible lowering of professional standards; there are fears that auxiliaries might try to "take over" professional functions in the classroom or, worse, that administrators under pressure of staffing a given number of classes might themselves assign auxiliaries to professional duties without the supervision of certified personnel. To teachers imbued with the ideology of a small teaching load, it seems questionable to apply funds to employ auxiliaries that might otherwise be used to reduce class size.

Other fears of professionals relate to the actual working out of necessary relationships. They question whether adequate time for planning would be provided for teacher and auxiliary teams, and even if the time were available, whether most teachers have the leadership skills necessary to manage such a team effort. A few wonder whether pupils might not respond better to their auxiliaries, and thus damage the relationship between pupil and teacher.

The auxiliaries themselves have a number of apprehensions related to the differences between their own and the professional staff's backgrounds, values, and patterns of speech. In some situations, particularly preschool programs, their own lack of training prevents them from realizing the diagnostic skills required of the teacher in designing activities for children; seeing only the end results of the process, they are likely to feel that they do the same things as the teachers and should be paid the same.

All of these problems are ones that emerged from a survey of fifteen demonstration programs operating in 1966. The survey authors, Garda Bowman and Gordon Klopf, concluded that "it is not likely that the desired outcomes from the utilization of auxiliary personnel in a given school situation would be realized unless certain pre-conditions to their use were established."[33] Their recommendations included the following suggestions:

Clarification of Roles. To prevent either an underutilization or an overutilization of auxiliaries, there is need for a careful definition of job content and activities, although the function of any individual auxiliary should continue to be developed in response to the immediate situation. Bowman and Klopf suggest that the whole range of teacher activities be reexamined, to identify those that might readily be assigned to nonprofessionals and those that should be performed by the teacher alone.

Training. The authors recommend that preservice training of auxiliaries include development of communication and other basic skills, to give them more confidence in the school milieu; and that they be trained for the specific school levels to which they will be assigned. Administrators and professionals who are to work with auxiliaries should themselves undergo some orientation training, including an opportunity to voice any doubts about the new situation. Institutes at which teachers, administrators, and auxiliaries can learn to work well together are also recommended.

After the auxiliary is on the job, the authors propose a continuing and comprehensive program of in-service training, to proceed at each level of responsibility on the career ladder. Further, that the coopera-

33. Garda W. Bowman and Gordon J. Klopf, *Auxiliary School Personnel: Their Roles, Training and Institutionalization* (Bank Street College of Education, March 1967), p. 8.

tion of the community college and colleges of teacher education be sought in developing a variety of programs that will help auxiliaries to advance generally or to move into roles requiring more skill, such as becoming library aides.

Institutionalization. Bowman and Klopf see as crucially necessary the incorporation of this program as an integral part of the school system, rather than as an extraneous appendage. Otherwise, training for jobs that are not stable or that are "dead end" would be frustrating, and the ultimate aims of the program unlikely to be realized.

Teacher Training Programs

Whatever peripheral aid may be supplied by classroom auxiliaries, the more fundamental problem persists of an adequate supply of relevantly trained professionals. The requirements discussed at the beginning of this chapter are complex ones; the skills involved in creating an adequate consideration structure in the classroom are particularly difficult to develop.

One excellent idea that has languished because of Congressional hostility is that of a Teacher Corps. Inspired by the success of the Peace Corps, the proposal was to recruit the same type of dedicated youth to serve in a national corps of teachers, most of them to be assigned to urban ghetto schools. If we could afford to send people to help communities in remote parts of India, it was argued, it made sense to extend the same services to the underprivileged in our own cities. Congress never warmed to the idea, however, and although the Teacher Corps is a going institution, it has been starved for funds and has not, so far, been able to do the kind of job that was originally envisaged.

In fact, although most observers of the urban school scene seem to be convinced, correctly or not, that the teacher is the crucial variable in reversing the retardation of the slum school pupil, and in the face of the manifest complexity of the training task involved in providing first-rate teachers, remarkably little of the money available for urban education is earmarked for teacher training. If innovative activity is not noticeably widespread, however, there has been enough talk about what needs to be done and a sufficient scattering of experimental projects to suggest the nature of current trends.

The clearest emphasis is on providing actual *experience* with lower-class youth in slum school settings. There is a conviction among teacher trainers, supported by numerous reports from beginning teachers, that it is necessary to prepare neophytes for the "culture shock" of the lower-class schoolroom. Participants in four regional conferences for student teachers and beginning teachers of the disadvantaged recently produced suggestions for teacher-training programs at the college level; the key factor, in their view, was experience, as embodied in the following proposals:

1. Beginning in the freshman or sophomore year, students interested in becoming teachers should work with children as teacher aides, teacher assistants, tutors, or recreation aides through school and community based programs. A case study of one child involving discussions with the child's teacher, as well as home visits, would be an easily planned introduction into the practical realities of teaching.

2. Early experience should be more than simply "learning about"; it should involve the student in serious effort to provide genuine services.

3. A community "live-in" experience should be made available for all students in those communities which present a social context different from the student's own social background. This exchange should be multidirectional with students moving freely from the inner city to the suburbs to the country, if feasible; and among all possible socioeconomic, ethnic, and racial groups.

4. Experience should be planned for all grade levels, to allow the students to get a first-hand view of the general development of the child.

5. Observation of, if not direct contact with, children with special problems —the mentally retarded, the physically handicapped, the emotionally disturbed—should be provided.

6. The experience of student teaching should be subjected to immediate analysis and evaluation for the student's own use in learning about himself as a teacher. Videotaping, demonstration teaching through role playing, student observation of other students are some ways in which a dynamic evaluation program could be developed to effect a continuous interaction between the student teacher and his teaching coach.

7. The bulk of the teacher training time should be spent on the actual scene of the future teaching. The schools themselves should become the college laboratories and it is there that the teachers of teachers should be located.

8. Student teaching assignments should be the result of a joint decision of the individuals concerned—the student teacher, the college coordinator, the school administrator, and the supervising teacher.

9. The student teacher should be treated as a full member of the professional team, contributing as much as possible within the limits of his professional skills and abilities.

10. The student teaching experience should be as long as possible—a year, ideally, and remunerated, particularly if it is set up as a fifth year or internship program.[34]

34. Helen J. Kenney, Polly Bartholomew, and William C. Kvaraceus, *Teacher Education: The Young Teacher's View* (Project Report No. 2, NDEA National Institute for Advanced Study in Teaching Disadvantaged Youth, July 1968), pp. 9-10.

Some of the most effective experimental programs in this area have involved an enrichment of the student teaching segment of the college program. The "120 Project" at Hunter College was one of the earliest of these, and was based on a close and continuing relationship between Junior High School 120 and the college. Students beginning their student teaching semester were permitted to volunteer to have their practicum experience at that school, with the understanding that when they graduated, they would accept a teaching assignment there.

In addition to the normal supervision provided by the school, a college faculty member spent much time at the school meeting with students at lunch and for more formal conferences, taking them on field trips to meet knowledgeable members of the community and to become acquainted with its resources, giving support, guidance, and counseling.

Over a period of years a large proportion of the school's faculty came to be made up of Hunter students who had been part of the 120 Project, and the turnover problem was much improved.

This model for providing on-the-spot experience for teachers-to-be is an ideal one, but far from common. The rising demand for a great increase in field work in teacher colleges serving large urban communities is not often accompanied by any concrete plans for supporting services that will help the student in the field to interpret and understand her experience. Field work of any kind is itself time-consuming, and often enough there is little or no time left after or during the experience to discuss what happened. Moreover, faculty time is costly and can seldom be assigned in large enough blocks to provide the real help in interpretation which is necessary. Although suggestion number 7 in the preceding list, that teacher trainers move into the schools, sounds admirable as an ideal, because the number of teacher-trainees in any school must be limited, stationing a college faculty member in the school is hardly practical without a very large increase in both funds and college faculty.

Aside from student teaching, the trend in preservice training in the colleges has been to increase field work experience in slum schools (tutoring, classroom observation, community visits, and so on) and to shift the emphasis in some of the academic work to a consideration of the problems of the lower-class child. Many courses in both the social and psychological foundations of education now focus on applicable generalizations from the behavioral sciences, and a few colleges offer sensitivity-training experiences. Some current planning is in the direction of constructing special tracks within the general teacher training curriculum which offer students intending to teach in the urban slum school a sequence of academic work and field experience tailored for them alone.

Robert Strom has suggested that the summer after graduation and just preceding the teacher's first classroom experience is a crucial period of time for specific preparation for the slum school assignment.[35] During the summer of 1966, he conducted a pilot project to test the idea in Columbus, Ohio. The major portion of the program consisted of a six-week summer session that included a variety of lectures on poverty, the lower-class family, self-concept and motivation, and so forth; a two-week team-teaching experience with eighteen children from a disadvantaged area; visits with a welfare worker; and a visit to the juvenile court. During the school year following, the participants were visited by project staff and were brought together for conferences once a month in a continuing in-service program.

Although the project staff did not undertake the difficult task of comparing the instructional effectiveness of their participants with a control group, they did gather evidence of attitude change toward the teaching assignment itself. As Table 7.7 shows, they were remarkably successful in shifting attitudes in a positive direction.

Table 7.7 Change in Teacher's Preference of Neighborhood for Assignment

Type of neighborhood	Preference indicated in June 1966	Preference indicated in January 1967	Preference indicated in May 1967
Low income	8	17	20
Middle income	8	1	1
No preference	5	0	0
Undecided	0	3	0
Total	21	21	21

SOURCE: Robert D. Strom, *The Preface Plan* (Project No. 6-1365, U.S. Department of Health, Education and Welfare, August 1967), p. 75.

In-service training has also come in for a major share of attention. The clearest emphasis here appears to be on the desirability of concentrating on help during the first year or so of teaching, when the beginner is most overwhelmed by her problems and when any gaps or inadequacies in preservice training provide the greatest trouble. Indeed, there is a minority view in the profession that suggests abandonment of undergraduate teaching preparation in favor of a two-year apprenticeship, the model for which is a growing number of masters-in-teaching programs. In such programs the student enters with a B.A. without teaching preparation, spends the summer in an intensive course, then begins teaching halftime. The other half of her day is spent either in small seminars in the school or in courses at the university. In such a situation the irrelevance of training, of which many beginning teachers

35. Robert D. Strom, *The Preface Plan* (Project No. 6-1365, Washington, D.C.: U.S. Department of Health, Education and Welfare, August 1967).

complain, is sharply reduced, and one does not have to face the problem of first training, then retraining, during the first year of teaching.

However desirable such a model is, from many points of view, it is unlikely to become very popular. Professional status depends in large measure on the existence of a sizeable academic preservice program, and a group interested in advancing as a profession will not willingly accept the concept of apprenticeship without preceding academic preparation.

It is difficult to assess the effectiveness of any of the foregoing proposals or experimental programs for the simple reason that almost no teacher training of any kind is ever subjected to evaluation on the basis of the most crucial variable: classroom instructional effectiveness. In part this is because, as we noted earlier, that variable is difficult to measure reliably. But it is unfortunate that the numerous experimental programs for teachers in the slum schools do not at least attempt to measure their effectiveness in terms of their *own* criteria for teacher ability. If, in recruiting for the program, they had selected double the number of participants required, then invited a random sample of half of that group to attend the program, they could compare the classroom performance of their trainees to that of a reasonably comparable control group. Government-supported training efforts seldom provide funds for such measurement, which explains some of the lack of interest in rigorous evaluation.

But another part of the explanation may well lie in what seems to be an absence of real conviction among teacher trainers that they have the answer to the instructional needs of the urban school. The literature on this specialized form of training heavily emphasizes, for example, the *form* rather than the content of training. It is very well to propose that we train young teachers *in* the school, rather than in the academy; but are we more likely to find firm solutions to offer for her problems there than in the college classroom? Although there are now beginning to emerge some responsibly detailed and practical discussions of teaching in the slum school,[36] we are at this writing some distance from the goal of a tested body of instructional practice that can be confidently built into a training design.

Recommended Reading

One of the most insightful books available on teaching the culturally different child is again Sylvia Ashton-Warner's *Teacher* (New York:

36. *See,* for example, Hilda Taba and Deborah Elkins, *Teaching Strategies for the Culturally Disadvantaged* (Skokie, Ill.: Rand McNally & Company, 1966).

Simon and Schuster, Inc., 1963), or the novel she wrote about her experiences as a teacher of Maori children, *Spinster* (New York: Simon and Schuster, Inc., 1959). Herbert Kohl's *36 Children* (New York: New American Library of World Literature, 1967) is a comparable account of classroom experimentation of a New York City teacher in a slum school.

A number of analyses of classroom observations in the New York schools have been published as an outcome of Project TRUE at Hunter College. They include G. Alexander Moore's, *Realities of the Urban Classroom* (New York: Doubleday & Company, Inc., 1967); Elizabeth Eddy, *Walk the White Line* (New York: Doubleday & Company, Inc., 1967); Estelle Fuchs, *Teachers Talk: A View From within the Inner City Schools* (New York: Doubleday & Company, Inc., 1968).

Hilda Taba and Deborah Elkins have written one of the most detailed and sensible manuals of methods for the slum school in *Teaching Strategies for the Culturally Disadvantaged* (Skokie, Ill.: Rand McNally & Company, 1966); and Robert D. Strom has edited a book called *The Inner City Classroom: Teacher Behaviors* (Charles E. Merrill Books, Inc., 1966) to which ten specialists have made useful contributions. The special problems of training teachers for the inner city school is the subject of a recent symposium edited by Bruce Tuckman and John O'Brian, *Preparing to Teach the Disadvantaged* (New York: The Free Press, 1969).

8

ADMINISTRATION AND THE URBAN SCHOOL

Although a great deal of criticism for the failure of urban schools has been directed at the classroom teacher, in the last three or four years the system itself and those who administrate it—that is, the urban administrator who plans and supervises both in the school and the central office of large city school systems—have been increasingly indicted. In this chapter we will attempt to explore the present nature of urban educational leadership, some of the problems associated with it, the characteristics of effective educational leadership, and perhaps a crucially important question—to what extent can better professional leadership in urban schools actually make a difference in the effectiveness of those schools?

Much criticism has been focused on the "bureaucratization" of urban schools. This generally refers to the growing complexity of the administrative tasks associated with large systems. We begin with a fairly lengthy examination of three important concepts related to the administration of the urban school: bureaucracy, leadership, and decision-making. A considerable amount of both theoretical and empirical writing dealing with these three concepts is available. We have attempted to select those aspects of bureaucracy, leadership, and decision-making which seem to relate to the urban school situation. However, a general review of these concepts seems essential for understanding the material in this chapter and the relationship between the school and community, the role of the classroom teacher, the nature of curriculum, and possible curriculum changes needed in urban schools.

BUREAUCRACY

Peter Blau, the American sociologist, defines bureaucracy as "the type of organization designed to accomplish large scale administrative tasks by systematically coordinating the work of many individuals."[1] The European sociologist, Max Weber, was the first to develop a theory of bureaucracy.[2] The predominant characteristics of a bureaucratic structure according to Weber are:

1. "The regular activities required for the purposes of the organization are distributed in a fixed way as official duties."[3] This implies a great deal of specialization. That is, a person with high skill in a particular task is assigned to do that task and no other. It also makes clear the duties of each position, since each is clearly defined. A school system has its specialists hired to perform particular functions: classroom teacher in first grade, English teacher in senior high school, principal, assistant principal, superintendent, curriculum coordinator, board of education member, and so on. This characteristic of specialization may lead to the situation in which one department or division is totally unaware of what another department is doing.

2. "The organization of offices follows the principle of hierarchy. That is, each lower office is under the control and supervision of a higher one."[4] Each person in a bureaucracy is responsible to someone else, a superior who may judge his work and also may give him orders which it is his duty to carry out. Each bureaucrat is also responsible not only for his own efforts but for those of all who work for him. A school system is clearly organized hierarchically, with superintendents giving orders to principals, who give orders and directives to teachers, who in turn give orders and directives to students.

3. Operations of a bureaucracy are governed by "a consistent system of abstract rules and the application of these rules to particular cases."[5] Explicit rules and regulations define the responsibility of each person in the bureaucratic structure and the relationships between these people. Sometimes rules and regulations may be very simple, and at other times very complex. They exist, in all bureaucratic structures. As any teacher or principal knows, a school system contains rules in the form of legal responsibilities, administrative directives from boards of

1. Peter M. Blau, *Bureaucracy in Modern Society* (New York: Random House, Inc., 1956), p. 14.
2. Max Weber, *The Theory of Social and Economic Organization,* A.M. Henderson and Talcott Parsons (trans.), (New York: Oxford University Press, 1947).
3. *From Max Weber: Essays in Sociology,* H.H. Gerth and C. Wright Mills (trans.), (New York: Oxford University Press, 1946), p. 196.
4. Weber, *op. cit.,* p. 331.
5. *Ibid.,* p. 330.

education, principal's directives to teachers, and teacher's classroom regulations.

4. "The ideal official conducts his office in a spirit of formalistic impersonality without hatred or passion and hence without affection or enthusiasm."[6] Personal considerations, likes and dislikes must be eliminated from the conduct of official business in a bureaucracy. This supports the contention that bureaucracies are cold and impersonal organizations, but it is important to realize that these qualities are vital to one of the fundamental requirements of bureaucratic organization—objectivity. In public school systems objectivity in evaluating administrators, teachers, and students is held to be of very high value.

5. Hiring and promotion in the bureaucratic structure is based on skill and ability and individuals are protected from arbitrary dismissal. "It constitutes a career. There is a system of promotions according to seniority, or to achievement, or both."[7] Protection from arbitrary dismissal, a carefully worked out rational system of promotion, licensing, examinations, tests, special educational qualifications for administrative positions, and tenure for teachers are part of all public school systems.

6. "Experience tends universally to show that the purely bureaucratic type of administrative organization . . . is from a purely technical point of view capable of attaining the highest degree of efficiency."[8] Weber is claiming here that bureaucracy, the main characteristics of which were outlined in the five previous points, is the most efficient system of organization that man has yet devised. Weber is describing the ideal type of bureaucratic structure. If everyone performed his duties in accordance with the highest development of the first five characteristics, there is no question that the result would be efficiency as total as any human organization could achieve. The purpose of this ideal type is not to describe reality, but to provide a set of criteria against which real educational bureaucracies may be judged. The ideal type of bureaucratic structure of the school system may be represented by the pyramid seen in Figure 8.1.

Real bureaucratic structures depart in significant ways from the ideal pyramid pictured, although we are not suggesting that the pyramid is totally inaccurate. It does, however, make at least four assumptions which must be questioned as far as educational systems are concerned.

Assumption one: the rationality of a bureaucractic structure. Given Weber's ideal type, a bureaucratic structure is completely rational. An alternative view is that human relations are so important in any structure that one cannot define an individual bureaucrat simply by identify-

6. *Ibid.*, p. 340.
7. *Ibid.*, p. 334.
8. *Ibid.*, p. 337.

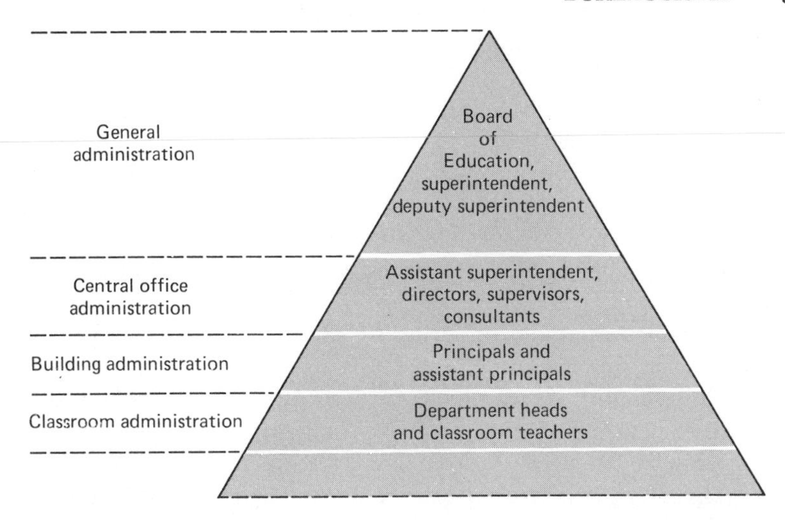

Figure 8.1 An organizational pyramid for public-school administration.
SOURCE: S.J. Knezevich, *Administration of Public Education* (New York: Harper & Row, 1962), p. 63.

ing his duties. We do not know, for example, the real relationship between a teacher and a principal by reading the handbook and guide published by the school system. The performance of people even in a bureaucatic setting depends to some extent on their own values and personal relationships. Many recent studies of bureaucracy have tended to concentrate attention on the development of informal organization and structures or, as Charles Page describes it, "bureaucracy's other face."[9] Informal organization in a bureaucratic structure may parallel to some extent the official hierarchy, but certainly does not duplicate it. It is not set up on the principle of rationally defined specialized jobs and a system of hierarchy. Here is how an informal organization works in a school setting:

One of the writers is acquainted with a superintendent of a medium sized midwest school system who is publically noted for his insistency on official chains of communication. Yet this administrator is also an active Rotarian, as are key persons in each department of the secondary school. By tacit agreement among department heads, any of the group whose department needs help is allowed to walk back to the office from the weekly noon luncheon with the superintendent. Other department heads stall a few minutes and return as a group. These five minute walks are off the cuff, never mentioned at school, and produce results. Any other direct approach by a department head is rebuffed by the question, "Have you talked to your building principal?"[10]

9. Blau, *op. cit.,* p. 46.
10. Willard R. Lane, Ronald G. Corwin, and William G. Monahan, *Foundations of Educational Administration* (New York: The Macmillan Company, 1966), p. 212.

However important informal organizations are to understanding the true operation of a bureaucracy, the attitude of many administrators toward them is likely to fall in either of one or two categories. Administrators may judge personal relations to be irrelevant to the real functioning of the bureaucratic structure. This is certainly a shortsighted view, as shown by the Rotarian-walk illustration above. Other administrators may view aspects of the informal organization as subversive to the efficiency of the bureaucratic structure. In fact, informal relations may actually *increase* efficiency. For example, a principal may phone a friend in charge of ordering supplies to expedite the processing of an order for new materials desperately needed by his teachers. If the call is effective and the materials arrive quickly, then this principal using personal relations outside the formal organization has increased the efficiency of his school. Informal groups and informal organizations are very likely to cut across different departments and different levels in the hierarchy. In doing this they tend to promote coordination and cooperation between separate parts of the organization. An informal group or organization within a bureaucracy may also provide certain kinds of flexibility which are not spelled out or written into the formal structure. These informal structures may actually help bureaucratic structures to change and remain flexible. Although they are more difficult to study, informal organizations are an indispensible element of any large urban school system.

Assumption two: rules are infallible. Rules serve a very important function in a bureaucracy. For example, they contribute to the predictability of work performance. They also serve as a form of communication, substituting for a superior constantly having to repeat instructions to a subordinate. Rules also—and this is particularly important for school systems—provide some standards of public evaluation. Rules and procedures which are written down can be checked not only by the teacher or principal but by the members of the bureaucracy at a higher level or even by people outside of the bureaucracy, such as boards of education or parents. There are, however, certain kinds of situations in which rules are inadequate.

Rules by themselves are fallible, for in almost every case they require interpretation by individuals in the bureaucracy. They are written before the fact and function as general guides in specific cases. Since each situation differs, no possible set of rules can anticipate all consequences. It is in the application of rules relating to the particular event that human judgment, personality conflicts, likes and dislikes come into the picture.

Clearly, rules exist from which no particular benefit derives and whose application might be contrary to the long-range purposes and goals of the organization. Historically, school systems have had rules denying certain kinds of pay increases and tenure to married women teachers. It is hard to see how this rule contributed anything to the overall effectiveness of the organization of the school; one could argue that it was detrimental to the long-range purposes of the school, particularly in a time of teacher shortage.

Rules and regulations may also be violated because they are considered contrary to the fundamental traditions of the organization and/or the community in which it is located. Any new rule in an organization faces the possibility that it may contradict or violate a traditional way of behaving. For example, the introduction of the time card and the routine of punching in and out of schools has been resisted bitterly by teacher organizations because it is judged to violate the traditional and more "professional" method of making teachers responsible. This resistance exists in spite of the fact that in many, and probably most, large school systems, some form of mechanical time accounting has already been established.

The facts that rules must be interpreted and that there are resistances to rules points to their inadequacy as a total definition of the bureaucratic relationship and bureaucratic performance. When one adds the informal to the formal bureaucratic structure the inadequacy of rules becomes apparent. It may be possible and desirable in certain situations to get around rules or "cut red tape" by using the informal structure.

Assumption three: goals exist for the entire organization. Actual bureaucracies depart from the "ideal" in the assumption that the goals which the organization has set for itself are pursued by all subdivisions. Barnard defines formal organization as a system of consciously coordinated activities or forces of two or more persons working toward a common goal.[11] What frequently happens is that one particular part of a bureaucratic structure may develop "a functional autonomy." It may work independently and pursue goals and objectives of its own. The independent financing of some school activities is an example of functional autonomy. Many athletic programs operate out of receipts from paid admissions to athletic contests and events. This separate financing may permit the athletic department to make decisions about purchasing new uniforms and equipment, quite apart from the general budget of the school. Those special academic schools which accept only students with the very highest scores and send their graduates on to prestigious colleges and universities may develop a functional autonomy and make curriculum and program decisions independent of the larger system of which they are a part. Functional autonomy *need* not be con-

11. C. Barnard, *The Functions of the Executive* (Cambridge, Mass.: Harvard University Press, 1938), p. 88.

trary to the goals and purposes of the larger organization, but may actually be.

In addition to functional autonomy, there may be real internal conflict, which produces resistance and opposition to the stated overall goals of the bureaucratic structure. Conflict may develop between individuals of different ranks within the bureaucratic structure or across subdivisions. In school systems, teachers frequently tend to identify with each other and on some occasions at least to resist and to object to policies and practices of the central administration. The organization of teachers' unions is based on the assumption of conflict along this line, since no one above the rank of department head may join the union. The assumption clearly is that above a certain level the interests of the individuals within the bureaucracy are not identical with those below a certain level.

Internal conflict may also develop between subdivisions of the bureaucratic structure. One school or one group of schools in a particular district may develop special goals which do not necessarily fit into the overall plan of the school system. The demands of both teachers and principals of urban schools in New York City, serving large numbers of poor youngsters, resulted in these schools being designated by the board of education as "special service" schools, and recipients of additional money and special personnel.

Internal conflict may develop around a number of different characteristics: age, sex groups, race, and ethnic backgrounds. Some urban black teachers see their own interests and goals with relation to the education of black youngsters in the public schools as being somewhat in conflict with the goals of both the teachers' union and the board of education of New York City.[12]

Assumption four: a single form of bureaucracy. There is an assumption that one single bureaucratic form and structure exists because of its efficiency and effectiveness. The most developed example of this ideal is the military establishment, with rules and disciplinary measures or punishment used for control.

Recently, however, social scientists have identified what they describe as two bases of bureaucratic authority which lead to two quite different kinds of structures. Gouldner suggests that some rules are established by agreement and others are established by imposition.[13] This author terms a bureaucracy "representative" when based primarily on agreement with technically justified rules established by consent. The

12. The New Coalition, for example, is a faction within the United Federation of Teachers in New York City; it is headed by Keith E. Baird, a black mathematics teacher.

13. A.W. Gouldner, *Patterns of Industrial Bureaucracy* (New York: The Free Press, 1954), pp. 11ff.

second type of bureaucracy Gouldner calls "punishment centered," in which authority and rules are based on imposition. Obedience to the rules is used as a criterion of performance. There is no assumption in making the distinction between these two types that one is necessarily more effective or efficient or in some sense better than the other. Bendix, however, has discovered that in the representative bureaucracy more initiative is expected and rewarded.[14] This in turn permits more flexibility in the performance of duties and tasks by bureaucrats. One might argue that this would be an advantage, especially in a rapidly changing industrial society such as the United States has today. Schools and school systems can be of either type. In fact, investigations by Nordstrom, Friedenberg, and Gold have clearly identified different patterns of bureaucratic structure and their effect on students in the schools.[15]

The distinction and conflict between the bureaucratic structure of school systems and the professional nature of teaching must be briefly mentioned. This distinction might be made clearer by examining administrative practices in another professional area. A study of physicians working in hospital bureaucracies points up the distinction between professional and bureaucratic decisions.[16] It was discovered that administrative and professional decisions were rigidly distinguished by both the doctors and their supervisors. Physicians were willing, for example, to grant supervisors the right to make purely administrative decisions, such as scheduling. Complying with these purely administrative requests apparently did not imply loss of professional dignity for the doctors. Physicians themselves retained the freedom to make decisions about strictly professional matters, including the entire area of patient care. Decision-making in this hospital structure was carefully distinguished from advice. When administrators ventured into the area of professional care, they did so in the form of offering advice and not handing down orders. Finally, the supervisors in the hospital setting were themselves highly trained physicians. Conflict seemed to be avoided by assigning supervisory duties only to those who had gained professional respect.

Without assuming that teachers as a professional group can be compared with physicians, this study seems to have implications for educational administration. It suggests that in so far as possible conflict can be reduced in the school setting by delegating professional decisions

14. R. Bendix, "Bureaucracy: The Problem and Its Setting," *American Sociological Review,* Vol. 12 (1942), pp. 498-502.

15. Edgar Z. Friedenberg, Hilary A. Gold, and Carl Nordstrom, *Society's Children: A Study of Ressentiment in the Secondary School* (New York: Random House, Inc., 1967).

16. M.E.W. Goss, "Influence and Authority among Physicians in an Out-Patient Clinic," *American Sociological Review,* Vol. 26 (1961), pp. 39-50.

Table 8.1 The following chart depicts both models; the New York City school system fits the monocratic, authoritarian one. The chart provides an encapsulated summary of the system's many characteristics that would have to be changed radically for reform to take place:

Authoritarian, monocratic model	Professional model
High degree of centralization (even of routine operating decisions).	Flexible centralization (to set standards and provide leadership; but with many routine and non-routine decisions decentralized).
Authoritarian leadership ("boss rule").	Professional leadership ("collegial rule").
Hierarchy (many levels, "tallness").	Limited hierarchy (few levels).
Assumed omniscience of top officials (accompanied by).	Flexible, consultative relationships with top officials (accompanied by).
Hierarchical, "upward" orientation of field staff, with periodic tendencies toward widespread rebellion and noncompliance.	Lateral, "collegial" orientation; no problems with rebellion; internalized professional standards regulate performance.
Complete discipline enforced from the top down.	Colleague groups informally enforce conformity to professional standards; administrative looseness; limited emphasis on authority based on office.
Responsibility owed from the bottom up.	Responsibility to live up to professional standards that one has internalized as inner controls.
High degree of specialization (departmentalization, parochialism; separate units function by their specialist logics; fail to be concerned with the broader organizational implications of their actions and their politics).	Limited, flexible specialization (free, open communications; little separatism and departmental chauvinism).
Recruitment and promotion practices that reinforce adherence to traditional bureaucratic codes (inbreeding).	Regular recruitment of outsiders.
Fragmentation of authority and power of top administrators, despite centralization (separate power blocs corre-	Consolidation of power and authority at top; extradepartmental ties result in more commitment to organization-

Table 8.1 Two models (*continued*)

Authoritarian, monocratic model	Professional model
sponding to major subunits—divisions, bureaus, separate levels); each bloc is a veto group, opposing changes that threaten its position.	wide goals than to personal career and empire building.
Weak chief executive.	Strong chief executive.
High degree of politicalization of bureaucratic functionaries (function as political bureaucrats; oriented toward *extrinsic rewards* of power, status, promotion, to the exclusion of professionalism).	High degree of professionalism oriented toward *intrinsic rewards* of professional recognition and status.
Limited planning (segmental, localistic, short-range reactivity, fire-fighting).	System-wide, long-range planning.

SOURCE: David Rogers, *110 Livingston Street* (New York: Random House, Inc., 1968), pp. 525-526.

involving teachers' classroom behavior to department chairmen or to teachers themselves.

David Rogers in *110 Livingston Street* points up the conflict between the professional role or professional model of the teacher and the authoritarian role or authoritarian model, which he contends characterizes the public school bureaucracy of New York City. Table 8.1 depicts the two models and identifies some of the problems of professional people working within a bureaucratic structure.[17]

Before leaving the subject of bureaucracy, one additional point must be raised about the relationship between bureaucracy and the concept and practice of political democracy. Blau suggests that to look internally at bureaucratic structures is to find "efficiency" as the organizing principle; while in a democratic structure the official organizing principle is "freedom of dissent."[18] There is a very clear and obvious tension between these two principles. Blau concludes that there is a particular state of tension within those organizations that have the responsibility of identifying majority opinion on some policy and then carrying it out. One obvious example is a political party presumed to poll the membership in some sense on choice of candidates, organize the campaign, and obtain the election of that candidate. Criticisms of the lack of democracy and the lack of the freedom of dissent in both major parties were increasingly heard during the campaigns of 1968. School systems perhaps

17. David Rogers, *110 Livingston Street* (New York: Random House, Inc., 1968), pp. 524-526.
18. Blau, *op. cit.,* chapter 6.

do not exhibit as much of this tension as political parties do, since it is assumed that the general purpose of school systems is widely accepted and that a board of education does not really need to poll the community to discover the most appropriate general goals and objectives for adoption. However, the school as a bureaucracy poses a different problem, since it is the particular institution designated to teach democratic values. The tension arises between the objective of teaching the values of a democratic society, including, certainly, the value of dissent, and the structure of the school which is most often bureaucratic, hierarchial, and antidemocratic.

LEADERSHIP

Leadership in an educational system, as in any complex bureaucratic structure, cannot be understood apart from its environment. In considering the context of educational leadership there are a number of problems which must be taken into account. First, complications arise from the competing demands of various pressure groups. Second, educational leaders are expected to delegate some of their authority and at the same time maintain control over the school or school system. When and to what degree delegation of authority to subordinates is appropriate provides a continuing dilemma for the educational administrator. Third, problems develop because of inconsistencies and conflicts between bureaucratic demands and societal demands. The recent and increasing movement on the part of residents of urban ghetto communities toward a greater say in the operation and control of schools clearly illustrates this kind of problem. The local community in its demands for greater influence are in direct conflict with some of the traditional rights of the big city school bureaucracy.

In examining the leadership setting one must also consider the formal bureaucratic structure and the informal structure discussed in the previous section of this chapter. The existence of the informal structure provides the leader with two possible sources for his authority—respect and popularity. Respect may be derived from technical skills which a particular leader possesses or from a respect for the office itself which the leader holds. Popularity is related to the informal structure. Many times the leader must choose between popularity with his subordinates and upholding rules and regulations. It is probably best to think of the leader in an educational institution as in a sense a middleman negotiating conflicting interests and values within the school and between the school and the larger society. Almost all educational decisions, for example, are unpopular with someone or some group. Leadership in this sense is best seen as compromise.

Definitions of Leadership

1. Historically, the first attempts to define leadership related it to the personality of individual leaders and described the personal traits necessary for effective leadership. The "great man" theory of history falls into this definition of leadership, that is, the attempt to explain historical events and movements not by economic, social, or cultural conditions but rather by the personality and character of certain powerful leaders. With the growth of behavioral science research, however, it is quite apparent that the search for the ideal personality of a "born leader" has simply not been productive. Studies which attempt to relate leadership to such factors as energy, health, emotional stability, appearance, IQ, self-confidence, or even height and weight do not seem to provide us with any very clear characteristics that might be used to develop a personality type. We are not saying here that personality is not important in leadership, but merely that the attempts to define it by personality traits and characteristics have been fruitless. It is clear, for example, that motivation plays an important part in leadership. Certain social skills —such as language fluency, humor, diplomacy, and tact—also seem to be important characteristics for leaders to possess. Yet it is still possible to find effective leaders who exhibit none of these.

2. A better approach to understanding the nature of leadership is to ignore the leader himself and his personality and focus on what the leader does—the functions of leadership. At least three necessary functions of leadership can be identified.[19] First, in the formulation of policy the leader of any organization is expected to relate the abstract goals or long-range purposes of the organization to the day-by-day working policies. Depending upon the setting, the leader's power to affect these two elements varies considerably. A principal of an urban school, for example, while he can certainly affect directly the day-to-day operating procedures in his school, has very little to say about the long-range goals and objectives of the school system. The second necessary function of leadership, the implementation of the policies formed, is the development of a specific form of operation and everyday routine decisions which will help to achieve established policies. The third essential function is the maintenance of "functional autonomy." This is particularly important in school leadership, since one of the main roles of a principal or superintendent is to obtain what the school or school system needs from the larger society and at the same time protect the institution, the teachers, and subordinate administrators from outside interference. The increasing demand for more public involvement and control over urban schools presents a particular problem as we have said. To what extent

19. Lane, Corwin, Monahan, *op. cit.*, pp. 307-308.

leaders in urban schools may allow community members to become involved and to make decisions without radically changing and possibly destroying the present structure of urban school systems is still to be discovered.

3. Another important attempt to define the nature of leadership focuses on the concept of leadership as a social process. Warren Bennis has characterized leadership in this sense as comprising the following fundamental elements:

a. an agent
b. a process of inducement
c. subordinates
d. the induced behavior
e. a particular objective or goal.

Putting these elements together, Bennis defines leadership as the ". . . process by which an agent induces a subordinate to behave in a desired manner."[20] The emphasis here is not on the leader, either in terms of his functions or his relations with subordinates and other members of the bureaucracy, but rather on the interaction process itself. It means essentially that leadership is not limited to one individual but may well be a continuum. Rather than looking for a set of rules, the administrator should attempt to understand certain basic principles of interaction.

When viewed as an interaction process, effective leadership is closely related to the leader possessing at least three basic skills:

1. maintaining his own position
2. supporting the interests of the subordinate
3. initiating ideas and commands.[21]

We will consider very briefly the first two skills and then in greater detail the third one, which involves the vital process of decision-making.

With respect to maintaining his own position a leader in any educational bureaucracy must view the problem as being twofold. He must maintain his position with respect to both his superior—whether a district superintendent, a superintendent of schools, or a board of education—and with his subordinates—principals, teachers, and students. With respect to his superiors a leader can attempt to maintain his position by either enhancing his own personal relations with them or increasing the objective standards of his work. Maintaining himself with his subordinates requires rather different tactics. He might, for example, prevent opposition to him from becoming unified and organized by

20. W.G. Bennis, "Leadership Theory and Administrative Behavior," in W.G. Bennis, K.D. Benne, and R. Chin (eds.), *The Planning of Change,* (New York: Holt, Rinehart and Winston, Inc., 1961), p. 440.

21. Lane, Corwin, Monahan *op. cit.,* pp. 315-320.

transferring subordinates who *are* in opposition from one department to another or out of the school system.

The second area of important leadership skills is in maintaining the subordinates' positions. This depends on a number of particular abilities and conditions, perhaps the most important of which is effective communication. Communication includes both clearly and definitely passing on instructions and decisions and, perhaps more important, the process of consulting with subordinates before decisions are made. This two-way communication is crucial for effective leadership, even when it is not absolutely essential for accomplishing the task. The use of praise and blame is also an effective device for supporting subordinates' positions. Homans asserts that an effective leader will neither praise nor blame a member of his group in front of other members.[22]

The third leadership task, that of making decisions, is crucially important in educational administration. Many writers on decision-making have described it as a series of steps. Griffith identifies the process as follows:

1. recognize, define, and limit the problem
2. analyze and evaluate the problem
3. establish criteria or standards by which a solution will be judged as acceptable and adequate to the need
4. collect data
5. formulate and select the preferred solution or solutions
6. put into effect the preferred solution.[23]

While this may be a very neat conceptual scheme, it does not go very far toward understanding what happens in actual practice. Perhaps a better approach is to consider what might be called the decision environment—general categories of concerns and commitments which infringe upon the logical order of Griffith's decision-making process. At least three commitments are important enough to comment on briefly.

1. It is particularly important for educational administrators to consider the effect of their decisions in relation to the interested public in the community. School systems are, after all, public institutions and do have very clear public commitments. The increased demands by parents for community control of urban schools (discussed at length in the final chapter) is clearly changing the kind of commitments which the urban public school system must make to the public. These redefined commitments must be taken into account in any decision made by an urban educational leader.

22. G. Homans, *The Human Group* (New York: Harcourt, Brace & World, Inc., 1950), p. 433.
23. D. Griffiths, *Administrative Theory in Education* in A.W. Halpin (ed.), (Chicago: Midwest Administration Center, University of Chicago, 1958), p. 132.

2. Past decisions of the school system also are an important part of the decision-making environment. Any decision sets a precedent and is likely to involve a necessary chain of other decisions. Possible actions are determined to some extent by the history of the system. A decision that is completely at odds with past decisions is likely to meet with considerable opposition from subordinates in any bureaucratic structure.

3. The educational leader must understand the nature of existing personal relationships within his school or school system. Some knowledge, for example, of the existing informal structure is extremely useful. If a leader does not know how a particular decision might affect the informal structure and the informal relations among his subordinates, his decision is likely to be that much less effective. This part of the decision-making environment implies that to some extent the subordinate should be brought into the decision-making process and play a part in it, but some problems are thus created, especially in an hierarchially structured bureaucracy like a school system. Principals or superintendents find it difficult to initiate contact on a colleague basis with their subordinates, and yet there is considerable evidence that consultation with subordinates and particularly with persons who may disagree is an effective problem-solving device.

Cert and March suggest that instead of considering decision-making as a step-by-step progression it would better be viewed as a bargaining process in which two or more sides make demands that may require modification of organizational policy and perhaps eventually modification of its goal.[24] The role of the leader in this conception of decision-making is that of a bargainer or mediator between competing demands of outside pressure groups, professional associations, teachers' unions, subordinate administrators, and boards of education. Decision-making viewed as bargaining becomes in a sense much more complex, less logical, but probably more closely related to real life. The level and complexity of decision-making varies considerably within school systems as Figure 8.2 illustrates.

RESEARCH ON URBAN EDUCATIONAL LEADERSHIP

How do urban principals relate to their teachers? How does the principal and his performance relate to the type of student who makes up the school population? What role does social class play in urban administration? Robert Herriott and Nancy Hoyt St. John look at these

24. R.M. Cert and J.G. March, "A Behavioral Theory of Organizational Objectives," in Mason Haire (ed.), *Modern Organizational Theory* (New York: John Wiley & Sons, Inc., 1959), pp. 80ff.

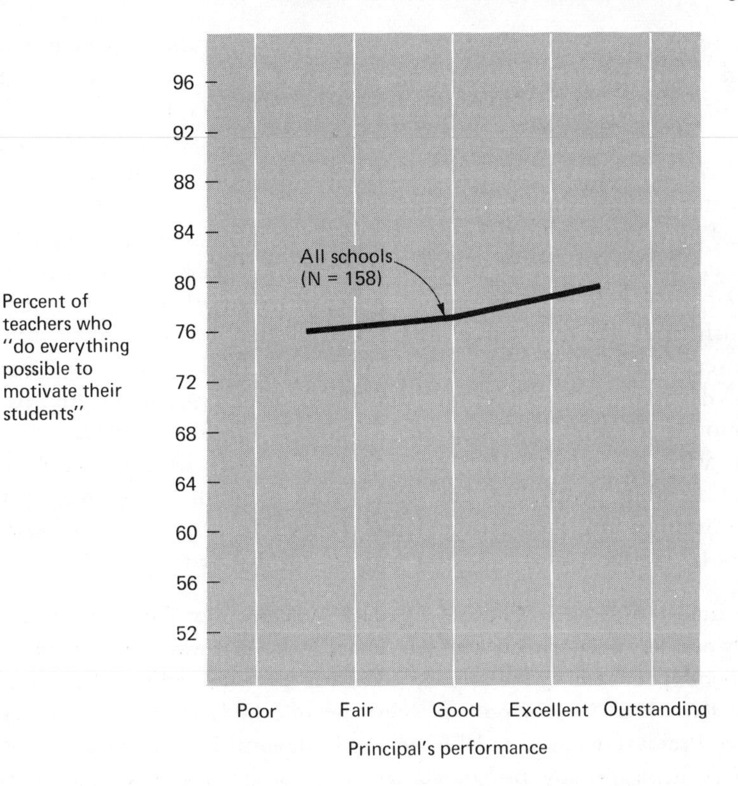

Figure 8.2 Relationship within 158 schools of the average proportion of teachers who "do everything possible to motivate their students" to the principal's performance in "giving leadership to the instructional program."

SOURCE: Robert E. Herriott and Nancy Hoyt St. John, *Social Class and the Urban School* (New York: John Wiley & Sons, Inc., 1966), p. 150.

questions in their study, *Social Class and the Urban School,*[25] which was based on a sample of 501 principals and 3367 teachers in 41 cities throughout the United States. The study points out a number of interesting differences between the urban principal in the slum school and in the middle-class school. For example, the lower the socioeconomic status of the school, the greater the proportion of principals who are themselves from working-class backgrounds, whose father's occupational status is blue collar. When one looks at the career characteristics of urban principals across social class lines one finds that, on the average, principals in schools at the bottom of the SES ladder are younger, less experienced, and more apt to be male than those at the top of the ladder. Principals in lower-class schools, like teachers in lower-class schools, place

25. Robert E. Herriott and Nancy Hoyt St. John, *Social Class and the Urban School* (New York: John Wiley & Sons, Inc., 1966).

greater emphasis on teaching professionalism, indicate less job satisfaction and a greater desire to move to a different assignment. For principals, this includes an interest in moving either horizontally or vertically, that is, moving up the ladder of increased responsibility to a superintendency or moving laterally to the principalship of a school in a better neighborhood with higher socioeconomic status.

The relationship between principal performance and socioeconomic status of the school is much less clear. Teachers in the schools were asked to rate their principals on a list of twenty-three aspects of the job of principal. On only three of the twenty-three items were the differences between the rated performance of principals in the lowest socioeconomic schools significantly different from those principals in the highest socioeconomic schools. The three items were: 1. "obtaining parental cooperation with the school," 2. "publicizing the work of the school," 3. "attracting able people to the school staff." In analyzing why principal performance on these three items is significantly lower in lower-class schools, Herriott and St. John suggest the following:

The data presented in Chapter 3 [which indicates that there are fewer parent visits and less cooperation with the school in lower socioeconomic status neighborhoods] concerning the relation of SES to parental visits and to cooperation with the school may in part explain why principals in slum schools are considered relatively unsuccessful in parental relations. Their relative lack of attention to publicity may be caused by the poor achievement and behavior of pupils and lower social prestige of parents in these neighborhoods while the relative lack of success in staff recruitment may be explained by the preference of teachers for schools in better neighborhoods.[26]

One of the most important hypotheses tested by Herriott and St. John is that ". . . the performance of the principal is more closely related to that of his teachers in schools of low socio-economic status than it is in those of high socio-economic status."[27] They found that

. . . for the schools of high socio-economic status none of the twenty-three indexes of the principal's administrative performance is significantly related to the teacher performance score. On the other hand within those of low socio-economic status nineteen of the twenty-three co-efficients are statistically significant. In addition for all twenty-three indexes of the principal's performance the correlation co-efficient for the low SES schools is greater than that for the high SES schools. Thus, the hypotheses that the performance of principals is more closely related to that of their teachers in schools of low SES than of high SES is supported.[28]

26. *Ibid.*, p. 135.
27. *Ibid.*, p. 146.
28. *Ibid.*, p. 153.

Table 8.2 Rank Order of 23 Aspects of the Performance of 79 Principals in Schools of Low SES, According to the Magnitude of Their Relationship with the Teacher Performance Score

Aspect of the principal's performance	Coefficient of correlation
19. Planning generally for the school.	.45*
18. Keeping the school office running smoothly.	.40*
6. Resolving student discipline problems.	.37*
4. Getting teachers to use new educational methods.	.35*
11. Improving the performance of inexperienced teachers.	.35*
21. Getting teachers to coordinate their activities.	.35*
20. Knowing about the strengths and weaknesses of teachers.	.34*
22. Attracting able people to the school staff.	.34*
1. Running meetings or conferences.	.34*
16. Handling parental complaints.	.33*
23. Knowing about the strengths and weaknesses of the school program.	.32*
13. Giving leadership to the instructional program.	.31*
15. Revising school procedures in the light of modern educational practices.	.31*
17. Publicizing the work of the school.	.30*
12. Getting *experienced* teachers to upgrade their performance.	.25*
5. Obtaining parental cooperation with the school.	.25*
14. Developing *esprit de corps* among teachers.	.23*
2. Handling delicate interpersonal situations.	.22*
10. Communicating the objectives of the school program to the faculty.	.21*
9. Maximizing the different skills found in the faculty.	.19
7. Directing the work of administrative assistants.	.17
8. Cutting red tape when fast action is needed.	.16
3. Working with community agencies.	.08

* $p < .05$.
SOURCE: Robert E. Herriott and Nancy Hoyt St. John, *Social Class and the Urban School* (New York: John Wiley & Sons, Inc., 1965), p. 156.

In Table 8.2 the twenty-three areas of administrative behavior which the authors use in their study have been ranked in terms of the relative magnitude of each behavior's correlation within the schools of low SES. From this one can see that in schools of low socioeconomic status the impact of the principal's performance on that of his teachers is likely to be most pronounced with respect to his ability to plan generally for the school, keep things running smoothly, and resolve student discipline problems. On the other hand his ability to work with community agencies, cut red tape, and direct the work of administrative assistants apparently has little effect on teacher performance. In presenting this evidence the authors make it very clear that they are not proving a causal relationship. They have only proved a correlation between principal performance and teacher performance, not that improved principal performance causes improved teacher performance. Nevertheless, the finding is important since, as the authors say, the "results of this analysis lend support to the proposition that performance of the principal is more crucial to that of teachers in schools of low as opposed to those of high socio-economic status."[29] The policy implication of this finding would seem to be that urban school systems should pay particular attention to the effectiveness of principals assigned to urban slum schools, since the study suggests that their performance may have significant effects on the performance of teachers and thus, one might argue logically, on the performance of youngsters in the school.

Another important study, *Staff Leadership in the Public Schools,* by Gross and Herriott attempts to deal with two aspects of the problem of public school leadership.[30] The authors identified the quality of Executive Professional Leadership, or EPL, a concept defined as the "efforts of an executive of a professionally staffed organization to conform to a definition of his role that stresses his obligation to improve the quality of staff performance."[31] The measurement of EPL was obtained from a sample of urban elementary school principals across the nation, by obtaining the responses from teachers to eighteen statements about the behavior of their principals. Teachers were asked to rate their principals on such items as "has constructive suggestions to offer teachers in dealing with their major problems." "Considers what is best for all the children in the decisions affecting educational programs." Or, "Treats teachers as professional workers."[32] After obtaining a measurement of EPL, the investigators were interested in seeing what, if any, were the effects of those principals with high EPL on other conditions in their schools. The investigators selected teacher morale, teacher professional performance, and pupil performance as three important variables. They found that where the EPL score of the principal was higher, teacher morale, teacher professional performance, and pupil performance also tended to be higher, as is shown in Figure 8.3.

Through the use of partial correlation (*see* Appendix for a discussion of this concept) the investigators indicated the relationship between

29. *Ibid.,* p. 157.

30. Neal Gross and Robert E. Herriott, *Staff Leadership in Public Schools* (New York: John Wiley & Sons, Inc., 1965).

31. *Ibid.,* p. 8.

32. *Ibid.,* pp. 27-29.

the four variables with which they were concerned and a fifth variable, family income. Their findings indicate that teacher morale is very likely a link in a causal chain between the EPL of principals and the performance of their pupils.[33]

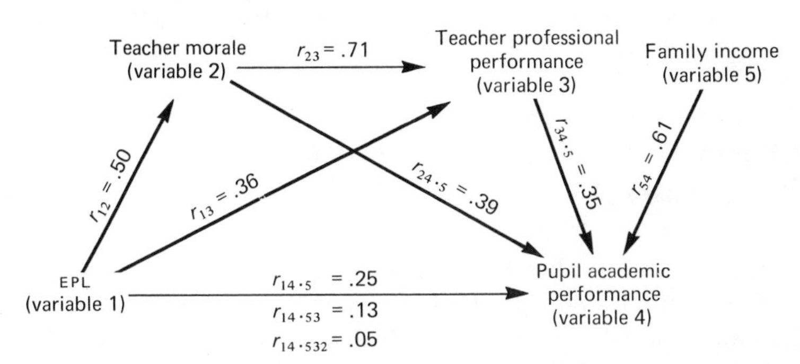

Figure 8.3 A five-variable schema for representing elected relationships among EPL, teacher morale, teacher professional performance, pupil academic performance, and family income.
SOURCE: Neal Gross and Robert E. Herriott, *Staff Leadership in Public Schools* (New York: John Wiley & Sons, Inc., 1965), p. 57.

The possession of EPL or a high EPL score makes a difference in how teachers view the school, in how they perform their tasks, and in how pupils learn. Effective professional leadership can and does make a difference in the effectiveness of the urban school.

The second objective of the study was to determine what characteristics determine the elementary-school principal's capacity for professional leadership. A negative relationship was found between the size of the student body and EPL. That is, the smaller the school enrollment the greater likelihood that the principal would have high EPL. As far as selecting principals was concerned, the authors summarized their findings as follows:

> If executive professional leadership is to be the criterion, many school systems are selecting principals on grounds that appear to have little empirical justification. Type or amount of teaching experience, experience as an assistant or vice-principal, number of undergraduate or graduate courses in education, number of graduate courses in educational administration, sex and marital status. On the other hand, characteristics that should be preferred in appointing elementary principals are a high level of academic performance in college, a high order of interpersonal skill, the motive of service, the willingness to commit off duty time to their work, relatively little seniority as teachers.[34]

33. *Ibid.,* pp. 52-58.
34. *Ibid.,* p. 157.

These findings seem to contradict several widely-held assumptions, particularly that the amount of teaching experience and experience as assistant or vice-principal produces better educational leadership scoring on EPL. On the positive side perhaps most surprising was the relationship between a high degree of EPL and high-level academic performance on the undergraduate level.

DECISION-MAKING IN NEW YORK CITY PUBLIC SCHOOLS

These research studies tell us something about urban administrators and effective professional leadership, but how are urban school systems really administered? In *Participants and Participation: A Study of School Policy in New York City* Professor Marilyn Gittell provides us with a study of decision-making in the largest public school system in the United States.[35] Professor Gittell begins by identifying three forms which participation in school policy formulation can take:

1. *Closed.* Only the professionals in the system participate
2. *Limited.* The board of education and/or the mayor and specialized educational interest groups participate
3. *Wide.* Groups not wholly concerned with school policy participate.

Professor Gittell suggests that the board of education's role has been and continues to be one of balancing conflicting views on various policy issues rather than providing the long-range educational planning which is a stated function of the board. She also points out that without a strong staff, that is, professional educators assigned to the board itself, rather than to the superintendent and his office, the board of education is really unable to evaluate effectively any educational proposals put forth by the superintendent or other parts of the educational bureaucracy. She concludes: "The bureaucracy and special interest groups have gained power by means of their expertise while the Board, lacking expertise and political leverage has lost power."[36]

The local school boards in New York City, except for certain experimental districts, are presently appointed by the central board of education. These local boards have not been given any real authority in the determination of school policy. They have acted rather as community forums at which hearings and discussions may be held about issues

35. Marilyn Gittell, *Participants and Participation: A Study of School Policy in New York City* (New York: Center for Urban Education, 1967).
36. *Ibid.*, pp. 6-7.

related to the community. Professor Gittell states flatly that the central board of education has been reluctant to delegate powers to local boards for fear that they would encroach upon its authority. District superintendents have also been reluctant to delegate any authority to the local boards, since they are afraid of interference with their own local school administration.

The superintendent in New York City is described by Professor Gittell as a "relatively limited chief executive." The main reasons for the limited nature of his power seems to be the strength of the bureaucracy over which he presides.

The superintendent in New York City lacks the most essential power of a strong executive, the power of appointment and removal. The system's supervisory staff is developed completely through promotion from the ranks. Tenured supervisors hold top policy making jobs allowing the superintendent little flexibility in appointments. All assistant superintendents receive tenures after a three year probationary period.[37]

Thus, no superintendent can rely on his own group of trusted advisors, nor can he develop his own advisory staff.

In *Participants and Participation* the educational bureaucracy in New York City was placed in two separate categories: the headquarters staff and the operational field staff. The author was unable to obtain a precise figure on the size of the headquarters staff, but makes an estimate of about 3000 professional employees. The operational field staff includes 2200 principals and assistant principals, 31 district superintendents, and 740 department chairmen. Professor Gittell identifies a core supervisory group which she believes holds much of the decision-making power in the New York City public school system. Included in this group is the executive deputy superintendent and the deputy superintendent in charge of instruction and curriculum, the board of examiners, and 20 of the 30 assistant superintendents who are attached to headquarters, plus a few active directors of special bureaus. Only 2 of this core group of 30 supervisors have any professional experience outside of New York City. All of the rest have spent their entire professional lives inside the public school system in New York.

In almost every area of school policy, there was evidence that those at headquarters, particularly the core of thirty odd supervisors were major policy makers. They exercised power individually as heads of divisions and departments and as a group they act to reinforce their individual decisions.[38]

37. *Ibid.*, p. 9.
38. *Ibid.*, p. 13.

The supervisors in the field in New York City are the district superintendents. Professor Gittell suggests that these men are essentially the only means under which the present structure of public education in New York City can achieve any administrative decentralization, and they are also the system's only source of liaison with local school needs. When asked in a questionnaire, the district superintendents indicated that they do not participate in the formulation of school policy:

. . . district superintendents have no discretion in the distribution of funds and only the most limited kind of discretion in the assignment of personnel. Their staffs are small and largely clerical. In practical terms district superintendents act as a buffer for parent dissatisfaction that remains unresolved by the school principal. The superintendent's lack of participation in policy decisions gives support to the central conclusion of this study that the central supervisory staff has cornered the power market.[39]

The Council of Supervisory Associations in New York City is a professional organization made up of the individual supervisory associations including those for high-school principals, junior-high principals, elementary-school principals, assistant principals, high-school chairmen, the board of examiners, assistant superintendents, and associate superintendents. The Council has approximately 3000 members. Professor Gittell states that both the individual associations and the Council itself, although having no formal position in the school system, exert a strong influence on educational policy. She notes that the Council has openly opposed the Princeton Plan, school bussing, the Comprehensive High School Plan, the dropping of IQ examinations, and school pairing, *after* these were adopted as official policy by the board and by the superintendent. With the one exception of dropping the IQ examinations, none of these policies were implemented by the superintendent or the board of education.

The United Federation of Teachers is the largest single organization of professionals within the public school system. Membership is now over 30,000. Professor Gittell maintains that the potential power of this large professional association to participate in a wide variety of policy areas has not been realized because the union, at least the union leadership, has decided to concentrate its attention on salary scales and related benefits. She suggests that in those cases when the union has taken a public position on issues outside of salary and related matters, it has generally been motivated by a desire to maintain the status quo. "The union has publically and privately fought the transfers of experienced teachers to difficult schools and the rotation plan has remained a volun-

39. *Ibid.*, p. 13.

tary program." It has also questioned the advisability of a 4-4-4 school reorganization because the plan threatened the status of the junior high school teacher. Since Professor Gittell wrote her study, the union has also come out very strongly opposing the Bundy proposal for school decentralization and policies of the Ocean Hill-Brownsville experimental district in New York.

From interviews conducted with union leaders, it was clear that they themselves saw conflict between on the one hand educational and professional goals and on the other the narrow interests of its membership. It some instances the union leaders expressed concern that their own positions of power might be threatened if they violated the narrow interests of their membership.[40]

Professor Gittell identifies two interest groups in New York City which share the responsibility for publically overseeing educational policy, the United Parents Association and the Public Education Association.

On the whole the role of both associations as overseers of educational policy is supportive rather than critical. Their inclination is to work within the structure focussing on particular problems. Neither has suggested any radical change. [Both have opposed the Bundy proposal for school decentralization.] Both groups exercise little influence in the area of curriculum. On occasion one or both have made general statements regarding the need for the inclusion of certain material in the curriculum or for greater emphasis in a given field but such concern is sporadic and unfocussed. Both have supported increased school expenditure and larger city and state appropriations.[41]

The final participant in school decision-making in New York City is the press. *Participants and Participation* suggests that newspaper reports in New York City have been generally mild and favorable toward the school system, with criticism reserved for very minor problems. Reporting in New York papers on educational matters has not been probing.

Professor Gittell selects two important decision areas and looks more closely at just how decisions are made. School budgeting in New York City is a central operation closely controlled and supervised by the core supervisory staff within the bureaucracy. In describing the procedure by which the budget is prepared annually for the school system, Professor Gittell points out that there is virtually no time available for public review and discussion of the budget. In fact, even the superintendent

40. *Ibid.,* p. 15.
41. *Ibid.,* p. 16.

has very little time for review or making comments, criticisms, or suggestions. Each budget, when presented to the board of education, focuses the board's attention on a small number of items which have been increased or decreased from the previous year. The budget document, Professor Gittell says, is never reviewed as a whole in the sense of reevaluating existing programs and activities.

The importance of the budget as a plan for school program and policy cannot be underestimated. New programs never see the light of day if they do not have the support of the superintendents in charge of the special divisions. The four or five headquarters superintendents who review budget requests are the first and final authority in the translation of programs to budget policy. This tightly structured procedure establishes inflexible standards for 80 to 90% of the budget. The central budgeting staff establishes standards for the entire school system tying the hands of the local school administrators and undermining their ability to respond to individual needs. The staff uses none of the existent methods for advanced program planning and evaluation, thus greatly restricting the consideration of policy alternatives. Public discussion of the budget is virtually impossible and civic and interest group participation is severely limited. Even the Board and the Superintendent of Schools are chained to a document that may have little to do with their hopes or intentions. At present the budget cannot be viewed in any way as a tool of the superintendent and it is even less a statement of the Board of Education's policy.[42]

Another important decision-making area in which central bureaucrats are predominant is curriculum. The Bureau of Curriculum Research at school headquarters is the officially designated agency for the development of curriculum. It has a fulltime staff of about twenty-seven individuals that function under an assistant superintendent. The Bureau has the responsibility for reviewing and rewriting all curriculum bulletins and recommending and implementing changes in curriculum areas. In some cases Professor Gittell suggests people in the field have been able to influence the bureau in making certain curriculum changes. Most school personnel actually used on special committees in the bureau to revise a particular curriculum area are administrators rather than classroom teachers. There is no evidence that classroom teachers have any influence on the development of curriculum in the New York City system. Evaluation of curriculum is almost never done in New York City except as part of a special program, such as Higher Horizons or the More Effective School program. Certain public pressure groups have occasionally been able to influence curriculum in the public schools in particular areas. For example, civil rights groups have in recent years

42. *Ibid.*, p. 27.

succeeded in securing greater emphasis on black history in the social studies curriculum. Professor Gittell concludes:

For all practical purposes, however, the continuing participants in curriculum policy making are the professionals at the headquarters. The deputy superintendent and the assistant superintendent in charge of the Bureau of Curriculum Research are the key initiators of policy and the curriculum coordinators, its implementers. Even though the principals and teachers are the final determinants of what is done in the school and in the classrooms.[43]

In several other decision-making areas more of the participants identified earlier play some role. In the selecting of a superintendent and the setting of a salary policy, for example, the board of education in the first case and the Teachers' Union in the second play significant roles. In the implementation or rather nonimplementation of New York City's integration policy Professor Gittell sees the board of education and the bureaucracy yielding to pressure groups in the community. In the case of integration policy Professor Gittell notes a possibly important development.

All this interest [pro and con on integration] has produced perhaps the most significant development in school decision making. For the past two decades superintendents, boards, and school bureaucracies have been freewheeling with little outside pressure, more or less entirely independent of public opinion. They have successfully closed off school policy formulation from elected local government officials and civic groups. The integration issue now has broken open the monopoly of power vested in this small core of school officials.[44]

Since Professor Gittell's study was completed in 1966, she did not have available to her information relating to the conflict surrounding school decentralization. This additional and rather different issue also raises ". . . serious questions regarding the role of professionals, their goals, and interests in school policy."[45]

In conclusion, Professor Gittell quotes Sayre and Kaufman: "On balance the school official enjoys an unusual capacity for self government."[46] As a political subsystem the New York City schools can only be described as "narrow, convergent, and dominated by a consenual elite." In an epilogue to *Participants and Participation* the author goes on to suggest a plan for improving what she views as the problems of the decision-making process in New York City public schools. Since this

43. *Ibid.,* p. 31.
44. *Ibid.,* p. 45.
45. *Ibid.,* p. 46.
46. *Ibid.,* p. 52.

plan has been superceded by the Bundy proposal and counterproposals by the board of education and other groups, we will defer a discussion of decentralization to the final chapter of this book.

Nat Hentoff, a New York journalist, provides a close-up view of an effective urban principal in his book, *Our Children Are Dying*.[47] In the introduction, teacher and author, John Holt, suggests that this educational biography of Elliot Shapiro, the principal of PS 119 in Harlem, raises important questions. What is the job of an educational leader? What is a principal or superintendent for? Holt argues that we are torn between two views. One, which generally prevails in practice, might be called the corporate or military view. The job of an educational administrator, particularly in urban slums, is to tell everyone under him what to do and to make sure that they do it. Holt describes the superintendent of a large school system who at one point pulled his watch out of his pocket, laid it on the table, and said with considerable satisfaction, "I can tell you what every teacher in this system is doing right now." The second view suggests that educational administrators should be no more than business managers and should have nothing to do with the process of education at all. Their jobs should simply be to keep school buildings equipped, lighted, heated, and to stay out of the teachers' way. Holt, a teacher himself, prefers the second alternative—no administration, no leadership over a dictatorial military approach to education. He concudes, however, that Dr. Shapiro fits neither stereotype.

> But the example of Dr. Shapiro shows us that the head of a school or a system of schools need not choose between being an absolute boss or only a sweeper of floors and payer of bills. What the good teacher can do for children, the good administrator can do for his teachers. Create and maintain an environment in the highest degree favorable to their learning and growth. In a part of the city from which most teachers flee as soon as they can, Dr. Shapiro has stabilized his teaching staff by making PS 119 a school in which teachers felt free to experiment and in which they could depend on further support from an actively interested parent body. In short he has seen that his duty to teachers is neither to boss nor to ignore but to inspire, reassure and protect.[48]

Based on a long series of interviews with Dr. Shapiro in PS 119 and its surrounding neighborhood, Hentoff describes the school as a bleak and forbidding five-story, "sickly beige" building crowded with 1100 children in classes from prekindergarten through the sixth grade. The Harlem neighborhood served is what social workers call a high delin-

47. Nat Hentoff, *Our Children Are Dying* (New York: The Viking Press, Inc., 1966).

48. *Ibid.*, pp. viii, ix.

quency area. About 35 percent of its families are on welfare; the rest have low incomes ranging from $40 to $70 a week. Housing conditions for many of the children are very bad. A building directly across the street from the school had been built for eight families, but now houses forty-five. Hentoff describes the effect of his first visit to Dr. Shapiro's school:

The office I note is distinctly different from principal's offices in most other elementary schools I have visited. Instead of the customary, unsmiling, impersonal attitude of the secretaries, the office personnel seemed to erect no barriers of "not to be questioned authority" between themselves and the children who come in and out bearing messages or wanting to see the principal. Busy but relaxed secretaries talk to rather than at the children. At the back of the room on the left is Dr. Shapiro's small private office. Its door is almost always open. In his mid-fifties, six feet tall but slightly stooped, grey haired, Shapiro has the face of a watchful but gentle eagle. He is softspoken and often wry. "It's like a medieval castle, isn't it?" He points to the battlements outside his window. "When it rains and the yard gets flooded all you need is a drawbridge."[49]

Dr. Shapiro's relationship with the educational bureaucracy in New York City, particularly the central office, can only be described as rather unusual. In 1961 Dr. Shapiro and his staff at the school became so enraged at the physical conditions in the school and especially at the lack of response from either the district superintendent or the board of education itself that they took the unusual and in fact unprecedented step of placing an ad on the school page of the May 22, 1961, New York *World Telegram*.

HELP! HELP! HELP!

Help Us to Get a New School to Save Our Children
Give Us a Building Without

1. Rats and Roaches on every Floor
2. A Leaking Roof
3. Broken Door Frames
4. Split Sessions ($\frac{1}{2}$ an education)
5. Refrigerator Temperatures in the Winter and Oven-Like Sweltering During Spring
6. Irreparable Plumbing, Resulting In: Backups, Leaks, Flooded Yards and Corridors and Lunchrooms

49. *Ibid.*, p. 5.

7. Sagging, Dangerous Walls
8. Overcrowding in Lunchrooms and Classrooms
9. Unsanitary Children's Toilets
10. Wasteful Temporary Patching of Obsolete and Intrinsically Inadequate Scrap-Pile Facilities Without Shoving the Taxpayers Money Down the Drain
11. Condemnation of Nine Classrooms of Our Old (1899) School Where Our Entire Building Is Wrought with Fire and Health Hazards

OUR CHILDREN DESERVE

A NEW SCHOOL

NOW!!

The Teaching, clerical and administrative staff of Public School #119—Manhattan

As might be imagined, the ad aroused a considerable amount of interest in PS 119. Television and radio newsmen descended and Mayor Robert Wagner arranged to visit the school. During the Mayor's tour of the building a rat, spotted by several teachers and students, was chased with a broom. It escaped under a radiator, but the press made much of the rat's appearance during the Mayor's visit. In spite of the publicity associated with the newspaper ad and the rat incident, the school was not repaired over the summer. In the fall, on the first day of school, workmen arrived and began to make major repairs requested and promised the previous spring. Parents in the district, angry about the chaos in the school and the torn-up schoolyard, declared a boycott. For two days 900 children out of the 1100 school population were absent. Dr. Shapiro, speaking about the boycott said: "I couldn't tell them to keep their children out, but they knew I was sympathetic." After meeting with angry parents, a representative of the board reluctantly agreed that time and a half for work done after three in the afternoon and on Saturdays would be paid, and that the school's rehabilitation would be accomplished as quickly as possible. The relationships between Dr. Shapiro and the central office at 110 Livingston Street in Brooklyn were not, as can be imagined, very good. Dr. Shapiro's main criticism of the bureaucratic structure of the school was not so much in its specific operating procedure but rather in its judgment about what was realistic or what was possible in the area of urban education. Hentoff mentions hearing an assistant superintendent of schools making a radio speech to Harlem parents saying that "educationally we have nothing to be ashamed of here in Harlem."

> It was an honest opinion [Shapiro said], and it is shared by many people in the system. They mean that they are doing about the best they can with the present resources, but they fail to recognize that resources are not so limited as they have taken them to be. We ought to be ashamed, I mean those of us in the school system, that we have not been leaders for dramatic improvements, and that we do participate in a process in which two-thirds or maybe three-fourths of the children are being so badly educated that we are giving them a lifetime of unemployment.[50]

Dr. Shapiro in his years at PS 119 was also drawn into a great number of community problems and associations with what he calls extracurricular concerns of the community. "It was very important to batter at the welfare agencies. To beat down the doors, to get people accepted. I spent hours on the phone." During this early period an assistant to the then Commissioner of Welfare, James Dumpson, said to Shapiro one day, "Considering all the time you spend with us, I don't see how you get much else done in that school. You seem to have departments of home welfare, housing and community service at PS 119. Don't you have a department of education?"[51]

In addition to involving himself, Dr. Shapiro encourages the teachers in his school to become aware of the home and family life of their pupils. For example, when the decision was made to construct the replacement school for PS 119 next door, Dr. Shapiro encouraged members of his staff to find apartments for residents who would be displaced by the new construction.

In addition to involving himself and his faculty in neighborhood and community problems, Dr. Shapiro has introduced curriculum changes in the school. Because of his concern with the lack of emphasis on American Negro and African history and culture in the curriculum, Dr. Shapiro encouraged Miss Beryl Banfield, now an assistant principal, to prepare a manual for teachers on ways of introducing African material into elementary-school classrooms. The resulting seventy-five-page manual includes sections on African folklore, family life, games, music, dances, art, and history, along with a bibliography for teachers and one for children. The manual was popular with the teachers in PS 119 and soon requests came from other schools, church groups, and social agencies who wanted copies. In the summer of 1964 copies were also used by the Mississippi Freedom Schools.

50. *Ibid.*, pp. 44-45.
51. *Ibid.*, p. 74.

Since Hentoff wrote *Our Children Are Dying* in 1966, Dr. Elliott Shapiro has left the principalship of PS 92, the school which replaced 119, spent a year as a visiting professor at the University of Rochester, and has now been rehired as a district superintendent on the lower East Side of Manhattan. This area does not include his old school but it does serve large numbers of impoverished blacks and Puerto Ricans. In light of his move from principal to district superintendent it is interesting to look at Shapiro's response to Hentoff's question of what he, Shapiro, would do if he were to become superintendent of schools in New York City.

I'd go to all the poorest neighborhoods and stir up the parents. I'd have a few offices, not just one and most would be in the poor communities. I'd travel to them on a regular schedule so that the parents would know when I'd be there if they wanted to see me. My main office would be in Harlem or in Bedford-Stuyvesant. I'd also approach as many groups throughout the city as possible to get as much community support for the funds we need. The middle class, the business community—I'd make it very clear to them they haven't been helping nearly enough. And I would constantly urge the Board of Education to demand larger budgets. Constantly. Also I'd set up a permanent office in Washington because much of the funding from now on has to be federally based. In that office we'd develop specialists in formulating programs, and in knowing how to get through all the various agencies in that governmental maze. Then we'd have to relate their specialized knowledge to the political strength of New York City. In other words we'd have to devise ways to keep the populace alert as to who has been helping education and hopefully their votes would signify their continuing concern. That's the beginning.[52]

From this description one would be safe in saying that Shapiro would score high on Gross and Herriott's EPL. The problem for urban school systems seems to be one of attracting more Elliott Shapiros, more high EPL principals who are committed to an idea of service rather than to bureaucratic stability and personal advancement.

An additional question must be asked. Would one thousand Elliott Shapiros in the New York City school system complete the job of significantly improving the educational performance of urban youngsters? Or, in addition to bringing in more effective leadership to urban education, are there structural or organizational bureaucratic changes which need to be implemented? In the last chapter of this book, we will explore several suggestions for bringing the school closer to the community in which it is located, in particular we will discuss the contro-

52. *Ibid.*, p. 133.

versial and fiercely contested proposal for school decentralization and community control.

Recommended Reading

Peter Blau's short incisive volume, *Bureaucracy in Modern Society* (New York: Random House, Inc., 1956), is still probably the best general introduction to the study of bureaucratic organization. A classic work dealing with groups and leadership is George Homans' *The Human Group* (New York: Harcourt, Brace & World, Inc., 1950). A recent collection of articles dealing specifically with leadership is Edwin P. Hollander's *Leadership, Groups and Influence* (New York: Oxford University Press, 1964).

110 Livingston Street by David Rogers (New York: Random House, Inc., 1968) is a highly critical case study of educational bureaucracy in New York City. *The Public School of Chicago* by Robert Havighurst (Chicago, Ill.: The Board of Education of the City of Chicago, 1964), although not focusing on administration, provides insights into another large educational system.

Neal Gross, Ward S. Mason, and Alexander W. McEachern's *Explorations in Role Analysis: Studies of the School Superintendency Role* (New York: John Wiley & Sons, Inc., 1958) is an excellent analysis of this important administrative position. John Holt's *Why Schools Fail* (New York: Pitman Publishing Corporation, 1967) gives the author's personal view of how school administration and atmosphere affect learning. A more systematic view of this relationship is presented by Edgar Z. Friedenberg, Hilary A. Gold, and Carl Nordstrom in *Society's Children: A Study of Ressentiment in the Secondary School* (New York: Random House, Inc., 1967).

9

DESEGREGATION

The underlying assumption of this chapter, although obvious, must nevertheless be stated: Forced segregation of any group on any level in public life has no legitimate place in a professed democracy. The acceptance of the statement does not help very much in dealing with the complex problems of desegregation in American public education. Almost every urban school board in the United States has committed itself in theory to desegregation, yet the number of communities which have, in fact, desegregated their schools are few. While not exclusively an urban problem, it is fair to say that our largest cities have the most difficult job, one that is in some sense qualitatively different from the desegregation problems facing smaller communities.

Two very recent factors are not dealt with in detail here because their impact is as yet impossible to measure. The first is the effect of the black power movement on the thrust toward desegregation. It seems clear that black power at the very least is already reducing support for desegregated schools among younger and better-educated black Americans. Another unknown factor is the effect various proposals for decentralizing urban school systems will have on efforts toward desegregation; New York City has at this writing made a very modest move in that direction. Critics of decentralization suggest that with powerful local school boards, moving youngsters across school attendance or city lines to achieve desegregated schools will become more difficult, if not impossible.

The chapter begins with the historical background of the problem, moves to a descriptive statement of the current situation, and examines methods of desegregation—both those tried and those proposed. We then look with particular care at the relationship between desegregation and school performance. This evidence is crucial, since the argument for desegregation is based on the assumption that better learning by minority group youngsters will take place upon desegregation. An evaluation of the various plans and programs designed to solve this fundamental educational problem concludes the chapter.

THE EDUCATION OF BLACK AMERICANS

It is important to realize that the problem of desegregation in American schools is not just a recent phenomenon. Before the Civil War, when most black Americans lived in the South, those few slaves who were educated attended mixed schools along with the owner's children on plantations. In addition, some free blacks received education along with white youngsters in the cities. After the Civil War, Reconstruction governments in the South put considerable emphasis on public education and in all cases legalized mixed schools. Ex-slaves in positions of power for the first time believed strongly that education would be crucial in solving problems for their race. Not only black children but adults as well were involved in formal education.[1]

When federal troops departed from the Southern states as part of the settlement of the disputed Tilden-Hayes (1876) presidential election, Southern whites once more took over complete power. They were virtually unanimous in their opposition to desegregated schools, which they viewed as having been forced on them by Northern carpetbaggers. Black leadership had not had enough time to develop, which left the black community unable to mount any successful opposition or in any way retain what had been gained under Reconstruction. Throughout the remainder of the 19th century the educational position of black Americans in the South deteriorated seriously. Those organizations established by Northern antislavery groups after the Civil War, such as the Freedman's bureau and other private philanthropic groups, had died out. The historic *Plessey* vs *Ferguson* Supreme Court decision firmly established the right of states to segregate the races as long as the two groups were provided with equal facilities. After 1896 it became legal as well as traditional to keep blacks and whites separate in public facilities, such as waiting rooms and schools.

It is difficult for us today to understand just how desperate the educational situation was for blacks at the turn of the century. Conditions

1. Henry Allen Bullock, *A History of Negro Education in the South* (Cambridge, Mass.: Harvard University Press, 1967), chapter II.

forced many black leaders to regard the struggle for equality as unrealistic. They believed that gains could only be achieved though policies of conciliation and appeasement of the white power structure.

The best-known spokesman for this position was undoubtedly Booker T. Washington (1856-1915). Born as a slave, Washington worked for higher status beginning as a janitor, educating himself, becoming a teacher, and finally, in 1881, founding the Tuskegee Institute, a school devoted to the practical training of Negro-Americans. It was Washington's clearly stated philosophy that black Americans should cultivate the soil and gain economic stability by acquiring ownership of land. He urged them to secure the good will of white persons and accept their philanthropy.

. . . to those of my race who depend upon bettering their condition in a foreign land, or who underestimate the importance of cultivating friendly relations with the Southern white man who is their next-door neighbor, I would say, "Cast down your bucket where you are"—cast it down in making friends, in every manly way, of the people of all races by whom we are surrounded.

Cast it down in agriculture, mechanics, in commerce, in domestic service, and in the professions. And in this connection it is well to bear in mind that whatever other sins the South may be called to bear, when it comes to business, pure and simple, it is in the South that the Negro is given a man's chance in the commercial world, and in nothing is this Exposition more eloquent than in emphasizing this chance. Our greatest danger is that in the great leap from slavery to freedom we may overlook the fact that the masses of us are to live by the productions of our hands, and fail to keep in mind that we shall prosper in proportion as we learn to dignify and glorify common labor, and put brains and skill into the common occupations of life; shall prosper in proportion as we learn to draw the line between the superficial and the substantial, the ornamental gewgaws of life and the useful. No race can prosper till it learns that there is as much dignity in tilling a field as in writing a poem. It is at the bottom of life we must begin, and not at the top. Nor should we permit our grievances to overshadow our opportunities. As we have proved our loyalty to you in the past, in nursing your children, watching by the sick bed of your mothers and fathers, and often following them with tear-dimmed eyes to their graves, so in the future, in our humble way, we shall stand by you with a devotion that no foreigner can approach, ready to lay down our lives, if need be, in defense of yours, interlacing our industrial, commercial, civil, and religious life with yours in a way that shall make the interests of both races one. In all things that are purely social we can be as separate as the fingers, yet one as the hand in all things essential to mutual progress. . .[2]

2. Booker T. Washington, *Atlanta Exposition Address* (delivered at the opening of the Cotton States' Exposition, Atlanta, Georgia, September 1895) in *Selected Speeches of Booker T. Washington,* E. Davidson Washington (ed.) (New York, Doubleday & Company, Inc., 1932), pp. 31-34, 35.

Many Negro-Americans accepted Washington's philosophy. However, when economic forces caused migration to Northern cities, a more militant spirit emerged. This led to the establishment of the National Association for the Advancement of Colored People in 1909. By 1917 the NAACP launched an educational program to obtain decent elementary schooling for blacks in the rural South, where tens of thousands were getting none at all. No mention was made in this campaign of the goal of desegregation. The early NAACP strategy was to bring cases of unequal educational facilities into the courts, accepting, in other words, the *Plessey* vs *Ferguson* decision of 1896. After achieving considerable success over the years with this policy, the NAACP developed larger goals. The organization was no longer satisfied with so-called equal facilities; rather, the goal gradually became desegregation and the admission of nonwhite children, youth, and college students to previously all-white institutions.[3]

THE ROLE OF THE SUPREME COURT

The NAACP first won cases in the federal courts on the grounds that public educational facilities for black Americans were not equal. Court victories were based on the narrow ground that pointed to certain inequalities in teacher salaries, libraries, availability of courses, and so on. The fiction of separate but equal still remained. However, in 1950 a crucial Supreme Court decision (*Sweatt* vs *Painter*) paved the way for the eventual overthrow of the separate-but-equal doctrine.[4] Texas, by this decision, was required to provide a law-school education for a single black student. It did so by actually establishing a second law school with a highly paid faculty and a good library—for the one student. This student and the NAACP did not consider such an exclusive school to be equal and took it to the courts. The argument was no longer about physical facilities, salaries, or any of the tangible things upon which previous cases had been decided. The unanimous *Sweatt* vs *Painter* decision declared that the state university must admit the black student to its own law school because a school established for one student was inferior in "those qualities which are incapable of objective measurement but which made for greatness in a law school." The court pointed to the lack of interaction with other students who would become future lawyers and possible judges in the state.

In that same year the Supreme Court heard another important case, that of *McLaurin* vs *Oklahoma State Regents,* and again delivered a unanimous decision.[5] In Oklahoma the black applicant was admitted

3. Bullock, *op. cit.,* chapter IX.
4. *Sweatt v. Painter,* 339 U.S. 629, L. Ed. 114, 70 S. Ct. 848 (1950).
5. Bullock, *op. cit.,* p. 230.

to the state university's graduate school, but was required to sit in a specially assigned seat, to use a separate section of the library where books were brought to him, and to eat at an isolated table in the cafeteria. The Supreme Court found this unequal for virtually the same reasons as in *Sweatt* vs *Painter,* arguing that intangible but important qualities were being denied to the student.

Technically these two decisions still fell within the doctrine of separate but equal. However, the interpretation of equality had become so difficult that, it seemed to many observers of the Supreme Court, any kind of separation was soon going to be judged to be unequal. This final step occurred on May 17, 1954, when the *Brown* vs *Board of Education* decision was handed down.[6] This case, involving school children from five different states, included in the decision reports of social science studies indicating that segregation made black children aware that whites considered them inferior and thus impaired their learning.

. . . in these days, it is doubtful that any child may reasonably be expected to succeed in life if he is denied the opportunity of an education. Such an opportunity, where the state has undertaken to provide it, is a right which must be made available to all on equal terms.

We come then to the question presented: Does segregation of children in public schools solely on the basis of race, even though the physical facilties and other "tangible" factors may be equal, deprive the children of the minority group of equal educational opportunities? We believe that it does.

In *Sweatt* v *Painter,* in finding that a segregated law school for Negroes could not provide them equal educational opportunities, this Court relied in large part on "those qualities which are incapable of objective measurement but which make for greatness in a law school."

In *McLaurin* vs *Oklahoma State Regents* the Court, in requiring that a black student admitted to a white graduate school be treated like all other students, again resorted to intangible considerations: ". . . his ability to study, to engage in discussions and exchange views with other students, and, in general, to learn his profession." Such considerations apply with added force to children in grade and high schools. To separate them from others of similar age and qualifications solely because of their status in the community may affect their hearts and minds in a way unlikely ever to be undone.

. . . we conclude that in the field of public education the doctrine of "separate but equal" has no place. Separate educational facilities are inherently unequal.

6. *Brown* v. *Board of Education,* 347 U.S. 483 (1954), in David Fellman (ed.), *The Supreme Court and Education* (New York: Bureau of Publications, Teachers College, Columbia University, 1960).

Therefore, we hold that the plaintiffs and others similarly situated for whom the actions have been brought are, by reason of the segregation complained of, deprived of the equal protection of the laws guaranteed by the Fourteenth Amendment. . .[7]

This unanimous decision effectively overturned the *Plessey* vs *Ferguson* separate but equal doctrine.

Several things need to be emphasized about the Supreme Court decision. First, while it is true that reports of social scientists were admitted, the decision itself was not based on these studies but rather on the logical recognition that to be separate but equal was impossible and, in fact, that segregation had been instituted to create and implement inequality. Secondly, the Brown decision was not in any sense an abrupt about-face for the court. It was the culmination of a long process beginning in the 1930s and gradually leading toward the illegality of racial segregation in public schools.

THE STRUGGLE FOR DESEGREGATION

Cities and communities in the border states—such as Missouri, Oklahoma, West Virginia, Kentucky, Maryland, and Delaware—responded positively to the Supreme Court's order: "To admit to schools on a racially non-discriminatory basis with all deliberate speed the parties to these cases." Baltimore was the first large city to adopt a policy of desegregation. Its method was simply to offer every child the opportunity to attend the school of his choice on a first-come first-served basis. There was some resistance by white extremists; no violence resulted, however, and the move brought about considerable desegregation within the Baltimore school system. A number of communities in the North patterned their own plans after Baltimore's, especially those large cities where residential segregation had created large concentrations of black children.

Other early attempts to desegregate school systems did not come easily or quickly. Little Rock, Arkansas, was undoubtedly the most publicized example of reaction to desegregation. In September 1957 America, and indeed the entire world, was treated to the spectacle of howling mobs of white adults being held back by federal troops while nine black students entered the previously all-white Central High School. Trouble in Little Rock was by no means over in 1957. The following year, for example, schools were closed by a decree of the governor and remained closed through the school year. It was not until 1961 that some seventy-

7. *Ibid.*, pp. 88, 89, 90.

five black students entered Central and two other high schools without violence. In a poll conducted in 1961 the majority of Little Rock's citizens still favored segregation, but nevertheless believed that the law must be obeyed. In 1968 Little Rock voters rejected a proposal designed to achieve effective racial balance in the city's high schools, and turned the control of the school system over to racial conservatives.

Clinton, Tennessee, was another center of considerable violence and opposition to desegregation. In 1956 desegregation of the high school was followed by rioting. National guardsmen were called out, and the school was closed. In October of 1959, when it seemed that the community had finally adjusted to a change, the school was blown up with dynamite. This destruction apparently had the reverse effect from that intended. Since the school's rebuilding, desegregation has gone ahead modestly but peaceably in Clinton.

In 1960 a new element was added to the desegregation conflict. In New Orleans the efforts of white mobs (mostly women) to stop four black girls from entering two formerly all-white elementary schools was the first desegregation conflict to be covered live and extensively on television. Many observers believe that the extent of the violence and hostility shown by white New Orleanians was in part due to this new kind of visability. Although cause-and-effect relationships are difficult to establish, it seems likely that the widespread publicity given to conflict may add fuel to the fire. Many observers believe that the riots of 1967 and 1968 were spread to some extent by exposure on national television.[8]

Violence has not been the only, nor the most effective, means by which communities have opposed the Supreme Court decision. The commonest device in Southern communities is the "pupil placement plan" used now in at least ten states. Under this plan at the beginning of the school year a black child is placed in the school (all black) that he attended in the previous academic year. He may then seek a transfer to another school. When black parents attempt to challenge this placement and actually do apply for a transfer, a variety of pressures are brought to bear against them. If these fail, technical and bureaucratic mishandling of the application may lose the request or slow the process of transfer. School officials may further block a transfer by applying such criteria as emotional adjustment, home background, morals and health, and adequacy of the child's former training. Economic and, finally, physical pressure has been brought to bear against black parents applying for a transfer. There is no doubt that this type of plan, com-

8. For the best account of these attempts see *The New York Times* for the months and years to which we refer.

bining lip-service legality with a firm, deep-seated opposition to desegregation, has been extremely effective.[9]*

So far we have been dealing with the struggle surrounding desegregation in the South. But the upheaval caused by the Supreme Court decision of 1954 was not geographically confined. After 1954 many civil rights leaders and liberal politicians began to take issue with de facto segregation existing in all Northern cities because of discrimination in real-estate practices as well as the historical tendency for minority groups to develop in separate communities. Prior to the Supreme Court decision most educators in the North had not accepted the argument that desegregation was an educational problem. They tended to view it as unfortunate, perhaps, but clearly the result of residential patterns beyond their control. In some cases civil rights leaders discovered school districts in a number of large Northern cities that had been deliberately gerrymandered to prevent mixing of the races. They also became more clearly aware that in general the facilities—including the age of the building, class size, quality of programs offered—were not equal when one compared the all-black schools in urban centers with the predominantly white schools in more affluent neighborhoods.[10]

As pressures began to mount urging Northern school desegregation a variety of plans, outlined below, were developed. Some have been tried with varying degrees of success, while others are still proposals for the future.

Open enrollment. Open enrollment has proven to be a popular plan for educators in Northern communities because it is voluntary, an important political ingredient lacking in other proposals. Under open enrollment, schools with available space are authorized to receive pupils from crowded and/or otherwise less-desirable schools. The sending schools are in almost every case heavily segregated and tend to be located in the inner city. The receiving schools generally have a more even racial balance or are all-white. Under this plan, then, minority group youngsters are "bussed" to predominantly white schools. While open enrollment improves racial balance in the receiving school, it has virtually no effect on the sending school, other than to make it slightly less crowded. Teachers in sending schools complain that most often children participating in the plan tend to be the better students from upwardly mobile families, not the group for which the program was

* Although some state pupil placement laws have been declared illegal by the courts, the practice still exists in many Southern communities.

9. Bullock, *op. cit.*, pp. 258-260.

10. *Equality of Educational Opportunity, Summary Report* (Washington, D.C.: U.S. Department of Health, Education and Welfare; Office of Education, 1966), pp. 10-13.

designed. In 1965 New York City abandoned the open enrollment plan because it involved at its height only a few thousand students and was not effective in promoting desegregation. Also the program did not significantly improve the performance of those transferred. At this writing Chicago is having considerable difficulty in implementing a modest voluntary bussing program which would carry black youngsters into previously all-white schools. The hostility from white communities has slowed the program to a virtual standstill.[11]

Princeton Plan. A second method of desegregation, called either the "Princeton Plan" or "school pairing," has proven to be useful in situations where adjacent attendance districts enroll white students in one school and black students in another. Under the Princeton Plan the two schools are brought together in one district and reassigned—School A, for example, taking all the youngsters in the combined districts for grades one, two, and three; School B taking all youngsters for grades four, five, and six. This plan creates larger districts, presenting possible problems of transportation. Its usefulness is also limited to those communities where different ethnic populations live in close proximity, those generally called border or fringe areas. The plan would be of little use to a black child living at 127th Street and Lenox Avenue, the center of Harlem, or in the black ghettos of Los Angeles or Cleveland. From that point one must travel several miles in any direction before encountering sizable numbers of white families. However, this method has been tried in smaller communities, such as Princeton, New Jersey, which gave the plan its name, and may well continue to be a viable method of producing desegregation in towns and moderate-sized cities.

Changing attendance districts. A simpler and in some cases effective method of desegregation is to draw attendance lines for certain schools. This method has the virtue of requiring no additional monies or new legislation. The right of boards of education to change attendance patterns is a reasonably well-established legal principle. Generally, school districts in our larger cities follow neighborhood lines, although in some cases, as mentioned above, lines were purposely drawn to separate racial groups. Here, as in pairing, the effectiveness is greatest in fringe areas.

Educational complexes. Under this proposal for desegregation a group of adjacent schools, perhaps a junior high school or a middle school (5, 6, 7, 8) and the elementary schools feeding into it would be brought together as a small school system within a larger one. The boundaries of this smaller system would be carefully drawn to include different ethnic and racial groups. Within the cluster several types of

11. Henry W. DeZutter, "When Folks Get Together to Talk about Busing," *The New Republic,* Vol. 158 (March 2, 1968), pp. 13-14.

arrangements could be made. Pupils might be assigned and reassigned among the schools to achieve better racial balance. Special educational activities and services which could not easily be carried on in each of the buildings could be conducted in one or two locations and students could be brought to them. According to its supporters the educational complex combines the advantages of the neighborhood school with the advantages of the larger educational community, such as wider contacts for the students and expanded program offerings.

Educational parks. This plan would bring all of the schools in a large section of a city or in an entire city to a single educational park or campus. A central educational site to service a large geographic area is not at all new in American education. It is actually the application to urban America of the rural consolidated school, under which hundreds of thousands of children have been educated for several generations. Nonwhite youngsters would be assigned to classes in a central school with students from a wide variety of neighborhoods. Some advocates of this plan recommend that all elementary, junior, and senior high school students attend school on one site. Others would prefer separate campuses for each level. A reasonably conservative estimate for establishing educational parks in our twenty largest cities is $20 billion.

Metropolitan schools concept. The most ambitious and far-reaching plan yet advanced for reorganizing urban public schools was developed by the University of Chicago's Robert Havighurst. In 1964 Professor Havighurst directed an extensive analysis of the problems of the Chicago public school system. He concluded that under the present system of city government and city-suburb conflict, effective education in the Chicago metropolitan area was virtually impossible. What was needed was legal unity, at least in the area of education, between the city and suburbs surrounding it. His plan called for a single areawide (city and suburb) taxing unit with local community school boards exercising considerable control over districts with 100 to 200 thousand people. The areawide or metropolitan authority would have the power to plan and construct schools and certify teachers. The local boards would administer schools, establish teacher salaries, and to a large extent determine curriculum. Havighurst also suggested that the local community school board should have supplementary taxing powers and should be free to raise money locally or from foundations for special programs within their communities. Open enrollment, school pairing, changed attendance patterns, school complexes and parks could then all take place in the context of the entire metropolitan area rather than the city or individual suburb. What is clearly involved in Havighurst's plan is quite a radical change in the economic and social outlook of suburban residents. It seems a fair question to ask whether suburbanites, many of them new arrivals from the city, would be willing or could be persuaded to shoulder directly the educational burdens of the central city.

TEANECK AND ENGLEWOOD

The success of Northern school desegregation efforts depends upon a complex of local factors, well-illustrated by contrasting two neighboring Northern communities and their attempts to deal with the problem of segregation. Reginald Damerell in his *Triumph in a White Suburb* describes in considerable detail the process of growing concern, conflict, and resolution of school desegregation in Teaneck, New Jersey.[12] Teaneck, a suburb of New York City just over the George Washington Bridge in Bergen County, has a population of approximately 35,000 people, about 10 percent of whom are black. Most of the black residents of Teaneck arrived there after 1954, and the majority settled in one part of the community. By 1963 Teaneck had a small ghetto and a school in which over 50 percent of the students were black. At first an open enrollment plan was tried by the board of education; it did not succeed. Damerell describes the slow and sometimes exceedingly painful process of educating the community to admit the fact that segregation in housing and schools existed, and then to produce and support a workable plan for desegregating the schools. Teaneck's story is a happy one and Damerell ends his book with the crucial school board election of 1965, which produced a slate of candidates committed to a program of desegregation designed by the superintendent of schools. In judging the importance of this example it must be noted that black residents were virtually all middle class and most of them, like other Teaneck residents, were professionals and businessmen who worked in New York City. The problem of social class conflict was not present. Although it is difficult to judge how much impact this had on the successful solution to the problem, it seems fair to say that had there been sizeable numbers of lower-class blacks among Teaneck residents, the outcome might have been different.

Unlike Teaneck, Englewood has had a black population for several generations.[13] Many of the early black residents were servants in the wealthy homes of Englewood and surrounding communities. By 1960, out of this community's total population of 26,000, 27 percent were black. For many decades racial imbalance in Englewood schools amounted to almost total de facto segregation. Segregation occurred for

12. Reginald G. Damerell, *Triumph in a White Suburb* (New York: William Morrow & Company, Inc., 1968).

13. Robert La Frankie, "Englewood: A Northern City in Crisis," in Robert A. Dentler, Bernard Mackler, and Mary Ellen Warshauer (eds.), *The Urban R's* (New York: Frederick A. Praeger, Inc., 1968), pp. 24-43.

two reasons: a conscious policy on the part of leaders of the white community to contain blacks in one section of town; and the economic conditions that forced blacks to live and to buy houses where they could, namely in that same section of town. From the Supreme Court decision in 1954 until 1962 the board of education resisted all efforts on the part of civil rights organizations to insist on desegregation. In February 1962, when the board turned down an ultimatum concerning open enrollment from the NAACP, an all-night sit-in at city hall resulted in the arrest of eleven persons on charges of disorderly conduct. These arrests were the first that resulted from sit-ins north of the Mason-Dixon line.

The situation in Englewood at the present time is extremely precarious in terms of desegregation. Although an all-black elementary school has been closed, the situation is tense. Unlike Teaneck, the community has not in any sense committed itself to desegregation.

It is important, when looking at these successes and failures, to keep in mind that though both towns are located in a large metropolitan area, Teaneck has a population of 35,000 and Englewood only 27,000. What may be possible with good public and professional leadership in small communities, where nonwhite citizens and pupils are in a reasonably small minority, may not be possible in large central cities where the number of nonwhite youngsters is rapidly approaching or has surpassed the number of white youngsters in public schools.

Berkeley, California, home of the University of California, is the largest city in the United States to desegregate its public schools through a program of bussing.[14] A city of 120,000 located in the San Francisco Bay Area with a nonwhite population of approximately 48 percent, Berkeley accomplished desegregation through a carefully planned campaign, which took five years. In September of 1968 the plan was completed when 3500 of Berkeley's 8700 elementary students began to travel to school outside their neighborhoods.

While indicating the possibility that larger cities can be desegregated, it must be noted that Berkeley (perhaps because of the university) is a more liberal community than any other in the Bay Area, which itself constitutes a liberal metropolitan region in California. It seems doubtful that one can generalize from the Berkeley experience for other cities of comparable size.

THE PRESENT STATUS OF DESEGREGATION

How segregated are the public schools of America? The best sources of information on segregation and desegregation are the U.S. Office of

14. Thomas Wogaman, "Desegregation in Berkeley," *The Urban Review*, Vol. 3, No. 5 (April 1969), pp. 13-16.

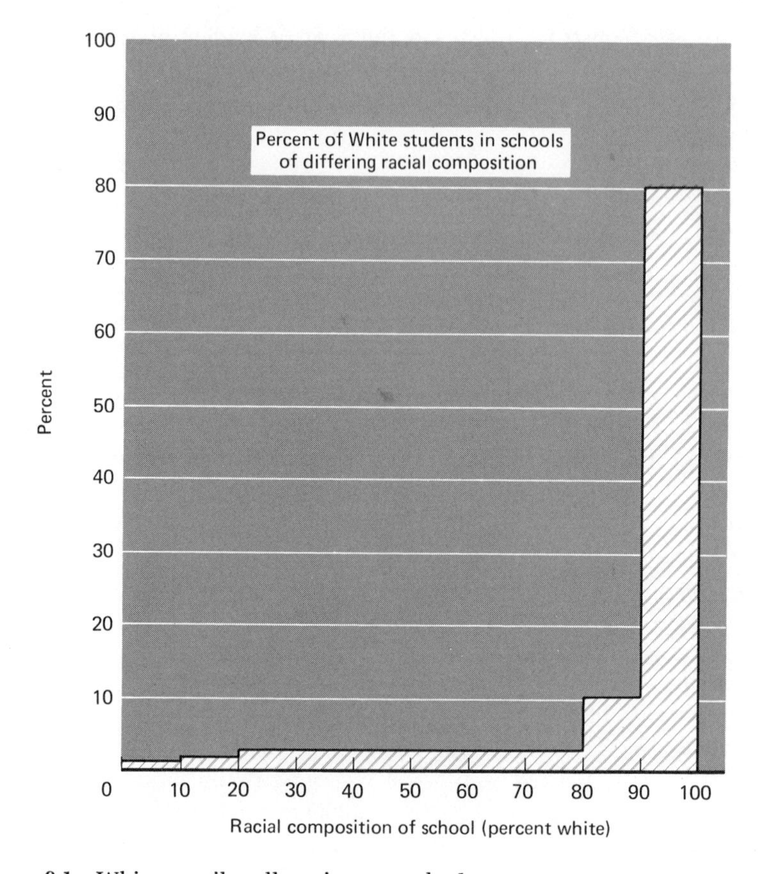

Figure 9.1 White pupils, all regions—grade 1.
SOURCE: U.S. Department of Health, Education and Welfare; *Equality of Educational Opportunity, Summary Report* (Washington, D.C.: U.S. Office of Education, U.S. Government Printing Office, 1966), p. 4.

Education survey, *Equality of Educational Opportunity,* published in 1966, and *Racial Isolation in the Public Schools,* a report of the United States Commission on Civil Rights published in 1967.[15] *Equality of Educational Opportunity* says in part: "The great majority of American children attend schools that are largely segregated, that is, almost all of their fellow students are of the same racial background as they are." A look at the bar graphs in Figures 9.1-9.4 shows that about 65 percent of all first-grade black pupils attend schools that have an enrollment 90 percent or more black, while about 77 percent of all first-grade white

15. A Report of the United States Commission on Civil Rights, *Racial Isolation in the Public Schools* (Washington, D.C.: U.S. Government Printing Office, 1967); and U.S. Department of Health, Education and Welfare, *Equality of Educational Opportunity* (Washington, D.C.: Office of Education, U.S. Government Printing Office, 1966). All numbers and percentages used in this section are from these two reports.

students attend schools that are 90 percent or more white. A much greater proportion of black students attend schools that are 90 percent or more black. Almost 90 percent of black first-graders fall into this category: 72 percent in the urban North and 97 percent in the urban South.

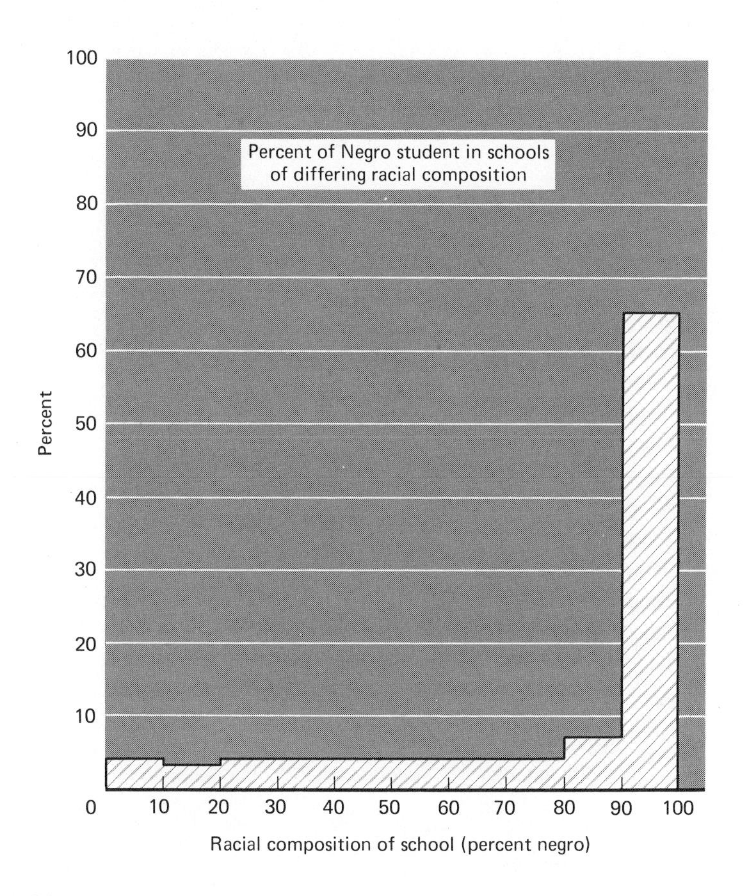

Figure 9.2 Negro pupils, all regions—grade 1.

SOURCE: U.S. Department of Health, Education and Welfare: *Equality of Educational Opportunity, Summary Report* (Washington, D.C.: U.S. Office of Education, U.S. Government Printing Office, 1966), p. 5.

As startling as these figures may appear, they do not tell the whole story by any means. The Office of Education study found that in the major urban areas, in which about two-thirds of the nation's black and white population now live, school segregation is considerably greater than the national figures might suggest. *And it is growing.* In our largest metropolitan areas about 80 percent of the nonwhite enrollment was in central city schools, while almost 70 percent of the white enrollment was suburban, outside of the city itself. In Cleveland, 98 percent of the nonwhite public school children in the metropolitan area went to school in the central city in 1960, while about 70 percent of the whites were in suburban public schools. Cleveland city schools were 47 percent nonwhite in 1960. By 1965 they were more than 51 percent nonwhite. In Philadelphia 77 percent of the nonwhite public school children attended schools in the city, while 73 percent of the white children went to school in suburban areas. In 1960 Philadelphia schools were 48 percent black; by 1965 this figure had jumped to 60 percent. This pattern of racial segregation is typical of all major metropolitan areas.

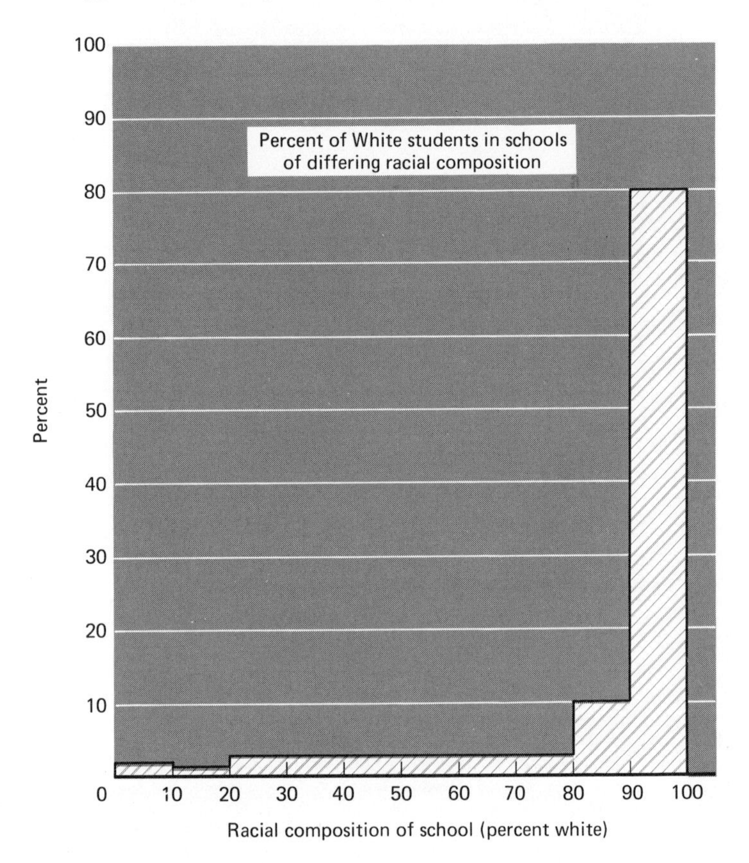

Figure 9.3 White pupils, all regions—grade 12.

SOURCE: U.S. Department of Health, Education and Welfare; *Equality of Educational Opportunity, Summary Report* (Washington, D.C.: U.S. Office of Education, U.S. Government Printing Office, 1966), p. 6.

Segregation is also severe within the central cities. Table 9.1 shows the extent of elementary-school segregation in seventy-five cities. In these cities three-quarters of the black students are in elementary schools with enrollments that are nearly all black, while 83 percent of the white students are in nearly all-white schools. Nine out of ten black elementary-school children attend majority black schools. This high degree of segregation is true all over the nation—East, West, North, and South. In some Northern cities the proportion of black children attending predominantly black schools is higher than the national average. In Flint, Michigan, 86 percent of black elementary-school children are in majority black schools; in Milwaukee 87 percent, in Chicago 97 percent. This pattern persists regardless of the size of the school system. It is true of large cities and small cities, of the major metropolitan areas and small satellite cities. Nor does the pattern necessarily vary according to the proportion of blacks enrolled in the school system. Blacks make up only 25 percent of the elementary-school enrollment in Milwaukee and almost 60 percent of Philadelphia. Yet in both cities about three out of four black children attend nearly all-black schools.

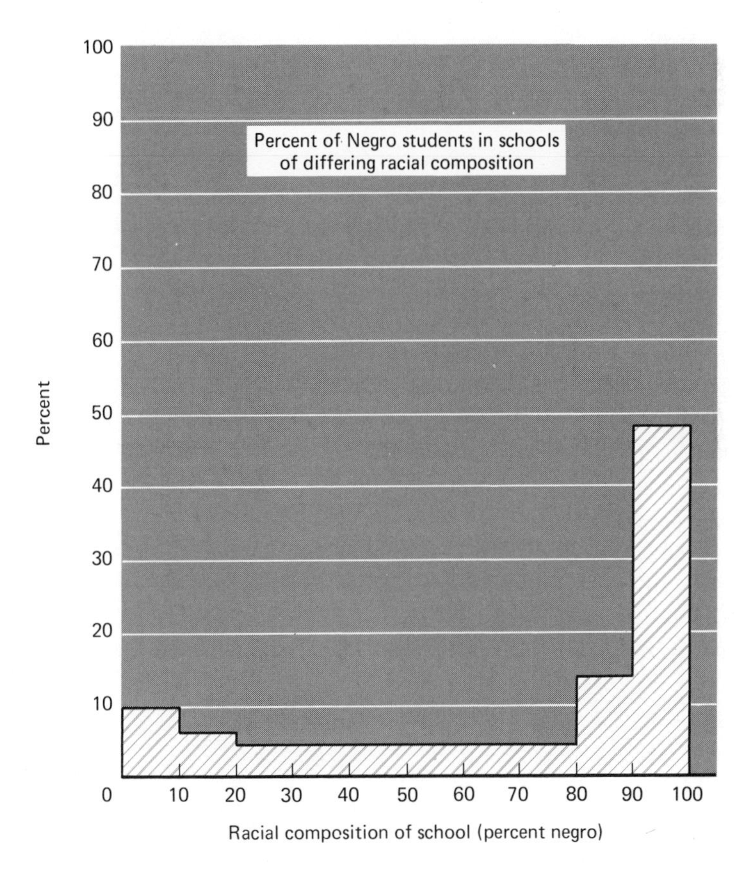

Figure 9.4 Negro pupils, all regions—grade 12.

SOURCE: U.S. Department of Health, Education and Welfare; *Equality of Educational Opportunity, Summary Report* (Washington, D.C.: U.S. Office of Education, U.S. Government Printing Office, 1966), p. 7.

Table 9.1 Extent of Elementary School Segregation in 75 School Systems*

City	Percentages of Negroes in 90 to 100 percent Negro schools	Percentage of Negroes in majority-Negro schools	Percentage of whites in 90 to 100 percent white schools
Mobile, Ala.	99.9	99.9	100.0
Tuscaloosa, Ala.	99.6	99.6	100.0
Little Rock, Ark.	95.6	95.6	97.1
Pine Bluff, Ark.	98.2	98.2	100.0
Los Angeles, Calif.	39.5	87.5	94.7
Oakland, Calif.	48.7	83.2	50.2
Pasadena, Calif.	None	71.4	82.1
Richmond, Calif.	39.2	82.9	90.2
San Diego, Calif.	13.9	73.3	88.7
San Francisco, Calif.	21.1	72.3	65.1
Denver, Colo.	29.4	75.2	95.5
Hartford, Conn.	9.4	73.8	66.2
New Haven, Conn.	36.8	73.4	47.1
Wilmington, Del.	49.7	92.5	27.3
Miami, Fla.	91.4	94.4	95.3
Tallahassee, Fla.	99.7	99.7	100.0
Americus, Ga.	99.3	99.3	100.0
Atlanta, Ga.	97.4	98.8	95.4
Augusta, Ga.	99.2	99.2	100.0
Marietta, Ga.	94.2	94.2	100.0
Chicago, Ill.	89.2	96.9	88.8
East St. Louis, Ill.	80.4	92.4	68.6
Peoria, Ill.	21.0	86.9	89.6
Fort Wayne, Ind.	60.8	82.9	87.7
Gary, Ind.	89.9	94.8	75.9
Indianapolis, Ind.	70.5	84.2	80.7
Wichita, Kans.	63.5	89.1	94.8
Louisville, Ky.	69.5	84.5	61.3
New Orleans, La.	95.9	96.7	83.8
Baltimore, Md.	84.2	92.3	67.0
Boston, Mass.	35.4	79.5	76.5
Springfield, Mass.	15.4	71.9	82.8
Detroit, Mich.	72.3	91.5	65.0
Flint, Mich.	67.9	85.9	80.0
Minneapolis, Minn.	None	39.2	84.9
Hattiesburg, Miss.	98.7	98.7	100.0
Vicksburg, Miss.	97.1	97.1	100.0

* Percentages shown in this table are for the 1965-1966 school year, except for Seattle, Wash. (1964-1965), Los Angeles, Calif. (1963-1964), and Cleveland, Ohio (1962-1963).

Table 9.1 Extent of Elementary School Segregation *(continued)*

City	Percentages of Negroes in 90 to 100 percent Negro schools	Percentage of Negroes in majority-Negro schools	Percentage of whites in 90 to 100 percent white schools
Kansas City, Mo.	69.1	85.5	65.2
St. Joseph, Mo.	39.3	39.3	91.3
St. Louis, Mo.	90.9	93.7	66.0
Omaha, Nebr.	47.7	81.1	89.0
Newark, N.J.	51.3	90.3	37.1
Camden, N.J.	37.0	90.4	62.4
Albany, N.Y.	None	74.0	66.5
Buffalo, N.Y.	77.0	88.7	81.1
New York City, N.Y.	20.7	55.5	56.8
Charlotte, N.C.	95.7	95.7	94.7
Raleigh, N.C.	98.5	98.5	100.0
Winston-Salem, N.C.	88.7	95.1	95.6
Cincinnati, Ohio	49.4	88.0	63.3
Cleveland, Ohio	82.3	94.6	80.2
Columbus, Ohio	34.3	80.8	77.0
Oklahoma City, Okla.	90.5	96.8	96.1
Tulsa, Okla.	90.7	98.7	98.8
Portland, Oreg.	46.5	59.2	92.0
Chester, Pa.	77.9	89.1	37.9
Harrisburg, Pa.	54.0	81.3	56.2
Philadelphia, Pa.	72.0	90.2	57.7
Pittsburgh, Pa.	49.5	82.8	62.3
Providence, R.I.	14.6	55.5	63.3
Columbia, S.C.	99.1	99.1	100.0
Florence, S.C.	99.1	99.1	100.0
Sumter, S.C.	99.0	99.0	100.0
Knoxville, Tenn.	79.3	79.3	94.9
Memphis, Tenn.	95.1	98.8	93.6
Nashville, Tenn.	82.2	86.4	90.7
Amarillo, Tex.	89.6	89.6	98.3
Austin, Tex.	86.1	86.1	93.1
Dallas, Tex.	82.6	90.3	90.1
Houston, Tex.	93.0	97.6	97.3
San Antonio, Tex.	65.9	77.2	89.4
Richmond, Va.	98.5	98.5	95.3
Seattle, Wash.	9.9	60.4	89.8
Milwaukee, Wis.	72.4	86.8	86.3
Washington, D.C.	90.4	99.3	34.3

SOURCE: *Racial Isolation in the Public Schools* (A Report of the United States Commission on Civil Rights, 1967), pp. 4-5.

As gloomy as this picture of desegregation may appear, it is even worse when one considers the changes over the past decade. It is quite clear that more and more black youngsters are attending basically segregated schools in all parts of the United States. In Oakland, California, for example, the percentage of black enrollment in schools 90 to 100 percent black increased from 8 percent in 1959 to 48 percent in 1965. In Pittsburgh, Pennsylvania, between 1950 and 1965, the percentage in almost all-black elementary schools increased from 30 to 49 percent. In Cleveland, Ohio, between 1952 and 1962, the increase was from 57 to 82 percent. Not only are more black youngsters attending segregated schools but a higher proportion of black youngsters are attending these schools.

The pattern is somewhat different in Southern urban areas where, naturally, the *proportion* of black students in totally black schools has decreased since the 1954 Supreme Court decision. Before that date 100 percent of black youngsters attended 100 percent black schools. But the *number* of black children attending all-black or nearly all-black schools has risen sharply. In Houston, Texas, where public schools were segregated until 1960, the number of black children in all-black elementary schools has increased by 20 percent from 1960 to 1965.

In considering these patterns of separation it is important to keep in mind that they are also associated with differences in physical facilities often considered to be a part of "quality education." Although, as we noted earlier in chapter 3, nationwide differences in school facilities for pupils of varying socioeconomic levels are not very striking outside the very largest cities, differences related to ethnicity show up fairly consistently in the Coleman data. For the nation as a whole, for example, white children attend schools with a smaller average number of pupils per room than do any of the minorities (29 verus 30-33), though there is a reversal of the pattern for some regions (nonmetropolitan sections of the North, West, and Southwest).

Nationally, black pupils have fewer of many kinds of facilities important for academic achievement: physics, chemistry, and language laboratories; fewer books per pupil in their libraries; fewer available textbooks. Two important general conclusions emerge from the report of the Coleman data:

1. Though there is not a wholly consistent pattern of disadvantage in the matter of facilities, there are definite and systematic differences.
2. Majority-minority differences are not striking at the national level but are often sizeable and significant when one looks at regional averages. For example, 95 percent of black and 80 percent of white high-school students in the Far West have access to language laboratories, compared with 48 percent and 72 percent respectively in the metropol-

itan South. In the metropolitan Midwest the average black student shares his classroom with 54 pupils, compared with 33 per room for whites.

DESEGREGATION AND ACHIEVEMENT

Many of the pressures for school desegregation are justified on the simple premise that separate schooling for blacks and whites is unfair and undemocratic; segregation, whether deliberately imposed or the incidental result of existing neighborhood patterns, harms youngsters of both groups because it nurtures feelings of estrangement and hostility among both and erodes the social order into which they grow up.

This would appear to be sufficient grounds for a vigorous effort to desegregate schools both North and South. But Americans, apparently, can live fairly comfortably with profound conflicts between the ideals they voice and actions or social arrangements that violate those ideals, as Gunnar Myrdal pointed out in his monumental study of the black in America in the thirties.

Most advocates of school integration, consequently, seek more immediate and practical reasons for undertaking the vast and expensive task of desegregating urban school systems whose attendance patterns are grossly unbalanced by the existence of extensive inner-city ghettos. Indeed, the landmark Supreme Court decision on school desegregation, as we have seen, argued its necessity not only on the legal and moral issue but on the premise that the black child is denied equal opportunity to learn in a segregated school.

During the fifties and sixties advocates of urban school desegregation developed several significantly different versions of this reasoning. Black militants, on the one hand, tended to focus the issue on the qualitative differences between ghetto schools and middle-class white schools. Only by getting their children into a *white* school could they get them into a *good* school with a stable, experienced teaching staff; up-to-date materials; and adequate, modern facilities. They pointed to such surveys as Patricia Sexton's in Detroit which proved the sharp differences in quality between schools in high and low socioeconomic areas, and demanded integration as the only way they could get equal treatment.[16]

It should be noted, however, that black leadership in this instance is supported by only minorities of their constituencies. In one study the need for integrated schools was ranked near the bottom of eighteen needs by the black community, though they ranked "better schools" in second place. Katz observes: "Even in the large cities of the North civil rights

16. Patricia Cayo Sexton, *Education and Income* (New York: The Viking Press, Inc., 1961).

advocates who agitate for an amelioration of de facto segregation are disheartened by the lack of grass roots support."[17] The rise of black separatist doctrine since that statement was written makes it even more applicable at the present time.

On the other hand, white intellectuals arguing for integrated schools tended increasingly to see the problem in terms of the self-image of the black child, just as the Supreme Court did. The segregated school, they pointed out, is a daily reminder for the child of his socially inferior status, no matter how good a school he attends. More positively, the integrated classroom gives the lower-class child not only an opportunity for a better self-concept but exposes him to the middle-class values of his classmates. Christopher Jencks has put the case persuasively in this way:

> In my observation, the most important single factor in shaping an alumnus of a school is neither the physical facilities, the content of the curriculum, the erudition or imagination of the teachers, nor the size of classes, but the habits and values of the pupil's classmates. . . If, as often happens in the slums, the school is dominated by the "hoods," it doesn't seem to matter how small the classes are; the most ambitious and often the most gifted students will concentrate their attention on learning how to jump the wires on a car rather than on learning the theory of electromagnetism. . . If I am right about the importance of the student culture, the quality of education depends largely on the spontaneous interplay of habits, interests, and ideals which each group of classmates brings from its homes, partly on the ingenuity of teachers and administrators in controlling this interplay, and hardly at all on the quality of formal instruction offered by the teachers. It seems to follow, moreover, that if you want to improve the education available to a child from the slums the most important thing to improve is the attitude of his classmates toward "brains," and toward work generally.[18]

While white intellectuals developed this argument and looked for both experimental and empirical evidence to support it, the black civil rights revolution suddenly shifted course in the mid-sixties, resulting in a change in attitude about school desegregation among black leaders. As Livingston Wingate, a New York civil rights leader, put it:

> The greatest need today is the immediate establishment of *quality education* in the ghetto. We must no longer pursue the myth that integrated education is

17. Irwin Katz, "Problems and Directions for Research in Public School Desegregation," in Harry L. Miller (ed.), *Education for the Disadvantaged* (New York: The Free Press, 1967), p. 248.

18. Christopher Jencks, "Slums and Schools," *The New Republic* (September 17, 1962), p. 315.

equated with quality education. Bussing a disadvantaged and isolated child out of Harlem on a segregated bus to an "integrated" classroom downtown will *not* give him quality education. Once in a classroom downtown, the disadvantaged Harlem pupil would find himself below the achievement level of his white classmates and suffer a more demoralizing experience of frustration than he had in the ghetto inferior school. Moreover, he would return at night to the same ghetto conditions he left in the morning.[19]

The road to quality education, Wingate and others argued, lies in the control of the ghetto school by its own community, an issue we shall examine in detail in the last chapter. In relation to desegregation this viewpoint defines a new position entirely.

It is clear, however, that both the proponents of integrated schools and those who advocate "quality education" in ghetto schools, with community control of education, are primarily concerned with the child's self-image and recommend a radical reconstruction of his environment. The diagram below roughly schematizes the relationship of integration positions to the more conservative remedial proposals we have looked at earlier.

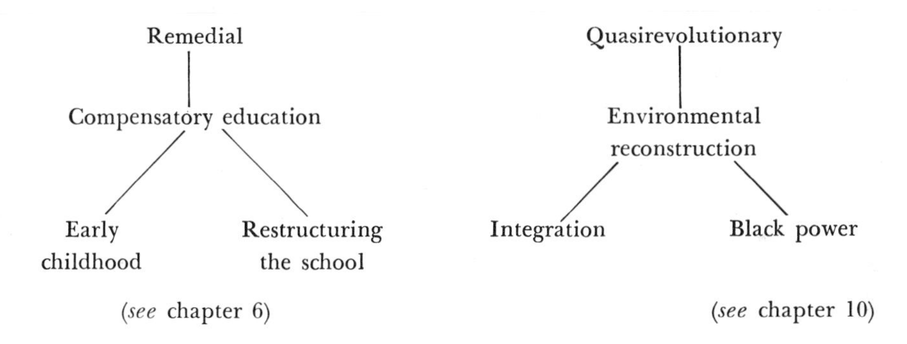

The question of whether the achievement of the minority group child will improve with community control over his ghetto school may be answered as we know the long-range results of some experiments with school-community relations only now beginning in several cities around the country. On the other issue, whether integration promotes better achievement, we have a large body of both experimental and empirical evidence to which we now turn.

The relationship between integration and achievement is particularly a crucial one to determine because of the very great cost of any large-

19. Livingston Wingate (from an address to the 25th Annual Work Conference for Superintendents, Teachers College, Columbia University, July 9, 1966), in Harry L. Miller (ed.), *Education for the Disadvantaged* (New York: The Free Press, 1967), p. 220.

scale and feasible system of school integration in large cities. Minority group children respond more readily than do majority children to better school facilities, according to the Coleman study, but the record of compensatory efforts appears to indicate that these are not enough to close the gap. Entirely aside from possible differences in school quality, it must be determined if the difference in school climate that results from the presence of white middle-class students affects the achievement and aspirations of their black and other minority group classmates. The evidence deserves a close look, if the spending of billions of dollars in transportation and new school plants depend on the results.

Even more important than the financial issue is the question's bearing on the current policy controversy about the future of the urban ghetto. Black militants are presently in fundamental agreement with economic conservatives on a policy that some observers call "gilding the ghetto," the assumption that because urban areas are unlikely soon to become integrated, capital should be injected into business and industry in the ghetto itself to create jobs and income. The possibility of any degree of meaningful integration in the near future is shrugged off as a mirage.

Some moderates agree that if one means by integration a house-by-house dispersion of blacks and whites within the central city and in the suburbs the hope is indeed a mirage. But they argue that the enormous inner city ghettos that now exist constitute not merely a moral blot on the cities but that they also distort the structure of the entire metropolitan area. The increasing proportion of low-income blacks within the central city separates masses of low-skilled workers from the jobs they need in increasingly distant outer rings of the area, where most new industry is established. It also operates to keep whites outside the central city, where most of them work, thus creating severe tax problems for the city government and imposing an intolerable burden on municipal transit systems that must bring these groups to their jobs every day and return them every evening.

The moderate's answer to the problem is ghetto dispersal at whatever cost and without waiting for a change in white attitudes toward neighborhood integration. Their assumption is that it is immediately useful to have black communities growing in the suburbs, whether these communities are integrated or all-black. From this viewpoint the situation in which enough black families settle in a community to "tip" the balance so that whites move out entirely may be a desirable one rather than a cause for concern.[20] If enough situations of this kind occur, the central city ghetto will begin to shrink in size.

To return to the issue of school integration, the type of community

20. John F. Kain and Joseph J. Persley, "Alternatives to the Gilded Ghetto," *The Public Interest,* No. 14 (Winter 1969), pp. 74-87.

integration that is perceived as most immediately necessary is in part influenced by the evidence of educational effect in mixed white and black classrooms. If putting black and white pupils together has a direct influence on the academic achievement of the blacks, then either we must wait for genuine metropolitan area housing integration or find the money for effective school integration, wherever the children live. If school integration does *not* have such a direct influence, the policy option of dispersing inner city ghettos, even if it does little to change the pattern of de facto segregated schools, seems more attractive than before.

EXPERIMENTS IN INTEGRATED SITUATIONS

There is a sizeable body of experimental literature in psychology that bears either directly or indirectly on the question of how minority group members perform in integrated situations. Most of the research is based on the possible psychological meaning of those situations to the minority child, an analysis that contains the following assumptions:

1. Because the society as a whole is a segregated one, many children who find themselves in an integrated classroom face a new type of contact with white strangers. Furthermore, they are likely to feel academically inferior to their classmates, an estimate based partly on white prejudice and partly on realistic differences in the quality of their schooling.
2. The child's own expectation of mistreatment, his feelings of *social threat,* may arouse anxieties that impair his performance of classroom tasks. To the extent that he encounters actual hostility from his white classmates, or indifference, the probability of his experiencing threat should, theoretically, increase; and the same result should obviously flow from similar attitudes expressed toward him by authority figures in the school.
3. It is further theoretically possible that in a defensive reaction to feared or actual threat, the minority group child may give up any effort to excel in order not to arouse further hostility.[21]

The same body of theory, however, suggests that when the minority child is accepted by his classmates and by the school authorities, his motivation should be affected positively. Several studies provide evidence that black children, at least initially, want the friendship of their white peers.[22] Under such circumstances, most of what we know of the dynamics

21. Irwin Katz, "Review of Evidence Relative to the Effects of Desegregation on the Intellectual Performance of Negroes," *American Psychologist* (June 1964), pp. 371-389.

22. Marian R. Yarrow (issue ed.), "Interpersonal Dynamics in a Desegregation Process," *Journal of Social Issues,* Vol. 14, No. 1 (1958), entire issue.

of groups suggests that they would respond to the standards of those with whom they seek to be accepted. If the white teacher is friendly and approving, one might expect even greater effect on the minority child's motivation, depending, of course, on his initial attitude toward white authority.

Another aspect of the situation that should influence the child's performance is his perception of his probability of success. To a child who finds himself in a new school that he knows is academically superior to the one from which he comes, the knowledge of such a disparity may well serve to discourage him from trying hard. A number of experiments with white students support this hypothesis: Motivation is highest when the student sees his probability of success as about 50-50; motivation declines as the probability falls below that level.[23] Presumably, then, if the black pupil sees the scholastic standards of his new school as so considerably higher than his own that his likelihood of meeting them is small, his motivation is likely to fall.

A third source of possible difficulty is *failure threat,* the fear and anxiety aroused by the expectation of the social consequences of failure. Although laymen usually assume that this fear should operate as a motivational force in a consistent way, the experimental evidence indicates that it is by no means a clearcut motivator. If the child's fear of social disapproval of failure is strong, psychologists suggest, and he expects to fail, he may develop unconscious feelings of hostility for the adults from whom he anticipates disapproval. Such feelings, which are difficult for children to deal with, may be turned inward and be expressed as the much safer attitudes of self-derogation and inadequacy, which *increase* the expectation of failure.

These three mechanisms have been tested in a variety of laboratory situations where one or more of them has been deliberately manipulated. Several examples of these are described here to illustrate the resulting trends of such experiences.

In a typical situation, two black and two white students are asked to work as a team on some intellectual task. Although each member of the group has the same IQ, the black students make fewer contributions than the whites; and, when asked afterward to rank each member's intellectual performance, give the whites a higher rank. They also tend to prefer one another as work companions, and to express less satisfaction with the group experience than do their white counterparts.[24]

In a similar experiment involving pairs of subjects, one black and one white, each person was assigned either a difficult or easy version of

23. J.W. Atkinson, "Motivational Determinants of Risk-taking Behavior," in J.S. Atkinson (ed.), *Motives in Fantasy, Action and Society* (Princeton, N.J.: D. Van Nostrand Company, Inc., 1958), pp. 322-340.
24. Katz, *op. cit.,* pp. 371-389.

the same task. Even when the black member of the team had the easier version, he tended to accept passively his white companion's suggestions for a solution. When each was tested privately on the task before being assigned a partner, the black students produced fewer errors than they did later in the team situation working with a white.

The results of these trials clearly suggest that social threat operates to lower the performance of black students and to make them more passive.

In one set of experiments, however, blacks were forced to announce their solutions openly before entering the discussion to reach a team agreement. In this circumstance there was an increase in the amount of influence black students exerted over white partners in subsequent trials. Significantly, observers noted some hostility among the white members of the team in response to this evidence of black competence.

The presence of a white authority can have a facilitating effect, as the theory suggests, but only when the black student has a reasonable expectancy of success. Individual subjects worked on tasks with both white and black experimenters present; tasks were either easy or difficult at different times and were presented under two conditions. In Condition 1 tasks were not labeled as intellectual ones; in Condition 2 they were so labeled. Black subjects worked more efficiently at difficult tasks with a white administrator than with a black one under Condition 1, where there was no reason to doubt their own abilities to perform. When the task was presented as a test of intelligence, however, performance with black testers rose slightly and declined markedly with white testers. The presence of a white authority has incentive value, apparently, unless a low expectancy of success arouses fear of white disapproval.

In a similar experiment with groups of black students, both hard and easy versions of a test of digital manipulation were presented under a variety of conditions:

1. some groups were told that it was not a test at all
2. others were told that this was a scholastic ability test and scores obtained were to be compared with norms determined at their own colleges
3. this group was told they were taking a scholastic ability test with scores to be compared to national norms.

The largest differences between the groups taking the test under the three different conditions were produced by the more difficult version of the test; presumably, a very easy task does not arouse enough motivation to make a difference. Groups achieved highest scores under Condition 2, where motivation was high but where there was little threat involved in the comparison. The poorest performance was under Condition 1, where there was little motivation to do well. When the comparison with a national norm apparently aroused a low expectancy of success, performance was medium.

The results of a considerable number of such laboratory tests may be summarized this way:

There is a low probability of success for a minority group child in a situation where he has a low expectation of success due to inferiority feelings or marked discrepencies between his scholastic preparation and that of his classmates, in a situation where he feels rejected by white classmates or teacher, in a situation where failure is likely to bring disapproval by others.

There is a good probability for success in a situation in which the child feels accepted by classmates and teacher and in which he has reason to anticipate that good performance will win white approval.

We shall return to a consideration of these conclusions in a later section of this chapter, where we will suggest some general criteria for a desegregation policy.

EMPIRICAL EVIDENCE ON THE EFFECTS OF DESEGREGATION

Few observers are willing to accept laboratory evidence on performance in integrated situations as conclusive and final. What happens in the laboratory under controlled conditions may or may not be true of complex and real school settings. Most of the claims for the influence of racial balance on school achievement, consequently, rest on studies that compare actual academic performance under segregated and integrated conditions.

The available evidence is of several kinds: studies of change in groups of children who have undergone some shift from a segregated to an integrated situation, and studies that are crosssectional in that they look at different groups of children who are in different conditions of integration at a given time. The problems of evaluating the conclusions are different, but almost equally formidable.

BEFORE/AFTER STUDIES

The weakest support for the claim that integrated schooling has a direct effect on achievement comes from a source that, on the surface, looks strongest, the data describing the rise in achievement levels in systems that have recently been desegregated. As a result of the Supreme Court decision, Louisville schools integrated during 1955-1956. Two years later the median scores for all pupils had risen, with the greater gains achieved by black pupils.[25] But the report does not show any relationship between these gains and actual changes in the racial balance of the schools, and indeed the gains were greater where black children chose to remain with black teachers. Since the teaching staffs were *not* desegregated at that point, black children apparently gained the most where they remained segregated.

Washington, D.C., schools made a year-by-year study of the post-integration achievement of their students and found a consistent rise in all academic subjects tested for every grade level from 1955 to 1960.[26] By 1960, however, three-quarters of all pupils in Washington schools were black, and a rigorous system of ability-grouping made it unlikely that there was much classroom integration even in schools with white children attending. As with Louisville, the most reasonable explanation for the rise in achievement levels lies in the upgrading of curriculum and instruction that occurred at the time of desegregation.

One small but much better-controlled study in Tennessee seems to offer more trustworthy evidence. Anderson matched a group of children who were going into a newly-integrated school system with others who remained in all-black schools; the match included sex, age, socioeconomic circumstances, and, to some extent, family environment. The experimental desegregated group were doing significantly better academically at the end of the school year.[27]

All of these Southern instances, however, even Anderson's, present the same problem of interpretation: Southern schools for blacks are generally so far below the standards of white schools that desegregation means a very sizeable jump in school quality. Whatever the ambiguity about the impact of school factors on achievement, it is difficult to believe that there is not some point of school inferiority beyond which the school begins to contribute substantially to educational retardation. Most Southern schools for blacks probably *are* beyond that point.

The data from Northern cities, then, is particularly important, because the differences between ghetto schools and middle-class white schools are not so great as in the South. The evidence comes from a variety of not-very-adequate studies of school bussing programs. A typical example is Wolman's study of New Rochelle's transfer program, initiated after a court fight over an old elementary school with a 90 percent black population.[28] A court decree required the system to permit optional

25. *Ibid.,* p. 376.
26. *Ibid.,* p. 376.
27. L.V. Anderson, *Effects of Desegregation on Achievement and Personality Patterns* (Doctoral dissertation).
28. T.G. Wolman, "Learning Effects of Integration in New Rochelle," in Meyer Weinberg (ed.), *Integrated Education* (Beverly Hills, Calif.: Glencoe Press, 1968), pp. 318-320.

transfers from the school for black children, and about half the parents elected that their children do so. A study of the pattern of growth in reading scores from grade to grade showed "a pattern of growth consistent with those for comparable socio-economic and ethnic groups."[29] Wolman goes on to point out that "when one considers the factors militating *against* success in achievement for these transfer students, their ability to sustain a working level at least comparable to non-transfer students must be credited."[30]

Considering the evidence cited earlier on the stress involved in integrated situations, one can only agree; but this seems cold comfort. The report notes that the most striking gains for transfer students occurred among the kindergarten group, who achieved higher scores on the Metropolitan Reading Readiness test than the comparable non-transfer group to a statistically significant degree. But we are not given the actual score differences, and statistical significance in these cases is not necessarily meaningful, as we have noted before.

Similar ambiguities are the common case in most published reports of this kind, where school officials claim that bussing programs have resulted in improved academic achievement levels for ghetto pupils but seldom provide the actual data. The more careful studies—New York City's evaluation of its open enrollment program, for instance—tend to produce negative conclusions, at least for reading achievement.[31]

These studies of New York's programs found that bussed children were somewhat more favorable about their receiving schools than their former schoolmates were about the schools from which they were being bussed, but not overwhelmingly so. In their new schools, hearteningly, observers found that the children were not being stereotyped by the resident children and were readily accepted into friendship relationships. But studies of reading gains are contradictory. In the first study of the program a group of open enrollment pupils were matched with a group that stayed in the sending schools. In that study no gains were found in reading achievement for the bussed pupils. In a second study the following year reading scores of bussed children were found to be superior to the median-reading levels of the schools from which they came. These findings can most reasonably be explained by supposing that the bussed children represented a superior group in their sending schools rather than by attributing their higher scores to the effect of bussing. Fox substantiated the first of these conclusions by finding that the majority of principals involved agreed that the bussed pupils were indeed a selected group.

29. *Ibid.*, p. 318.
30. *Ibid.*, p. 318.
31. David J. Fox, *Expansion of the Free Choice Open Enrollment Program* (New York: Center for Urban Education, September 1967, mimeographed).

CROSS-SECTIONAL STUDIES

The Coleman study has given the most recent impetus to the belief that there is an established link between integration and achievement. The minority group children in his sample of schools who were doing academically better than most others were in schools with majority children. One acceptable interpretation of this finding is that integration *does* have a direct influence. But another equally plausible explanation is that children who live in neighborhoods in which their schools are naturally integrated belong to upwardly mobile families, who have gone to considerable trouble to provide better schools for their children. However, a reanalysis of Coleman's data by McPartland shows that the important variable seems to be the proportion of white children *in the actual classroom* rather than in the school generally.[32] That is, black children in classes where white children are in the *majority* have higher verbal ability scores, whatever the racial composition of the school. McPartland concludes further that verbal differences between black children in white-majority classrooms and those in black-majority classrooms cannot be explained by the selection or grouping practices used by the school.

If McPartland's analysis holds up, it constitutes the single most important piece of evidence of a direct relation between integrated schools and minority achievement. Other studies are subject to the same difficulty as the original Coleman findings, as an examination of Alan Wilson's Berkeley research indicates.[33]

In his first study Wilson collected data on sixth-graders in Berkeley who attended schools in one of three distinct parts of the city: the Berkeley Hills, where most of the students are from professional or executive families; the Flats, where most of the black population is concentrated; and the Foothills, which is between these extremes both geographically and in terms of social composition. The Hills schools were overwhelmingly white; the Flats schools had 62 percent black students; and the Foothills comprised 71 percent white and 14 percent black (the remainder was Oriental).

Gross differences in achievement level between the three groups of schools are reported in Table 9.2, and conform to most of the known data on social class in relation to school achievement.

An examination of achievement-test scores of the students, grouped by their father's occupation, indicates that, as one might expect, the

32. James McPartland, "The Relative Influence of School Desegregation and of Classroom Desegregation on the Academic Achievement of 9th Grade Negro Students," Report No. BR 6-1610 (Baltimore, Md.: Johns Hopkins University, September 1967).

33. Alan B. Wilson, "Social Stratification and Academic Achievement," in A. Harry Passow (ed.), *Education in Depressed Areas* (New York: Bureau of Publications, Teachers College, Columbia University, 1963), pp. 217-236.

Table 9.2 Mean Test Scores, Percentages Reading at Grade Level and Percentages Receiving A or B Marks in Reading and Arithmetic, by Sex and School Strata

	Boys			Girls		
Variable	Hills	Foothills	Flats	Hills	Foothills	Flats
Reading test	106	92	73	105	96	82
Arithmetic test	83	67	54	79	71	60
IQ test	126	112	101	123	115	103
Percent reading at grade level	97	50	40	98	69	62
Percent receiving A or B in reading	61	41	21	63	60	35
Percent receiving A or B in arithmetic	56	50	19	51	65	34

SOURCE: Alan B. Wilson, "Social Stratification and Academic Achievement," in A. Harry Passow (ed.), *Education in Depressed Areas* (New York: Bureau of Publications, Teachers College, Columbia University, 1963) p. 221.

differences revealed by this table are mainly due to differences in the backgrounds of the children attending schools in various areas of the city. Wilson's question is: Are there differences in the achievement of children *from the same occupational level* who are attending different schools? Taking reading achievement as a crucial test, he compared

Table 9.3 Mean Reading Achievement-test Scores of High-sixth-grade Students, Classified by Sex, School Strata, and Father's Occupations

	Boys			Girls		
Father's occupation	Hills	Foothills	Flats	Hills	Foothills	Flats
Professional and executive	107	100	—*	107	108	—*
	(94)	(21)	(2)	(93)	(15)	(1)
White-collar and merchant	106	93	81	102	99	81
	(46)	(31)	(18)	(55)	(38)	(16)
Manual and artisan	—*	91	71	103	93	84
	(3)	(55)	(72)	(11)	(46)	(87)

* Means are not reported for cells containing fewer than ten cases.

SOURCE: Alan B. Wilson, "Social Stratification and Academic Achievement," in A. Harry Passow (ed.), *Education in Depressed Areas* (New York: Bureau of Publications, Teachers College, Columbia University, 1963), p. 223.

children whose fathers were in roughly the same occupations with the same grouping in other schools; the results are reported in Table 9.3. This data strongly suggests that the school itself has an "homogenizing" effect on students, and seems to confirm Jencks' belief (quoted earlier) in the potency of the peer group. Indeed, Wilson collected data on boys' peer groups in the Berkeley schools which indicates that in the Flats schools the boys who are not interested in going on with their education are well-integrated among their classmates and are overrepresented among the leaders of the school.

There are some significant objections to this interpretation, however. It is possible that the heavy concentration of black students in the Flats reduces the average reading scores. To test the effect of a number of variables within each occupational grouping, Wilson performed a complex analysis that resulted in a series of weights indicating how much each variable contributed to reading scores. In Table 9.4 the weights for each of the variables is a measure of how much the variable *independently* contributes, holding all other factors constant.

Table 9.4 Estimates of the Main Orthogonal Effects of Sex, Race, School Strata, and Fathers' Occupations upon Reading-test Scores

Source of Variation	Main effect
Sex	
Male	− 1.7
Female	+ 1.5
Race	
White	+ 3.0
Oriental	+ 0.9
Negro	−12.7
School Stratum	
Hills	+ 2.3
Foothills	− 0.1
Flats	− 4.3
Father's occupation	
Professional and executive	+ 3.7
White-collar and merchant	+ 1.1
Manual and artisan	− 4.4
Mean	97.7

SOURCE: Alan B. Wilson, "Social Stratification and Academic Achievement," in A. Harry Passow (ed.), *Education in Depressed Areas* (New York: Bureau of Publications, Teachers College, Columbia University, 1963), p. 226.

One can predict the average reading score for any particular group by adding or subtracting the appropriate effects to the total mean of 97.7. Thus, the predicted reading achievement of black working-class boys in Flats schools is 97.7 — 1.7 — 12.7 — 4.3 — 4.4 = 74.6. But the prediction for the same boys in Foothills schools is only 4.2 less or 70.4. Although Wilson has produced evidence that the schools have *some* effect, it does not seem to be a very substantial one.

Furthermore, there is an alternative explanation for the fact that boys of the same class and race do better in schools in areas outside the ghetto. As Wilson himself points out:

> It is doubtless true that one of the reasons manual workers choose to live in the Hills is to obtain greater educational and social advantages for their children. Very likely they place an emphasis upon the value of school success which is more comparable to other residents of the Hills than to their educational compeers in the Foothills and Flats.[34]

Wallin and Waldo, in another San Francisco study, tested this possibility by gathering data on parental educational aspiration for their children.[35] The sample included about 2400 eighth-grade boys and girls, of whom 135 were black boys and 133 were black girls. The researchers found a sizeable association between school climate (based on the proportion of students from middle-class families in the school) and student's level of aspiration. But, when the parents' aspirations for the child (reported by the child himself) were controlled, the relation between school climate and the child's educational aspirations was considerably reduced. The children in the schools with greater numbers of middle-class pupils tended to have parents with high aspirations for them. Although Wallin and Waldo did not investigate achievement levels, their findings suggest that parents of lower-class children in mixed schools have higher aspirations for their children and probably exert more pressure on them to achieve.

Though the case for the claim that an integrated elementary school climate has any substantial effect on *achievement* of black students thus is, at best, unproven, one cannot ignore the possibility that high-school climate at least may have a considerable influence on *aspiration.* Wallin and Waldo's negative findings on the effect of integrated elementary schools are confirmed by at least one other study.

Nancy St. John analyzed the aspiration level of black high-school

34. *Ibid.,* p. 224.

35. Paul Wallin and Leslie C. Waldo, *Social Class Background of 8th Grade Pupils, Social Composition of Their Schools, Their Academic Aspirations and School Adjustment* (Washington, D.C.: U.S. Office of Education, Cooperative Research Project No. 1935, 1964).

students in a Massachusetts city, using as a reference point the state of integration or segregation of the elementary school they had attended.[36] Her conclusion was that the racial balance of the earlier schooling had no significant effect on educational aspiration.

But a later San Francisco study by Wilson suggests that regardless of elementary-school conditions the high-school climate itself may influence aspiration for advanced education.[37]

He divided a sample of high schools into A (upper white collar), B (lower white collar), and C (industrial). Although Wilson does not examine race separately, the concentration of black boys in Group C schools permits one to make at least cautious inferences from the social class data applicable to the problem of integration. Group A schools, for example, have only 2 percent black students; Group B have 22 percent; and Group C 34 percent.

Wilson's most striking evidence for the influence of high-school climate lies in the differences in aspiration between schools when achievement level and IQ are held constant, as reported in Tables 9.5 and 9.6.

Table 9.5 Percentages Aspiring to Go to College by School Groups and Grades

	School group (percent)		
Median academic grade	A	B	C
"A"	98	96	78
	(60)	(24)	(9)
"B"	90	89	72
	(152)	(90)	(46)
"C"	72	55	41
	(145)	(207)	(184)
"D"	43	21	25
	(47)	(120)	(169)

SOURCE: Alan B. Wilson, "Residential Segregation of Social Classes and Aspirations of High School Boys," in A. Harry Passow, et al., *Education of the Disadvantaged* (New York: Holt, Rinehart and Winston, Inc., 1967), p. 279.

It is clear that high achievers as well as those with academic potential are "less likely to wish to go to college if they attend a working class school and, conversely, that low achievers are more apt to want to go to

36. Nancy Hoyt St. John, "The Effect of Segregation on the Aspirations of Negro Youth," *Harvard Educational Review,* Vol. 36, No. 3 (Summer 1966), pp. 284-294.

37. Alan B. Wilson, "Residential Segregation of Social Classes and Aspirations of High School Boys," in A. Harry Passow, *et al., Education of the Disadvantaged* (New York: Holt, Rinehart and Winston, Inc., 1967), pp. 268-283.

college if they attend a middle class school."[38] And, as Wilson points out, though it is reasonable to suppose that working-class families have moved to middle-class areas in order to give their children educational advantages, ". . . it is not so persuasive to argue the corollary that middle class families would act to depress the aspirations of their children if they live in a predominantly working class neighborhood."[39]

Table 9.6 Percentages Aspiring to Go to College by School Groups and IQ Scores

	School group (percent)		
IQ score	A	B	C
120+	96	83	33
	(100)	(81)	(18)
110–119	93	72	51
	(128)	(108)	(53)
100–109	76	52	41
	(87)	(89)	(82)
90–99	47	24	35
	(30)	(63)	(68)
89–*	25	29	25
	(12)	(69)	(111)

* This relationship disappears among those with IQ's below 89, that is, those for whom collegiate aspirations are unrealistic.

SOURCE: Alan B. Wilson, "Residential Segregation of Social Classes and Aspirations of High School Boys," in A. Harry Passow, *et al., Education of the Disadvantaged* (New York: Holt, Rinehart and Winston, Inc., 1967), p. 279.

Thus, the case for the influence of school climate on aspiration is a far better one for the high school than for the elementary school. Nor is it difficult to find an explanation for this difference. The influence of peer groups is notably greater during the high-school years in contrast to the larger influence of the family during preadolescence. Moreover, the self-contained classroom of the elementary school and the administrative tendency to group by ability restricts the influence of the larger peer society on the child. It seems reasonable to conclude that both racial and social class integration is more important at the secondary level, at least as regards a hoped-for influence on aspiration levels.

38. *Ibid.*, pp. 278-279.
39. *Ibid.*, p. 280.

SOME POLICY IMPLICATIONS

We may now reexamine desegregation policies, and particularly the specific methods for school integration in metropolitan areas, in the light of these findings from both experimental and empirical studies. It is reasonably clear that as a technical answer to the problem of de facto segregation, school bussing needs to be sharply reevaluated.

Although the transfer of groups of elementary children from one school neighborhood to another represents the only immediately practical means of desegregation in cities where extensive black ghettos exist, it is doubtful that it accomplishes much more than a perhaps spurious air of democratic mixing. In order for the technique to achieve its educational objectives much would have to be done to the receiving schools to make them more beneficial to the bussed-in child. On the basis of his review of the literature on desegregation and performance Katz suggests that we must at least exercise caution to insure that children moving into a new school have a reasonable chance of succeeding academically, that in-service training of teachers and others in the newly integrated school be instituted to develop an awareness of the emotional needs of children in these situations, and that ability grouping practices be modified.[40]

Some observers go considerably beyond this prescription. Nathaniel Hickerson, a black educator, has concluded:

> If we reject *de facto* segregation as inimical to American democracy, then we must reject mere physical integration of Negroes and whites in schools as inimical to the best interests of Negro children . . . we must decide that this integration is to be more than placing of Negro and white children in the same school building.[41]

Hickerson proposes nine basic steps that must be taken to improve education in the integrated schools of the North:

1. A realistic proportion of Negro teachers, counselors, and administrators, should serve in the public schools, particularly integrated schools.
2. Teachers, both white and Negro, with special interests and training in education of minority groups should be employed whenever possible in integrated schools.
3. Teacher training institutions must offer courses in minority-group education, and should sanction for employment in schools with an integrated student body only those teachers who have successfully completed these courses.
4. Race-minded and bigoted faculty members, employed in integrated

40. Katz, *op. cit.*, p. 386.
41. Nathaniel Hickerson, "Physical Integration Is Not Enough," *Journal of Negro Education* (Spring 1966), p. 115.

schools should be identified and ruthlessly removed wherever possible. Perhaps expressions of racial hostility could be grounds for immediate dismissal as a violation of policy of the board of education. . .

5. All schools, but particularly those that are integrated must place emphasis upon the historical contributions of Negroes to the development of man's culture and American institutions. . .

6. Business, professional, union, civic and sports leaders, both white and Negro, should be encouraged to come to the school in the community to discuss with students the kinds of employment opportunities available for those who do well in school and who plan to continue in advanced training. . .

7. Schools, through home visits by faculty personnel, should encourage Negro parents to attend school functions and to become identified with the school and its problems.

8. Negro students (together with whites) in junior high and high schools should be sent as missionaries into the lower grades of the elementary schools to talk with children and impress upon white and black alike the necessity of taking school seriously. . .

9. Special programs such as Compensatory Education and Operation Head Start should be used always by school districts in integrated situations.[42]

These criteria fit well with those developed by the staff of a school system which successfully built an integrated program with a significant impact on the achievement levels of black children in the system in Westchester, New York. The Greenburgh District 8 experiment included an intensive plan of counseling, remedial work, and community involvement that, over the course of almost a decade, considerably narrowed the gap between white and black pupils on all important measures.[43] To the list above, one might add the following criteria as a result of this experiment:

1. Heterogeneous grouping.
2. Early remediation to bridge the cultural gap.
3. Controlling class size to permit individualized instruction.
4. Intelligent, sensitive management of situations with racial overtones to combat them openly and without defensiveness and to turn them into positive learning experiences.

Taken all together, these criteria are clearly most difficult to put into practice in schools which receive groups of black children from distant parts of the city. Greenburgh is a small community with a manageably small school system. In the very different context of a large city it is manifestly impossible for the school personnel in a receiving school

42. *Ibid.*, pp. 115-116.

43. Naomi and Arnold Bucheimer, *Equality through Integration* (Anti-Defamation League of B'nai B'rith, undated).

to have much to do with the community from which the children come, to take only one of the objectives. Nor is it easy to see how a large bureaucratic civil service system with a strong, protective union could find ways of identifying and dismissing teachers who express racial bigotry. The receiving school itself, committed to its surrounding community, is likely to view the bussed-in children as an alien element, no matter what the skin color, simply as a result of the way organizational systems work.

Other attempts at urban integration fare somewhat better when measured by these criteria. School pairing, for example, maintains the closeness of the school to the communities it serves and thus makes more probable the identification of school personnel with the student body. Although the educational park plan appears to have many of the disadvantages of bussing, in its removal of the school and the child from the community of origin, its counterbalancing advantages offset the problems. First, it pulls the white children out of their communities along with black children, so that both groups are on an equal footing. Under such conditions the peer culture might well become more important than in the usual neighborhood elementary school. Second, children will be attending school over a long period of time within the same relatively small system, permitting the administration of the complex to develop a consistent program of teacher training and to work toward the establishment of a helpful student culture. The economics of the plan would actually encourage the employment of highly specialized human-relations experts to help toward such a goal. Third, the large complex will permit the employment of expert personnel to develop workable plans of early diagnosis and remediation, one of the key elements in the success of the Greenburgh experiment.

It is unlikely, however, that the educational park idea will be realized in the near future, and the stubborn realities of the present still confront us. If our interpretation of the available evidence on elementary-school desegregation is correct, the fight to integrate at this level in the very large cities has an aura of futility about it; even if it were to succeed, and even if we could make the receiving school a psychologically helpful situation, we could not expect very great gains in achievement. As an alternative, the demands of the black community for greater control over ghetto schools makes a great deal of sense.

A greater amount of attention might be devoted to a more positive integration of the urban high school, if it is indeed the potential breeding ground for aspirations among the academically able black poor. High-school children can make their own way about the city, so that it is considerably easier to obtain a reasonable racial balance in high schools than in elementary schools. From this point of view Havighurst's metropolitan school plan deserves serious examination for its potential contribution to a general scheme of useful desegregation.

Recommended Reading

A good survey of black education under conditions of total segregation is provided by Henry Bullock in *A History of Negro Education in the South* (Cambridge, Mass.: Harvard University Press, 1967).

The United States Department of Health, Education and Welfare's *Equality of Educational Opportunity,* "The Coleman Report" (Washington, D.C.: Office of Education, 1966), at least the summary edition, should be high on the reading list of any prospective urban teacher. *Racial Isolation in the Public Schools* (A Report of the United States Commission on Civil Rights, Washington, D.C.: Government Printing Office, 1967) presents the strongest case to date for school desegregation on educational grounds.

Perhaps the most diverse collection of articles dealing with school desegregation is Meyer Weinberg's *Integrated Education* (Beverley Hills, Calif.: Glencoe Press, 1968), selected from the journal of the same name. Part III of *Policy Issues in Urban Education* edited by M.B. Smiley and H.L. Miller (New York: The Free Press, 1968) contains some excellent articles on this topic. *Triumph in a White Suburb* by Reginald Damerell (New York: William Morrow & Company, Inc., 1968) describes the painfully slow and difficult process of desegregating a Northern suburban community.

10

SCHOOL AND COMMUNITY

This chapter deals with what is perhaps the most sensitive and crucial of urban school problems: the relationship between the school and the community which it serves. Historically this association has been assumed to be close and mutually supportive. The substantial power given to local school boards across the country assumes that in a very real sense the school belongs to and should serve the community in which it is located. This traditional relationship does not characterize urban schools and particularly urban schools serving lower-class communities. Leaders of poor urban communities have been increasingly insistent that the school in fact does *not* belong to them and in no way represents or relates to their neighborhoods.

We begin with an examination of the concepts of community and community power, including a variety of ways in which the school can relate to its community. A case study of decentralization in New York City is provided, as well as an examination of the community school concept. The chapter concludes by describing the growing black power movement in relation to urban schools.

THE CONCEPT OF COMMUNITY

Perhaps no concept in social science is as cloudy or confused as the concept of community. A considerable amount of empirical study and theoretical material has failed to provide an adequate definition. The term seems to mean many things to many social scientists. Charles

Adrian, for example, argues that for most purposes the community is a functional concept rather than a geographic one. "Its spacial boundaries do not coincide with the legal area encompassed by a local unit of government." To the citizen, the concept of community may simultaneously include an area both larger and smaller than a given city (as discussed in an earlier chapter, the urban community is a special case). It differs for purposes of water supply, community chest campaigns, retail trading, educational facilities, hospital service, religious worship, police protection, and other activities. The community, as a symbol of direct social relationships in grassroots government, has been highly romanticized in recent years by both popular and scholarly writers. People were never so interested in it as they have become now that they feel they have lost it.[1] Some social scientists would argue that the term, local community, refers simply to people who live close together, which could mean in a neighborhood, small town, suburb, section of a large city, or a metropolis itself. Other social scientists would maintain that people, land or geographical area, and organization are the three essential concepts of community.[2] Still other definitions stress purposive interaction, such as the following classical definition by John Dewey:

> Where there is conjoint activity whose consequences are appreciated as good by all singular persons who take part in it and where the realization of the good is such as to affect energetic desire and effort to sustain it in being just because it is a good shared by all, there is insofar a community. The clear consciousness of a communal life and all its implications constitutes the idea of democracy.[3]

Some authors in fact have managed to write an entire book about an important aspect of community, namely school-community relations, without once providing a definition.[4]

James Coleman, a scholar whose studies have encompassed both communities and schools in the United States, offers the following definition:

> To the sociologist and the layman alike the term community concerns things held in common. Some of these things may be tangible objects such as the

1. Charles R. Adrian (ed.), *Social Science and Community Action* (East Lansing: Institute for Community Development, Michigan State University, 1960), p. 3.

2. Luvern L. Cunningham, "Community Power: Implications for Education," in Robert S. Cahill and Stephen P. Hencley (eds.), *The Politics of Education in the Local Community* (Danville, Ill.: Interstate Printers & Publishers, 1964), p. 30.

3. John Dewey, *The Public and Its Problems* (Denver, Col.: Alan Swallow, Publisher), p. 149.

4. Merle R. Sumption and Yvonne Engstrom, *School-Community Relations: A New Approach* (New York: McGraw-Hill, Inc., 1966).

common property of a family or the common pastureland held by a tribal community. Others are less tangible. Common ideas, beliefs and values. Common customs and norms held by all. And finally, common or joint actions of the community as a whole. Furthermore when we speak of a community, we ordinarily mean a set of people who have not just one element in common but many.[5]

When we use the concept of community in this chapter, and elsewhere in the book, we will not be referring to metropolitan areas or to cities themselves. "Urban community" will refer to more limited geographic areas within the city, which seems to fall within the general definition provided by Coleman. However, before we are able to relate the concept to the school we will need to consider to what extent certain parts of our large cities possess characteristics of a community. Sumption and Engstrom, in *School-Community Relations,* identify five characteristics of the modern community.[6]

1. *A community is changing.* There seems no doubt that this characteristic applies to urban ghetto areas. We know that because of in-migration, out-migration, as well as population movements within cities, there is considerable change. Over a longer period of time housing conditions, and economic opportunity may change within a given area. Racial and ethnic composition is also a constantly changing factor in most parts of our large cities.

2. *A community is diverse.* Here we are on more questionable ground. There is no doubt that in any reasonably-sized geographic area —for example, central Harlem, which stretches from 110th Street to 150th Street in Manhattan—there is considerable diversity in terms of socioeconomic background, in terms of educational level, occupation, and so on. Ethnic diversity, however, does not characterize Harlem. Ninety-eight to a hundred percent of the population is black. In many areas of our largest cities, ethnic and social class diversity seems to be decreasing. We are getting an increasing concentration of lower socioeconomic, nonwhite citizens in the central city. One must question whether the characteristic of diversity applies to many urban areas.

3. *A community is structured.* It possesses economic structure upon which the inhabitants depend for a livelihood, a social structure which regulates social life to some extent, and a political structure which dictates the government of the community. At least two of these must be seriously questioned. The economic structure of urban ghettos is in

5. James S. Coleman, "Community Disorganization," in Robert K. Merton and Robert A. Nisbet (eds.), *Contemporary Social Problems,* 2d ed. (New York: Harcourt, Brace & World, Inc., 1966), p. 671.

6. Sumption and Engstrom, *op. cit.,* pp. 5-8.

local terms nonexistent. Although some industry may be located there, it does not provide a livelihood for very many inhabitants. Most residents must travel outside the ghetto to seek employment. The political framework, although it may exist to some extent, is generally tied in and subordinate to the larger power structure of the city itself. With rare exceptions the power to make political decisions which directly affect the lives of ghetto residents is not found in the local community. References to "the man," "to the boss downtown" clearly indicate that ghetto residents know where the power is. Social structure, insofar as it regulates social life, is also very weak or absent from many urban areas.

4. *A community is organized.* This characteristic seems notably absent among the metropolitan poor. The experience of the "war on poverty" conducted over the last four years points up the extreme difficulty of creating local organizations or strengthening those already existing in urban areas. Engstrom points to organization provided by professional and occupational groups, such as teachers, doctors, longshoremen, bricklayers, or special interest factions (that is, tax reduction, conservation)—all of which are particularly lacking in urban ghetto areas. Groups designed to put pressure on public agencies exist, if at all, in rudimentary form. "Maximum Feasible Participation of the Poor," that attempt to assist the disadvantaged to organize themselves, seems to be the most drastic failure of the "war on poverty."

5. *A community makes decisions.* Quite clearly urban ghetto residents in whatever city we choose to observe do not make important decisions about their own lives. The public institutions, the political parties, and the special federal programs designed specifically for them —all have their power center and owe their fundamental allegiance to structures outside the ghetto.

It should be apparent from this analysis that in many ways urban ghettos, those neighborhoods predominantly nonwhite and lower class, may not qualify as "communities." This situation like so many others is changing and a number of forces are at work attempting to develop communities in slum areas. Later in this chapter we will discuss how the school itself may contribute to the process of developing urban communities.

COMMUNITY POWER STRUCTURE

Urban teachers and administrators should be aware of the power structure that exists in a given city or community, since the nature of this structure can directly affect the school and its relationship with the local community.

Two general theories of social power are advanced by social scientists. The first, the "structural or power elite theory," has been put forward by Floyd Hunter, C. Wright Mills, and other sociologists.[7] Studies which make use of the concept of social stratification and which relate a given community power structure to social stratification make five important assertions about power as it is exercised in communities.

1. The upper class rules in local community life. These studies differ in their description of what constitutes the upper class—whether the upper class is divided on economic grounds or status ascriptions. Despite different definitions of class, all of these studies seem to agree that the upper class, usually the group with the highest socioeconomic standing, has the most power.

2. Political and civic leaders are subordinate to the upper class. These studies maintain that political and civic leaders as a group possess less power than the upper class as a group. In addition, they are usually supposed to take orders from or do the bidding of the upper class.

3. A single "power elite" rules in the community. One may probably best picture this concept in terms of a pyramid of all-purpose power dealing with a wide variety of community issues. On the national level, for example, C. Wright Mills develops a case for a power elite which consists of national political figures, including the president of the United States, the presidents or board chairmen of the largest corporations, and the leaders of military services.[8] Stratification studies of individual cities as well as small communities indicate the same pyramiding of all-purpose power in the hands of a few individuals, all members of the upper class.

4. The upper-class power elite rules in its own interest. Stratification studies find that the main reason for the wielding of power by this upper-class power elite is the perpetuation of its own existence as a social class and as an elite.

5. Social conflict takes place between the upper and lower classes. The reasoning behind this assertion is that social conflict will generally follow divisions of interest in the community, and stratification studies find that the divisions of interest follow a social class line. The interests of factory workers are different, for example, and conflict with the interests of factory owners.

An alternative theory which attempts to explain community power is the "pluralist" theory associated with the work of Robert Dahl and

7. Floyd Hunter, *Community Power Structure* (Chapel Hill: University of North Carolina Press, 1953); and C. Wright Mills, *The Power Elite* (New York: Oxford University Press, 1956).

8. C. Wright Mills, "The Structure of Power in American Society," *The British Journal of Sociology,* Vol. 9, No. 1 (March 1958), pp. 29-41.

Nelson Polsby.[9] The basic assumptions of the pluralist position may be summarized as follows:

1. The assumptions of the stratifications studies (Hunter-Mills) about the invariable association between power and other social conditions—such as position, wealth, and prestige—are open to question and should be subject to empirical research.

2. The real measurement and identification of community power requires very intensive study of the actions of participants in processes of community decision-making and issue resolution. Rather than identifying individuals in groups on a social class ladder, actual observation and analysis should be made of the actions of individuals in making important community decisions.

3. The determination of overlap among decision-making personnel, that is, the concept of general or all-purpose power is only possible if one looks at several issue areas in a particular community and then analyzes who actually makes decisions in each area.

4. The final and most important assertion of the pluralist school is that community power is accorded to individuals and groups not on the basis of their perceived status or reputation, not, in other words, on who they are, what their family or social connections are but rather on the basis of what they do, their participation in the decision-making process, and the actual impact that they have in this process.

These two sharply divergent theoretical positions paint rather different pictures of how power in a given community is likely to operate. There are strengths and weaknesses in each. The pluralist position is quite clearly more democratic, a more palatable picture of power in a democratic society. It points not to one pyramid of all-purpose power for American communities but rather a large number of small pyramids. Power and decision-making are spread much more widely. At the same time, the pluralist school is based quite clearly on the analysis and measurement of one particular process in the community, that is, "decision-making," not, clearly, all decision-making but that which is available for study—public or semipublic meetings of city councils, boards of directors, and so forth. This method does not take into account, for example, the possibility of a late night private telephone call from one of the "power elite" to an elected official. What the pluralist focuses on is the official vote at the meeting the next day. Limiting the definition of community power to decision-making, results in a widely spread picture of power, since all communities have a considerable number of boards, committees, councils, and so on.

In spite of these reservations the more recent pluralist community

9. Robert A. Dahl, *Who Governs? Democracy and Power in an American City* (New Haven: Yale University Press, 1962); and Nelson W. Polsby, *Community Power and Political Theory* (New Haven: Yale University Press, 1963).

studies have raised serious questions about the adequacy of the stratification or power elite theory. Robert Dahl's highly respected study of power in New Haven, *Who Governs?*, points to a plurality of power figures with very little overlap between different areas of concern.[10]

Criticism has been made of the research techniques of the stratification school as well. One of the common tools of the stratification methodology is to use the reputational technique to identify the power elite. Allowing some citizens to make judgments and identify other key individuals in a power structure leads, the critics say, to the identification of *both* status figures—those who have high social position, family connection, and so on—and actual power figures, and offers no way of distinguishing between the two.

Ronald Corwin's *Sociology of Education* contains a view of the power structure somewhat different from either pluralists or elitists, which may have particular relevance for urban ghetto areas.[11] He suggests that a distinction can be made between those individuals in power positions who are predominantly local and those who are "cosmopolitan." He seems to be defining whole cities as communities. With slight modification the distinction between local and cosmopolitan might be a useful tool for looking at power in poor neighborhoods. Certain individuals and certain institutions, such as churches and block associations, are local; while social welfare institutions and some elected officials on the state and federal levels are cosmopolitan. Their orientation, their influence, and the source of their power while including the local community encompasses a wider geographic area. The public school system of any large city using this distinction must then be considered a cosmopolitan institution. Its line of authority, structure, and the source of its power come from outside the urban ghetto.

Regardless of the theory of power which seems most useful and appropriate, social power does exist in metropolitan areas. Whether or not ghettos are defined as communities, power exists there as well. The urban school and school system must in some way develop a response to the power environment in which it finds itself. Corwin has identified five possible responses which schools can make.[12]

The first, *passive adaptation,* refers to more or less intentional and self-imposed restraint on the part of the school, either to please external groups or to avoid actions which might displease them. If it is true, as we have suggested earlier, that the urban slum is not in some senses a community, then it is not surprising that the school has in general avoided passive adaptation with regard to the urban slum. It is only in recent years that organized demands and pressure have been brought

10. Dahl, *Ibid.*
11. Ronald G. Corwin, *A Sociology of Education* (New York: Appleton-Century-Crofts, 1965), pp. 380-383.
12. *Ibid.,* chapter 12.

to bear against the school by parents and other groups in inner city neighborhoods. One must look to smaller rural communities and to suburban schools to find any evidence of this response. There are certainly elements in the American philosophy of education which support it; that is, the tradition of decentralized community control over education which suggests that lay citizens and not professionals ought to determine school policies and practices. The demands by some black power groups seem to point in the direction of urging, insisting, and demanding passive adaptation on the part of schools toward the local community. We will look later in this chapter at a case study of this kind of demand in New York City.

The second response of the school to its power environment is that of *coalition.* This may be defined as a form of open combination between the school and one or more other organizations or groups for a specific common purpose. Public schools in slum areas have at various times sought coalition with certain community groups. Also interesting is the coalition sought and maintained at certain periods of time between the school and teacher organizations, such as the United Federation of Teachers in New York. Coalition is usually adopted either to defend the school from attack in one direction, which is considered to be unfair by the system, or to achieve some particular purpose. In New York City again, the close, indeed almost incestuous, coalition between the public school system and the division of Teacher Education in the City University clearly represents coalition, the purpose being to keep the system operating with as little outside interference as possible.

Corwin argues that often what appears to be a coalition is in fact a form of *cooptation.* These two responses, he argues, differ not so much in external form but in motive. Coalition, as we have defined it, is a way in which the school can cooperate with some other group in order to achieve a shared goal. Cooptation on the other hand is a combination designed by one organization, in this case the school, as a means to gain control over another. It is an attempt on the part of the school to extend control to groups and individuals who may be hostile to the school, and incorporate these individuals and groups under its own leadership. Corwin suggests that many Parent-Teacher Associations and/or parent organizations are in effect cooptated by schools. Arthur Vidich and Joseph Bensman uncovered cooptation in their study, *Small Town in Mass Society.*[13] They found that the principal of the school, since he was looked to by parents as an educational leader with ideas and ability, secured most of the speakers for the Parent-Teacher Association programs. Because of his position the principal was able to use the PTA and its elected officials to support his own proposals. Although there

13. Arthur Vidich and Joseph Bensman, *Small Town in Mass Society* (New York: Doubleday & Company, Inc., 1960), chapter 7.

has been little research on the relationship between inner city schools and their parent associations, informal impressions gathered by the authors and their colleagues point to cooptation in some urban slum schools. Here the parent association appears to be not a means of communication between the school and the neighborhood in which it is located but rather an organization which supports and restates policies and decisions which the school administrator has developed.

The fourth school response to its power environment is that of *bargaining*. Bargaining may be defined in this context as negotiation between the school and some other institution, organization, or group in which the school may forfeit some of its goals in return for that particular group's support. It is obvious that as demands from urban ghetto parents increase, bargaining will certainly take place. Educational bargaining of this kind goes on outside the ghetto area as well. The delegations of parents from various parts of a metropolis presenting petitions and making demands to the central school board represents another level of bargaining. Quite often, in return for agreement not to picket or boycott, or to stop picketing, boycotting, and so on, some of the demands of the groups are agreed to by the school system. It seems likely that this response and the skills necessary to use it will need to be developed to a high degree in urban ghetto schools, especially as the spokesmen for various positions become more articulate. The response of the school administrator and the school system to these demands must become more sophisticated; and the skills of bargaining and negotiation are likely to become indispensable for urban administrators.

The fifth response of the school is that of *competition*. Unlike the other four, competition is a form of overt resistance to outside demands and pressures. It does not involve a compromise, giving in, or establishing any kind of rapport with outside groups. This form of response has probably most frequently characterized the relationship between inner city schools and the neighborhoods in which they are located. Certain kinds of competition in urban areas have been established by outside pressure groups—for example, the Freedom schools established during several of the boycotts of the public schools in New York City. Tutorial and remedial programs established by community agencies may be viewed and have been viewed by some educators as competition. This response may very often take the form of a counteroffer being made to a demand by a local group or institution. When the Bundy proposal for decentralizing the New York City schools was prepared for the Mayor's office, the board of education very soon "competed" by developing its own plan.

These five responses are, of course, not mutually exclusive and many of them are likely to be going on at once. It is important to realize that the particular response which a school makes to its power environment can have significant effects on the school itself, on the teachers, and on the learning that takes place in its classrooms. We have not been describing merely administrative games but real action and conflict which clearly and directly affect the urban school.

URBAN DECENTRALIZATION: A CASE STUDY OF NEW YORK SCHOOL—COMMUNITY RELATIONS

In Washington, D.C., in Chicago, in Philadelphia, in fact in almost all large cities the last three or four years have seen growing demands for "decentralization" or "community control of public schools." Although these demands vary in intensity and in patterns of development, there are enough common elements to justify the use of a case study approach. We have selected New York City since it is the largest public school system in the nation and has in other areas, such as teacher organization and certain special programs, been a trend setter for other cities.

A number of factors have contributed to the creation of the rather dramatic problems of control in New York City public schools. For many years there has been a demand on the part of poor, and especially nonwhite parents, for better education and an increased voice for the community in the operation of New York City schools. Organized efforts along this line have been going on for the past six or seven years at least. More recently other factors have developed that will inevitably change school-community relationships considerably in New York. The school aid provided to local school districts discriminates against those districts with a large number of students. This formula obviously hurts New York City, the largest public school district in the nation covering five counties and enrolling over 1,000,000 children. New York City's Mayor John Lindsay was informed by leaders of the state legislature that in order to receive more aid, New York's one gigantic school district must be decentralized into a number of smaller ones. A commission to design a decentralization plan was appointed by the Mayor and headed by McGeorge Bundy, president of the Ford Foundation. The panel's report, usually referred to as the "Bundy report," says in part:

> We are deeply concerned with the need of participation, responsibility, shared authority, and concern. The schools have become dangerously separated from many of New York's communities. Pupils cannot be aroused and led upward or even kept in good order. If their parents are offered the reality of responsible participation then the school should prosper.[14]

14. *The New York Times* (November 8, 1967), p. 94.

The major recommendations of the "Bundy report" are as follows:

1. The New York City public schools would be reorganized into a community school system consisting of a federation of largely autonomous districts and a central board of education. The number of districts suggested in the report was from thirty to sixty ranging in population from 12,000 to 40,000 pupils.
2. Community school districts would have authority over the regular elementary and secondary education within their boundaries and would be responsible for adhering to state education standards.
3. A central education agency, together with the superintendent of schools and his staff, would be responsible for special educational functions and citywide educational policy, and would provide certain centralized services to the community school districts when requested.
4. Community school districts would be governed by boards of education elected for the most part by parents in the school district and also in part appointed by the mayor from lists of candidates maintained by the central educational agency.
5. The community school board and the district would receive a total annual allocation of operating funds which they would then be free to spend with considerable latitude, always, of course, staying within the bounds of state law.
6. Community school districts would have broad personnel powers, including the right to hire and fire community superintendents on a contract basis.
7. All tenure rights of teachers and supervisory personnel would be preserved as the system goes into effect. Afterward the local district itself would award tenure.
8. Community schools would have the power to hire teachers meeting state certification requirements. This would eliminate existing special city qualifications and examinations.

After the Bundy report was made public, other educational groups, realizing that some form of decentralization would probably come into existence in New York City, proposed their own programs. The board of education, itself a very interested party, proposed a much more modest program of decentralization. Their plan included such items as:

1. Local school boards would have the authority to grant or deny permanent tenure on the recommendation of the district superintendent. Any person denied tenure would have the right to appeal to the board of education.
2. The central board itself would remain in power performing most of the centralized functions that it now performs with certain exceptions.
3. Local districts would adapt curriculum and methodologies to

their needs and have more freedom in choosing textbooks and materials which, of course, would still have to meet city and state requirements. Local districts would also receive lump sum money to be spent on maintenance, repairs, painting, and so forth, at their discretion. The power to license teachers, to appoint them, and to appoint administrative staff —all would remain with the central school board.

The New York State Board of Regents also presented a plan for adoption by the state legislature, in some ways more radical than the Bundy proposal. It would, for example:

1. Replace the present board of education with a five-man executive body whose main job would be to work out the details of the planned reorganization.
2. Abolish the thirty present local school boards (these existing boards serve only as advisory bodies), and replace them with eight to twenty separate districts that would be run by new locally elected school boards.
3. Establish temporary small districts in areas of particularly low educational achievement.
4. Transfer to the community and the special temporary district boards full operational authority over the present school personnel in their areas.
5. Abolish the New York City Board of Examiners, which prepares and administers special examinations for New York City teachers and administrators, and accept state certification as the requirement to teach in city schools. The local school districts would have the power to hire and dismiss school personnel, control the spending of funds; and the authority to determine curriculum, instructional materials, and methods within the framework of state standards. Local districts would be headed by superintendents serving under contract to local boards.

How would one or any combination of these proposals for decentralization be likely to work in New York City? The answer to this question can only be very tentative. There have been in existence, since the spring of 1967, three "experimental" districts in New York City. Supported with planning grants by the Ford Foundation, these districts were designed as self-governing school complexes. The board of education designation was "demonstration school projects." A serious controversy developed in the so-called Intermediate School 201 district before the establishment of the Ford Foundation-financed experimental program. The beginning of the school-community conflict at IS 201 goes back to 1958, when the city board of education announced that it was going to build a special five-million dollar school in central Harlem. The Intermediate School designation meant that students would be drawn from surrounding elementary schools at the fifth-grade level and sent on to high school at the ninth-grade level. Local parent groups in the community argued against the selected location because they wanted an integrated school which would be impossible on the block surrounded by 127th and 128th streets, Madison Avenue, and Park Avenue, close to the center of Harlem. They suggested a number of alternative sites on the edge of Harlem, which they hoped would result in an integrated school. The board did not change its building site, but assured parents that every attempt would be made to integrate the school. Their main effort was the mailing of ten thousand leaflets to white parents in nearby communities, urging them to enroll their children in IS 201. This request for volunteers was totally ineffective.

Finally, in the fall of 1966, as the school was about to open, the board of education admitted its failure to achieve integration. At this point the opposition of parent groups in the community changed in both style and content. With the realization that the school would be totally segregated, the parents' demands changed to advocating a stronger community role in IS 201's operation. The shift went from a plea for integration to a demand for control. The controversy increased rather quickly in intensity. First, the white principal, Stanley Lisser, voluntarily requested a transfer, since a black principal was one of the parents' key demands. This brought the United Federation of Teachers into the picture. Teachers at IS 201 threatened to walk off the job if Lisser did not stay on as principal. Within twenty-four hours the board of education had rejected Lisser's request for transfer, which considerably increased the hostility of the parents' negotiating committee toward the school and the board of education. In October the board of education offered the community a council of parents and teachers that would be purely advisory. The parent group flatly rejected this offer. Later in the fall the already existing local advisory school board, which covered the IS 201 area, resigned en masse claiming that the board of education totally ignored its advice. This was the first time that such a resignation had ever occurred in New York City.

The infusion of Ford Foundation money in the spring of 1967 changed the situation somewhat. However, this history of conflict and antagonism, at times approaching the level of violence, has seriously affected what IS 201 has been able to do. There still exists a considerable degree of hostility between the teachers and the planning board established with the help of the Ford Foundation. For example, after the original principal, Stanley Lisser, left in the fall of 1967 the school's acting principal took a sick leave and two of four assistant principals left to do graduate work at Fordham University.

In the fall of 1967 IS 201 hired sixty new teachers. Many of them were inexperienced. Teachers have complained about a lack of cooperation between themselves, the parents, and the planning board. One member of the planning board stated:

Our critics say the demonstration projects have failed. But the fact is we have not yet started to demonstrate. We haven't really yet negotiated a complete proposal with the Board of Education. The Board wants this project to be a glorified parents association but we feel when you are given the responsibility you must also be given the authority. The authority to effect the achievement of children. That means authority in two key areas: personnel and fiscal control. Anything else is game play.[15]

What about the situation in the other two experimental districts? In Two Bridges—a district on the lower east side of Manhattan with a Puerto Rican, black, and Chinese population—the project initially seemed to get off to a good start. John Brumer, a forty-year-old British-born professor of education at Long Island University, was hired to serve as the education director. He described his immediate problem as making contact with the people in the district who were largely Spanish- and Chinese-speaking. Although Brumer seemed to most observers to be moving slowly yet significantly in building up a sense of community, while encouraging and reassuring professionals in the district, he finally resigned. His reason for leaving was much the same as those complaints voiced in other experimental districts: lack of cooperation from the central board of education and, particularly, an unwillingness to turn over real authority and responsibility to the experimental districts.

The third district, Ocean Hill-Brownsville in Brooklyn, has been involved in controversy since it was organized. The controversy has received national attention and has seriously affected the relationship between New York's teacher's union and the black community, both parents and students. At this writing a tentative and probably temporary peace has been established by the New York State Department of Education. The following chronology identifies the main events of the Ocean Hill-Brownsville case.

Chronology

1958. Board of education decision to construct IS 201 in Harlem as an essentially segregated school.

1967 July. Ford Foundation provides funds for three demonstration projects: (local districts) IS 201, Two Bridges, and Ocean Hill-Brownsville.

15. *The New York Times* (November 19, 1967), p. 11.

August 3. Ocean Hill-Brownsville parents elect their local governing board. The board of education accepts the election and grants the board power to elect the unit administrator and principals for the eight schools in the district.

September 2. Teacher representatives on Ocean Hill-Brownsville local governing board refuse to vote for local principals. They never return to the board.

1968 May 10. Local Ocean Hill-Brownsville governing board orders transfer of nineteen teachers, charging them with attempts to sabotage the demonstration project.

May 14-22. United Federation of Teachers lobbies in Albany and defeats strong decentralization bill for New York City (predicted by Governor Rockefeller).

September 9. First strike by UFT to protest refusal of the Ocean Hill-Brownsville district to reinstate teachers transferred in May.

September 10. Agreement reached providing for the return of the teachers to Ocean Hill-Brownsville.

September 13. Teachers strike again charging Ocean Hill-Brownsville governing board with failure to honor the agreement.

September 14. State Commissioner of Education James Allen enters the picture and becomes party to the negotiations.

September 30. Schools reopen under a plan providing for the return of the disputed teachers under the surveillance of observers from the union and the board of education.

October 14. Teachers union goes out on strike again charging that members have been terrorized and threatened with death at JHS 271 (Ocean Hill-Brownsville).

November 19. Strike settled. Ocean Hill-Brownsville district to be operated as a trustee of the state.

December 3. JHS 271 closed by the state after disorders break out in and around the school.

December 4. Trouble erupts in PS 39 (IS 201 district) as nine union teachers charged with insubordination are barred from entering school by community residents.

December 6. Teachers escorted to PS 39 by police, but school boycotted by students and other instructors.

Led by black and Puerto Rican men and women who are willing to risk their jobs and their careers in the educational establishment, by neighborhood people who are angry at promises unkept, at educational colonialism, and at their own powerlessness, the urban poor are making demands that shake the educational bureaucracy of the New York City schools to its foundation. At this stage activists are few in number, but their claim of wide support by ghetto residents is probably correct. When unit administrator McCoy was ordered

transferred out of Ocean Hill, an unofficial school boycott resulted in 80% of the students and teachers remaining away from schools in the district.

The leaders want control of their schools—not next month or next year, but now. The militants are often in the vanguard, testing the establishment for weaknesses, taking power whether it be delegated or not, exerting pressures to retain whatever powers they have gained. Such actions do little to ensure peace of mind for those with a vested interest in the status quo. The major fear in the minds of many school people is that community control will result in the destruction of the teaching profession's hardwon rights, and that race, religion, and politics will become criteria for the selection and retention of personnel.

Under any plan for community control the guidelines must be carefully spelled out—something that was not done when the Ocean Hill-Brownsville demonstration district was set up. There must be a commitment on the part of those now in control of education to see that decentralization will work and to mobilize their resources to that end. Had the central Board recognized the aspirations of Ocean Hill-Brownsville and provided greater cooperation, much of the chaos might have been avoided.

The attention focused on Ocean Hill-Brownsville may have delayed but has not stopped the movement toward community control of local schools. Educational power groups such as the UFT and the Council of Supervisory Associations, which supported the UFT during the 1968 strikes, will at best accept a limited form of decentralization with strong central controls. The attitude of the Union, judged by black and Puerto Rican leaders as not only antidecentralization but antiblack and Puerto Rican, has, if anything, intensified their desire for complete community control.[16]

The recently passed New York State Education law of 1969 has done little to bring a real settlement or even a satisfactory compromise to New York schools. The law calls for the absorption of the three experimental districts into larger local districts (about thirty in number with very limited powers). Both IS 201 and Ocean Hill-Brownsville have indicated their unwillingness to be absorbed. Serious conflict seems inevitable.

ANOTHER TEST CASE: WASHINGTON, D.C.

Other cities besides New York have been conducting experiments in urban school decentralization and community control. An interesting and possibly far-reaching experiment has been conducted in Washington, D.C.[17] The Morgan School is located in a district serving a neighbor-

16. Philip A. Alsworth and Roger R. Woock, "Ocean Hill-Brownsville: Urban Conflict and the Schools," *Urban Education*, Vol. 4, No. 1 (April 1969), pp. 38-39.

17. Susan L. Jacoby, "The Making of a Community School," *The Urban Review*, Vol. 2, No. 4 (February 1968), pp. 3, 4, 29.

hood known as Adams Morgan, an area about two miles north of the White House. The population includes blacks living in poverty, middle-income blacks, and some remnants of white Washington "society." In addition, it has a number of young white couples moving in to live in restored houses. The area's community council waged an intensive and ultimately effective campaign in 1967 which finally persuaded the board of education and school officials in Washington that the Morgan School should be contracted out to Antioch College. The college, although located in Yellow Springs, Ohio, had for a number of years been conducting a teacher-training program in Washington. The community apparently was almost unanimous in supporting the invitation to Antioch to take over the school, although a few black power militants objected to an affiliation with a "white" college. The board of education in Washington not only approved of the program but promised to provide the usual budget allotment for the Morgan School and put this allotment completely under the control of Antioch and an elected school board. "We just about gave them carte blanche," says John A. Sessions, a school-board member who has pressed vigorously for more neighborhood control of the schools. "If decentralization can't work here, I don't see how it can anywhere."[18]

The local school board began functioning in September of 1967. Eleven members of the board were black, four were white. Seven members had children in the Morgan School, three were community residents over twenty-five without children, three were teenagers, and two were teachers.

Despite the enthusiastic support for the project there were a number of problems which developed very quickly. Even with the backing of the central board of education in Washington the relationship between the community school board and the central board was not clearly defined. This far-from-clear relationship lent itself to a situation in which buckpassing developed. For a variety of reasons Antioch failed to fulfill its original commitment of two fulltime and two parttime members to the school district. Only one fulltime member had been assigned to the project by the end of the school year 1968. Paul Lauder, the original coordinator, was never replaced when he was removed from that job.

Another and perhaps more serious problem was the development of a clear split in the community over what kind of a program the school should offer. All groups wanted a better education for the children, but they did not agree on how that was to be attained. Some of the older black residents in the district had been disturbed by what they considered to be a lack of discipline in the school; while the younger, better-educated group, including some who might be called white intellectuals, favored a more progressive school program. Parent attendance at the

18. *Ibid.*, p. 3.

school board meetings had fallen off; generally only twenty to thirty parents attended. This represented a considerable decline since the public meetings with the central school board in 1967, when the plan for the Morgan School was being considered. Children at Morgan School were placed in heterogenous groups from 100 to 110 with seven adults for each group. The staff team was supposed to have included three or four licensed teachers, one Antioch graduate student, a student teacher, and two community interns. The school, however, did not have on its staff the three experienced teachers needed for each team. In fact, when school started in the fall of 1967 the majority of teachers had had no previous classroom experience.

Despite these problems there are some indications that the school is improving. Vandalism and the breaking of windows are at an all-time low in Morgan School. The local school board is becoming more effective as its political and educational sophistication increases. Foundation representatives are reported to be extremely impressed, and have indicated that they would channel any monies given through the board rather than through Antioch. One thing is clear, if the Morgan School is judged to be a success it will have to show considerable improvement in the learning abilities of the youngsters. So far, it has been unable to do this. Parents expect to see better performance as measured on the standard performance tests, and however inadequate and imperfect, they are one measure of the gap between urban ghetto blacks and the rest of white society.

Experiments in closer school-community relations and movements toward decentralization are not limited to New York or Washington, D.C. Many cities in the United States have been tentatively and experimentally moving in the direction of encouraging more involvement on the part of the city's residents. Philadelphia, for example, has given superintendents of its eight school districts some power over curriculum, and is now studying a plan to permit them to decide on distribution of available school funds within their districts. Atlanta, Georgia, public schools are divided into five districts, and area superintendents can transfer teachers and pupils and adjust curriculum to some extent within each district. Los Angeles has organized eight separate elementary-school districts and four secondary districts, each of which has its own administrative staff. In 1954 Chicago broke its public school system into twenty-seven districts; however, the superintendent of schools at that time, Benjamin Willis, continued to keep much of the important decision-making in the hands of the central board of education and the superintendent. New superintendent James Redman is developing a plan for three self-governing districts, each containing middle- and lower-class youngsters, both white and black. These three independent school districts will do much of the administrative work currently done by the central office of the superintendent, as well as have some jurisdiction over curriculum matters and leeway in budget expenditure.

Though none of these proposals or divisions have moved as far as either the experimental districts in New York or the Morgan School in Washington, they do indicate that school-community problems are being acknowledged and taken into account by educators in urban areas. Some oppose real decentralization, since they believe it may well freeze the process of desegregation. Others are concerned with political problems and the possibility that local district boards would be taken over by extremists, either of the left or the right.

BLACK POWER AND THE SCHOOLS

Although most educators do not speak frankly about it, there is a good deal of concern among urban school superintendents and principals over the growing phenomenon known as the black power movement. Since it is a matter of growing concern, prospective teachers should understand the nature of this phenomenon and the possible ways in which it may relate to the process of decentralization. Considered on one level, black power seems to be part of an historical pattern of attempts by minority groups to organize and consolidate themselves for gains in economic, social, and political power. The black power movement seems to be very much like the consolidation of power in Eastern cities, such as Boston and New York, by the Irish in the late 19th and early 20th centuries. Many of the suggestions and attempted goals that have been outlined by black power leaders are similar in scope and in substance to the kinds of power moves made by earlier immigrant groups in American cities. These goals are modest and represent sensible social and political objectives to which few valid protests could be raised. They include the consolidation of black political power through the election of congressmen, city aldermen, and mayors. In 1967 two major cities elected black mayors for the first time—Cleveland, Ohio, and Gary, Indiana.

Economic goals include the establishment of increasing numbers of black businessmen in disadvantaged communities, and a general upgrading in the skills and educational levels of black Americans. The programs for the school, while perhaps more controversial, still seem to be a reasonable and natural development on the part of the black community.

Stokely Carmichael and Charles Hamilton, writing in *Black Power: The Politics of Liberation in America,* suggest:

. . . control of the ghetto schools must be taken out of the hands of professionals, most of whom have long since demonstrated their insensitivity to the needs and problems of the black child. These experts bring with them middle class biases, unsuitable techniques and materials. These are at best disfunctional and at worst destructive.[19]

Although this is certainly not the whole story, each of these assertions points toward a truth about public urban education. The authors later quote with approval a motion adopted by the "People's Board of Education" led by the Reverend Milton A. Galamison of New York City, an active leader attempting to improve black education in New York. Galamison organized a very successful one-day school boycott by black students in 1964. This "People's Board of Education" set up in opposition to the central board of education of New York City stated its goal as:

1. We seek to alter the structure of the school system so it is responsible to our individual community needs in order to achieve real community control. This may require legislative or state constitutional convention action. This means, of course, decentralization, accountability, meaningful citizen participation, etc.

2. To develop a program which will get grass roots awareness for understanding of and support for the goals stated above. It is suggested that we give top priority to organizing and educating parents and citizens in the poverty areas [approximately fourteen].

3. We recognize that power should not rest in any central bureau including our own and that by every means possible we should encourage the development and initiative of local people's groups.[20]

Reverend Galamison in the summer of 1968 was appointed to the expanded board of education of New York City by Mayor John Lindsay.

Matching these statements with the main points of the "Bundy report," it becomes very clear why black power advocates are in favor of either the Bundy or the New York Board of Regents decentralization plans. Their only complaint is that these proposals do not go far enough toward complete community control.

Another element within the black power movement must be mentioned. Considerably clouding and, in fact, overshadowing the demands and programs mentioned above is the support for and encouragement of "defensive violence" by black Americans against white Americans. Statements by black power figures like Stokely Carmichael or Rap Brown advocating violence have had a good deal of press coverage, while their

19. Stokely Carmichael and Charles V. Hamilton, *Black Power* (New York: Vintage Books, 1967), p. 166.

20. *Ibid.*, p. 171.

more modest programmatic statements go ignored. Although these "newsworthy" items are unpleasant and perhaps unfortunate in terms of tactics, it would nevertheless be inappropriate to conclude that the black power movement is bent on the total destruction of American society. There are groups which seem to be definitely committed to a revolutionary program, but making as reasonable an estimate as is possible, these seem to be considerably in the minority within the black power movement. Much attention has been given by the press in the United States on the relationship between black power and the summer riots of 1965, 1966, and 1967. Some reports initially traced the cause of riots to organized insurrection. Mayors of cities afflicted with riots attempted to blame them on "outside agitators." Yet the two most careful studies, *Rivers of Blood, Years of Darkness* by Robert Conot, a study of the Watts riot of 1965, and the *Presidential Commission Report on Civil Disorders,* found literally no organized activity behind the riots.[21] Quite explicitly, the cause was traced to discontent and despair growing out of the treatment of black Americans by their more fortunate white brothers.

In considering the black power position in relation to public schools an interesting theory has been advanced by editor and writer Jason Epstein.[22] He suggests that the militant black movement, in fact urban blacks as a group, are moving toward eventual control of the institutions of the city itself. The first institution against which they are mounting an attack is the public schools. He suggests that this is natural and should arouse no particular alarm among white citizens since they have seen it happen before in terms of political machines, police departments, and sanitation departments of many cities. One or another ethnic group has gained control of these institutions in the past. Simply organizing political power and developing more black businessmen in urban ghettos will not be enough. Epstein concludes:

> It was not after all Malcolm X's plan to destroy the American middle class but to build a black version of it from the proceeds of black dry cleaning stores and service stations. The flaw in Malcolm's vision was its modesty. [And, by implication, the vision of most black-power advocates.] The necessary goals of Black Power are the fundamental institutions of the city itself. If these goals are not met, it is impossible to see how the schools can transmit their language and their culture to tens of thousands of ghetto children and then what would be left of the city.[23]

21. Robert Conot, *Rivers of Blood, Years of Darkness* (New York: Bantam Books, Inc., 1967); and *Report of the National Advisory Commission on Civil Disorders* (New York: Bantam Books, Inc., 1968).

22. Jason Epstein, "The Politics of School Decentralization," *The New York Review of Books,* Vol. 10, No. 11 (June 6, 1968), pp. 26-32.

23. *Ibid.,* pp. 31-32.

Epstein sees black power moving outward from the ghetto to take over citywide institutions, the first of which may well be the school. Concentrating on local power and independence within the ghetto is really only the first step in this process.

THE COMMUNITY SCHOOL—ITS POSSIBILITIES FOR URBAN LIFE

In considering the various changes in school-community relations and proposals for decentralization we have not yet looked at the concept of a community school. Although some elements of a community school have existed and now exist in many American cities, the most outstanding example of a total community school system is found in Flint, Michigan.[24] The program in Flint, originally known as the Mott Foundation program of the Flint board of education, was at first privately financed, although it was established in the public schools. The program was begun in 1939, partly in an attempt to provide increased community activities and educational opportunities in an industrial community during the depression. In 1958 almost 28,000 individuals were involved in the adult education center in activities ranging over arts, crafts, sewing, business, insurance, evening college, and high school. Prehigh-school programs, home and family living, home arts, mechanical skills, and music were also offered. Other activities of the community school included athletic programs, a children's theater, and Flint College and Cultural Center, which was newly developed. Planners of the Flint project judged that the elementary school was particularly important, and established elementary-school programs as a transition from the conventional to the community-educational center. Almost all of the newer elementary schools, for example, have a separate wing consisting of a community room, a kitchen, a gymnasium, and an auditorium. In the elementary school special health and safety programs now include a health center for the needy, and special facilities for the blind preschool and the deaf preschool. A teenage traffic court was organized in junior high schools where violators are tried and sentenced by a teenage jury. Provisions were made in the school curriculum for leadership training, fresh-air summer camp, music enrichment, and a physical fitness program—including citywide tournaments, a science fair, teen club, work experience program, and special counseling for potential dropouts. A number of community offerings operated out of the schools provide home and family-living counselor service.

24. Leo E. Buehring, "New Pattern: Community Schools," *The Nation's Schools* (January 1958), pp. 35-39.

Considered to be extremely important in the overall functioning of the program is the Flint Cooperative Teacher Training Program. The student attends junior college for the first two years and then is placed as a fulltime teacher in an elementary classroom under the direction of a trained teacher and a field cooperative teacher. In addition to this classroom experience the student takes twenty semester hours per year, including the summer session. At the end of five years this program awards a bachelor of arts degree and the Michigan State Provision Teaching Certificate. Scholarships are available for the first two years of college if needed. A recent visitor to the Flint school system gives the following description:

Neighborhood elementary schools are busier on almost any evening than during the day. Five hundred youngsters attend junior high school on Saturday morning on their own accord to acquire skills they haven't found time for during the regular school week. An elderly woman goes back to high school [one of 3000 persons enrolled each year in adult high-school education]. A family re-upholstering dad's easy chair in the school's arts and crafts room [part of 3500 enrolled annually in the 776 adult education courses]. Community players rehearsing their next production in the auditorium of the elementary school. A school person making neighborhood calls.

The Flint community school also provides facilities for the regular session of the neighborhood teen club; [one of 43 such groups with a card-carrying membership of 13,000]; for 6000 children on top lots during the summer; for meetings in the community rooms of men's clubs, PTA's, and various other organizations, for square dances for parents, teenagers, and the younger ones and other recreational activities held in the large gymnasium; for a Christmas party attended by 700 adults in a school with an enrollment of only five hundred.[25]

It is true that almost any single part of this overall, comprehensive school-community program is not new and many of the particular ingredients can be found in other systems. What is unique about the Flint concept is that all of these programs are coordinated by and most operate out of the local school. The school literally becomes a community center.

Most philosophers of the community-school concept, however, go beyond even the idea of the school as a total community center.[26] They also envisage the school as an agency in which problems of the community will be studied and, hopefully, solved. Havighurst and Neugarten suggest that in a true community school both school-age and

25. *Ibid.*, p. 36.

26. Joseph K. Hart, *The Discovery of Intelligence* (New York: King's Crown Press, 1924).

adult students would collect facts concerning the neighborhood, study local problems, participate in group deliberations which would include important planning and decision-making, and work on both individual and group projects.[27] In theory, then, the community school should use the community as a laboratory for learning and the school should be designed for use by all of the local residents seven days a week, daytime and nighttime, summer and winter. Two things are expected to result from the establishment of a true community school—first, an increase in learning and interest in learning on the part of both children and adults; and, second, actual changes in the community.

Havighurst and Neugarten, in discussing the urban community school, contrast the general approach outlined above with that of the "four walls" type of school.

> The alternative to the community school in the city system may be called the "four-walls" school. It focuses attention upon doing the best possible job of teaching every boy and girl who comes into the school, whoever he is, whatever his color, nationality, or IQ. It minimizes any activities which might "distract" school personnel from this task. This means building good school buildings, equipping them well, and staffing them with well-trained teachers. It means making clear to parents and interested citizens that the schools are run by professionals who know their business and who do not need help from other people in the community. It means keeping the schools "out of local politics." In contrast to the community school, it means relatively limited cooperation with other social institutions, public and private. The school may ask help from public aid and public health agencies, but the help must fit in with school policies and programs.
>
> The four-walls type of school system works for efficiency, economy, and high educational standards, and attempts to free the teacher to do the best possible job under conditions that maximize his independence from outside groups. The community outside the school is regarded as introducing problems of undesirable complexity for school personnel, and the attempt is made to keep the boundary between community and school clearly defined and respected lest tensions arise to interfere with school operations.[28]

What can we say with any confidence about the possibilities for the development of urban community schools? One thing is obvious. For truly effective urban community schools to become a reality decentralization must become an accomplished fact. It is quite impossible to imagine the dynamic Flint project and the two-way relationships described earlier in this chapter to flower under the heavy monolithic, bureaucratic struc-

27. Robert J. Havighurst and Bernice L. Neugarten, *Society and Education,* 3d ed., (Boston: Allyn and Bacon, Inc., 1967), pp. 222-229.

28. *Ibid.,* pp. 229-230.

ture of present-day, large city public education. There is, however, no assurance that decentralization would guarantee a true community school. It is perfectly possible to imagine a system of fairly complete and far-reaching decentralization which would simply not include the programs and relationships with the public that make up a community school.

It would also be incorrect to assume that there is any fundamental and massive demand for community schools by inner city residents. Support for decentralization seems to be motivated more by a desperate conclusion that urban educators are simply unable or unwilling to teach poor youngsters and that therefore some other attempt must be made to improve education for the poor. The case of the Morgan school in Washington, D.C., suggests that lower class, poor parents in urban areas may want a rather intensive, conservative, highly disciplined, traditional academic course of instruction for their youngsters; that is, the kind of schooling which they believe most white middle-class youngsters are receiving.

There is no doubt that extra school-community programs held evenings and weekends, plus new construction, will tremendously increase the costs of public education. The Flint program, as was stated, was begun with private financing. Supporters of the community school might argue that over the long run this kind of institution would pay for itself through savings in welfare payments, police protection, court costs, and less social disorder, as well as increased purchasing power for a better-educated and better-employed generation of urban youth.

The political and bureaucratic problems of establishing urban community schools would be considerable. Since the scope and extent of the school would be so greatly increased, it means significant readjustments in a variety of other social institutions, that is, welfare, police, housing, and urban renewal. It seems likely that many local politicians would view the development of community schools with considerable suspicion. Already local political opposition has all but wiped out the federal Office of Economic Opportunity's Community Action Program, which attempted to set up local community organizations for the poor to act in some sense as a countervailing force to the city power structure.

Any planners of community schools must also face the problems of developing interest in the schools and organizing the poor. To the extent that one accepts Oscar Lewis' theory of the "culture of poverty" (*see* chapter 2), it is clear that to organize the lowest levels of the poor or to help them to organize themselves effectively for anything is an extremely difficult job. However, it is true that the disadvantaged are becoming increasingly interested in the education of their children, although this interest does not at the present time take the form of a demand for community schools.

Charles V. Hamilton, professor of political science at Roosevelt University in Chicago and co-author with Stokely Carmichael of *Black Power: The Politics of Liberation in America,* proposes what is clearly a community school system for Harlem.[29] He implies that similar systems could be set up for other black ghettos in large cities. Professor Hamilton suggests a completely autonomous Harlem school system which would be chartered by the state of New York and responsible to the state. The elected school board members would be residents of Harlem and the entire planning for the school system would be the work of the Harlem community. The school would become the focal point of the community, with education family-oriented and not simply child-centered. He calls this proposal "The Family-Community-School-Comprehensive Plan." In true community school fashion it would function year round, day and evening, providing education and training for the entire family. Health clinics and recreation facilities would be included. Public assistance would be funneled through the community education program. Case workers with substantially reduced case loads, in addition to being investigators, could be teachers of budget management. Teachers, Hamilton suggests, would be specially trained in a program similar to the National Teacher Corps. Mothers would teach classes in skills which they possess. The curriculum would be both academic and vocational. There would be a special emphasis on the culture and history of black people. The law enforcement agency would also be a part of this comprehensive system and would train community service officers. Local police precincts would be based in the school and would focus much of their work on crime prevention. Hamilton concludes:

> . . . the school would belong to the community. It would be a union of children, parents, teachers, school workers, psychologists, urban planners, doctors, community organizers. It would become a major vehicle for fashioning a sense of pride and group identity. . . . Black power structures [for which one might substitute community school] at the local level will activate people, instill faith, not alienation, and provide habits of organization and a consciousness of ability. Alienation will be overcome and trust in society restored.[30]

In spite of possible opposition to the specific proposal which Hamilton offers, reorganization of urban public schools is necessary. The present system dissatisfies too many groups and is actually failing to perform the task assigned to it by society.

29. Charles V. Hamilton, "An Advocate of Black Power Defines It," *The New York Times Magazine* (April 14, 1968), pp. 82-83.

30. *Ibid.*, p. 83.

Recommended Reading

Stokely Carmichael and Charles Hamilton's *Black Power* (New York: Vintage Books, 1967), although not totally accepted by black militants, can serve as a useful introduction to the concept. The writings of Eldridge Cleaver, especially *Soul on Ice* (New York: Dell Publishing Company, 1968), provide unusual insight into the mind of a sensitive black radical.

The nature of community is analyzed from a conservative perspective in Robert Nisbet's *Community and Power* (New York: Oxford University Press, 1962). The best single collection of articles dealing with the Ocean Hill-Brownsville crisis in New York City is *Confrontation at Ocean Hill-Brownsville,* edited by Maurice R. Berube and Marilyn Gittell (New York: Frederick A. Praeger, Inc., 1969). For an account heavily slanted in favor of the Teacher's Union, see Martin Mayer's *The Teachers Strike New York, 1968* (New York: Harper & Row, 1968). Ronald Corwin's *A Sociology of Education* (New York: Appleton-Century-Crofts, 1965), especially chapter 12, presents a good analysis of how schools respond to the community environment.

A FINAL NOTE TO TEACHERS AND PROSPECTIVE TEACHERS

The general conclusions from the evidence reviewed throughout the book are clear: A combination of deprivation, inequalities of opportunity, environmental structure, and a set of different values in lower-class children creates educational problems that are more resistant to attack by changes in school practices and resources than educators originally had thought. If this summary statement is true for lower-class children in general, it seems even more applicable to black youngsters, whose backgrounds include centuries of exploitation and prejudice. Although in the long run there is little question that our society will have to face the general issue of improving the lot of the entire lower class, the most pressing and immediate item on the national agenda should be to eliminate inequalities of income and occupational status between black and white.

It is possible that because the pressures behind the demand for equality are so dangerously explosive these inequalities will be dealt with successfully within a generation, without waiting for the slow processes of school reform. The development of special admission standards to colleges, making skilled jobs available to people without the paper credentials for them, increasing access to subprofessional career ladders, encouraging private employers to hire the "hard core" by insuring them against any special losses involved, reforming the welfare system, perhaps in the near future the federal government assuming responsibility as the employer of last resort—all of these and other programs are more-or-less independent of changes in the school's productivity.

The process of equalization would be greatly accelerated, however, if the school's resources were also more effectively deployed, and although the effectiveness of many of the school programs reported here have been disappointing, a decade of experimentation has taught us which directions are likely to be most fruitful:

1. Simply increasing the magnitude of available school resources in a shotgun approach seems to do little to close the achievement gap, but intensive, carefully executed programs over a long period of time have a significant effect on at least those children from the more stable families of the disadvantaged population. That they do not work for

everyone suggests not that we should abandon compensatory programs but that we need better targeting.

2. Perhaps the most immediately useful conclusion of the Coleman study is that the total environment of the school needs to change if its effectiveness is to be improved. Whether the school is reconstructed by educators or by the community is perhaps not so much an issue as it may appear in this text; most reconstruction designs depend heavily on opening the school to community influences.

3. The "wash-out" effect observed in many early childhood programs may be due, as some experts suggest, to a delay in intervention. Some form of training beginning at the age of six months may be far more effective than later training, particularly if it involves concomitant maternal education.

4. Although the effect of school integration on achievement is still in doubt, integrated classrooms may very well, on evidence, influence aspiration. The educational park may be the only feasible way of integrating schools of the largest cities, but Berkeley and others have shown that it is possible to integrate the smaller ones.

Any of these efforts on a reasonable scale cost a great deal more than we are currently investing in educational reforms; together, they demand a vastly increased expenditure by the federal government because the budgets of the cities are already overstrained. Given the present constellation of political forces it is unlikely that Congress will make available the funds necessary for a large-scale attack on the problems of urban education, or will even increase sizeably the effectiveness of those more direct nonschool programs of occupational equalization.

Thus, the educators professionally concerned with these problems have first of all a responsibility as citizens to exert what pressures they can to insure that a more adequate proportion of the society's resources are allocated to the task of equalizing opportunity, both in school and out, even while they try to improve their effectiveness as professionals.

Although methodology is not within the authors' purview, we have come to one general conclusion from this psychosocial examination of the urban school which has implications for the professional classroom role of the teacher. The key, it seems to us, is attention to the individual child. It is the same tired truism of all teacher training, to be sure, but the evidence is clear that most teachers in the large-scale urban school systems seldom apply the principle of individualization, possibly because it is much more difficult in practice than it appears in theory to be.

This is crucial for a number of reasons that the text may have made obvious at various points but which are worth summarizing here:

1. To take the time and effort to understand each child is the best

possible antidote to stereotyping on the basis of class or race and the setting up of unfair negative expectations.

2. Individual attention makes possible the development of personal relationships within the teacher-pupil role relation, which is far more consonant with the value system of the lower-class child than are large group methods.

3. It provides a basis for varying curriculum and methods to suit the often different learning styles one finds in the urban slum school classroom.

4. It provides for the teacher a greater opportunity for professional satisfaction derived from seeing the results of his own work. The reward of seeing some children make more progress than predicted can be significant.

Individualizing instruction is a good deal easier at the elementary than the secondary level, but we suggest that it is even more desirable at these upper grades, where the peer group makes more important counterclaims on the goals and behavior of the child. The ultimate effect of greatly increased financial resources, should we ever get them, may well depend on the willingness and ability of the professional to change what he habitually does in the crucial arena of the classroom.

APPENDIX

RESEARCH AND THE PROBLEMS OF CAUSATION

The discussion that follows deals in a very simplified way with an extraordinarily complicated problem: "How do we come to *know* something?" There is still a small society in England whose members insist that the world is flat as a saucer; even the pictures of earth brought back by the first astronauts to circle the moon failed to convince them that their belief was incorrect. Most of us carry about some beliefs that are just as resistant to new evidence or to particular forms of evidence.

There are a number of ways in which we come to know, or believe, something. One is the method of sheer *tenacity;* what has been so in the past is right—a method that is gradually disappearing at least among the better-educated members of modern societies.

A second basis is *authority;* we accept as true a very large number of facts and generalizations because someone who is competent to know about them assures us of their truth. We could not get along very well without such a method of knowing, since it is impossible for us to learn everything first hand. The better-educated and more sophisticated, however, also tend to be cautious about granting authority to people who might not really have it.

A third method of knowing is based on *intuition;* we accept truth that we think is self-evident or appears reasonable to us. For a long time people believed that punishment ought to serve as a deterrent to antisocial behavior; the stronger the punishment, the greater the deterrent. But evidence that has been accumulating over the past twenty-five years of psychological research indicates that this is a very unreliable deterrent; it may work under some conditions, but most of the time it does not.

That kind of research constitutes the fourth method of knowing, *the method of science,* which tries to build in its own corrections for possible error, which considers alternative explanations, and which is open to public criticism and inspection.

Science and common sense involve many of the same processes, but science goes about the process of knowing systematically and with controls over the possibility of error. Thus:

1. The man in the street develops theories and hypotheses, just as the scientist does, but he does so loosely. During the thirties many people believed that the economic depression was caused by Jews, as a small group nowadays theorizes that all of our political and economic problems are the result of the machinations of a widespread Communist conspiracy. Scientific hypotheses are, in contrast, based on some empirical evidence, are tested for consistency, and must be proven by further empirical test.

2. The layman tests his theories, but he does so selectively. If his theory is that blacks are intellectually inferior to whites, every time he comes across an instance of stupidity in a black he chalks up another successful test of the theory. But he ignores any instances that disprove his notion, as the patent existence of black intellectuals or daily encounters with *white* stupidities.

3. If several things occur together in the experience of laymen they are likely to assume that one *causes* the other, a tendency that has led some primitives to the conclusion that pregnancy is due to a particular phase of the moon or some other astral event. When scientists test the possibility that one factor causes another they try systematically to rule out the operation of any other factor that might be a cause.

The Problem of Causation

The field of education is not yet so advanced as to be concerned with what scientists would generally consider genuine theories. But it is very much interested in finding out what does and does not operate as a cause of children's learning in school. Will a new instructional technique work better than the old? Does grouping children by ability help or hurt the child? Can we improve learning by eliminating formal grade levels? These and other such questions can be answered not only by informed hunches or chains of reasoning leading to self-evident propositions but by formal research. Whether the research deserves to be treated any more respectfully than the expert's hunch, however, depends on how well it has satisfied some scientific criteria for the establishment of causation:

1. It must show that the causal variable *precedes* the variable it is supposed to effect. This is a simple-minded enough requirement, but one that can occasionally cause some trouble. Does academic success, for example, contribute to the development of a good self-image or is it the other way around?

2. The two variables that are presumed to relate to one another in some causal fashion must co-relate or vary together strongly enough

to rule out a purely chance association. If one throws a pair of dice only five times, they may by a fluke come up "seven" four out of five times. One must be cautious about the claim that they are loaded, at least not before trying them out twenty or thirty times to see if the oddity persists.

3. Knowledge that there is a correlation between two variables does not help much in determining the question of whether one variable *causes* another. This is reasonably obvious as soon as one examines some widely-known correlations. High-school grade-point-averages predict college grades fairly well, but do not *cause* college grades. Clearly, the same factors that influence how well a person does academically in high school are likely to be influential in his doing similarly well in college; the two sets of grades are causally connected not to each other but to some set of third factors. There is also a high correlation between sales of ice cream and deaths by drowning because both go up together in hot weather and decline in cold. To show that variable X precedes variable Y in time and that the two correlate fairly well still leaves a major question unanswered: Is there some *other* variable that might be responsible for Y that was operating in the situation?

Eliminating the question of timing, which needs to be examined in each specific situation, we suggest some general guidelines for interpreting correlation figures and for judging the degree of control the research has maintained over variables that might be the *real* causes of the particular effect under consideration. For convenience, we will adopt for the following discussion the conventions of the field and refer to any event or thing that causes something as an *independent variable* (or X); the thing that is influenced is the *dependent variable* (or Y).

Correlation

Suppose we know the IQ scores of a group of pupils and, having given them a test in vocabulary knowledge, we are interested in the connection between their IQ's and their verbal ability on our test. One way of putting it is: Can we *predict* how they will do on the test if we know their IQ's? Still another way of expressing it is: How much of the variation in test scores among this group of children can we *explain* by examining the variations among their IQ scores? Table A-1 shows the two scores for each student.

A careful examination of the two sets of scores will show that for each three-point increase in IQ score there is exactly a six-point increase in test score. If we plot each set on a graph, as in Figure A-1 (called a scattergram), the dots form a straight line. Each of the dots in this graph represents two scores; for example, the one with the circle shows the position of the student with an IQ score of 91 and a test score of 52.

Table A-1 IQ Scores and Test Scores Showing a Perfect Positive Correlation

Student	IQ score	Test score
1	85	40
2	88	46
3	91	52
4	94	58
5	97	64
6	100	70
7	103	76
8	106	82
9	109	88
10	112	94

This is a perfect positive correlation and is an exceedingly unlikely state of affairs. It would mean that IQ alone is a *sufficient* explanation for how well the students in this group did on the test, without regard to such factors as attention, motivation, previous experience with the words, and a host of other variables, most of which we would expect to have some effect on test performance.

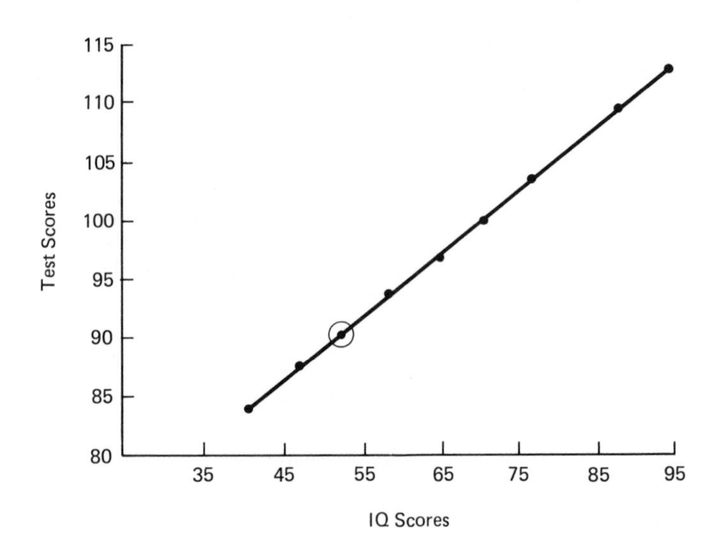

Figure A.1 Scattergram of test scores in Table A-1.

There are a number of ways to show that one variable bears a consistent relationship to another, but most of the studies reported in this book demonstrate a relationship through the use of correlation, and report the degree of the relationship in the form of a *correlation coefficient, r*. In the perfect example above, $r = +1.00$; it is positive because there is an *increase* of test score with each increase in IQ. Table A-2 shows test-score data for the same range of IQ scores, indicating a correlation of $r = -1.00$; the scores *decrease* with each increase of IQ score; again, clearly, an improbable situation. If IQ was no help at all in explaining the performance on this particular test, the two sets of scores would bear no relation to one another, and in this case r would equal 0.00.

Table A-2 IQ Scores and Test Scores Showing a Perfect Negative Correlation

Student	IQ score	Test score
1	85	94
2	88	88
3	91	82
4	94	76
5	97	70
6	100	64
7	103	58
8	106	52
9	109	46
10	112	40

Thus, the correlation coefficient fluctuates between -1.00 and $+1.00$; the closer it is to zero the less important is the relationship between the variables being studied.

The question of how to interpret its importance as it grows larger can be answered in several ways. If the sample under investigation is small (including only 20 or 30 persons, for example) even a fairly sizeable-seeming r (.40, for example) might not be an indication of significant correlation. The statisticians would put it this way: It is possible to obtain a coefficient this large in such a small sample simply by chance.

On the other hand, in large samples, which tend to be characteristic of educational studies, a very small correlation coefficient, even one as low as $r = +.05$, may be statistically significant. In this case it is not necessary to accept the finding as important just because it exceeds chance; one must make an independent judgment of the magnitude of the relationship it indicates between the variables, and a coefficient of .05 is rather trivial by anyone's definition.

As coefficients go beyond .20, however, it becomes more difficult to judge their importance. Because of the way in which it is calculated, for instance, one cannot consider an r of .40 as twice as great as an r of .20. The simplest and most accurate basis for judging significance is to square the correlation coefficient to obtain a coefficient of determination. With a correlation of .40, r^2 becomes .16 and may be interpreted this way: 16 percent of the variation in the scores of Y can be explained (or predicted) by the variations in the X scores. This leaves a good deal of the variation in Y unaccounted for, but it is still a respectable proportion to have explained; science comes to understand relationships slowly, and to understand almost a fifth of something is a step forward.

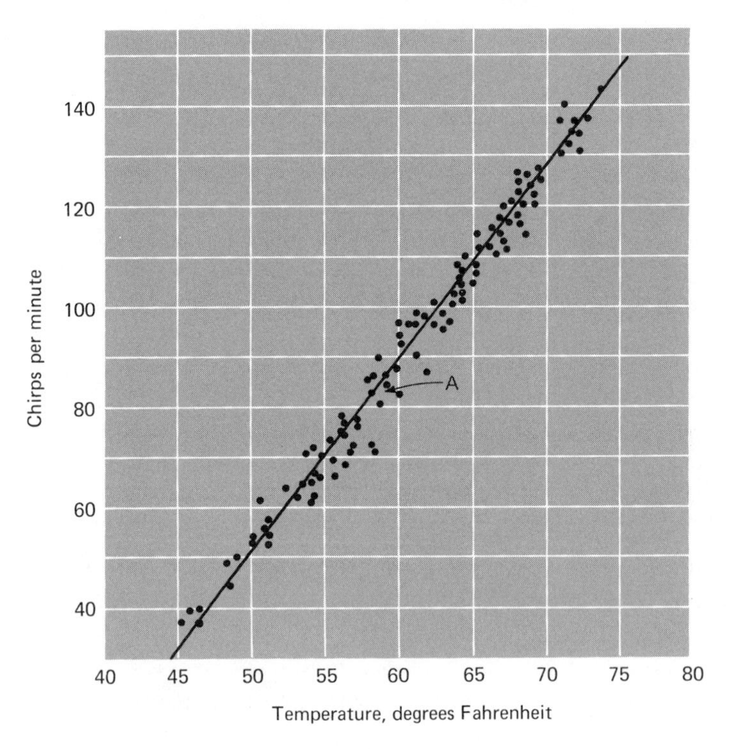

Figure A.2 Temperature and cricket chirps per minute of 115 crickets.
SOURCE: Frederick E. Croxton, Dudley J. Cowden, and Sidney Klein, *Applied General Statistics*, 3d ed. (Englewood Cliffs, N.J.: Prentice-Hall, Inc., 1967), p. 390.

Implied in the foregoing is the assumption that in a complex world one is unlikely to find *one* cause for any phenomenon, an assumption that social scientists generally make. One finds occasional very high correlations in nature; Figure A-2, for example, shows the scattergram of temperature readings and the related chirps-per-minute of crickets. In this case $r = +.99$, and one can be fairly certain that nothing else in cricketdom has much to do with a cricket's frequency of chirping. Man, however, is more complicated, and if we are interested in what causes different levels of academic achievement, which is itself a complicated phenomenon, we can expect to find many interrelated factors having some influence.

In order to study the influence of a number of factors at the same time, simple correlation is an inadequate tool, because any one of our X variables may overlap with another. Variations in IQ influence differences in achievement level, and so do variations in social class; but we know that *some* of the variation in IQ itself can be explained by social class position. These two independent variables share some *common* explanatory powers. In the natural sciences it is often possible to control the influence of a number of independent variables by holding one constant at a time; for example, one can repeat the same experiment, keeping the same temperature each time and varying the humidity or some other relevant factor. This is difficult or impossible to do in social science research, but the statistical tool of partial correlation provides a way of holding one or more of the independent variables constant to permit one to observe what happens to another. An example of partial correlation is given below to demonstrate the process and the way in which it can be read and interpreted.

The example is taken from the Gross and Herriott study of school leadership whose general findings are discussed in chapter 8. The major independent variable of interest here is the measure of EPL, the aspect of the principal's leadership that involves his interest in and support of the teacher's professional role in the classroom. The higher the principal's EPL score, the greater his involvement with and support of his teachers as professionals. The study gives us first the simple correlations between EPL scores for the principals and a number of other variables (these simple correlations are in this context called "zero order r's"). Each one of the variables is assigned a number that will be used throughout to identify it:

1. EPL score of the principal
2. teacher morale
3. teacher professional performance
4. pupil academic performance

The zero order correlations are:

$r_{12} = +.50$ (that is, the correlation between the principal's EPL score and his teachers' morale)
$r_{13} = +.36$
$r_{14} = +.06$

We know that family socioeconomic level has a considerable influence on pupil academic performance by itself; and the study found some evidence that the low correlation between EPL and pupil performance indicated above was not true of all socioeconomic levels. Let us assign the subscript 5 to the variable "family income"; r_{54}, the correlation between family income and pupil performance, turns out to be a sizeable +.61.

Now we can "partial out," or hold constant, the effect of family income on our zero-order correlations. We will in effect be saying: To what extent do EPL and teacher morale (or professional performance or pupil performance) vary together when we look at groups of schools whose pupils have the *same* average family income? Or, for schools that have the same average family income but different levels of teacher morale: To what extent are the variations in morale accompanied by variations in the principal's EPL score? With family income held constant our zero-order correlations change:

$r_{12.5} = +.55$ (read: the correlation between EPL and teacher morale, independent of the family income of the school population, is .55)

$r_{13.5} = +.41$

$r_{14.5} = +.25$

This procedure has clearly increased the estimate of the EPL's influence on all these factors, considerably so in the case of its effect on pupil performance. The way the principal behaves makes more of a difference for some children than others, a fact that was obscured by our treating children as a total, undifferentiated group.

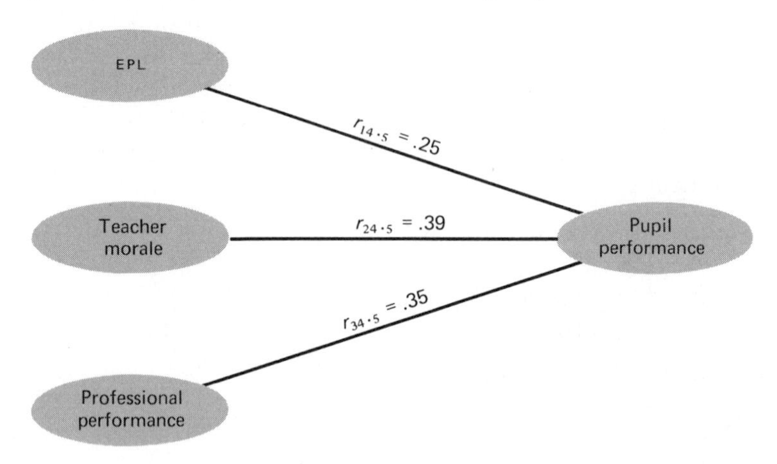

Figure A.3 Relation of three school variables to pupil performance holding family income constant.

SOURCE: Based on data from Neal Gross and Robert E. Herriott, *Staff Leadership in Public Schools* (New York: John Wiley & Sons, Inc., 1965), p. 55.

Gross and Herriott go on to examine another interesting question on which partial correlation can throw some light: Does the principal's interest and supportiveness have a *direct* effect on pupil performance or is it merely that his type of leadership helps to create high morale and more professional teaching, which in turn influences pupil performance? With pupil performance as the dependent variable, and with family income of the school population held constant, here is the situation as shown in Figure A-3. Taking EPL as the independent variable of major interest, we can hold constant not only family income but teacher morale. For schools of the same socioeconomic composition and the same average level of professional performance, $r_{14.5}$ turns out to be only .13. If we also remove the effect of teacher morale, $r_{14.532} = .05$. So, the influence of EPL falls almost to nothing. The original relationship between EPL and pupil performance is apparently due to its indirect influence on morale and professional performance.

The Direct Control of Causal Variables

The use of partial correlation to control the effect of independent variables after the fact is a useful method when the aim is to compare the influences of a number of major known variables that are probable causes of a particular result. But it can deal only with aspects of a situation for which measures exist, leaving all others uncontrolled. Of greater importance is the fact that the issue of causality is still unsettled; Gross and Herriott have shown that EPL and teacher morale vary together, but they have not eliminated the possibility that some other aspect of the principal's behavior is linked to morale or performance of which EPL is merely a misleading symbol. It is only when *all other* possible influences are controlled that one can properly infer a causal relationship. An illustration of a simple education experiment can make this point more explicitly.

Let us suppose that a teacher wishes to test the idea that writing comments on students' written work improves their performance more than merely putting a grade on the papers. The simplest test of the hypothesis is to select two groups of students, put grades only on the written work of one group, and write relevant corrective comments on the papers of the other group. At the end of the term submit the latest example of their writing to an objective judge to determine whether the average of the experimental group exceeds that of the control group.

Assuming that the experimental group does significantly better, how can one interpret the results? It depends on whether all of the other possible reasons for that groups' better performance can be eliminated as causal factors. If the teacher merely selects two convenient classes, nothing at all has been proven. The experimental class may have had a preponderance of better writers to begin with; they might be more verbal and would have improved over the control class in any case; more of them may have come from middle-class homes with helpful parents; it might have a larger proportion of girls, who tend to be more verbal than boys.

One way of holding some of these possible causes constant is to form two special groups instead of taking any two classes at hand. Each student in the experimental groups can be matched with one in the control group, so that each has the same IQ, the same score on a test of verbal ability, the same sex. This method has two drawbacks. One is that it takes a large pool of students to produce very many such matched pairs—and the difficulty grows with every additional characteristic used in matching them. The second is that for some very important variables, such as home environment, we seldom have the necessary information.

The only way of insuring that *all* personal characteristics that might influence the dependent variable are distributed without bias among both groups, and that the groups are consequently "equivalent," is to start out with the total group of students and determine which group to assign each student to on some chance or random basis—by tossing a coin for example. Each of the characteristics of every student then has an equal chance of appearing in either group. It is possible that some characteristic might by chance appear in one of the groups more than another, but the probability of that happening is known; the findings of the experiment can thus be assigned a precise margin of possible error, just as the election polls report their findings in terms of a plus or minus 3 percent of being accurate. The reason that pollsters can be so precise is that they, too, use a random or chance selection process in choosing their samples.

Such comprehensive control over possible independent variables is almost impossible to achieve where one cannot directly control which children will appear in which group. The uncertainty that this difficulty introduces into nonexperimental findings is illustrated by a number of the research studies cited in the text.

How can we know, for example, whether integration causes improved academic performance among black children? If children are bussed out of their ghetto schools into middle-class white schools, and in comparing their reading levels to those of children who remain in the ghetto schools we find that they are superior, are we then justified in claiming that integration results in better reading performance—only hesitantly at best. Too many other independent variables are left uncontrolled; ghetto schools may reasonably be bussing out their best pupils, which would be sufficient in accounting for the apparent improvement. The receiving schools may be separating the bussed children into segregated ability groups, in which case our supposed independent variable of integration is not even operating. If there is an equally plausible alternative explanation for the findings *that the research itself has not successfully eliminated from consideration,* some degree of doubt is justified.

The principle of an *alternative plausible explanation* applies to most of the other available data bearing on whether integration is a causal factor in achievement. In its national survey, the Coleman study found that minority group children in integrated schools do better academically than those in segregated schools. One must ask, who are these children living in neighborhoods in which it is natural for them to attend schools with whites? The plausible answer: Black families living in working-class or middle-class areas are quite likely to be upwardly mobile and ambitious for their children. So long as the variable or parental pressure remains uncontrolled in these studies, any conclusion about the causal operation of integration itself is suspect.

The only way to answer the question conclusively would be to divide a large group of ghetto school pupils into two randomly-selected groups, then bus only one group into white schools and insure that they would be placed into integrated classes, finally, then, compare the progress of the two groups over a period of two or three years. The obvious difficulties in such a test suggest the reason why we are so unsure about what causes what in education. There are so many variables, and there are so many ethical and practical barriers to experimenting with children in any rigorous way that would control those variables, that very little of a conclusive nature can be learned.

We must, nevertheless, continue to pay attention to the results of this type of research, though it should receive critical attention. First, it is better to know something than nothing, so long as one is aware of the limitations on what it is one knows. Second, tightly controlled experimental research has its own drawbacks; it must usually be so limited in scope that it creates some uncertainty about how widely applicable its findings are. An experiment limited to fifty children in a particular school in one special city may not have much to say about children everywhere in all types of schools. Third, medium-sized studies (between the large national survey and the small local experiment) are increasingly finding ways of instituting some controls over independent variables that might account for the changes that are expected. As noted in chapter 6, several fairly sizeable evaluations of compensatory education programs used either matched schools or control classes as a way of assessing the progress of experimental groups of children.

In the long run important questions of causation in education are not likely to be settled by single studies. What is ultimately convincing is to find a number of pieces of evidence from both small controlled

INDEX

A

B

C

E

F

G

H

I

J

K

P

S

T

U

Y